Open Hearted

Cheryl Barnes-Neff, PhD, MDiv

Also by Cheryl Barnes-Neff

Religion, Education, and Democracy: Exploring the
Intersection between Religion, Secularism, Democracy, and
Public Education in a Pluralistic America

Confessions of a Reluctant Pink Ribbon Girl

C.A.R.E. About What Matters

The Self-Care Toolkit

Open Hearted

ESSAYS ON BUDDHIST STUDY AND PRACTICE

Cheryl Barnes-Neff, PhD, MDiv

Laurel Oak Press

About the essays:
These essays appeared first as academic work and are used with permission
of the author. Quotations and concepts are used as critique and analysis of
the original work, and all source material content remains the copyright of
the original authors. A complete bibliography is included for reference. The
author acknowledges, and fully credits their work. The author welcomes any
corrections, or identification of missing citations; corrections will be made
in the next addition. All interpretation and analysis is the author's, not the
source material.

Disclaimer: The practices discussed here are meant for educational and il-
lustrative purposes only. Please do not attempt any meditation or other Buddhist practices without the guidance of a qualified Buddhist teacher, or
without the approval of your medical or mental health professional.

Contents

Introduction 1

Buddhism 9

Life of the Buddha 32

The Four Noble Truths 67

The Precepts 86

The Doctrine of Mahayana 106

The Myth of Freedom..161

Immeasurables & Paramitas 180

Agnostic Buddhism 200

Japanese Buddhism...213

The Compass of Zen 224

Korean Buddhism..244

Tracing Back the Radiance 273

Buddha Nature 290

The Diamond Sutra 314

Hua-Yen Buddhism 327

The Platform Sutra..349

Stages of Emptiness 358

Conclusion 375

Bibliography 387

Acknowledgements..403

About the Author...404

For

Matt

for

Everything

CHAPTER 1

Introduction

About the Book

I have a confession to make. This book is basically a collection of my home-work over my years of earning a Master's in Divinity. But before you put the book down, I do think that there is a point to reading on. This will be a different approach than you've probably read before. When you open the chapter on "Introduction to Buddhism," you won't actually be reading an introduction to Buddhism. What you will be reading will be my impressions of Peter Harvey's book *An Introduction to Buddhism*. As I wrote the various assignments for my classes, one of my goals was to look at each one from the point of view of how the academic study would affect my practice - what it meant to me.

Academic study of any religion is different from the devotional expression of that religion, and that's a good thing. By studying Buddhism objectively, we can learn about Buddhism in a variety of ways. The impact of every religion intersects many disciplines. When we study Buddhism, we can look at it's influence on art and culture, society, literature, politics, the history and development of Buddhism as a religion over the years, the influence of cultures and indigenous religions on Buddhism when it arrived in different countries, and the effects Buddhism has had on modern times. Perhaps most importantly, looking at Buddhism in context of the societies it has settled in, helps us see how Buddhist terms have entered our modern lexicon, and have influenced how we see ourselves whether we realize it or not.

I used the term "objectively" in the last paragraph. When I began my studies toward my first advanced degree, a Master's in Buddhist Doctrine, my assumption was that the authors of the text books I read, the professors I studied with, and that I would be objective in our analysis of Buddhist thought. I thought that I would be able to find the *bottom line* truth of Buddhism; find the Universal Truths about the tradition. In a sense, finding the Buddha's voice. What I learned, however, is the problem of objectivity - or believing that we can be truly objective.

Feminist scholar Donna Haraway has written extensively about the trap of objectivity. She asserts that all knowledge is "situated," meaning that no matter the object of our study, the only place we can actually see it, is in our own world view. She uses the colorful metaphor of calling the claim of objectivity a "god-trick" as though we can "see everything from no where." When we are honest with ourselves in how we define our analysis of religion, we not only present our conclusions within the context of our world view, we create an academic environment that values and works with the cross and multi-disciplinary nature of study.

I also owe a great deal of my understanding for how to study religion to Professor Diane Moore of Harvard's Divinity School, where I studied Religious Studies and World Religions. She and other religious scholars have identified three central assertions for study:

- Religions are internally diverse as opposed to uniform,

- Religions evolve and change over time as opposed to being ahistorical and static, and

- Religious influences are embedded in all dimensions of culture as opposed to the assumption that religions function in discrete, isolated, "private" context.

There is a Tibetan saying that just as every valley has its own language, so every teacher has his own doctrine. While an exaggeration, it does point out that even within Buddhism, there is an understanding that a teacher must mediate a received tradition and adapt it to the needs of the student. Even though Buddhists might say there is a shared moral tradition, and in a very real sense, that is true, it can be eye opening to see such diversity in the interpretations of what seem to be basic Buddhist concepts.

Buddhism may be somewhat unique, though, in its acceptance and understanding of this internal diversity. From the earliest days, the doctrines were not taught as something to be accepted blindly, but to be seen as a sort of medicine to cure the spiritual ill of suffering. While, at first, this realization leads to confusion and a bit of disillusion with the religion. When I began this study, I felt I had a good grasp on the basic concepts. I thought I would simply be elaborating on those essentials. I believed that concepts like the Four Nobel Truths, the Three Marks of Existence, and many others would simply have different ways of teaching the same thing when comparing the different schools. I thought that I already knew what Buddhism *is*, it would be simply learning more of the details.

What I learned instead, is not that the terms are so different between schools that they have no true meaning, but that the world view and context of the teachers of those schools were just as important to understand as the interpretations themselves. When confronted with such differences, I learned important lessons academically and in my practice. When interrogating the truth claims of a tradition, having an open mind - a beginner's mind - is key. Opening up my investigation and research to include a cultural approach to study, made my learning far richer than memorizing facts on a page. In practice, I feel I learned that famous phrase "only don't know" in an important way.

There is a real risk for someone like me who tends to be a methodical thinker, who finds comfort and security in being knowledgeable, to stop too soon in my spiritual insights. I could explain, describe, and analyze an abstract concept like "emptiness" all day long. It was only after learning about the different ways that term is used; in the many contexts, did I appreciate that learning about emptiness intellectually would only take me so far. And I feel very lucky. By studying sometimes conflicting explanations and even arguments between great Buddhist teachers, I got to have the best of all the worlds.

In most of the essays, I relate stories about my life and how the readings resonate with or challenge my understanding and practice. In an ideal world, it would be best for you to read each of the books the essays are about. While that's not realistic, or even necessary really, I do hope you'll consider looking into some of the books discussed here. You'll find a comprehensive list at the end of the book. I have tried to write enough about the work to make the commentary understandable, and have tried to rewrite some of the more scholarly passages to be more conversational.

One last note, and very important, is that in the summaries or descriptions of the books, articles, etc., I give full credit to the many wonderful authors, teachers, and Buddhist masters whose work I have studied. I have used quotes from many of these resources in my reviews of the work, and the ideas are theirs. I am very grateful to all of them for their insights, teaching, and revelations; any errors in the content or commentary are mine. There has been a generous handing down of the precious Dharma for over 2,500 years, and I hope that in some small way, my essays continue that tradition.

About Me

I was accidentally raised without a religion. We didn't go to church on Sundays, didn't say grace at the table, and didn't have bedtime prayers. My Dad used to say "I'm as close as you can get to an atheist without actually not believing in God." My sister and I did go to vacation Bible school with our cousins when we spent our summers on the farm in Nebraska, but I felt like an observer to something I didn't feel a part of.

One day when I was about 12 years old, I mentioned to my mother that, like her, I was not religious. I can't remember how that conversation started, but I do remember what happened next. Mom was pretty horrified that I would say such a thing. It hadn't occurred to her that my sister and I really didn't have any sort of religious education, but that was soon to change. She called her best friend, and that very Sunday, off we went to the First Presbyterian church.

I loved singing in the choir, but Sunday school was not my cup of tea. I asked lots of questions, but it was pretty clear that those questions were not welcome, and often went unanswered. And even when I did get answers to my questions, those answers didn't sit well with me. I was interested in having a religion, though, so I rode my bike to the library and asked for suggestions for books on religion. The librarian was used to me since I visited often, and frequently had requests for information not found in the kid's section. I've often wondered what she must have thought about a 12 year old coming to her with the research project of "finding a religion." She helped me find a variety of books and I found myself drawn to different aspects of many of them. The books available really weren't very sophisticated about the religious practices of especially the Eastern religions, but I was intrigued by their exotic nature. I didn't actually make a decision based on this reading, but it helped to plant the seed that it was not only ok to search, searching was a good thing!

It was about this time that I had what I can only describe as a religious experience. Things were not always peaceful at home, and sometimes the stress would take its toll. One night, I woke up while it was still dark and the family still asleep. My bed was next to the window, so I sat up and looked out at the starlight through the trees. A soft focus, triangular shape appeared. As it took shape, I was so curious about it that it didn't occur to me to be afraid. I shifted on the bed to sit cross legged, and simply looked at the shape. It didn't seem to do anything, nor was it trying to tell me something, but I found myself feeling peaceful. The trees and stars seemed more vivid; even alive. With my breathing deep and regular, my mind and heart peaceful and calm, the shape dissolved.

I went back to sleep, and began a rudimentary meditation practice from that day forward. I had no idea what meditation was, but I knew that sitting quietly each day, simply looking out the window and allowing my mind to settle helped me. It not only helped me face each day; it nourished my spirit.

Over the years, I've continued by search for meaning. I made the determination early on that I did not believe in the supernatural. Believing in God didn't make sense on so many levels, nor did having an "immortal" soul. Being interested in science and reason, made gravitating to Buddhism pretty natural. My journey in Buddhism hasn't been all smooth sailing; there have been plenty of bumps along the road. Like many others who are drawn to Buddhism have found, sometimes our idealized concepts about what we think Buddhism is, and what Buddhists should be like, don't live up to our expectations. But I kept up with my developing meditation practice, went on retreats, and continued my personal search.

Over the years I found, more and more, that my personal path and the path of Buddhism were going the same direction. I've been a student of Thich Nhat Hanh for many years, and, in 2003 during a retreat with him and the monks and nuns of the Order of Interbeing, I made the decision that I wanted to become ordained into the Order. I renewed my commitment to being a Buddhist by taking the Five Lay Precepts again, and sought out a Dharma teacher in our lineage to mentor me in the process. My partner Matt joined me on this journey, and it became another way to practice. By sharing what we were finding, bouncing ideas off each other, and sharing our opinions and insights, we saw the material in a new way. We joined another aspirant and set upon a two year journey that was challenging, fun, insightful, and filled with lovely people. It deepened my practice in ways I never could have anticipated.

Once started on a journey of education and learning, it's hard to stop! After our ordination, I realized that the process and the ordination were not the end, but the beginning. Thich Nhat Hanh told the group of ordinands at our ceremony that the brown jacket signifying our ordination is like a library card; it doesn't mean that we've read all the books in the library. Being a library rat from the time I was a child, that statement spoke my language.

One of the most important aspects of Thich Nhat Hanh's Order is Engaged Buddhism. Thay expects the members of his Core Community, monastic and lay, to look for ways to help others. In some cases, that is in Sangha building – to form groups to share the practice of mindfulness with others. In other cases, members find creative ways to reach out to people in need. As a hospice nurse, I wanted to incorporate these teachings in my patient care. After some discussions with hospice chaplains, I found that becoming a chaplain was something I wanted to pursue. Researching how to become a chaplain led me to look for a way to earn my Master's in Divinity. Because it was important to me to focus on Buddhism, I was happy to find out that there was a possibility of taking classes that could be considered in an equivalency process.

I knew that I wanted to study Buddhism from an academic point of view as well, and began looking for a way to do that. I couldn't relocate to any of the handful of schools in the U.S., but online education was beginning to come into its own. I found the Prajna Institute of Buddhist Studies (called the Five Mountain Buddhist Seminary when it first began), and enrolled. I was surprised at the rigor of the studies, and the demands on the students, but pleasantly so. I wanted a challenge, and I wanted the accomplishment of passing the courses to be meaningful. Three years later, those goals were met and surpassed. I was very proud of the body of work I had produced, and had made good friends of my classmates. I graduated with a Master's of Buddhist Doctrine, but without enough credit hours to meet the MDiv equivalent. I hoped to take additional courses to make up the hours, but that was not to be in the current setting.

Sadly, the Prajna Institute was not able to sustain the school. I was uncertain of what direction I could take, so was thrilled to find that one of the instructors let me know that the teacher who had founded the Five Mountain Order had been working to establish a "Sangha without Borders," and had founded the Buddha Dharma University. Best of all, they offered an MDiv! I enrolled, and was happy to find the degree of academic excellence I had hoped for.

Which leads us to this book. In looking at all of the assignments completed, I noticed something very important. Throughout this training and education, the instructors encouraged (insisted on!) that each assignment include how what we were learning would affect our practice. Each of the assignments developed my knowledge and my practice. When I re-read the assignments, I realized that they became a journal of sorts showing me where I was growing as a person, as a scholar, and as a practitioner.

This book is a collection of my homework, but it is more than just that. It's a way to chronicle a journey that became much more than a means to an ends. I am so grateful for the opportunity to have studied with the amazing teachers of these two schools. The exposure to many ways of thinking that I never would have found on my own, and the resources we were given that continue to enrich my practice. It became a running joke that sometime during nearly every course, I would write "where has this author been all my life??" I loved that all of the students were challenged and stretched, but most importantly, at every step of the way, it was understood that what we were learning had a purpose in practice.

One of the first patients that I visited as a Buddhist chaplain, had specific questions about Buddhist practice. Because of my work with these two schools, my answers to him were not simply factual replies. I could listen with stability, answer his questions, and help him look at how the practice could help him. We worked together for the weeks leading up to his death, and I can truly say that it was not just me visiting this young man, but a team of wonderful teachers going all the way back to the Buddha himself. We were able to help him on the greatest journey all of us travel. For that I am so grateful. My lineage name, given to me by Thich Nhat Hanh when I formally took my vows as a Buddhist, is *Tâm Bi Khai* in Vietnamese. The English translation is Compassionate Opening of the Heart. It's a wonderful name, that humbles me every day in the best possible way. Not because it describes me so well, (sometimes it doesn't describe me at all!) but because it is my greatest desire and aspiration. To open my heart to be filled with the great ocean of compassion for myself and for all beings.

I hope that reading these essays can help you on your journey as well. Perhaps you will be inspired to read some of the books that are referenced here, or perhaps look at this material in new ways. I do hope that it inspires you to bring any of the work that you study into your practice. In that sense, you can teach yourself the Dharma in a way no teacher can.

CHAPTER 2

Buddhism

When beginning a study of Buddhism, the logical place to start is with an introduction to basic Buddhism, of course. The text chosen was Peter Harvey's classic text, "An Introduction to Buddhism: Teachings, History, and Practices," written in 1995. The book covers the basics thoroughly in an academic way, but also strives to highlight the practices of Buddhism as well as the doctrine. The book reflects on the history and classic interpretations of Buddhism, but also relates the teachings to modern sensibilities. In that regard, the book was ahead of its time, understanding that religions are not monolithic, but change and adapt with the times. Viewing Buddhism as it intersects with modernity is an important approach.

The following essays are not an introduction to Buddhism themselves, but rather discuss, review, and critique key concepts from the text. In addition to an academic analysis, I built on Harvey's approach to emphasizing practice as the heart of Buddhism. In many of the essays I include personal stories that relate to the concepts, and illustrate how my understanding has evolved through guidance from my Buddhist teacher, academic study, insights from teachers and students at the seminary, and my personal practice. The sections in the chapter roughly reflect written assignments or are modified from discussion forums, but have been reworked for ease of reading and understanding.

Triple Gem

The first terms we encounter when being introduced to Buddhism are: the Buddha (most commonly considered the historical Buddha, Siddhartha Gautama), the *Dharma* (the teachings of the Buddha), and the *Sangha* (the practice community). These key terms are the core of how one becomes a Buddhist. By taking refuge in these three concepts, known as the *Three Jewels* or *Triple Gem*, the practitioner becomes a Buddhist. Taking refuge is also a form of practice, and many Buddhist communities renew the refuge vows during formal services.

Recitations of the refuge vows are repeated three times, helping the practitioner focus on each aspect of the Three Jewels. The history of the terms *gem* or *jewel* reflect the symbolism of a gem, being multifaceted, beautiful, and precious. A gem can be used as a prism to break light into a rainbow, can reflect images back, and has value as a rare thing crafted by a skilled artisan. When we look for a gem, we have to dig deeply, searching in hidden recesses even needing to be broken out of base material. When gems are found through the many layers, we then must refine the material which might, to the untrained eye, not look very special. The skilled craftsperson can see the potential beauty and transforms the rock into a jewel. We too might be diamonds in the rough, learning from the Buddha, the Dharma, and the Sangha who have made many trips into the mine of the mind, the heart, and life on this earth.

When one takes refuge, a number of images come to mind. One might think of refugees, fleeing from political or natural disasters, or we might think of finding a place protected and safe from the treacherous world. Woven into this concept of refuge is the idea of "faith." When we take refuge from the storm in a storm shelter, we have faith that the shelter will hold up to the wind and keep us safe. Harvey takes this symbol further, likening the refuge vows as an island safe from the storm, something that uplifts, sustains, and protects us. When we look at the Buddhist term for faith, *saddha*, it is commonly translated as "trustful confidence," but we can also find the translation "to place the heart upon." When a practitioner takes refuge, he or she has faith that the Triple Gem will sustain their spiritual life. That may start as a faith born of tradition, an intellectual confidence, or even dogged determination. This faith may mature over time into a heartfelt faith in the practice. Some of the teachings may be difficult, but when we have this trustful confidence, we can dive in without fear. If a teaching doesn't make sense, we can put it aside for a time until we can look deeper to understand. The fruit of the practice becomes like the very jewels of the Buddha, the Dharma, and the Sangha.

Each of the three is equally important; in fact, one could not exist for long without the other two. While the Buddha Gautama is an historical person, without the Dharma, his life would simply be an academic footnote. The Dharma without the Buddha as an exemplar, would be interesting and even helpful, but would lack the spark of life and would seem removed from the realm of our own lives and capabilities. The Sangha could not stand alone for long, no matter how well intentioned the members. The people, without a way of life to guide them, would become simply a political or cultural group, not different from any other group of people. Like the Celtic symbol the *triquetra*, the three points are interlaced together. One can focus on one of the points or the other, but when one delves deeply into one point, the other two are there also. According to Thich Nhat Hanh, in Chinese and Vietnamese Buddhism, a practitioner who takes refuge will add the phrase "within myself" to each of the aspects of the Triple Gem during the taking refuge ceremony. This shows that interwoven within the Triple Gem is the understanding that those qualities are woven within us as well. When we see the Triple Gem holistically, we see that each aspect helps us to identify with the Buddha, learn about the Dharma, gain support from the Sangha body, then to internalize those qualities to make them our own.

Faith

The difference between information and knowledge can be explained simply and can be looked at on deeper levels as well. Information is a collection of facts and data, knowledge is the ability to put the component parts together as a whole. When we have information, we may know a lot of facts, but we can't necessarily apply those facts to our lives. Knowledge puts the facts to use in the world and we can see how the parts connect with each other. With knowledge, we can look at the fine detail and nuance of the information and potentially extrapolate the data set into other areas of thought. When we're learning something new, we memorize all the facts and figures, but even though we might be able to talk a lot about the subject, we can't apply that information very well.

I may know all about the structure, development, and function of teeth, but it wouldn't be a good idea for me to pull your painful tooth! When we hear people talk about Buddhism on this level, we hear lots of information about the differences between the schools and details about the who, what, where, and when of history, traditions, and people. When we hear people speak who are knowledgeable about Buddhism, though, we'll hear far fewer facts about the differences in schools and traditions, and far more about how the information can be moved from our heads to our hearts – how the facts can change how we live our lives. One of the first concepts I learned about Buddhism was the not-self characteristic. When I learned the facts of this idea, it was just a concept, but while it's nearly impossible to explain fully how that information moved from a conceptual framework in my head, to knowledge in my heart, it was the single most important idea that awakened a profound feeling of compassion for all beings in me. Yet, when I was in grad school and talked with a fellow student about this, he couldn't understand how information about, basically, energy not being able to be created nor destroyed would make anyone more compassionate.

To engage the Dharma fully, we must take refuge in it, we must practice, and we must realize the fruits of our practice. Taking refuge is more than simply running into a shelter during a storm, but a commitment to the Buddha, the Dharma, and the Sangha as well. By placing trustful confidence, or placing my heart upon the Three Jewels, I undertake the practice wholeheartedly. If I don't make that commitment, I may be too doubtful, or decide to pick and choose what I'll believe and never have more than information about Buddhism. To practice is to use the advice of the Buddha to study the Dharma and to use the many tools given to us. Practice has a number of levels to help us focus our minds and gain insight into our nature. Realization isn't something that can be granted externally nor achieved by us. The realization of awakening, or Nirvana, is the fruit of practice. This last idea was a shocking one to me. As an achievement oriented person, I thought I would be able to accomplish a list of practices, and like building a ship in a bottle, have a neat awakening experience to put on the shelf. Instead, I've discovered that the Buddha, like all good healers and gardeners, has created a structure or healing space for us. Whether a human body or a radish, only the body can heal itself and only the radish seed can grow into a radish. What they do need is the right conditions to manifest. Taking refuge, for me, is about walking through the gate of this garden; practice is about using the tools available to me, and realizing the fruits of my practice is seeing the changes in my attitudes, ability to listen with stability to others, my ability to be more honest with myself, and to hear the Dharma sung by everything and everyone around me.

These three components are integral to one another. Taking refuge is more than just a ceremony to become a Buddhist. Many Buddhists recite the refuge vows daily to help remind themselves of the importance of this commitment. We take refuge for a variety of reasons, all equally important. Taking refuge can keep us safe in a chaotic world; giving us a place to rest in order to heal. When I consider the suffering that I have felt and still feel in life, having a father figure, comforting words, and a community of support is incredibly important. Refuge also gives me a structure that allows me to spend my time in practice, not reinventing the wheel of the Dharma. When we travel, the rules of the road, traffic signals, and maps gives us a structure so our energies can be focused on getting from point A to point B. It gives me friends on the path so the journey isn't so lonely, I can lean on the shoulder of support when I feel weak, they can help keep me honest, and that I can lend my support to others as well. Refuge without practice is merely becoming a member of some organization, like signing up for a grocery membership. Practice is crucial to fully engaging the Dharma. I might learn to meditate for stress reduction, for instance, and learn techniques designed to help me relax, but only feel that relaxation for the time I'm using the technique. Without having taken refuge, I haven't really committed myself to a way of life, nor do I find much more than self-improvement as the end result. A very important teaching I received from my first Zen teacher was that in taking refuge, I have a right to my feelings, opinions, and doubts – but I don't have a right not to practice.

Typically, I think of blind faith as a bad thing. If I have a faith that is based on what I think I have to believe in because of family, tradition, or my passion about a religion or religious figure, on some levels that might be enough. However, because I have a naturally analytical mind, I have to ask a lot of questions and work through everything logically. Blind faith wouldn't work for me. In Buddhism, we're encouraged to develop our practice ourselves. The Buddha told his attendant Ananda that no one should believe what they are told based solely on the person, even the Buddha himself, has said, but on working out the idea for ourselves. That doesn't mean that faith does not have a place in Buddhism, even blind faith from time to time. When the Buddha asks us to take the precepts, or live the Noble Eightfold Path, we might think that it's really not necessary to do certain things we don't see as making a difference.

Yet, one of the most important teachings I received early on in my adventure in Buddhism was to accept that what the Buddha taught was right and while it is ok to ask questions and doubt, it's also ok to put it on hold for the time being, but to follow the path and precepts anyway. There are times when I can fully take the plunge into the Triple Gem, and other times that I just don't think that it's all true in all cases. I think to myself "that person isn't suffering nor do they have any kind of good excuse for their behavior, they're just selfish!" or "I'm not suffering and I'm not in the mood to practice, I'm just cranky – sometimes a cigar is just a cigar, Mr. Buddha!" But, I go ahead with a faith that seems blind in that moment to go for walking meditation, or sitting, or taking a deep breath and just listening to that person I think I have figured out. At the very least, I always learn something. That version of blind faith is based on taking refuge and placing my heart on the path by practicing, knowing that walking in freedom is possible.

The Myth of Hinayana

Even in some modern religious studies text books, we can read a statements about the Buddhist schools being categorized as *Hinayana*, *Mahayana*, and *Vajrayana*. This is sloppy scholarship. It probably stems from the term Mahayana. It seems logical to assume that the "yana" part of the word is the consistent aspect, and having it in each of the schools only makes sense.

So, let's break it down. "Yana" is a Sanskrit word meaning "vehicle." "Maha" means "great" - so, Great Vehicle. A wonderful name for a religion, and often discussed as a vehicle with room for everyone. "Hina," on the other hand means "lesser," so Lesser Vehicle. Those who have learned Hinayana as a school of Buddhism, when asked, will make up a story about "lesser" not being an insult, but rather a vehicle for one person like a bike; the Great Vehicle, then, is like a bus carrying more people. To further the confusion, many people, especially in the West, believe that Hinayana practice is about becoming an Arahant, while Mahayana practice is to become a selfless Bodhisattva. The Arahant is judged, then to be selfish, only wanting enlightenment for himself, while the Bodhisattva will sacrifice his own enlightenment to the service of all sentient beings becoming enlightened. This is easily researched to be an erroneous interpretation. It may well be that the early Orientalists and translators, in their efforts to understand the texts, applied their own understanding and interpretations. The best example of this is the translation of the term "Bodhi" as "enlightenment," as though it is an equivalent of the European philosophy of Enlightenment. While there are some similarities in philosophy, the term is not the same. In fact, Bodhi actually means "awake," so "Buddha" is "one who is awake." However, both Theravada and the Mahayana schools agree that the Bodhisattva is the highest aspiration, and the Buddha was a Bodhisattva.

The other error, and a quite egregious one at that, is to equate Hinayana with Theravada Buddhism. This is insulting and historically inaccurate. In pre-sectarian Buddhism, there were a number of monastic groups that developed based on teachers who focused on different aspects of the Buddha Dharma. Many of these differing schools even lived in the same areas, studied together, and practiced together. When Theravada, "The Teaching of the Elders," migrated to Sri Lanka, Mahayana was born on the Indian mainland, and the Hinayana debate began. One of the old schools at the time, the Sarastivada, may be the target for the Hinayana invective. This argument, and that school, is long dead. However, the term carried forward and continues to be used in a variety of ways.

One of those ways is to equate Hinayana with earlier schools that no longer exist. This is not accurate, either. It's far more accurate to discuss pre-sectarian Buddhism, or to review pre-Mahayana schools from an historical perspective, since these schools no longer exist. Another is to use Hinayana and Theravada interchangeably. This is simply lazy scholarship. This is not a valid use for the term; no Theravadin would call themselves that term, and it's important even from that standpoint alone, to respect the identity of a given group.

Persistent confusion exists in the use of Hinayana in Tibetan Buddhist teaching. In a sense this continued use of the term in Tibetan teaching because of the translations from Sanskrit into Tibetan and choices made about word connotations and denotations. As we've said, "yana" as "vehicle" is not in question. "Hina," on the other hand, (or "hiina" in Pali) has been used in the suttas, as early as the *Dhammacakkappavattana Sutta*. This is the most important way to understand what the word means. In this context, the term hina is used to convey the meanings: low, coarse, vulgar, ignoble, and other undesirable qualities. The definitions go from bad to worse, and the early Mahayanists would have been well aware of this. The term "Hinayana" was certainly used as a pejorative, not a name for a valid school of Buddhism. However, when the translation of the word hina is translated into Tibetan, it is translated as "dman-pa." This word may well be the source of the confusion. While it does mean "low in quality: indifferent, inferior," it can also mean "low in reference to quantity, little." In the connotations of the word, the idea of "lesser capacity," enters into the understanding of the meaning. Therefore, what the Tibetan masters were explaining was based, not on the Sanskrit/Pali word hina or hiina, but the Tibetan word dman-pa.

Some Tibetan teachers use Hinayana to denote "lesser capacity," in the context of a practitioner who can only carry the burden of practicing for themselves, rather than the "greater capacity" of a Mahayana practitioner who carries all sentient beings on the path to liberation. Some Tibetan teachers attempt to mitigate the harsh definition by teaching that the "small vehicle" is for oneself and only for monastics, while the ideal "large vehicle" is for everyone, monastic and lay. This is not accurate either, since all early schools recommended monastic life and were skeptical that a lay practitioner would be able to devote the time to meditation that would lead to liberation. Instead, they believed that the lay practice was beneficial in gaining merit for the next life where the person could become a monastic.

In short, the term Hinayana should be retired from use except for historical context and linguistic curiosity.

Turtles All the Way Down

From a Mahayana perspective, what is the aspiration of someone practicing with a hinayana attitude? This is an interesting question, one that might give the term hinayana some purpose. Perhaps we could say that anyone other than a Buddha practices with an inferior attitude, since until that realization of waking up, we still cling to our sense of self and our practice can't help but be flawed on some level. On the other hand, we can say that cannot call anyone's practice inferior, since our attitude is our attitude and all attitudes are born of ignorance. Any practice is better than no practice at all, and all practice will yield fruit, even if it's just one in breath, following the sound of one ring of the bell, or the sight of one inspirational image. I certainly remember my practice along my adventure in Buddhism and there have been highs and lows in my attitude. If I had been deemed inferior or garbage, I might have been dissuaded from practice at all. I might have thrown up my hands "what's the use?" Yet, I still need helpful prodding to remind me that I'm not there yet; so my practice can still be brought to the next level.

When I was new to my current temple, I felt a bit like a fish out of water. I had been to traditional ceremonies in the past, but had looked at them like more of a cultural thing. As inspirational as they were, they were not integral to my practice. As I began to attend services, I understood that services are indeed important for a variety of reasons. But not speaking Vietnamese and not knowing the how's and whys of the components of the service was a handicap and I was wondered if I should keep attending. During one of the holiday times that first spring, many monks and nuns were visiting. The eldest Venerable monk was officiating and everyone was very excited to have him there. I arrived early for the service to watch the preparations and see if I could help out. I saw him sitting on the back porch of the temple watching some activity by the building that serves as kitchen and dining hall. He got up and walked over to the young men who had found a large turtle making its way toward the temple. They wanted to relocate the turtle, but the monk came over to them and, I found later when someone helped translate for me, that the monk wanted them to bring the turtle into the sanctuary.

The monk declared that the turtle wanted to hear the Dharma, and we needed to help him listen to this Dharma talk so perhaps he would achieve human rebirth in his next life. So, during this elaborate and beautiful service, there was a big old bucket up front with a large turtle plopped in it. At first, I shook my head at this silliness – poor turtle was probably terrified. The more I found myself looking at the turtle (and he did stretch his head out of his shell during the talk) I realized I could relate to the turtle. I felt out of place, struggling to understand the language, yet I was accepted and welcomed to have a place there whether anyone thought I could understand or not. I realized that not only did I have faith in the Buddha, that he has faith in me. Maybe the comparison between my understanding and the Buddhas is very much like the comparison between the turtle and the Venerable. After the ceremony, lots of people wanted to say hello and pay respects to the elder monk and he stayed, good naturedly greeting everyone. I held back to give others their time, but wanted to greet him too. I could greet him properly in Vietnamese at least. When I bowed and greeted him I pointed to the turtle, then to myself and said *cám ơn* – thank you. He chuckled and patted me on the shoulder with a twinkle in his eye.

Since then, I've been easier on others and myself in practice – we're all, after all, turtles in a bucket.

Vajrayana

The Vajrayana path developed into a new vehicle that according to Harvey, incorporated a number of factors and techniques from Hinduism and based on Mahayana concepts of emptiness which posited that any object or action could be used as a doorway to the ultimate dimension. The aspiration of someone practicing Vajrayana is much the same as the Mahayana practitioner, with the additional desire to attain Buddhahood in this very life. When taken literally, as Harvey describes the *Bodhisattva* path, the way of the Bodhisattva would seem hugely long, covering many lifetimes working through a series of steps. When viewed metaphorically, we can look at those steps as aspects of ourselves to understand on a deeper level as we unpeel the onion of what we perceive the self to be. Like the Mahayana, the Vajrayana path includes the aspiration of the Bodhisattva, to attain awakening to help all sentient beings achieve awakening as well. On any of the three vehicles, a person has the capacity of waking up to their original nature.

The practitioner of the Vajrayana path takes the role of student to the teacher who initiates the student to the rituals, mantras, and esoteric practices. Key in the motivation of the student, is the desire to attain Buddhahood and Vajrayana teaches that all efforts are to be practiced with the motivation to achieve awakening for the benefit of all sentient beings. The student must make his or her decision about what kind of practice and which teacher (*guru*) to follow with seriousness. Just as we look for guidance on the important matters of our day to day life or turn to experts for questions of our health, homes, or career, of even greater importance is to find appropriate guidance for our spiritual development. The next step in this role is the commitment to do the work. It is important to ask questions and it is normal to feel frustrated, but the student must work past these feelings. To paraphrase the Zen saying, "after the rant, the practice."

The way of the Vajrayana path consists of the basic steps of, 1) Empowerment in the esoteric practices, 2) Oral Transmission received from a qualified teacher which allows the student to follow a chanting text giving the practice a greater effect on the student, and 3) Explanation to clarify the stages of the practices and texts so the student exactly how to do the practice correctly. Esoteric practices are transmitted from teacher to student and are considered secret. Secrecy and transmission sound bizarre to Western ears, but the secrecy is a function of the context between the teacher and student.

The student/teacher method is important to create a sacred bond of commitment and integrity to the teachings; creating a context within which the student can understand the teachings and stay on track within this complex tradition. Outside of this context, the teachings would mean very little, or could be harmful from the standpoint that they might turn the student away from the Dharma if the practices did not help, or could be seen as worldly diversion. Vajrayana uses the concept of *upaya*, or skillful means, developed in earlier Mahayana teachings. These skillful means help the student see themselves in terms of their Buddha nature and ultimate truth, as opposed to the relative nature of the world seen in terms of duality. By practicing seeing and experiencing ultimate truth, we have the potential of nurturing our Buddha-nature so that it comes to fruition. The Dalai Lama explains further that the student is ripened within the tradition through his or her personal predisposition to attain Buddhahood, and experience a special state which is blissful yet empty, inseparable of space and awareness, and this special quality of mind can awaken.

An Ishtadevata or Meditational Deity is a fully awakened being who becomes the focus of meditation and devotion. Patrul Rinpoche explains that the Ishtadevata can be considered peaceful or wrathful, or neither peaceful nor wrathful depending on the practitioner's nature. The teacher generally guides the student for which Ishtadevata is appropriate for the student to meditate on, based on the student's inner qualities and subtle energies. There are many fully awakened beings and each of them represents an aspect of wholesome action or quality of enlightenment like: Quan Te Am, Bodhisattva of Compassion; Mahakala, the wrathful deity that destroys our mental chatter, replacing it with clarity of thought; Manjusri, the Bodhisattva of wisdom, or the Amitaba Buddha, guardian of the Pure Land.

The Ishtadevata is viewed to be the embodiment of awakening and a mirror for the student, reflecting the aspects of the student that are needed for awakening. This deity practice is a profound meditational state where the practitioner identifies with the deity fully. The student has the potential in this identification to understand that there is nothing that separates him or her from the deity through mind consciousness, as opposed to *seeing* oneself as the deity. This is not pretending to be the deity nor a delusion, like the psychiatric patient who thinks he is Jesus, but touching the awakened aspect of ourselves that resonates at the same frequency of the deity. Also important is to view ourselves within the context and environment of the deity; the Pure Land, for instance, and in the context of performing the actions of the deity for the benefit of others. The subtle energies are engaged and recognized by the student as being inseparable from the body and the student learns how to control and modulate these energies to focus and direct them. The student's experience of the self is transformed into a new experience of being the deity, awakening the potential that who we are is not the self we identify with, and that the boundaries of our physical bodies are not what we generally perceive them to be. In Celtic mythology this is present in the idea of seeing beyond the veil between this world and the eternal, yet recognizing that the eternal is not distant, that it is *fighte fuaighte* which in Gaelic means "woven into and through each other."

The teacher of the Vajrayana path is a skillful practitioner who can guide a student on the path and confer transmissions, pointing out the nature of the mind. Using *upaya*, skillful means, the teacher can identify the strengths and weakness of the student, assign practices that fit the student's inherent learning style and character type, and do what is necessary to help the student wake up. HHDL goes on to explain that the teacher must be skilled in the higher aspects of concentration, be able to speak about any aspect of the Dharma, be able to relate it to the entire cannon of the Buddha Dharma, and have the motivation to help others. This motivation is very important, and should come from a deep desire to help rather than for praise or other reward, just as we would not thank ourselves for eating our food because it is something we must do. The teacher must also realize that he or she is helping the student's achievement. The teacher cannot remove the student's negative actions or complexes, cannot transplant their realizations into the student, and cannot take away the student's suffering. One of the most important teachings about this, I received from the Buddhist teacher I had when I was a new nurse. Helping was very important to me and this teaching was about the importance of humility when we help. I had worked through some important issues with this teacher, and he asked if I felt some feelings of satisfaction at having accomplished this. I said that yes, it really felt great to have done the work and seen the fruits of my labor. I was very grateful for his guidance even though it seemed frustrating at the time. He had given me the tools, but allowed me to use them myself. He smiled and asked why I would want to take that feeling away from someone else. I was taken aback, but knew what he meant – I wanted to fix things for others, thinking that I was helping, but often actually fixing things to my liking. I needed to let go of what I wanted the outcome to be, certainly help the other person, but to help them on their path not mine.

The relationship between student and teacher on the Vajrayana path is a very important one because the student must have complete confidence in the teacher, and the teacher must maintain his or her vows and commitment to the student. HHDL explains that the teacher is the spiritual path to awakening because he or she is the person whom the student can relate to, who the student sees as the embodiment of awakening. The teachings must be comprehensive and authentic for the student to progress and the teacher is the guide to help the student avoid delusion or detours on the path. The

teacher is responsible to help the student understand the Dharma and to recognize false teachings. The student is responsible for taking the time to get
to know the teacher to be sure that this is the right teacher for them and is
also responsible for recognizing false teachings even from their teacher,
which is in keeping with the Kalama Sutra giving the guidelines for discernment in evaluating the truth of a teaching.

The commitments involved in following the Vajrayana path involve ad-
hering to the specific vows or *samaya* of behavior transmitted by the teacher.
These are aspects of the Bodhisattva and monastic vows, but always include
proper conduct based on generosity, ethics, patience, effort, concentration,
and wisdom. The practitioner of the Vajrayana path takes the traditional
Buddhist refuge in the Three Jewels, and adds to that taking refuge in the
guru (teacher), the *Yidams* (root of attainment or aspects of Buddha nature),
and the Dharma protectors who dispel obstacles to the path. The most important commitment is one's altruistic intention of studying and practicing
for the benefit of all beings. Additional commitments may include daily
practices such as numbers of chants, commitments to attend retreats, and
specific meditations. Commitment to the vows protects the mind from negativity and emotional distress, and strengthens the bond between the student
and teacher. Breaking the vows can cause the student to have further suffering because of confusion and delusion.

The fruition of the Vajrayana path is the attainment of full Buddhahood.
The Vajrayana is one of the three vehicles or routes through which one can
attain awakening, the others being Theravada and Mahayana. Additionally,
the fruition of the Vajrayana path is the maximum result that can emerge
from the four main areas of practice: view, meditation, and conduct. This
point is important – that the practice yields the fruit; the fruit is not something one can go get, create, or be given. Much as a seed contains the whole
of the tree and the future fruit, it is not yet a tree until it is planted in fertile
soil, watered, and cultivated by the experienced gardener. In Sylvia Plath's
Ode to a Bitten Plum, she spins a vision of taking a bite of a plum and looking ever deeper at the physical nature of the plum, its colors and textures,
then inside the seed to its secret potential as a tree, then further in: "Encased
in a wooden shell, enclosed in the small, tight darkness is the pale green
twilight; the timeless peace of centuries, the magic hush of deep grass and

deeper leaves wreathed in an enchanted garden." Then her consciousness shifts back to reality "Beauty of a bitten fruit, quiet in my warm hand."

The differences in method between *Sutra*-based Mahayana practice and *tantra*-based Vajrayana practice are a matter of perspective. Each of the vehicles recognizes the importance of the Buddha's words and the value of the *sutras*. In teachings-based practice, the student cultivates his or her mind and wisdom by reading the words of the Buddha and other great teachers. The *sutras* function to help us learn the basic methodology and practice, but they also serve to help us identify within ourselves and reflect on our body, speech, and mind. If our actions and thoughts are not in alignment with the sutras, by reading about the right thing to do, we can change to better reflect wholesome words and deeds. As we integrate the teachings and the actions, we become the teachings and our actions flow from that ground of being. In the mystery-based practice of Vajra-Tantra-Mantra, the student uses techniques given to her or him that connect to the subtle consciousness not engaging the intellect. Putting the books away, my take on the difference is that each looks at the process of making the connection to the ultimate dimension from a different point of view. The sutra-based practice looks from the outside in, and the tantric-based practice looks from the inside out. In our Sangha group when we were studying Thich Nhat Hanh's Fourteen Mindfulness Trainings, we were asked to re-write each one and relate them to our life. One of the things I noticed was that some of us related to the trainings first from the view point of the society and world, others from the view point of their personal experience.

From either point of view, we could explore the ideas, for instance loving speech, non-attachment to views, mindful consumption, etc. We can start considering how they relate to the world, how that affects our society, how that affects our community and family, and what impact those issues have on each of us personally and then what we in turn bring to the family, community, and world. Others might find that connecting with the trainings on a personal level, perhaps how we've suffered personally from our circumstances, then seeing how that relates to friends and family, the community, and the world as a whole. Much like the approach to a mandala, we can trace the lines from the inside out or outside in, we see the lines first, the interconnection of the lines, and finally the whole of the mandala. While any discussion of the teachings would fall into the sutra-based category, it was helpful to me in considering the bottom-line difference in the two.

In Tantra, when we connect with the universal energy within us, we make a shift from relative reality to the ultimate reality, seeing the world with the eyes of the Buddha. We're still in the world, but not of the world. In energy work we talk about that for some forms, we need to center ourselves first before we can effectively channel the energy. In Reiki, for instance, we learn a technique to start the flow of Reiki, to *be* Reiki, and that flow centers us. That analogy seems like what I perceive the differences between the two approaches is getting at.

Bodhichitta

The term Bodhichitta is made up of two components. Bodhi means *awake* or completely open, and *chitta* (also spelled *citta*) meaning *mind, heart,* (heart/mind) or *attitude.* This bodhichitta or completely open heart/mind is called the soft spot, the place that is tender and vulnerable and is equated, in part, with our capacity to love and experience compassion. The first step on the Bodhisattva path is the arising of bodhichitta; the aspiration to strive for Buddhahood for its own sake and for the sake of all suffering beings. The concept of citta has its roots in the *Anguttara Nikaya* (A.) from the Pali cannon which saw the mind as having many unskillful tendencies with deep roots, but below these roots is shining and pure. "Monks, this mind is brightly shining, but it is defiled by defilements which arrive" (A.1.10) The bodhichitta ideal is found in both the Madhyamikas and Yogacarins schools as well in the Tathagata-garbha writings. Tathagata-garbha is composed of Tathagata, the name the Buddha called himself meaning *one who has thus gone/arrived* or *Perfect One,* and *garbha* which means *embryo* or *womb.*

These writings helped develop the idea of the Buddha-nature or potential of all living beings to become fully awakened to their true Buddha nature. Harvey explains that there are a number of analogies that are used to describe this inner nature such as the shoots of a great tree piercing through the fruit, suggesting both the reality of the tree within the seed and its' potential which needs cultivation and care; a gem wrapped in rags suggesting the perfection that is obscured but that only needs to be uncovered; or the gold ore that must be refined of its impurities to bring out the intrinsic purity of the gold suggesting that skill is needed to successfully refine the ore. The diamond that needs to be uncovered; the very creamy, rich milk that can be made into butter with the work of churning it; the sesame seed filled with oil that we must pound out of the seed – all analogies reflecting that the Buddha nature is our potential, our heirloom, that we have to uncover by doing the work ourselves.

In the Perfection of Wisdom literature, bodhichitta, the thought of enlightenment, arises when the person becomes aware of the Tathagata-garbha, Buddha nature, within. A key passage states "'That thought is no thought, since by nature it is brightly shining', and that it is a state of 'no mindedness' which is beyond existence and non-existence." His Holiness the Dalai Lama writes that when we realize that we do not wish to suffer, we should work to uproot its causes, and when we can conceive of a state in which we have total cessation of ignorance, we will develop a strong desire to reach such a state. Specifically stating "Our understanding should be so profound that is shakes our whole being and induces in us a spontaneous wish to gain it. Once we develop this spontaneous wish to achieve cessation, an immense appreciation for the beings who have realized this cessation within their own minds develops and the recognition of the Buddha's accomplishments becomes powerful. The benefits and beauty of his teachings become clear."

To elaborate on the bodhichitta idea, two levels can be described: 1) aspirational and 2) engaged. Aspirational bodhichitta has two stages: 1) the heartfelt wish or desire to become a Buddha to benefit all sentient beings and 2) pledging to never abandon this aim until it is achieved. Engaged bodhichitta means engaged in practices that will cultivate this goal and assist in its attainment such as taking the Bodhisattva vows.

Zasep Tulku Rinpoche explains that without bodhichitta and without cultivating bodhichitta, the Vajrayana practices can have the danger of the practitioner experiencing the visualizations, mantras, and the like boosting their own ego coming away from the practices feeling that they are very accomplished and smart. To cultivate bodhichitta and the mind of shunyata, the stage is set for the practices to have a strong foundation in compassion. An analogy the Rinpoche uses is that bodhichitta is the juice of the fruit and when we eat the fruit, the juice is the essence of the fruit. When we develop and cultivate bodhichitta, we become the child of the Buddha, joining the family of the Buddha.

When we have this precious heart/mind, a pure love and compassion is shining toward all beings. By cultivating the aspects of bodhichitta: generosity, patience, compassion, etc. it will benefit and stay with the practitioner as illustrated in the verse "All other virtues are like the plantain tree; for after bearing fruit they simply perish. But the perennial tree of the Awakening Mind unceasingly bears fruit and thereby flourishes without end."

Thich Nhat Hanh explains that when we take refuge in the Buddha, we also take refuge in the Buddha in ourselves. When we touch the seed of awakening in ourselves, we open up the thought of awakening, awakening the desire to liberate ourselves from suffering and to help other living beings. When we are filled with the energy of bodhichitta, the highest mind, the mind of love, we become Bodhisattvas and we can confront any kind of danger or difficulty. An English translation of a chant from the Vietnamese service that is recited before taking refuge says: "The one who bows and the one who is bowed to, are both by nature empty. Therefore, the communication between them is inexpressibly perfect." This helps us understand that we are not different from the Buddha and that we are not separate from him either. The Buddha's nature is our nature.

Bodhichitta is, in part, compassion – our ability to feel pain, have empathy with others who feel pain, and the heartfelt desire to help others in pain. Yet another analogy for bodhichitta is the rawness of a broken heart. This broken heart sometimes leads us to have unwholesome feelings like anger, resentment, fear, and anxiety, but underneath all of that is the honesty of our suffering. The first Noble Truth explains that we all have suffering; it is something that we all share in. Considering suffering to be noble or holy seems strange, especially since we spend a great deal of time trying to avoid suffering or building walls to protect ourselves.

We armor our hearts emotionally from a personal standpoint and even from a cultural or societal one through racial, ethnic, sexual orientation, or other prejudices. Yet, when we connect with our pain it is an honest and courageous thing which breaks the barriers that separate us from others and from our Buddha-nature. That experience of bodhichitta, of connecting to our compassionate nature and of wanting to help others, can be powerful.

When I was a little girl, one of my aunts lived next door to us. She had multiple sclerosis and from the time I was a toddler, she was confined to her room either in bed or in a chair. She was my personal bodhisattva because she was a constant presence for me. My parents had many problems that unfortunately lead them to leave me to my own devices much of the time, but my aunt was someone who gave me her undivided attention and I was happy to visit her every day. As I grew older, I was more and more determined that I would become a nurse so I could take care of her. I was so grateful for her kindness that I wanted to return something to her. She died when I was ten years old, but the desire to help remained alive and well. When I graduated from nursing school and had my picture taken with my cap and white uniform on, I could feel her presence and happiness for me.

In the *Bodhisattvacharyavatara*, this verse rings true for me: "May I be the doctor and the medicine and may I be the nurse for all sick beings in the world until everyone is healed." (Chapter 3, Verse 8) I dove into my studies to help others and while my studies, my experiences as a student nurse, and my first job were exciting and fulfilling, it was all a challenge and at times overwhelming. I dove into the sea of compassion, but it sometimes felt like I would drown. The advice I got from the experienced doctors and nurses was to not get so involved, not to care so much. It is an unwritten rule for caregivers that we should armor our hearts against the pain that seeing so much suffering produces. I had been working in the pediatric intensive care unit for about a year and was beginning to feel pretty competent and confident. Working on the night shift one week, we had a child die each night and I was one of the nurses to help either during the events when the child died or to help after the death. I thought I could shrug it all off, after all, this was a string of bad luck, but next week will be better and I am a professional and not supposed to be affected by this.

When I arrived at my apartment in the morning at the end of the week, I lay down on the living room floor without even taking my coat off and slept there all day. When I woke up, I knew that denying my pain was not a good idea and this soft spot, this grief, was real and putting up walls to deny it was not real and not healthy.

Dr. Arthur Kleinman has written that the balance between science and the art of medicine has shifted too far toward the science and technology aspect and has nearly disabled the physician from being a care giver. Care giving is a foundational component of moral experience, he says: "It is a practice of empathetic imagination, responsibility, witnessing, and solidarity with those in great need. It is a moral practice that makes caregivers, and at times even care-receivers, more present and thereby fully human – it completes (not absolutely, but as a kind of burnishing of what we really are – warts and all) our humanity." When a young hospice patient that I currently visit, called upon by the team because he wanted to talk about his life and learn from a Buddhist perspective, asked me about karma and reincarnation, he wanted to know if it was something he did wrong in a past life that brought about his disability. I answered that perhaps that was the case, but perhaps it was people like me who had a need to learn about compassion and opening our hearts. Perhaps, it is you who are the bodhisattva, the one who choose the difficult life to be a gift to us who care for you.

Compassion is the word we often use to translate the Sanskrit word *karuna*, but karuna is a more complex word which includes the fragment *ru* – *to weep* and is said to be the anguished cry of deep sorrow when we experience the suffering of another as if it is our own and is born of a clear sense of unity with all living beings. As we awaken bodhichitta, we must work with it to soften and open ourselves to our limitless capacity for understanding. This is very powerful, and sometimes hardest to apply to ourselves. When we can connect with the feeling of compassion, we have the opportunity of encouraging and being with that feeling, then noticing the results. It is with that encouragement that we can expand our feelings from ourselves to our loved ones to others – the basis for the *Metta Bhavana* or loving kindness meditation.

We hear in the *Karaniya Metta Sutta*: "As a mother would risk her life to protect her child, her only child, even so should one cultivate a limitless heart with regard to all beings. With good will for the entire cosmos, cultivate a limitless heart: Above, below, and all around, unobstructed, without enmity or hate. Whether standing, walking, sitting, or lying down, as long as one is alert, one should be resolved on this mindfulness. This is called a sublime abiding here and now." This is the true state of affairs; seeing the world as it really is and connecting with it. This expansion cannot happen by force, by pushing our way to grasp or attain it.

We cannot make a strawberry. If we have all of the component parts and chemicals and colorings, we might make something that tastes something like a strawberry or looks a bit like a strawberry, but it will only be a pale substitute. When we plant a strawberry seed, water it, cultivate it, read gardening advice, maybe even some seasons fail in our efforts, but eventually the strawberry plant will manifest and we will find a beautiful red jewel of fruit that we can pluck. When we put it in our mouths, it will taste so sweet and pure. Virginia Fry shares her experience with giving talks about end of life care to primary physicians. In her lectures, she shares the Zen story of the tigers and the mouse. When she tells the story of the woman who is chased by tigers and tries to escape down a rope on a cliff, only to find that more tigers were below her and to add insult to injury a mouse started gnawing on the rope she was clinging to! What did the woman do? The only sensible thing she could do – she spied a ripe strawberry on a plant clinging to the cliff; it was so beautiful there in the sunlight, so she reached out, took it, and popped it into her mouth. Her last word was "Sweet!"

When the physicians who heard the story were asked to comment on it, they tended to be frustrated: if only she had thrown the strawberry to the tigers to distract them, or swung the rope away, or even what was she thinking being in that dangerous area in the first place? We fight so hard to be in control, to have the outcome we want, that we often fail to be present for our patients, fail to be honest with them, fail to help them find comfort and happiness even in the midst of suffering and confusion.

All too often it is because their pain reminds us of our own and makes us feel vulnerable and afraid. When I first started in nursing, it was so easy and exciting to help – so filled with happiness to chant "may all beings find peace!" But when I found that the suffering was all too often more than I could help, or patients seemed unwilling to be helped, or children died in spite of all of our efforts, I began to realize that my aspiration was less like a Hallmark card and more of a profound truth that I was not sure I was capable of.

Like hearing the Heart Sutra for the first time and thinking it is just wonderful, then really listening to it and feeling quite terrified, and then learning to relax into it to begin to understand a glimmer of its meaning. Yet, the end of that first stanza, that after this penetration he overcame all pain, gives us hope that we too can penetrate the veil of illusion that keeps us locked in our suffering. At the end of the sutra, the mantra is proclaimed "*Gate gate paragate parasamgate bodhi svaha.*" Pema Chödrön says: "Just as the seed contains the tree, this mantra contains the entire teaching on abiding in the *Prajnaparamita*, abiding in the fearless state." and she goes on to explain that we can look at the translation of the mantra as either "gone, gone, gone beyond, gone completely beyond..." as a process of a journey always stepping further and further; or we could translate it "groundlessness, groundlessness, more groundlessness, even beyond groundlessness..." taking our bodhisattva path stepping further into groundlessness, stepping beyond fear.

When my mother died, we returned from a long trip to Michigan and back for the funeral and then prepared for the ceremony at Chua Bao An, the Vietnamese Buddhist temple I attend, I bought yellow roses, her favorites, to place on the alter during the service. I spent some time alone in our meditation room, taking one of the blooms with me that morning. I didn't think I could meditate, but I did spend time with the rose, looking deeply into the petals just being with the rose thinking about what it once was as a little bud, what it would become wilted and thrown away, but to become the earth again to nourish other roses. I looked at my own hand, having looked in the mirror that morning and realizing how much I now look like my mother, seeing that chain of ancestors who brought me where I am today. I remembered pictures of my mother as a little girl, a young woman, beautiful and smiling, yet having lived through many hardships and suffering, holding me when I was a baby.

I knew that one day I would die, too and my son might look at pictures of me throughout my life and wonder about my life and consider his own mortality. I wanted to whisper to the rose, "mom, is that you?" and I felt a great relief. I felt that I could let her and myself off the hook for all the things in our relationship that were lacking, for all the things that did not go right, and for all the things that did: all these things were images from a kaleidoscope, beautiful in their own way yet ever changing and I could release them, no longer feeling resentment or longing for what could not be, or clinging to what was that I wanted to keep.

In his commentaries on the Heart Sutra, Thich Nhat Hanh talks about learning from a leaf that it is not afraid of the next phase of its existence when it is ready to fall from the tree, that we should not speak of the life of the leaf, or our life, but of Life. When the leaf was part of the tree, it worked hard to nourish the tree, but when it changes and falls to the ground it will become part of the soil and continue to nourish the tree, becoming a leaf yet again. The leaf is empty of a separate self; as is the rose petal, my mother, and me. I could take a step into groundlessness.

CHAPTER 3

Life of the Buddha

This course was a study of the book "Buddha" by Karen Armstrong and the PBS documentary "Buddha" directed by David Grubin. The book is an attempt to explore the life of the Buddha in an historical way. Armstrong explains that early on, she discovered that how we approach history has a cultural component. India had a different concept of what is important to know about a figure historically. In the West, we want to know the facts about a timeline, both from the standpoint of chronology, but also from a psychological standpoint - why is that person the way they are? In our culture, we believe that the formation of the self is the most important thing to know about. The early Buddhists were more interested in symbols, myth in its highest sense, and the significance of the stories for the reader to understand how the life of Siddhartha Gautama relates to the dharma; all in the service of helping us wake up.

The essays here consider Armstrong's writings, other histories of the Buddha, and compare the documentary to explore the difference approaches. The attempt is not to uncover the "truth" about the historical Buddha, but rather to look at the different angles to see the evolution of these approaches, and to consider all of them as a prism with different facets, producing a rainbow of understanding.

Buddha's Life

When Armstrong begins the story of the Buddha's life, she starts with the traditional story of the home life of Siddhartha Gautama at around the time he left his family to go forth into homelessness on his quest to find the answer to suffering. Armstrong explains the story of his life of luxury, all the best education, food, training in the way of the warrior, an arranged marriage and the birth of a son, and the potential to be a great leader. He was the pride of his family, friends, and community and no expense or effort was spared to make him happy. Yet he was not happy. He felt that this life was crowded and dusty; he longed for clarity and meaning. He was exposed for the first time to seeing old age, illness, and death; this changed his life and made him determined to find an answer to the suffering he saw.

So we went forth to the forest and a life of homelessness. He wandered, found teachers, and became an ascetic. He was so devoted that he nearly starved himself to death, becoming so thin that he could nearly touch his spine when he put his hand on his stomach, his skin was black and withered, and his hair fell out. He had learned from the many teachers he had listened to and followed that the self-conscious and eternally greedy ego was at the root of the problem of suffering, and their efforts had led them and him to try to kill this ego aggressively by doing violence to the body and trying to break the spirit of the practitioner. The Buddha finally realized that these methods had failed; he had practiced them flawlessly, yet they had not produced the transformation that he sought. He cried out "Surely, there must be another way to achieve enlightenment!"

The Buddha had a remembrance of a time in his childhood when he was taken to the ceremonial ploughing festival that was hosted by his father in the spring. All of the people were dressed in their finest and it was a time for the community to come together to celebrate and to honor the work of the fields, hoping for a good harvest in the fall. The legend has it that Prince Siddhartha was taken to the festival and he and his nurses found a perfect spot to watch the festivities, a bit away from the goings on but still close enough to see. King Suddhodana, Siddhartha's father, left his son in the care of the nursemaids to go participate in the ploughing and festivities. The nurses left their charge on a couch under a rose apple tree, and while he slept they stole away to catch a glimpse of the excitement. When Siddhartha found himself alone, he gazed at the ploughed field and saw there the earth that had been cut into, revealing the bugs and worms wiggling and torn apart, the new shoots and seeds destroyed. As he watched, birds landed in the furrows, feasting on the bugs and worms. A hawk swooped in from high in the sky, capturing a bird in his talons, flying away with it for a feast of its own. When he saw this, he was over-taken with sadness at the state of these creatures and felt tremendous compassion for them as though they were his own relatives. Unbidden, he felt a sense of powerful joy and expansiveness, an ecstasy that had nothing to do with the craving, desire, selfishness, or clinging of our normal state of being.

While we have all had a similar experience of feeling spontaneously and unselfishly joyful, that experience is often ruined when we stop experiencing it and start thinking or talking about it. Instead, the boy did the wise thing and sat in meditation, entering spontaneously the first *jhana*, feeling a calm happiness as he contemplated what he had seen. When the party returned to the rose apple tree, they saw the little Prince deep in meditation and were in awe of what they saw. The shadow of the tree had not moved with the passing of the sun, but had stayed to shade the boy so that his meditation would not be interrupted. This shadow was symbolic of the North Star or Axis Mundi; the center of the world. As a mirror of what would come later, sitting under this rose apple tree, little Siddhartha entered into the first jhana and had a glimpse of Nirvana.

Later, Gautama would remember this event and realize that he did not need to destroy his body to find liberation, but that even a small, untrained child could experience this meditation. He could feel the memory of the coolness of the shade of the rose apple tree, and could imagine that coolness of the state of Nirvana, curing mankind from the lifetime of the fever of suffering and strife. He realized the Middle Way which shunned the over-indulgence in the desires of the self, yet eschewed extreme asceticism which was equally as self-indulgent and asserted that neither of these ways would lead to happiness.

Going back to the child under the rose apple tree, we might like to explore the components of that experience of jhana. The first part of that experience, it seems to me, to be one of awakening bodhichitta or compassion for the beings of the field. The second part of the experience was the feeling of joy (*mudita*) and the boy's correct action of entering meditation (jhana) when the experience arose. Each of these component parts are important to look at more closely.

The term Bodhichitta is made up of two components. Bodhi means awake or completely open, and chitta (also spelled citta) meaning mind, heart, (heart/mind) or attitude. This bodhichitta or completely open heart/mind is called the soft spot, the place that is tender and vulnerable and is equated, in part, with our capacity to love and experience compassion. Bodhichitta is important because it starts the process of awakening our true nature, that of Buddhahood. There are a number of analogies that are used to describe this inner nature such as the shoots of a great tree piercing through the fruit, suggesting both the reality of the tree within the seed and its' potential which needs cultivation and care; a gem wrapped in rags suggesting the perfection that is obscured but that only needs to be uncovered; or the gold ore that must be refined of its impurities to bring out the intrinsic purity of the gold suggesting that skill is needed to successfully refine the ore.

The diamond that needs to be uncovered; the very creamy, rich milk that can be made into butter with the work of churning it; the sesame seed filled with oil that we must pound out of the seed – all analogies reflecting that the Buddha nature is our potential, our heirloom, that we have to uncover by doing the work ourselves. Not only did the young Siddhartha Gautama start his journey to Buddhahood with this spontaneous arising of Bodhichitta, he remembered the experience as the spark that led him to move past the teachings of the other gurus he had been working with and trust in his own inner knowledge; the trust that this organic experience he had as a child was a valid approach to the spiritual path.

Early Life

Siddhartha's birth was a miraculous one; while not virginal in origin it was unusual in that Siddhartha was born out of his mother's side. He is said to have immediately stood up and took his first steps in the cardinal directions. It was predicted at his birth to either become a great king, leader, and uniter of people or a great religious leader who would bring peace to the people.

His family decided that they liked the king part better, so they spared no expense or effort to prepare Siddhartha for this future. They assured that he had the best education, physical training, and was spared any unhappiness. But like anyone who has only known luxury and has no suffering to compare their material life to, he was not happy. He knew something was amiss, but he didn't know what it was. With divine intervention, Siddhartha did "go forth" into the city and saw for the first time a person who was ill, a person who was old, and a dead body. He was horrified by what he saw and decided to go forth to the religious life.

Psychologically, there is little difference between Siddhartha's journey and the one we take today. Many people were sheltered or have sheltered their own children the same way Siddhartha's parents did. We can see the hallways of our schools filled with children who have everything, yet are searching and who feel empty. Siddhartha experimented with spirituality, but because of his genius and ability to be completely honest, he was able to see the interconnectedness of how his life came to be, what it meant, and how to rise above the events that happen to transform his suffering. Armstrong says it well that rather than becoming a god, he became fully human. The story of the Buddhas life may have some elements of truth to it, but it is made up of symbolic images that mirror the later discoveries he would teach. The literal is transformed into the spiritual when he found that: "I am of the nature to grow old. There is no way to escape growing old. I am of the nature to have ill health. There is no way to escape ill health. I am of the nature to die. There is no way to escape death. All that is dear to me and everyone I love are of the nature to change. There is no way to escape being separated from them. My actions are my only true belongings. I cannot escape the consequences of my actions. My actions are the ground upon which I stand." (translation by Thich Nhat Hanh)

Life Events

When considering what to focus on in the Buddha's life, an approach is to consider the importance of looking at which events mirror or fore shadow the insights and teaching that would develop into the Dharma we know today. Siddhartha Gautama's birth and upbringing were sheltered and perfect.

He did not want for anything, yet as he grew, he also grew restless and increasingly unhappy. The story of Siddhartha Gautama is a charming one; one that could easily be told in contemporary terms. In today's Western culture, many children are raised like the little prince that was Siddhartha's childhood. He was protected from all bad things; guarded and sheltered, trained to be a leader of men, given all that money and position could offer. Siddhartha was his parent's pride and joy – perfect in every way – yet, he knew something was missing.

When first exposed to old age, illness, loss, and death he knew he had to go forth to find the reason and release from these horrors. He found that what he was at fist horrified by was actually a Noble Truth; our very nature is a gift to teach us the truth. In finding this perfection of mind, he created a method for awakening and came to develop a monastery of teachers who themselves were successful on this path. We can take refuge in the Buddha, the Dharma, and the Sangha as equal partners to protect us, guide us, and ultimately, share in the joy of our liberation from the suffering of the world. Going forth as he did was to shed himself of all of the things that made up his life before. Where there had been luxury, there was austerity; plenty of food, he could now count his ribs through his skin; family and friends, only companions on the path with competing philosophies and concepts. Having rid himself of everything associated with his old, unsatisfactory life, despite the accomplishments of his yogic training, he was still unsatisfied.

These pairs of opposites are important to consider, not because the Middle Way means "everything in moderation," (it does not) but in seeing that neither having everything nor having nothing will make a person happy. When he was able to awaken, he could see that he had everything he needed to be happy by dwelling deeply in the present moment.

We do not know how "factual" or accurate the story of the Buddha's life is, but as Jane Hirshfield says in her documentary, "People like stories. It is one of the ways we learn. The story of the Buddha's life is an archetypal journey. But it is a means to an end. It is not an end." When we look at Gautama's motivation for going forth, we see that he had an awakening in a relative way by seeing people who were ill, were old, and were dead. When he was able to touch the ultimate dimension, he could see that these things are a Noble truth; that touching our suffering is the first step in using that gift to look deeply into ourselves to find the truth and the key to unlocking the door to liberation. W.S. Merwin says eloquently, "Everybody understands suffering. It's something that we all share with everybody else. It's at once utterly intimate, and utterly shared. So Buddha says, 'That's a place to begin. That's where we begin.'."

Armstrong discusses the nature of the Buddha as being fully human. This is, perhaps, one of the best, most concise ways to describe the nature of a Buddha. The Buddha was able to see the world as it really is, which can be done by anyone and sometimes when people do see the world as it really is, they become profoundly depressed and discouraged when they recognize the level of devastation and violence in the world. The Buddha, on the other hand, looks at the world as it really is and in a holistic way; looking at the root causes of the suffering experienced and seeing the path to liberation from that suffering.

Armstrong discusses that while the Buddha spent most of his time in cities, most depictions of him are in pastoral settings deep in meditation. During his life, the Buddha traveled a great deal and established a number of monasteries around India. Often he had rich benefactors who would donate beautiful and valuable land to build simple huts for the monks to rest and study in especially during the rainy season. These benefactors, including kings, would be drawn to the teachings and wanted to build their own merit by giving generously to this charismatic holy man. Many of them also learned more about the teachings and followed them because they grew to understand them and took them to heart, not just for selfish reasons. The Buddha visited many of them in their palaces, and was unmoved by their riches, perhaps because of his upbringing and familiarity was this class of people left him unfazed. On the other hand, the Buddha is most often depicted in setting of solitude and beauty. Further in history, Buddhist art has created many images of the Buddha with serene expressions and showing the Buddha in repose or meditation. The symbolism of what the Buddha represented is more important that a documentary approach to his life and times. Seeing a statue or painting that gives us a hint at what it might have been like to sit in meditation with the Buddha is wonderful and inspiring.

As we read the scriptures, the more we can remember that they are filled with symbolism and do not emphasize a blow-by-blow history of the life of the Buddha and his disciples, the better we can examine what the stories, sutras, and legends are trying to convey to us. Armstrong speculates that when the stories talk about Gautama confronting Mara as he is approaching the Bodhi tree that the symbolism is most likely talking about Gautama's shadow self, confronting his own inner demons. Additionally, the story of Gautama's life is a mirror for the story of his life as the Buddha; he sees illness, old age, and death then transforms his suffering of those into a framework to help us understand the underlying reality of these states of being. The Buddha would go on to wake up to the understanding of sunyata (emptiness) by realizing that he could not do that by denying himself of his desires, but by looking deeply into them and transforming them. Or as Jane Hirshfield says so beautifully, "One great tap-word of Buddhism is compassion, which is the deep affection that we feel for everything because we're all in it together. Be it other human beings, other animals, the planet as a whole, the creatures of this planet, the trees and rivers of this planet. Everything is connected."

History

Deciding which events in the Buddha's life are important is a challenging task. Perhaps the best way to consider what is important is to look at which events mirror or fore shadow the insights and teaching that would develop into the Dharma we know today. Siddhartha Gautama's birth and upbringing were sheltered and perfect. He did not want for anything, yet as he grew, he also grew restless and increasingly unhappy. Going forth as he did was to shed himself of all of the things that made up his life before. Where there had been luxury, there was austerity; plenty of food, he could now count his ribs through his skin; family and friends, only companions on the path with competing philosophies and concepts. Having rid himself of everything associated with his old, unsatisfactory life, despite the accomplishments of his yogic training, he was still unsatisfied. These pairs of opposites are important to consider, not because the Middle Way means "everything in moderation," (it does not) but in seeing that neither having everything nor having nothing will make a person happy. When he was able to awaken, he could see that he had everything he needed to be happy by dwelling deeply in the present moment.

When we look at Gautama's motivation for going forth, as discussed in the last assignment, we see that he had an awakening in a relative way by seeing people who were ill, were old, and were dead. When he was able to touch the ultimate dimension, he could see that these things are a Noble truth; that touching our suffering is the first step in using that gift to look deeply into ourselves to find the truth and the key to unlocking the door to liberation. There is a book by Dr. Paul Brand called *Pain: the Gift that Nobody Wants*. In it, he relates his story of working with lepers in India, and the discovering that leprosy is actually a disease whereby the body loses its ability to feel pain. People continually injure and wear down their bodies, causing disfigurement leading others to be frightened and disgusted by their appearance.

This lead him to look at pain in a different way; to see that we need pain to protect ourselves as well as learn about ourselves. The pain that we feel whether physical, emotional, social, or spiritual is something we can explore and look deeply at to see what the root causes are. When we find those root causes or habit energies, with that insight we find the burden of suffering eased. When we recite the Five Remembrances, we touch not only the Buddha's motivation for going forth, but also what he learned; that our actions are the ground on which we stand, that: "...by relying on the compassion of the Buddha, The wisdom of the Dharma, The fellowship of the Sangha, May I discover my true nature, And liberate others beings and myself from *Samsara*."

The term *Kšatrīya* (or *rājanya*) was derived from the Sanskrit word kṣatra meaning umbrella, to govern, roof and was related to terms for ruler, warrior, and king. This warrior caste in Vedic times was not something one was necessarily born into, but was based on aptitude, talent, and experience. Of the castes at the time, the warrior class was ranked first, above the Brahmins, farmers and artisans, and laborers. Kšatrīya members were thought to be the protectors of the Dhamma (duty and justice) and they are assigned in rituals to carry a staff made from the banyan tree, a tree that grows root branches that hang from the tree creating a canopy that can cover a large area, symbolically protecting and shielding the people beneath it. According to Armstrong, the caste system in India was evolving to include the merchants, and while not integrated into the caste structure, the wandering mendicant monks were almost seen as a caste level themselves.

We can see that, whether Gautama was born into the warrior caste or not, symbolically, the qualities associated with this caste are the very qualities attributed to Gautama and then are mirrored on a spiritual level by the Buddha. The warrior caste members were seen as handsome and strong, highly skilled in martial arts, and possessed exemplary courage. The very qualities that the Buddha would demand of his followers mirror those same qualities found in the warrior caste, to be courageous in looking deeper into one's self with complete honesty, to become the refuge for all beings, and to protect all beings from suffering by transcending it and showing others the way to liberation.

It may be that Gautama also associated himself with the warrior caste for the same reason that his early life mirrors the ultimate realities of his liberation. He was destined, potentially, to become a king and ruler of men, taking what he needed and wanted by force, protecting his people by the sword. Instead, he became a spiritual leader, who learned to cut through illusion instead of flesh. As a spiritual warrior, he was no less courageous than a soldier because being honest with ourselves exposes us to our vulnerability, pain, and fears. The spiritual warrior takes off his armor instead of putting it on; walking into the fire with nothing to protect him, burning off the layers of "dust" that cloud reality. Mara would tempt Gautama to become a *cakkavatti*, a world ruler, a giant among men before Gautama made his final rejection of his householder life to go forth on his spiritual quest. He is tempted to consider all the good he could do in the world by ruling it with justice. Gautama realizes that kingdoms, even just and good ones, come and go; that for lasting peace, he must seek a different kind of life. Again, the vision of a world ruler in the relative world, is mirrored in the absolute when the Buddha becomes the personification of the ultimate spiritual development and achievement.

During the Axial age, the Vedic religion of India was changing. The mendicant monks and philosophers of the day were struggling to make sense of a changing world and in so doing, were also changing the way they thought about the old religions. Armstrong explains that the beginnings of

Hinduism can be thought to have started during this time. These new scriptures were called the Upanishads and they reinterpreted the Vedic literature making a connection with the individual's nature and the ultimate nature of *Brahman*. By looking inward, the goal was to see that Brahman was the essential nature of everything, and one could come to realize that this essence is identical to ones' own soul (*atman*). The spiritual seeker desired an experience of the self that was transformed into a new experience of being Brahman, the ultimate deity; that one is not the self we identify with and that the boundaries of our physical bodies are not what we generally perceive them to be. The hope is to obliterate the self, thereby ceasing suffering. In Celtic mythology this is present in the idea of seeing beyond the veil between this world and the eternal, yet recognizing that the eternal is not distant, that it is fighte fuaighte which in Gaelic means "woven into and through each other."

Alara Kalama was one of Gautama's teachers while he was on his journey. Kalama taught a version of *samkhya*, discrimination, which taught that ignorance rather than desire caused our suffering and separated us from our true Self. Armstrong goes on to explain that this school of thought teaches that we must become aware that the personal Self is identical with the Absolute Spirit (*purusa*) present yet dormant in all things but concealed by the material world (*praktri*). If one could learn to discriminate between these two, cultivate the intellect, and live above the emotions, one would have direct knowledge of samkhya and the praktri would depart from the uspura, liberating the practitioner from all suffering. One of the stories Armstrong relates from this period is teacher explaining the samkhya concept to his son by demonstrating putting salt into a glass of water. Even though the water looks clear once the salt is dissolved, one can still taste the salt. The father explains to his son that this is the same with Brahman and is the essence of the individual.

This is an appealing doctrine, and I would venture to say because there are elements of this teaching still in Buddhism and its' similarity to ideas about the concept of a soul, that many Westerners believe that this is what Buddhism is all about. There are many appealing and valuable contributions developed in samkhya, but when we explore samkhya more fully, we see that it is based on abstract, speculative concepts contrasted with the inductive reasoning of Buddhism. The problem is, that while elements remain in the teachings: the awareness that our feelings, emotions, physical conditions and circumstances are impermanent; that people can find the truth within themselves; and that ignorance is one of the roots of suffering, the searching for an eternal, Absolute Self (soul) and an external Absolute Spirit (god) will be in vain. Because, the Buddha found, we are empty of these concepts and that the answers are found within us; that final, direct experience of samkhya can never be achieved.

Nirvana

The Mahayana school considers the ground of all phenomena to be the intrinsically enlightened mind. What, then, is the ground of awakening? There are a number of possibilities. The Buddha taught that the First Noble Truth is suffering and toward the end of his life, he would say that the only things he taught in all those years are the truth of suffering and liberation from that suffering. We might say, then, that the ground of being for those of us who are not yet awakened is suffering. To find the ground of the awakened mind, we would need to turn to the Buddha's teachings on how to awaken. One of the basic principles is to learn to see things as they really are. This seems like an easy enough thing to do, until we realize how many layers we've learned to cover reality with. Like the proverbial dust that the legends and sutras talk about covering our eyes, we have cultural, religious, familial, psychological, and a host of other issues coloring our perceptions. We believe, to the point of dying and killing for, in the reality of a separate, concrete, eternal self.

The Buddha taught that this is an illusion and modern science shows us that each thing we consider separate and unique is actually made up of non-thing elements; that energy cannot be created nor destroyed, certainly showing that the Buddha was right. We can truly understand this concept and not have it change us at all. When I was first learning about the not-self characteristic, I remember talking with a fellow student about the elements of being, and how there is no uniquely *Cheryl* element. I relayed what an impact this had on me; that I felt connected to all other elements in the universe, and the feelings of compassion for all beings this brought up in me. He did not see it that way. He could not understand why these facts, which he agreed with as scientifically sound, could change a person's connection with others, let alone make them more compassionate.

Armstrong discusses this quandary, illustrating that while the program to become awakened, the Noble Eightfold Path, in and of itself, may change the behavior of a practitioner and make them a better, more moral person, but that is not what will transform their suffering into liberation. The practitioner must also practice what Armstrong calls the yogic discipline of meditation. The practitioner must learn the Dharma, much like a person must learn their scales, music, and understand their instrument but it will only be by looking deeply and understanding in a profound way that their virtuosity with their instrument can be realized. We must move our intellectual understanding from our head to our heart for the Bodhichitta to rise up within us. Just as the Buddha experienced under the rose apple tree, Bodhichitta must bloom for awakening to be experienced. My Dharma name means "True happiness is found in peace," so my answer to the question of the ground of awakening is Peace.

Churchill said of Russia that it is a riddle wrapped in a mystery inside an enigma. Armstrong explains (complains?) that we know very little about the life of the Buddha. We can consider cultural reasons for this, that the individual is less important in Asian cultures, or that the Buddha himself wanted to minimize his personal story, personality, and authority in favor of promoting a way of life and program to lead others to their personal liberation. Be that as it may, we do know some things about the man who would come to be known as the Buddha, one who is awake. The story of Siddhartha Gautama is a charming one; one that could easily be told in contemporary terms. In today's Western culture, many children are raised like the little prince that was Siddhartha's childhood. He was protected from all bad things; guarded and sheltered, trained to be a leader of men, given all that money and position could offer.

Siddhartha was his parent's pride and joy – perfect in every way – yet, he knew something was missing. When fist exposed to old age, illness, loss, and death he knew he had to go forth to find the reason and release from these horrors. He found that what he was at fist horrified by was actually a Noble Truth; our very nature is a gift to teach us the truth. In finding this perfection of mind, he created a method for awakening and came to develop a monastery of teachers who themselves were successful on this path. We can take refuge in the Buddha, the Dharma, and the Sangha as equal partners to protect us, guide us, and ultimately, share in the joy of our liberation from the suffering of the world.

What made the Buddha special enough to realize Nirvana? Well, other than Siddhartha Gautama being a genius, nothing. Saying that the Buddha wasn't "special" is not what my teacher calls an "equality complex" (where a person insists on being treated equally, not recognizing that each student has different needs) or on the modern notion that we are all special in our own special way. Buddhism teaches that we all have the seeds of all aspects of human nature in our store consciousness and these seeds need to be watered in order to flourish. When we listen to Dharma talks, share the energy of mindfulness with the Sangha, and practice honestly, we water the seeds of awakening. This is our responsibility. We cannot make a strawberry; if we try, it is a poor imitation of flavor, fragrance, and beauty. We can, however, plant a strawberry seed, cultivate it with care, learn from other master gardeners, and even learn from our mistakes. In the end, all of the elements needed for the strawberry to manifest must be present: the sun, the earth, the water, the work of the gardener, and many other factors that create the strawberry that tastes so sweet when eaten in this kind of mindfulness. The Buddha is our master gardener, helping us identify the unwholesome from the wholesome, giving us advice on how to grow those strawberries. We look to him and all the other wonderful teachers along the chain as the inspiration that, yes, we can do this!

Armstrong discusses the nature of the Buddha as being fully human. This is, perhaps, one of the best, most concise ways to describe the nature of a Buddha. The Buddha was able to see the world as it really is, which can be done by anyone and sometimes when people do see the world as it really is, they become profoundly depressed and discouraged when they recognize the level of devastation and violence in the world. The Buddha, on the other hand, looks at the world as it really is and in a holistic way; looking at the root causes of the suffering experienced and seeing the path to liberation from that suffering. Thich Nhat Hanh explains that as we practice, we develop our habit energies so that when we experience negative or unwholesome feelings, we do not act on them; we fully experience them, look deeply into them, and transform them. Or more directly: "you have a right to your feelings of anger, you do not have the right not to practice." So our relative nature differs like night and day from the Buddha on the surface, but ultimately, our nature is the same; it becomes our choice to water those seeds and bring the fruit of awaking into being.

The three baskets, or *Tipitaka* (Pali) or *Tripitaka* (Skt), is a traditional term for the cannon of sutras which are divided into three categories: the *Sutta Pitaka* (Pali)/*Sutra Pitaka* (Skt) – the teachings or sermons of the Buddha, the *Vinaya Pitaka* (Skt & Pali) – the precepts and rules of monastic order, and the *Adhibdharma Pitaka* (Skt)/*Abhidhamma Pitaka* (Pali) – the commentarial literature about the Sutras. Originally, these works were committed to memory and transmitted orally. About a hundred years after the death of the Buddha, the cannon was formalized by the Second Council which some scholars believe formed the present Pali Cannon.

Other research contends that the Tripitaka was not as finalized as first thought and there was considerable movement in which texts were included and in what form. The structure for the Tripitaka further divides the texts into sections which helps organize them for study. Armstrong goes on to explain that when schisms occurred within the monastic structures, texts were often rearranged, texts added, and further elaborations or additions were made, but rarely were substantive changes made in the texts themselves or their meanings. While we do not know about the monks who committed the works to memory or later transcribed them, there may well have been modification or misunderstanding of the words that were changed, purposefully or accidentally; so we have no way of knowing for sure what the actual words of the Buddha were or which works are authentic.

Interestingly, Armstrong does discuss the idea that an oral tradition is inherently flawed, despite, as she says, the "monk's yoga trained memories." I have heard this theory of oral traditions being less desirable than a written one by other authors, but having spent a number of years attending services at Buddhist temples, it is my opinion that oral traditions have the potential for being superior to written work. When words are chanted over and over, those words are more likely to be remembered accurately, especially in a public setting, because the people chanting know those words just as well as the person responsible for leading the chanting. At any rate, the Vietnamese ladies at our temple wouldn't miss a thing and would catch any mistake loud and clear.

Armstrong states that there is sufficient research to lead us to believe that Siddhartha Gautama actually lived, even though we don't know as much about his life as a modern biographer would like. It is a fair question to ask what the impact would be if research revealed without a shadow of a doubt that Gautama never lived. Modern Buddhism in the West might be quite different. In the West, we feel that individualism is a supreme value. In Asian countries it is hard to tell if there would be much, if any, impact. In cultures where the group is valued over the individual, it may seem an absurd question to worry about if one man existed out of many. I asked two of the monks who attended a recent mini-retreat at our temple that question. The older one laughed and simply said "that's a silly question" and the younger one thought about it and answered that because there are so many Buddhas to choose from it would be ok if there was one less. We take refuge, he explained, in the Buddha, not in the man Gautama. For me personally, it would make no difference because it seems like one of those thought puzzle questions. I can have confidence in what I learn that was discovered by people from just a few generations ago whom I do not know personally.

We use technology and science every day that, conceptually, do not depend on a single person for those concepts to produce the phones, medicines, surgical procedures, cars, etc. to exist. Armstrong even talks about that many of the basic principles that the Buddha taught were not new; she even goes so far as to compare similar ideas throughout what she terms the Axial age. Like scientific discoveries, there may be a number of people working on the same problems who come up with similar solutions, but it will be the first or most charismatic person who becomes famous and associated with the work. It is very likely the same with the development of Buddhism. Many of the sutras that were spoken by other bhikkhus in the presence of the Buddha, were praised by him and given his seal of approval, illustrating that the Dharma is a and on-going living thing, that is shared with the world by those with wisdom.

Disciples

The Buddha's first disciples were the brothers Tapassu and Bhallika who were traders traveling between India and Myanmar (Burma). Legend has it that they encountered the Buddha who had just spent the past week experiencing the bliss of his liberation under the Bodhi tree. Armstrong says they were informed of this encounter by the gods. In other stories it is said that they were amazed at the Buddha's radiance and calm. The brothers gave the Buddha his first meal of honeyed rice cakes. According to legend, they received eight locks of the Buddha's hair which they took to Ukkala and the locks of hair were later enshrined in stupas which still exist.

Bhallika went on to become a monk and became an arahant while Tapassu remained a householder and continued as a trader. The two brothers are credited with bringing Buddhism to Myanmar. There are a number of reasons that this is significant. These two were people who were not spiritual seekers, yet they recognized something special in the Buddha. By recognizing that they wished to follow the Buddha, it is telling us that the path to liberation is for everyone, not just monks, nuns, and spiritual seekers. There is something for all of us in the teachings. For me, it is also significant that they did not hear a talk by the Buddha when they decided to become disciples. They did not make the decision based on faith or authority, there was no one there to give them that idea. Instead, they could see in the Buddha the stability, peace, and equanimity in his face, smile, and posture. In a very real way, they were able to see the fruits of the Buddha's labor, the result of path.

I remember being on retreat and coming to the meditation hall early to get situated before our sit and seeing a monk there sitting with such stability that it took my breath away. I placed my cushion next to him and sat with him, connecting to that energy. It's always been a touchstone for me. When I've been asked in a kind of fun parlor game, what question would you ask a famous person living or dead, my answer for myself is that I would ask the Buddha if he would sit with me for a few minutes, knowing that I would always be able to come back to that perfect space. After sitting with that monk on our retreat, I've known that I have sat with the Buddha and I know how the two brothers felt when they saw the World Honored One.

Monk

According to Epstein in his *Buddhism A to Z* compilation, the three types of Sangha are: 1) the Sangha of Buddhas comprised of the infinite numbers of

Buddhas, 2) the Sangha of the Sages comprised of the fully awakened beings who have reached one of the stages of Arhatship or one of the Bodhisattva stages; and 3) the Sangha of the field of blessings which is composed of four pairs and eight kinds of holy people, the Bhikshunis and Bhikkhus who receive and uphold the moral teachings. The *Seeker's Glossary of Buddhism* goes on to explain that the Sangha is the second of the Three Jewels and is of equal importance with the other Jewels: the Buddha and the Dharma.

Each of the three Jewels is equally important; in fact, one could not exist for long without the other two. While the Buddha Gautama is an historic person, without the Dharma, his life would simply be an historic curiosity. The Dharma without the Buddha would be interesting and even helpful, but would lack the spark of life and would seem removed from the realm of our own lives and capabilities. The Sangha could not stand alone for long, no matter how well intentioned the members. The people, without a way of life to guide them, would become simply a political or cultural group, not different from any other group of people. According to Thich Nhat Hanh, in Chinese and Vietnamese Buddhism, a practitioner who takes refuge will add the phrase "within myself" to each of the aspects of the Triple Gem during the taking refuge ceremony, showing that interwoven within the Triple Gem is the understanding that those qualities are woven within us as well. When we see the Triple Gem holistically, we see that each aspect helps us to identify with the Buddha, learn about the Dharma, gain support from the Sangha body, then to internalize those qualities to make them our own.

At Chua Bao An, the Vietnamese Buddhist center I attend, I was taught to bow three times when I entered the sanctuary: once to the monks and nuns, lay men and women who make the center possible and give me such kindness and support; once to the unbroken line of wonderful teachers, some of whom brought the Dharma to us at great sacrifice to themselves; and once to the Shakyamuni Buddha, the Amitaba Buddha, and all of the Buddhas throughout history. The monks and nuns of the Sangha study, maintain the temple, teach, and contribute to their community as they can. More importantly, they serve as an example for all of us. At one of the retreats I attended a few years ago, we were having a ceremonial, mindful meal. I love attending these, because I find mindful eating and the connections found within everyday activities and the sacred nature of everything we do so powerful.

We had a large group of participants with a number of people who had not attended a retreat for a long time, so we were packed in the dining room. Some of the people at my table were reaching over the serving platters, scooping large amounts of food into their bowls, and eating as though someone was going to take the food away from them. It was hard to stay focused and I found myself feeling unhappy. But I looked over to the monastics table and there was my good friend and one of my teachers Tinh Tuyen, and she was eating mindfully with a look of calm peace on her face. I felt that energy within myself, and resumed eating mindfully, a half smile formed on my lips, and my peace was restored. I have such gratitude to all of the monastics of the world, because any time I feel ill at ease, I know that they are there: meditating, walking mindfully, eating peacefully, reciting the sutras, and showing the way to peace and happiness.

The mendicant monk movement was an old tradition in India where seekers would dress in yellow robes and travel the roads. They sought dharmas and gathered alms, which the people saw both as a way to honor the journey of the alms-seekers (which they may have secretly longed for as well) and as a way to gain merit for themselves. What was new was the birth of what Karl Jaspers calls the Axial Age, which Armstrong discusses within the context of her book as well. This was a time when there was a growing sense of unease and dissatisfaction with the status quo; the thought that the old ways were not quite enough anymore.

The Vedic faith had not changed or adapted to help the people understand how it related to their lives. So these holy men were thought to be the pioneers to help bring about transformations and develop new ideas that would benefit the world. People were very happy to support these wanders and that tradition continues to this day. My main mentor during the academic part of preparing for ordination with the Order of Interbeing spent time in India teaching meditation and the Dharma. He found that he was supported by the community and when he fell ill, the people were very generous in helping him by bringing him food, medicine, and being sure he was getting better. It was a culture shock to him when he returned and found that people in the West are not as supportive of *dana* offerings. They wanted to know what the fee for a class was, and didn't see the point of adding more to the "tip jar." There can be a feeling of resentment for monastics by people who are not steeped in this tradition, perhaps because they feel they are giving handouts to people who should be making their own living. What they fail to see is the very real support the monastics give to us, and that it is an honor to assure that this beautiful tradition continues for the benefit of all beings.

Nothingness

When the Buddha declared that he had achieved the final release and was liberated from Samsara, he did so because he was grounded in the perfection of disciplines that lead up to his ultimate understanding and the penetrating honesty that characterized his path leading up to this point. Armstrong explains that although he achieved amazing feats of concentration and ascended the levels of the yogic path, this honesty and self-awareness prevented him from being deceived that he had achieved what he truly sought: the full liberation from suffering. He could have rested on his accomplishments a number of times and was offered positions with the sanghas of the great teachers of the day, but he refused, knowing that he must continue searching.

While Alara Kalama practice of Samkhya allowed him to achieve high levels of jhana (meditative experience) and he claimed to achieve a plane of "nothingness" this state was still not the Ultimate Dimension – Nirvana – that the Buddha sought. Now, achieving the level of "nothingness" or samadhi or *Svarupa-Avirbhava* is nothing to sneeze at! To be the "knower" of the "un-manifest," prakriti, primordial nature and the "manifest" world that arises out of prakriti would certainly be meditative bliss. An early Buddhist teacher of mine who had studied with His Holiness the Dalai Lama talked affectionately about being reminded not to be complacent in his meditation, that these states were not the goal, were essentially meaningless, and not to become attached to them. He laughed with a wink about them being meaningless, simply meditative bliss – what use is that? So the Buddha was able to recognize the truth of this experience, that this was not an ultimate experience of the Self; he had created this experience himself.

This state of unity with all things, the "nothingness" of Samkhya may

well be the state that scientists are studying in mapping the mind of meditators. When looking at the potential for neuro-plasticity, neurologists have
turned to Zen meditators to see the changes in brain activity during deep
meditation using EEGs and fMRI scans. During meditation, brain scans
show a number of neuro-chemical and neuro-transmitter changes in the
brain, and its' relationship between the amygdala and the pre-frontal cortex,
leading scientists to believe that meditation can help a person create new
connections in the brain. The feeling of self-transcendence can be linked to
decreased activity in the right parietal lobe of the brain which can be brought
about through states of meditation or brain damage. The Buddha was able to
see the difference between a religious experience, as valuable and meaningful as it might be, from the full experience of Nirvana.

The Buddha realized that this version of "nothingness" was still not the
Nirvana that he sought. He would realize later, the perfect understanding of
emptiness, sunyata, and find the uncreated perfection that would lead to liberation.

Class

During the Buddha's time, the practice was embraced by the ruling class and
the intellectuals and the Buddha had kings as benefactors and even as good
friends. The class that seemed to be most open to the BuddhaDharma was
the merchants and businessmen who weren't really part of a class, per se, but
were part of a new movement to bring commerce and enterprise to India.
Kings are people who want to know what is happening in their kingdoms
and often will make a show of support for a popular religious leader to show
their spirituality, but according to the legends, the Buddha made genuine
friends with these leaders, inspiring them to do good for the people they led.
The businessmen and merchants could see the pragmatism of Buddhism as
an initial appeal; Armstrong explains that this was because they could see
that living a wholesome life could be a good investment in the future if merit
accumulated led to a better next life.

Buddhism spread to East Asia in a variety of ways, but the most important aspect of its spread was the ability to translate the sutras into the
native language. Buddhism took on some of the ideas in Taoism, for instance, because translators didn't have words for some Buddhist ideas and

used terms borrowed from Taoism, coloring people's concepts of Buddhism. The acceptance of Buddhism in these countries was regional in nature and monks were recruited to travel and spread the doctrine to the villages and establishing monasteries.

In the West, Buddhism has been a growing part of the culture because of trade and colonization to Buddhist countries. From the introduction of the *Tibetan Book of the Dead* published in 1927 which appealed to scholars and intellectuals, to the beat generation then hippie culture of the 50's and 60's who embraced Zen and Tibetan Buddhism.

It's not too different from the Buddha's day – it seems that intellectuals and those trailblazing a new way in the existing culture are attracted first to Buddhism. For the higher classes, one of the factors for wanting to be on the leading edge of a way of thinking may be because those are people who like to collect and acquire things and this would have been something new and appealing to be in the know about, but it would also be appealing for those who want to think things through to make sense of them; to analyze things to find truth. For those striving to make a new way in the world, Buddhism would have a distinct appeal since it promotes working things out for ourselves, just as these social trailblazers were doing, following their own impulses to something new.

Caste System

The caste system in India is ancient, but also complex and varied region to region. Gautama was not born into a society that embraced the caste system, but he did claim the warrior caste as his own (which at the time was considered above the Brahmins which now are considered first). While Gautama was certainly influenced by his upbringing and culture, when we became the awakened one, this influence was minimal in his development of his teachings, used only to create examples and metaphors to help teach others. The Buddha said (*Sutta-Nipâta*, 142):

> "Birth makes not a man an outcast,
> Birth makes not a man a Brahmin;
> Action makes a man an outcast,
> Action makes a man a Brahmin."

In rejecting the caste system, the Buddha was making a spiritual statement about the importance of taking personal responsibility for our lives. In
the story about his encounters with Kassapa, the Buddha demonstrated his
superior spiritual and psychic abilities, but important to note is that those
"abilities" didn't work to convince Kassapa. This is important because the
Buddha explained to Kassapa that it is by our actions that our worth is determined. Ethics becomes the ground of faith, not rituals that are empty of
any practical meaning or practice. In the Five Remembrances, we remind
ourselves that (as translated by Thich Nhat Hanh):

> *I am of the nature to grow old. There is no way to escape growing*
> *old. I am of the nature to have ill health. There is no way to escape ill*
> *health. I am of the nature to die. There is no way to escape death.*
> *All that is dear to me and everyone I love are of the nature to change.*
> *There is no way to escape being separated from them. My actions are*
> *my only true belongings. I cannot escape the consequences of my ac-*
> *tions. My actions are the ground upon which I stand.*

The Buddha made it clear that it is not by birth, or caste, or divine intervention that we will wake up and live a wholesome life, but by our own mind
and actions.

How does the Buddha's omniscience "square" with the account of the
establishment of the monsoon season retreat? The Buddha is said to have
omniscience not omnipotentence, for one. The Buddha, as we learn in the
Simsapa Sutra, said:

"Once the Blessed One was staying at Kosambi in the simsapa forest.
Then, picking up a few simsapa leaves with his hand, he asked the
monks, 'What do you think, monks: Which are more numerous, the few
simsapa leaves in my hand or those overhead in the simsapa forest?'

"The leaves in the hand of the Blessed One are few in number, lord.
Those overhead in the simsapa forest are more numerous.

"In the same way, monks, those things that I have known with direct knowledge but have not taught are far more numerous [than what I have taught]. And why haven't I taught them? Because they are not connected with the goal, do not relate to the rudiments of the holy life, and do not lead to disenchantment, to dispassion, to cessation, to calm, to direct knowledge, to self-awakening, to Unbinding. That is why I have not taught them." (SN 56.31)

I was taught that the Buddha was omniscient in regard to everything about awakening, not about everything in the universe. Many things in the universe, though, can certainly be known through inductive reasoning by an awakened mind, and the Buddha being a genius didn't hurt either.

The monsoon season was a time when most people stayed close to home, but the first monastics continued to travel afield. We really don't know if this was of their own initiative or if they were instructed to do so by the Buddha. According to Armstrong, this practice was criticized by others, including the Jains who, because of the principle of ahimsa (doing no harm), would not travel during the rainy season for fear of harming the new grass, bugs, and other critters. The addition of a growing number of parks donated to the forming monastic order that were close enough to the city that people could reach them, but far enough away to provide some peace and quiet for study came together to form the monastic framework we see to this day.

The Buddha seemed to want the way the order developed to be organic, so I just do not see any precognition that led the Buddha to set things up to happen the way they did, but rather that the disciples worked things out on their own to fit the world they lived in.

Monastics

The Buddha's disciples, at first, traveled and taught all through the year even during the monsoon season. This was met with criticism, especially from the Jains who practiced ahimsa, doing no harm. They felt that there was too much damage done by people traveling through the wet land, killing insects and crushing tender shoots. They were right, of course, but the Buddha was allowing his disciples to form their own way of being monastics and allowed them to give traveling during the monsoon season a try. To respond to the critique, the monastics were pulled back during monsoon season. An additional development was that the Buddha was given a number of pleasure parks which were converted into retreat centers for the monastics to use. These parks were close enough to the cities to allow people to come to visit, yet far enough away to be peaceful for the monastics to study, meditate, and practice.

Buddhist monastics, to this day, have maintained this practice of taking time in retreat for part of the year. Because the monks were not allowed to leave the retreat center for more than a week at a time, and only with permission, they had to develop a community and had to learn to work together. The long term impact was to create a structure that has borne the fruit of monastics having the time to develop their thinking about the basic teachings and produce sutras, doctrines, and treatises about the dharma that have enhanced our understanding of the practice. Because the various schools have time in one place, they also developed rituals and practices that the lay members from the community can participate in and benefit from.

The community of monastics also serves as inspiration for the community. The monastics develop ways to cooperate and work together, serving as a model of behavior. They also serve as inspiration in the practice. When I have gone on retreat, even the one day retreats at our temple, I have always come away refreshed by my contact with monastics. When I have a hard time settling in, or eating my lunch mindfully, I can look over at one of the monks or nuns and watch them sitting with a half- smile, peacefully attending to whatever they are doing. I can take in that energy that they are so willing to share. At any time of the day or night, when I am struggling, I can close my eyes and be grateful for the monastics that I know are practicing diligently to share that energy of mindfulness with me.

While the majority of what we learn about Buddhist teachings, women are held to be equal to men and equally capable of awakening. However, there are some things in the scriptures, which some scholars believe were added after the Buddha's death, showing a less than hospitable view of women. Most notably is the idea that the Buddha proclaimed that without women the sangha would last 1,000 years, but with women, it would now last a mere 500 years. Now, my personal opinion which I cannot back up with any scholarship or proof is that these attitudes about women were added or changed later. I do not believe that the Buddha was a misogynist – if he saw a distinction between male or female, young or old, rich or poor, or any other pairs of opposites, it would mean that he had not penetrated the duality of the relative world and did not see the unity and inter-being-ness of all things. This is clearly not the case. My personal opinion is an idea I had when I first heard this story in my 20's and was quite shocked by it.

Asking one of my first Zen teachers about the Buddha's attitude toward women and asking if he thought a woman could become enlightened, his response was: "So, are you a woman?" (Zen can be infuriating at times, can't it?) But as we discussed it more, he wondered out loud about how people can sometimes hear something and because they don't listen closely, they think they know what was said, but they may have missed something. My own take on this has been that the Buddha may very well have said that without women in the sangha, there will be teachings for 1,000 years, but with women in the sangha, there will only be teaching for 500 years – as a good thing. After all, when all beings have awakened, there will be no more need for teaching. We will all be teachers for each other.

Thinking about the other monastics and the treatment of women through the years, I really do not harbor resentments. It makes me very sad, but today in the news we hear about new regulations being proposed that would allow a hospital to not perform an abortion nor refer the woman to a facility that will even if the woman's life is on the line; that rape is only rape if it is forcible, that rape victims are not victims but accusers unless there is a conviction, and the newly proposed budget cuts come down hard on poor women, limited access to family planning and nutritional support. It is 2011.

How could I be shocked by a culture that considered women as property not changing their views in an instant? Armstrong goes on to talk about the Buddha's journey as one that is masculine in nature; to liberate himself from the mundane, domestic world; establishing a monastic order that would strive to learn to break attachments. Our life is characterized by attachments and losses; it is understandable that men who wish to break those bounds would see women as an irresistible force.

Further bolstering my personal opinion, though, is the Buddha's insistence that we go on this journey ourselves, that we take personal responsibility for ourselves and our actions. His monastics and followers had to work out their problems for themselves. The culture of his time (and, sadly, our own) is a paradigm that men really cannot help themselves. What else can they do but to act on their lustful feelings? At the beginning of his quest, Gautama felt that his son was a fetter – an attachment that was holding him back from his destiny. The pull of his love for his wife and son was so strong that he knew he could not even look at them as they slept before he slipped out the door. Yet, when he understood the true nature of things, the depth of his love for them and for all beings was a far greater depth of compassion.

In my own life, the depth of these attitudes has followed me around, despite living in a time when things are better and women are more outspoken about fixing the problems. Yet we still are expected to just go along with things – don't make a fuss. When I turned forty, I found out that I have a super power! I am invisible! Sometimes people can't even hear me talk – It's amazing! I can say things in meetings or whatever the setting, and because of my super power, they don't notice, yet some men have the power to hear and repeat what I said to the delight of the others.

Interestingly, when I do confront a man who has either ignored my contribution or downright stolen my idea, they figure out a way to blame me. Either, they say, they didn't realize I was making a contribution, that the contribution wasn't that good or they would have responded, that anyone could have had that idea, or I must be hysterical. It's tough to be patient. Yet, being patient is exactly what I have to do; to realize that this kind of behavior is done out of ignorance. It's up to me to take the high road – that doesn't mean being a wallflower, I'm still going to wave my hands and say "hey, guys, I'm here too!" but I do my best not to let the injustices get my goat. Hopefully, the quality of the work I do and my contributions will win over the ones who don't think women are up to the task.

Bodhichitta

Bodhichitta is, in part, compassion – our ability to feel pain, have empathy with others who feel pain, and the heartfelt desire to help others in pain. Yet another analogy for bodhichitta is the rawness of a broken heart. This broken heart sometimes leads us to have unwholesome feelings like anger, resentment, fear, and anxiety, but underneath all of that is the honesty of our suffering. The first Noble Truth is that we all have suffering; it is something that we all share in. Considering suffering to be noble or holy seems strange, especially since we spend a great deal of time trying to avoid suffering or building walls to protect ourselves. We armor our hearts emotionally from a personal standpoint and even from a cultural or societal one through racial, ethnic, sexual orientation, or other prejudices. Yet, when we connect with our pain that is an honest and courageous thing to do which breaks the barriers that separate us from others and from our Buddha-nature.

Mudita, or joy, is sometimes referred to as sympathetic or unselfish joy. This is the joy that we feel at the accomplishments and good things that happen to others. It is an important quality to cultivate because it helps us be more confident in the world and to understand that the world is a wide, abundant place and we do not have to be greedy or jealous of the good fortune of others. Mudita also has a wider definition of the infinite capacity for joy; an inner wellspring of joy that we have within us. Mudita is the ally of compassion, giving the practitioner a sympathy and brotherhood with the object of one's compassion.

On a personal note, an understanding of mudita has been one of the best practices I have utilized in dealing with disappointments and failures. When we wish we had something or some aspect of life that we feel is normal or expected it is a shock of disappointment when circumstances beyond our control prevent us from having that thing. We might wish for a specific kind of relationship, a long lasting marriage, that our children achieve what society and we expect, or any number of things that come into our minds. When see others with bigger houses, better careers, or that very thing we wanted so much but cannot have, it seems normal to be jealous or depressed. When we explore the idea of mudita, we learn that we have not only the capacity for joy that is not limited by the boundaries of what we have, but is big enough to encompass the world. When we pair this with the idea of the unity of all things, that we are in everything and everything is in us, we can allow this sympathetic joy to rise in us as we recognize that we do not have to experience or have everything possible personally; we already have everything that ever was and ever will be.

For a long time I was deeply disappointed because I could not have more children. I was very grateful for the child I had, and spent a lot of time with my son and found a lot of joy in raising him. That still did not take the sting away completely for that strong desire that I had from a young age and the expectation that, of course, I would have a nice large family. When it could not be, it was important to me not to just gloss my feelings over or stuff them down inside and make platitudes to myself that I should be grateful and get over it. Instead I turned to the Dharma and considered mudita to be my friend. How could I learn to have joy in the children of the people around me? I found that the more I cultivated this quality of finding joy in the lives and wellbeing of others, the happier I was inside. I would be fully present and listen to my friends talk about their children, and when I could step out of myself and listen deeply to them, I realized how interconnected we were and their happiness was part of mine and my happiness was part of theirs. Perhaps at first, this was akin to living vicariously in others experiences, but it developed into something deeper than that. Mudita had lead to loving kindness (metta) and metta had lead to compassion (karuna). I found that my longing had been cured by the good medicine of joy.

When we have these strong feelings of bodhichitta, compassion, mudita, and metta, we would do well to take the example of the young Siddhartha and learn to meditate and look deeply at these feelings. Jhana, the cornerstone of Right Concentration, also known as dhyana, is translated in a variety of ways to mean meditation and meditative states, trance, contemplation, musing and the like. Because the term meditation is so ambiguous, especially today with the word taking on secular techniques and copyrighted definitions from teachers developing their own forms and programs, and the other end of the scale being the wimpy musing; perhaps the term jhana or dhyana is best for Buddhists to use. The word jhana can also be traced to the Pali verb jhapeti, meaning to *burn up*, implying that jhana burns up mental defilements which prevent serenity and insight. There are four jhanas that are discussed in Buddhist literature: 1) the first jhana which is a state of one-pointedness, happiness, joy, examination, and applied thought, 2) the second jhana which is characterized by one-pointedness, happiness, and joy, 3) the third jhana which is characterized by one-pointedness, happiness, and equanimity, and 4) the fourth jhana which is characterized by one-pointedness, equanimity, and the six higher knowledge's of psychic powers, clairaudience, mind-reading, memory of previous lives, clairvoyance, and Nirvana.

To learn more about how to enter jhana, we can turn to both the *Anapa-nasati Sutta* and the *Satipatthāna Sutta*. In these sutras, we learn the importance of mindful breathing to enter into a relaxing, serene state, samatha to learn to pacify the mind and strengthen concentration, and go on to learn the four establishments of mindfulness which help us develop insight, vipassana. In learning to cultivate equanimity, we discover that whatever arises in us, whatever happens in our body or mind, we do not need to be swept away by it, intoxicated or terrorized by it, embarrassed or ashamed, enamored or covetous, excited or bored; we simply recognize what is there whether it is pleasant, unpleasant, or neutral.

When the little Prince Siddhartha was under the rose apple tree, and his parents returned to find him alone in his meditation, they were amazed to see him sitting with such serenity and ease. His mother burst into tears, she was so touched. His father bowed to his son, but felt troubled that the boy would not grow up to be a great political or military leader, but a spiritual leader. Siddhartha, unconcerned by the reaction of his parents and nurse-maids, stated "Reading the holy Veda cannot help the worms!" Through his experience of compassion, bodhichitta, and jhana, he realized that it would be the experience of wisdom that would lead to Nirvana, and this day called "Siddhartha gets a glimpse" by Arnold, would lead to the full experience of liberation and achievement of Buddhahood.

Perinirvana

The Buddha's life had a mythic quality from start to finish. His beginnings were rich in the physical and material, but poor in spirituality. As he gained spirituality by shedding the material, he also gained a large following, many monastic retreat centers, and the adulation of the rich and influential. Through it all, he taught how to be in the world yet not of the world. In his compassion to teach, he allowed himself to become surrounded by people who needed his help. Armstrong mentions that there were times he even had to admonish his monastics to be quiet! He probably would have preferred to sit in silence, enjoying the bliss of liberation, yet he went to the cities where the drama, chaos, and noise were to educate us how to understand the world, and to lead by example. Toward the end of his life, there is a journey of him going from big city to progressively smaller towns. Illustrating the shedding of all the things we accumulate over a lifetime. It also gave the Buddha a chance to teach, once again, in a very simple way; giving the last instructions for how to manage the sangha and to confirm the essence of his teachings.

At our hospice, we do an exercise with new staff. We have them write a list of the fifteen most important things in their lives. Then we tell them to cross off five items. There is some grumbling, but they do it kind of laughing a bit about it. Then we tell them to cross of five more items. Now there is a bit more grumbling and less laughter and sometimes some complaints. Now they have to cross off four items. This makes people a bit alarmed, but as we talk, we explore how it feels to start losing everything that is important to us as we approach death. Then we ask them to cross off that last item. Some people can't do it – they just can't bring themselves to take that step. Yet, it is important for them to understand that we all will have to cross off that last item one day.

While I have really loved this book, I do part company with Armstrong in this last chapter. I don't think she's reading the *Mahaparanibbana Sutta* with the right "accent." She talks about the Buddha being exasperated with Ananda, chiding him, or impatient with his devoted companion – the last person on the Buddha's list of important things. One of the things I've learned from my teacher is to always hear the compassion in the voice and words of the Buddha. Everything he says to Ananda is pure compassion, not scolding or irritation. Interestingly, Armstrong feels that Ananda was not up to the task of asking the Buddha to stay among the living for the coming eons to teach despite the Buddha "hinting" three times that it was possible. Of course Ananda understood what the Buddha was saying – he could only bring himself to be silent; he knew he had to refuse such a request. Only the death of the Buddha would show the truth of his words about impermanence and no-self. Only the death of the physical shows us the reality of the unity of all things: that the all is in the one; that the one is in the all.

When my mother died, I felt a great sense of relief. While on the surface that seems awful, the reality for me was that I realized that I could let her off the hook. I no longer had to struggle with what I felt I needed from her or what she needed from me. I found, after looking deeply for a long time, that I could look at my hand and see my mother's hand. That she had suffered a lot and was only able to give so much to my sister and me. Yet, I could touch my cheek with my hand and feel my mother's touch. I could give my child my full attention and feel the nourishment that I craved from my mother through that moment of mindfulness. In a very real way, I feel closer to my mother now than when she was alive.

The Buddha had his moment, not unlike Jesus prior to the coming crucifixion of asking out loud if this really had to be this way. Ananda did crumble and ask him to please continue, yet the Buddha knew this could not be and rejected the request. Ananda had done the right thing when it was important, and they both had taken their turn taking care of the other. It's so touching to imagine these two old friends going on this journey together, Ananda companioning the Buddha through life and now through death. I have to believe that it was meaningful for the Buddha to know that Ananda felt his grief so deeply and truly cared for him, not for what he could do for him or anyone else, but for himself. Having equanimity doesn't mean not being human; Armstrong talks about awakening not being some supernatural state, but being perfectly human. Yet she does interpret the Buddha being joyful at the deaths of Sariputta and Moggallana, perhaps she is still clinging to a belief in Nirvana as a place. Perhaps the Buddha felt the same feeling I had and these two brilliant disciples were no longer someplace else, but in the palm of his hand.

Life of the Buddha

In both the book and documentary, deciding which events in the Buddha's life are important must have been a challenging task. Both the book and documentary approached the early legends of the Buddha's life in a similar way. They considered the importance of looking at which events mirror or fore shadow the insights and teaching that would develop into the Dharma we know today. Siddhartha Gautama's birth and upbringing were sheltered and perfect. He did not want for anything, yet as he grew, he also grew restless and increasingly unhappy.

The story of Siddhartha Gautama is a charming one; one that could easily be told in contemporary terms. In today's Western culture, many children are raised like the little prince that was Siddhartha's childhood. He was protected from all bad things; guarded and sheltered, trained to be a leader of men, given all that money and position could offer. Siddhartha was his parent's pride and joy – perfect in every way – yet, he knew something was missing. When first exposed to old age, illness, loss, and death he knew he had to go forth to find the reason and release from these horrors. He found that what he was at fist horrified by was actually a Noble Truth; our very nature is a gift to teach us the truth. In finding this perfection of mind, he created a method for awakening and came to develop a monastery of teachers who themselves were successful on this path. We can take refuge in the Buddha, the Dharma, and the Sangha as equal partners to protect us, guide us, and ultimately, share in the joy of our liberation from the suffering of the world.

Going forth as he did was to shed himself of all of the things that made up his life before. Where there had been luxury, there was austerity; plenty of food, he could now count his ribs through his skin; family and friends, only companions on the path with competing philosophies and concepts. Having rid himself of everything associated with his old, unsatisfactory life, despite the accomplishments of his yogic training, he was still unsatisfied. These pairs of opposites are important to consider, not because the Middle Way means "everything in moderation," (it does not) but in seeing that neither having everything nor having nothing will make a person happy. When he was able to awaken, he could see that he had everything he needed to be happy by dwelling deeply in the present moment.

We do not know how "factual" or accurate the story of the Buddha's life is, but as Jane Hirschfield says in the documentary, "People like stories. It is one of the ways we learn. The story of the Buddha's life is an archetypal journey. But it is a means to an end. It is not an end." When we look at Gautama's motivation for going forth, we see that he had an awakening in a relative way by seeing people who were ill, were old, and were dead. When he was able to touch the ultimate dimension, he could see that these things are a Noble truth; that touching our suffering is the first step in using that gift to look deeply into ourselves to find the truth and the key to unlocking the door to liberation.

W.S. Merwin says eloquently, "Everybody understands suffering. It's something that we all share with everybody else. It's at once utterly intimate, and utterly shared. So Buddha says, 'That's a place to begin. That's where we begin.'" Armstrong discusses the nature of the Buddha as being fully human. This is, perhaps, one of the best, most concise ways to describe the nature of a Buddha. The Buddha was able to see the world as it really is, which can be done by anyone and sometimes when people do see the world as it really is, they become profoundly depressed and discouraged when they recognize the level of devastation and violence in the world. The Buddha, on the other hand, looks at the world as it really is and in a holistic way; looking at the root causes of the suffering experienced and seeing the path to liberation from that suffering.

Armstrong discusses that while the Buddha spent most of his time in cities, most depictions of him are in pastoral settings deep in meditation. During his life, the Buddha travelled a great deal and established a number of monasteries around India. Often he had rich benefactors who would donate beautiful and valuable land to build simple huts for the monks to rest and study in especially during the rainy season. These benefactors, including kings, would be drawn to the teachings and wanted to build their own merit by giving generously to this charismatic holy man. Many of them also learned more about the teachings and followed them because they grew to understand them and took them to heart, not just for selfish reasons. The Buddha visited many of them in their palaces, and was unmoved by their riches, perhaps because of his upbringing and familiarity was this class of people left him unfazed. On the other hand, the Buddha is most often depicted in setting of solitude and beauty. Further in history, Buddhist art has created many images of the Buddha with serene expressions and showing the Buddha in repose or meditation. The symbolism of what the Buddha represented is more important that a documentary approach to his life and times. Seeing a statue or painting that gives us a hint at what it might have been like to sit in meditation with the Buddha is a wonderful and inspiring thing.

As we read the scriptures, the more we can remember that they are filled with symbolism and do not emphasize a blow-by-blow history of the life of the Buddha and his disciples, the better we can examine what the stories, sutras, and legends are trying to convey to us. Armstrong speculates that when the stories talk about Gautama confronting Mara as he is approaching the Bodhi tree that the symbolism is most likely talking about Gautama's shadow self, confronting his own inner demons. Additionally, the story of Gautama's life is a mirror for the story of his life as the Buddha; he sees illness, old age, and death then transforms his suffering of those into a frame-work to help us understand the underlying reality of these states of being. The Buddha would go on to wake up to the understanding of sunyata (emp-tiness) by realizing that he could not do that by denying himself of his de-sires, but by looking deeply into them and transforming them. Or as Jane Hirschfield says so beautifully, "One great tap-word of Buddhism is com-passion, which is the deep affection that we feel for everything because we're all in it together. Be it other human beings, other animals, the planet as a whole, the creatures of this planet, the trees and rivers of this planet. Every-thing is connected."

CHAPTER 4

The Four Noble Truths

The book "Buddhism: Plain and Simple," by Steve Hagan was reviewed and analyzed, comparing other Buddhist authors and teachers on this, the most basic tenet of Buddhism, the Four Noble Truths. Each of the Four Noble Truths are explored here, but only three of the Noble Eightfold Path are discussed. Volumes could be, and have been written about this topic, and an over-all meta analysis would be very interesting. Perhaps a suggestion for a future dissertation.

First Noble Truth

The first Noble Truth is the reality of life, characterized by dissatisfaction and suffering. Interestingly, none of us like that definition. We hide from this reality all the time, and argue against it. We decide that we can choose not to suffer and to just let go, a little like the "Just Do It" campaign. Then something smacks us in the face and we can't say no to suffering. But the first Truth is a Noble thing as well. There is a book by a Christian missionary who worked with people with Hansen's disease (leprosy) called *Pain, the Gift Nobody Wants*. He explains that the reason people with leprosy have the deformities of missing body parts and disfigurement because they can't feel pain – they literally injure themselves into these horrible states because they pick up a hot object and don't know they are burning their skin, or keep running even after twisting their ankle. When we experience pain, we can stop and notice what is happening with us; what are we experiencing? Even if that's as far as we get, there is wisdom in that. As we practice and train our minds, we can look deeply at what is happening in our pain and learn about the origins of that pain. We can recognize and benefit from our pain, but we can also come to have compassion and empathy for others going through similar pain. If we never felt pain or suffered, we couldn't really fully experience the joys of life, nor could we fully feel a kinship with others who suffer.

Karma is simply cause and effect. Simply put, we know from observation and science that the present is made from the events that happened in the past. We can see the chain of causality, the chain of experience, our relatives, nature, culture, religions, society, and all the rest changing and blending from the old to the new. We can have total confidence that the events of the present will create the future. When there is hate or aggression in the world, it will contribute to hate and aggression being manifested in the future. When we have love and kindness in the world, it will contribute to love and kindness being manifested in the future. Because we all inter-are with everyone else, we really can't consider ourselves fully innocent of the hate and aggression that is present in the world. I've never liked that fact. Yet, I know that I have contributed to aggression through my thoughts, words, and deeds. Karma has helped me see how important it is to find true peace of mind and happiness within myself so that I will only contribute those qualities to the future.

The cause of the First Noble Truth is craving, longing, thirst, clinging, attachment and similar other words, all pointing to our tendencies for looking at the world and not seeing it as it really is. We have preferences and those likes and dislikes permeate all that we perceive in the world. There is a lot of conflict in the political scene right now and a lot of it has to do with things that people like and don't like – in fact, things that they feel passionately about one way or the other. Amid all the screaming, there is no space for listening. The ideologues on both sides create a stand-off while the politicians pander to the positions for their personal gain. It seems like everyone involved is clinging to their position for dear life; having made up their minds before the discussion even starts.

The effects of all this creates feelings that range from dissatisfaction to flat out suffering; suffering that feels like torture. Sometimes when we feel so strongly about our opinions and beliefs, we feel we might die if we don't get our way. History is filled with stories of people who are willing to fight, kill, and die for their preferences. It's one thing to prefer vanilla to chocolate ice cream, but when we allow ourselves to suffer if our preference isn't available; we close ourselves off from the potential of what else might be possible. This is something I know very well; I can think of lots of times when I've been so frustrated about situations because, after all, it just shouldn't be this way! Things should be different and better – preferably my way, of course.

The three types of suffering are sensual desire, clinging to life, and the desire for release from pain. We want sensual desire and are constantly searching for something new, something to stimulate us. We have so many more choices today than ever before, and many people walking down the street are talking on their cell phones, hurrying to get to their computers to retrieve voice mail, and then rushing home to watch TV. When I'm really busy at work with lots of computer work to accomplish, lots of questions to answer, classes to teach, and all the rest, sometimes when I finally get into bed, it feels like my brain is still firing away with little lights going off behind my eyes.

An important part of my practice is an energy healing technique called Reiki. One of the simplest things to do with Reiki is a self-treatment. By placing the hands at various points on the body, the energy flows to reconnect the body with the universal flow of energy. I find that it really helps me center myself, resting my eyes especially, and is a very good way for me to transition into *samatha* meditation. Over and above the noise and distractions of sensual desire is our desire to live. Until we are confronted by life and death situations, we might feel cavalier about this, denying that we fear death. Then death comes calling, either nearly taking us or through the death of a loved one. Sometimes we may be touched by the death of others that we don't even know, and it wakes us up to the impermanence of our own lives. When I gave birth to my son prematurely, I almost bled to death. I had felt until then that I had a pretty good bead on the whole life and death thing; that I didn't think I feared death and would be able to face it well. The reality was quite different. I think that when we do experience some of those flashes of fear, it actually helps us to connect in compassion to others who are in life and death circumstances, helps us to understand how precious life is, and it helps move us to want to understand and wake up, knowing that there is no time to spare. It seems ironic that we also suffer in our desire to be freed from suffering, but that, too, can help motivate us to learn the way to liberation.

The way we come to see this, is to pay attention. We all have buttons that are available for pushing. Sometimes people around us are particularly adept at finding them too, even though we think we've hidden them very well. And they delight in pushing those buttons, or so it seems. But the reality is that we're actually the ones pushing the buttons; buttons that are push pins that are hurting us. We could choose to observe the other person behaving badly – maybe even making some popcorn to enjoy as we watch. Instead we allow what happens to affect us and cause us pain. When we learn to pay attention to what is happening, we have an element of wisdom in that; some prajna (wisdom). Pema Chödrön teaches on the Tibetan term *Shenpa* meaning the attachments (kind of like the stickers on burrs) that hook us and cause us to shut down. So when we get our buttons pushed, our shenpa, causes us to come up with excuses for our bad behavior or leads us to behaviors what we believe make us feel better whether that is through alcohol, over-eating, gossiping, arguing and getting aggressive, or any number of bad habits. The advice the Buddha gives is to stop and be aware of what is going on, to stop pushing on the button that is hurting us, and loving ourselves enough to apply the medicine of practice.

The result of seeing and paying attention is that we can get more wisdom about what is happening, and stop feeding the cycle of the habit energy. When we learn about the store consciousness and the *bija* seeds of human nature, we learn that when seeds are watered, they tend to manifest. So when bad things happen to us, a seed of aggression or self-destruction might be watered and manifest itself in harsh words or worse. When good things happen, a wholesome seed might be watered and manifest itself as kindness and understanding. When we pay attention to this process, we can learn to look deeply at the unwholesome seeds and invite them not to grow. My mentor during the process of becoming ordained in the Order of Interbeing, Ian Prattis, tells a story about a Native American grandmother explaining the power of these inner habit energies to her grandson, likening them to wolves warring inside of her. One wolf is kind and gentle, the other was angry and hateful – both wolves are doing their utmost to take over her spirit. The grandson is awe-struck and asks which wolf will win this battle. The grandmother explains, "The one that I feed."

Other terms for *dukkha*, which is traditionally translated as suffering, are unease, disquiet, discontent, dissatisfaction, and Hagen describes a feeling of being off-kilter like a wagon wheel not quite on track. By looking at these varieties of ways to speak about dukkha, we get a sense of the range of what the term is pointing at. The big three of suffering, disease, old age, and death were the motivation that led Gautama to seek liberation from suffering. Yet, we can experience dukkha in many more ways than those three major sufferings. Each day we are confronted with things that just aren't the way we think they should be; we rail against change, yet we crave variety and the new. I think of the royal family who has a large staff of people who have the job of keeping everything the same for the royals, replacing wilted flowers with fresh, ironing the newspaper, putting out a fresh bar of soap every morning, preparing perfect breakfasts, laying out clothes, all done while keeping themselves nearly invisible to maintain an illusion of perfection. Yet, even with every precaution taken, reality does intrude causing pain and suffering. How do we think we can insulate ourselves?

The Second Noble Truth

The Second Noble Truth is about the arising of Dukkha, showing us the origin, roots, nature, and creation of suffering. When we approach the First Noble Truth, we come to recognize that the world contains suffering. This is no small accomplishment; many people go through their lives without ever examining themselves or wondering about their circumstances. They blame external causes or circumstances for all of their suffering. They (and by *they*, I mean, I) think that if everyone else would just shape up; just drive by the rules; do what's right instead of looking out for themselves first; just change to be more like me, I would be happy. When we have our first little awakening by recognizing suffering and looking at it, we then need to wonder what causes this suffering or discontent. Discontent becomes a habit that is hard to break and we tend to find fault in all sorts of silly things all day long until we can barely find pleasure in anything or anyone. My sister and I did an online workshop together a couple of years ago that asked the participants to keep a gratitude journal. That is a really good idea to help develop a habit of stopping to appreciate the wonderful things that are available to us every day, every where we look. Helps keep things in perspective. Thich Nhat Hanh talks about the importance of understanding what feeds our suffering, and paying attention to the spiritual and material nutriments we have ingested that cause us pain.

The commitments one takes when entering the Buddhist path are taking refuge in the Buddha, the Dharma, and the Sangha followed by taking the Five Lay Precepts. These three are equally important; in fact, one could not exist for long without the other two. While the Buddha Gautama is an historic person, without the Dharma, his life would simply be an historic curiosity. The Dharma without the Buddha would be interesting and even helpful, but would lack the spark of life and would seem removed from the realm of our own lives and capabilities. The Sangha could not stand alone for long, no matter how well intentioned the members. The people, without a way of life to guide them, would become simply a political or cultural group, not different from any other group of people. Like the Celtic symbol the triquetra, the three points are interlaced together. One can focus on one of the points or the other, but when one delves deeply into one point, the other two are there also. According to Thich Nhat Hanh, in Chinese and Vietnamese Buddhism, a practitioner who takes refuge will add the phrase "within myself" to each of the aspects of the Triple Gem during the taking refuge ceremony, showing that interwoven within the Triple Gem is the understanding that those qualities are woven within us as well.

This is called taking refuge in the three jewels. When one takes refuge vows for the first time, it can be done in a ceremony with ones teacher, repeating each refuge vow three times to help internalize the vows. As part of most Buddhist ceremonies, the refuge vows are repeated during each ceremony to renew those vows. One does not have to take their refuge vows in a public ceremony; one could take the vows privately in a way that is meaningful to them. I had taken my refuge vows by myself on a beautiful beach at sunset many years ago because it just felt right. I wanted the commitment, but I didn't have the support system in place to have a nearby sangha to join. For a long time, I thought that because I didn't have a sangha that the last refuge was missing for me. But when I attended my first retreat with Thich Nhat Hanh a number of years ago, he talked about that. He explained that if we really are solo practitioners that we can always come back to our true home within ourselves and have confidence that the sangha around the world are practicing in stability and are there to help us, too.

When one takes refuge, a number of images come to mind. One might think of refugees, fleeing from political or natural disasters, or we might think of finding a place protected and safe from the treacherous world. Woven into this concept of refuge is the idea of "faith." When we take refuge from the storm in a storm shelter, we have faith that the shelter will hold up to the wind and keep us safe. In Harvey's book "An Introduction to Buddhism" he takes this symbol further, likening the refuge vows as an island safe from the storm, something that uplifts, sustains, and protects us.

When a practitioner takes refuge, he or she has faith that the Triple Gem will sustain their spiritual life. That may start as a faith born of tradition, an intellectual confidence, or even dogged determination. This faith may mature over time into a heartfelt faith in the practice. When we look at the Buddhist term for faith, *saddha*, Harvey translates it as "trustful confidence," but we can also find the translation "to place the heart upon." I love that translation, because it says how I feel about the Dharma. While I do have faith in the Buddha, the Dharma, and the Sangha, the term faith seems too much like something one has to do to be allowed to stay in the group. Even refuge isn't my favorite way to talk about it; since it implies somewhat that we're running away and hiding. But the term "to place the heart upon" really hits the right note for me; there is a feeling of vulnerability because we have to be open and honest, yet a feeling of trust and confidence that even though this path can be very hard, it's also holding my heart in its hand, wanting me to achieve awakening.

The Third Noble Truth

The Third Noble Truth helps us understand that everything that comes into being will cease to be. The cessation of creating suffering is something within our grasp. Thich Nhat Hanh explains that the Third Noble Truth teaches us that healing is possible. Central to this third truth is the concept of interdependent origination. The Dalai Lama explains that all conditioned things come into the universe as a result of the interactions of the various causes and conditions present at any given time. We could ask our loved one "why are you not a tree?" since all of the component parts of any of us could easily have been reconfigured as something very different had conditions and the chain of causality been even slightly changed. Yet we tend to take everything in this present moment for granted, thinking that if only something here or there were different, I would be happy. We get that the present is made up of the past, yet we doubt that the future will be made up of the present, so we worry and live everywhere but here and now. Working in hospice, we meet families with a variety of reactions to the dying process; some who are very fearful, some who are in denial, and even some who have no regrets and face the process as a natural part of life. Seeing that impermanence seems so simplistic, yet it's the most profound thing we can face.

Cessation is used in a few ways: that our suffering can cease, implying hope for the future; that everything that exists will cease to be, implying impermanence, and that we can attain cessation, that cessation is liberation. The Third Noble truth begins the process of pointing us toward an understanding of emptiness. While many people have tried to claim that Buddhism is pessimistic because of the First Noble Truth, I would think that the Third Noble Truth is really the controversial one. This is the first hint at emptiness, and if we look deeply at it, we can understand it properly. But at first glance at cessation, we might be tempted to think that Buddhism is a nihilistic way of thinking, since we might believe that if everything that comes to be will cease to be, what is left? But as we go through layers of understanding of cessation, we can remember that cessation means liberation, not nothingness. We can take the Middle Way on our journey to first solve our problem of suffering and attaining true liberation.

Cessation entails looking deeply at emptiness so that we can understand, first through logic and deductive reasoning. One of the methods for looking at emptiness is to work through the process of deconstructing an object. When we try to find an intrinsic nature to an object, we fail to find one. When I was really concentrating on emptiness and the science of our material world, I found that the process of meditating on a flower, for instance, and thinking through its past and future and the inter-being-ness of all things, it awakened a lot of compassion in me for others. On the other hand, when I was explaining how I felt to a good friend who was in the geology program when I was in school, he absolutely understood the concept of emptiness as scientifically sound, but couldn't understand how that knowledge would make anyone feel anything in particular. This was a very important lesson for me. It seemed a shocking statement to think that knowledge didn't change feelings or behavior. At first, I figured that I just hadn't explained it well enough, but I later would understand that it's not the knowledge of emptiness that changes us, but looking deeply at it. I use the saying "moving the knowledge from the head to the heart," to describe it, but the Buddhist term might best be prajna, inner wisdom.

Steve Hagen talks about the importance of seeing things as they are as a mindfulness practice to help engender understanding of cessation. In mindful walking or sitting, a Zen teacher of mine used to ask us "what are you missing?" from time to time, and I still ask myself that when I'm out for a mindful stroll. As someone who loves to think, it's important for me to pause often to look at what degree of tunnel vision I've developed as I'm going along. The other phrase that is important to ask ourselves throughout the day is "are you sure?" Thich Nhat Hanh recommends that we print that on a piece of paper and hang it where we can see it during the day. That way, as we go along our day, making all sorts of judgments about this and that, we might look up and remind ourselves that we're probably not really seeing things as they are, but valuing them for how much we like or dislike them. I have a picture of a cardinal, my totem bird (the cardinal represents finding our voice – the male cardinal has a loud chirp, and he tends to attack his own reflection, a good reminder for me not to fight myself) and I added the "Are you sure?" phrase under it and have it tacked to the wall beside my office door. I've had people ask me what that means, and I'll just say it's a question I ask myself about things – some seem puzzled, and others think about it and have some interesting comments about their own surety about things.

The Fourth Noble Truth

The Fourth Noble Truth is a path that leads to liberation. It's important to understand the three turnings of the wheel for each of the Noble Truths: recognition, encouragement, and realization. Thich Nhat Hanh explains this by describing that for each truth we need to be able to recognize that basis for the truth. We need to be able to do a thorough assessment of the fact of suffering, the arising of suffering, the cessation of suffering, and finally the path leading to well being. The Fourth Noble Truth is a systematic approach to living a wholesome life, and sets eight aspects of understanding in place for us to look deeply at. These eight are not a linear process, but a holistic approach. In fact, the whole of the teachings is contained in each of the components if we look deeply at them.

We also need encouragement, or understanding that the path has to be lived, not just studied and understood as a mental or philosophical concept. It's kind of like studying all about the sun, but living in a sealed off basement never having seen the sun. The experience makes all the difference. The third turning of the wheel is realization; the understanding that the path is being lived and is helping us. Through my time in practicing Buddhism, there have been ups and downs, but there are a number of major ways that the tools and instructions I've received have helped me a great deal. I still need a lot of help, but I do know that if I hadn't experienced any change or difference, I wouldn't still be at it in some hope for enlightenment out of the blue.

The term "right" certainly makes us think of right and wrong, and that we want to do the right thing. But "right" in this case can also mean "wholesome" or "appropriate," and the word is not meant to produce a pair of opposites or a way that we can make ourselves right and someone else wrong. Being in the quality field, I have a slightly different take on this term. When we use quality principles to make a change in a process, we have to gather data to see what the reality of the situation is, not just what we want it to be or our opinion based on a couple of personal observations. Then we make a problem statement specifying what we see and what we would like to see happen. Then we make a goal based on our belief that the original problem can be solved. (Sound familiar?) Then we need to take a look at steps we can take to change the process and produce a new outcome.

Many people at this stage confuse the tools with the actions. One of the examples I give when I teach classes on quality principles is to say that a New Year's resolution might be to lose weight and get in shape. We make that general goal into a more specific one, and then I say that my actions toward my goal are to buy a treadmill and buy a diet book. Some folks actually think that those are good items for the process. Then we have a laugh when someone mentions that I will have to actually walk on the treadmill and follow the advice in the book, and I tell them that my treadmill is under a load of laundry and that I can't find the book! To me, "right" in this case is like that action item, using the tool of mindfulness or intention or the rest. If each of the qualities of the path simply sits on the shelf, they will not produce a change in us. We have to put them into action for them to work for us.

Right View is about having a direct experience of something. If I've never tasted an orange, I can't really have a right view of it. If you've never tasted an orange, all the explaining I could do won't help you until I hand you a section and you eat it. Steve Hagen explains that right view is not about having a view or concept, but being free from concepts and seeing things as they really are. The idea is to go beyond our views and arrive at "don't know mind" or "suchness" by asking ourselves all the time "are you sure?" I have a picture of a cardinal with that phrase printed underneath pinned to the wall of my office so I can see it often. When someone comes in to ask a question or complain about something or to ask me to help solve a problem, it's very helpful to keep asking myself that question so that I don't get taken down the garden path to a one sided point of view.

I actually prefer the term "right thinking" to "right intention," I suppose because of that phrase "the road to hell is paved in good intentions." Steve Hagen also calls it "right resolve" which is good too, since it points to the meaning of our desire for waking up to help others. When we look deeply at this aspect of the path, we can see bodhichitta right from the beginning of the Buddha's teachings. The story about Socrates holding a potential student under water to test his resolve that Hagen relates is one that I've heard with different characters in the roles, but the same idea underlying it. It's a really good point for all of us to remember as we're on the path.

When our lives are going pretty well and we're lighting candles, drinking green tea, and meditating, we're also pretty complacent and not all that motivated in our practice. But when something big happens to us, a loved one, or something that really touches us, that resolve is newly awakened in us. I had that experience when I visited a young man on our hospice service who wanted to learn more about Buddhism. The visit with him was quite remarkable, and on the drive home, I found myself in tears with the desire to practice awakened so strongly in me. I realized the profound reality of how important it is to have that inner peace, stability, and compassion within us in order to really be of support and help to not only this young man, but everyone I meet.

Hagen mentions an analogy for right intention of someone whose hair is on fire. There is no choice in the matter, weighing pros and cons, doing an opinion paper, or calling together a committee. The person acts – right now – to put the fire out. Not only for our personal desire to awaken, when we practice right view and right intention, we see the reality of the situation and act from that understanding and wisdom, producing a way to understand ethical actions. Hagen also explains that right view is wholesome, whole, and contains everything within it, so there is nothing to oppose or contradict. This, too, helps us act in the best interests of the situation.

One of the things Thich Nhat Hanh talks about when he writes about the Avatamsaka sutra, is that the reality is that we're all in the Pure Land, we just can't see through the veil of our discriminating perceptions of duality. When we wake up to that view, we find ourselves surrounded by gems, flowers, and beautiful birds. What is there to give someone when they have all those gems at their feet – it seems absurd to come over to them to give them a gem as though we are something special and they are in need. Instead, all we need to do is give that person our stability, presence, and practice so that they will be drawn to open their eyes. It's the peace and stillness that we have to cultivate, it's the only thing we really have to offer, but it's more than enough.

Right Speech

Right speech is, perhaps, the toughest part of the eightfold path – at least for me, anyway. It's more than just not telling a lie or something simple like not bearing false witness, although both of these can lead to ethical dilemmas. Right speech is more about communicating the other aspects of the eightfold path. Without right mindfulness or right view, we are tempted to use unskillful means when we speak, or we're tempted to believe and spread things we've heard before we're sure they are true. There is a sutra that the Buddha says that lying is worse than murder because when we lie we further a person's delusion about the world. I think what the quote is getting at is that we should pick our words carefully; we should say that we're hungry, not that we're starving, for instance. When we hear a rumor about someone, we should withhold our judgment about it, and certainly not spread the rumor until we know if it's a fact or not, and still maybe not talk about it true or false. The other component is our relationship with others. At the heart of right speech needs to be deep listening. When we listen deeply to another person, we learn what they are really about and develop a lot of compassion for them. Then when we speak, we're speaking with a mind of understanding and compassion, not to make a point, prove them wrong, or to impress.

When I was growing up, we spent our summers in Nebraska on the farm with some of our other relatives. My mother was the youngest of seven, and most of the aunts and uncles lived there. We would spend time with each family, and one of the bonding experiences was talking about the other families. I can remember being both upset by this, but also kind of delighted too. It was very stimulating, kind of like watching some of these guilty pleasure TV shows that show people behaving badly; a train wreck that you know you should turn your head from, but can't help but watch! At any rate, there are lots of times that I find myself being sucked into some of these types of conversation, even though the topic is more about issues at work than what people are wearing or doing in their personal lives. What really helps is saying "hello, habit energy – I know you." And remembering that this is part of a pattern that I learned as a child, it's not who I am. It can take courage to buck the trend of what is going on around us, but part of right speech is also about recognizing our habit patterns and learning how to break those patterns in a way that will also help the other person. Sometimes, the step in the right direction is knowing that we're not using right speech as well as we should even if we can't quite break the habitual pattern. Knowing can help us take responsibility and open doors to a better way to speak.

The ethics of all this can be a bit thorny. The classic example is asking if you would lie to protect a Jewish family from the Nazis and there are people who answer in a variety of ways depending on their personal ethical point of view. It's kind of a silly question, though, because even if you think you would lie convincingly to protect the family, in the real situation, you might find that your fear would overcome your intention to do the right thing. The other problem compounding the decisions we make is that we really don't know what the outcome will be of our actions. Something can happen that seems really bad, only to find that it was a blessing in disguise.

We have an ethics committee at work and I've sat on the committee for a number of years now. Most of the ethical dilemmas stem from people not listening to each other, but in trying to do what they fully believe to be the right thing and wanting to force their opinion on the rest of the family. It can be a real challenge for the staff who visit these patients and family to help them, since the family can have such a hard time believing that acceptance is possible. They can believe that if they accept a person's point of view, it's the same as condoning actions they believe to be wrong. Sometimes there is no fixing the situation, and we have to help the staff come to grips with a situation that they find very difficult, especially if they feel the patient isn't getting the kind of care they should.

Ultimately, we have to keep practicing so that we see things the way they really are, listen deeply so that we truly understand people, then act in a way that comes naturally from that place of peace and compassion.

Right Action

Right Action is ultimately about our actions being in the flow of our proper perception of reality. Hagen talks about us being like a leaf drifting on the breeze, not having to consider or decide what to do; we simply do what is appropriate in the situation. Now, for the rest of us, having some guidelines so that we don't get into too much trouble is a good thing. The Buddha thought of that, though, so we have precepts that help us behave in a way that will minimize suffering for ourselves or that we might cause others. I often hear Buddhists say that the precepts aren't commandments that will cause us to burn in hell if we don't follow them, but this isn't really a correct thing to say. It's not that we'll be punished by some big daddy in the sky if we don't follow the precepts, it's more about that the pain and suffering we cause ourselves and others does create a hell that we live in here on earth.

Right Livelihood is a pretty amazing part of the Eightfold Path to me; I'm not sure if any other religion acknowledges the fact that we all have to work to make our living. So, in Buddhism, we need to consider what we do for a living so that our work doesn't do further harm to ourselves or others. While there are a few professions that are off limits for Buddhists, for the most part nearly every job has its good and bad parts that we need to look at. Even if we're in a job that is thought of as "good," there will be aspects that are harmful that we should learn to work with to be sure we're not participating or encouraging that aspect. In a job that might be considered "bad," we may also find that we can bring our practice to that job to make things better for the people involved.

In looking at the ethics of these two, Hagen talks about the legal profession as an example, but I have a disagreement with one of his examples. He talks about the potential of doing good in the legal field, and that is very true. While regulatory issues and laws seem very boring and not at all spiritual, having regulations and laws on the books that protect people and having people in the legal field that make sure those protective laws are being followed appropriately can save lives and reduce suffering. On the other hand, Hagen makes the example that if a lawyer has to defend someone who is guilty, then maybe he or she should reconsider being in that field of law. I disagree with that statement. While we can say that it isn't "good" for a guilty person to get away with what they've done, the defense of that person is a vitally important part of our legal system. Not all of the defendants will be guilty, not all will be innocent, but without a vigorous system that demands that both side work hard to find as close to the facts as possible, the system would fall apart to the detriment of all of us.

It is worthwhile to think about the ethical implications of the precepts as well. The five precepts are a commitment on the part of the practitioner who takes them as vows to abstain from killing, lying, sexual misconduct, stealing, and intoxication. We can strive to simply follow the precepts in a very basic way, and following them will help us lead a better life and help keep us from generating more negative karma than need be. We can also consider that we follow the precepts not only for ourselves, but for others as well. I've heard lots of practitioners who have problems with one or more of the precepts saying that they don't have a personal problem with an aspect of one or more of the precepts, so why should they be held to that commitment?

For instance, someone might feel that they don't have a problem with alcoholism, so why shouldn't they drink socially? In a lecture I heard while still in college by a Theravadin monk that I've always remembered, he listened to a fellow student who felt strongly that Buddhism isn't about rules and the Buddha doesn't demand anything of us, so he wouldn't feel compelled to follow a precept unless he experienced the reason for it himself. The monk answered that if you can't follow these simple rules on faith, there is little hope that you can tackle the larger questions.

If we expect that Buddhist teachings can be sorted through and we can just pick out what we like and leave what we don't like behind, we're just constructing our own philosophy, not allowing Buddhism to change us. While I had not yet taken the refuge vows or precepts yet, I did stop drinking after that. Interestingly enough, I attended a department cocktail party with a friend and thought it was all so mature and cool to be there with professors, grad students, and other guests. They were serving wine and I almost reached for a glass, thinking that no one knew about my commitment, and after all, what could it hurt to just sip a glass of wine the way everyone else was doing? But I stopped myself and asked for water with lemon instead. I realized that I didn't feel uncomfortable with carrying the water, that it was better for me to make that choice. I thought that was the lesson for the evening. But the next day a young man I really didn't know very well, but remembered had attended the party came up to me. He told me that he just wanted to thank me. He saw that I just had water to drink, but that I was still having a good time and looked very comfortable just carrying the glass of water. It had been very painful for him to see all those glasses of wine and he was struggling with his alcoholism. It was like he had a friend on the path and he had been able to drink his soft drink and got through the evening ok. Knowing that has given me a lot of courage to strive to follow the precepts in a more complete and full way and to look more deeply into each one to see the richness that is present in each of them, even though I still fall short of that ideal.

Right Effort

Right Effort or right diligence is important for us to practice on the path. However, the Buddha recognized that not all diligence or effort is "right" or helpful to us. We can be diligent in our pursuit of selfish gain and we can even be diligent in our practice, but if that effort causes our minds or bodies to suffer or takes us further from reality, that effort is harmful to us. The classic story is of the monk who practices meditation very hard, harder than anyone else, and who takes great pride in his effort. The teacher asks why he is sitting so hard; his reply is "to become a Buddha" so the teacher picks up a tile and starts to rub it very hard with a rock. The monk asks his teacher what he is doing, and the teacher replies "making this tile into a mirror." The monk asks "how can you make a mirror out of a tile?" and the teacher replies "how can you become a Buddha by sitting?" Now, some people might take that reply literally to mean that you can't wake up through meditation practice, but the story is more about right effort than sitting. The Buddha himself taught that a musical instrument must be strung at just the right tension. Too loose and the sound will just be noise when one plucks the string, too tight and the string will break, just right and music is possible.

Thich Nhat Hanh teaches that Right Diligence has four practices associated with it: 1) preventing unwholesome seeds in our store consciousness that have not yet arisen from arising, 2) helping the unwholesome seeds that have already arisen to return to our store consciousness, 3) finding ways to water the wholesome seeds in our store consciousness that have not yet arisen and to ask our friends to do the same, and 4) nourishing the wholesome seeds that have already arisen so that they will stay present in our mind consciousness and grow stronger. It is important to realize that the other aspects of the eightfold path are integrated with each other so that we're using practices that bring us peace and compassion. It takes energy to look into suffering, especially when we've turned out eyes away from our suffering and suppressed our feelings pretending it doesn't exist. When we look at this suffering with honesty it may feel painful for awhile, but we can go through this pain and transform it into peace by using the energy of right effort.

The use of right effort correlates to Buddhist ethical system by reminding us that all of the elements of the eightfold path need to be kept in mind when we practice, they never exist by themselves. We can work very hard to help people but if what we do is the wrong kind of help, we may do more harm than good. We can become caught up in how much effort we're making and either become prideful or arrogant, or resentful if we feel our hard work isn't being rewarded or recognized. The efforts we make in our practice need to be done for the sake of practice alone, not for hope of reward or fear of failure. Otherwise, we are wasting our time.

Lineage

Traditionally, Buddhist lineage refers to the unbroken chain of transmission from the Buddha to the present time. Buddhist schools can generally trace their lineage through many generations and there are archaeological artifacts in the form of stupas, shrines, and documents that can support some of these names. For many schools, lineage is considered of high importance and is taken very seriously. In Vajrayana Buddhism, some teachers advise students to be certain of a teacher's lineage before taking an empowerment to assure that the lineage is not broken or manufactured, with the belief that such an empowerment would do the student more harm than good. Other traditions are just as strict, and there have been incidents of monks leaving Buddhist congress meetings because of the presence of individuals that they felt were not properly ordained in an intact lineage. Lineage trees have many branches today and it can be complicated to trace them. Realistically, it is impossible to fully verify each and every individual on a lineage tree, so these are accepted with a certain degree of faith.

Lineage is important, but we need to think through why we think it's important. After all, if all is one, and we all have Buddha nature, what can lineage do for us that we can't do for ourselves? When we wake up, isn't our lineage directly tied to the awakened nature of the Buddha? And it's certainly true that even some very traditional, well certified, teachers with impeccable lineage have acted badly; hurting themselves, their students, and tarnishing the reputation of their school and lineage. There is a lot of debate currently over Zen teachers, transmissions, and lineages.

Some people would regulate Zen teachers and consider them to be professionals like lawyers or psychiatrists; others say that this is a religious issue and Zen teachers and students need to take care of problems within the context of their organization. A student is left wondering who to believe and what to make of these controversies. Ethical guidelines could certainly help, especially here in the West, since this is a format we're familiar and comfortable with. More simplistically, we already have a very good set of ethical guidelines in the form of the precepts and a student would do well to observe that a potential teacher follows the basic five precepts as a start. After all, these precepts really are easy to follow in at least their simplest form.

The lineage of my tradition goes back to Dhyana Master Liễu Quán (1670-1742) of the Lâm Tế School (Bamboo Forest School) of the lineage of the Lin Chi (Rinzai) school. From there, the Tiep Hien (Order of Interbeing) and the order that Chua Bao An is part of are cousins in the same lineage; the head of that order, Thich Man Giac, being 43rd generation (Clarity of the Source) and Thich Nhat Hanh is 42nd generation (Compassion of the Heart). Both have their roots in Liễu Quán. In my ordination as a member of the core fourfold community of Tiep Hien, first my lineage name is Tâm Bi Khai (Compassionate Opening of the Heart) – Tâm being the 9th classical Chinese character of the gatha Liễu Quán wrote. My Dharma name is Chân Lac An (True Happiness in Peace), belonging to the 43rd generation of the Lâm Tế School and the 9th generation of the Liễu Quán Dharma Line. The gatha that Liễu Quán wrote is this:

> *"The great way of Reality, Is our true nature's pure ocean. The source of Mind penetrates everywhere. From the roots of virtue springs the practice of compassion. Precepts, concentration and insight - The nature and function of all three are one. The fruit of transcendent wisdom, Can be realized by being wonderfully together. Maintain and transmit the wonderful principle, In order to reveal the true teaching! For the realization of True Emptiness to be possible, Wisdom and Action must go together."*

CHAPTER 5

The Precepts

"The Heart of Being: Moral and Ethical Teachings of Zen Buddhism," by John Daido Loori is a book that a summary doesn't really do justice. This is a book that I always recommend to students of Zen Buddhism because it satisfies a need for an intellectual understanding, but calls on us to look deeper. Taking what might be thought of as simple - the Buddhist Precepts - and exploring them in a symbolic as well as historical way, we begin to realize that we could spend our whole lives working with the precepts. Not only moral and ethical instructions, but also a way to touch the foundations of Buddhist understanding. It is a way to experience the precepts, not simply to know and follow them. When we sit with the challenges of modern life and its questions of what is right and wrong, the precepts help give us a guide, but more important a framework for how to explore the nature of our minds and how we can relate to the world.

During the time of this class and writing this material, I was diagnosed with breast cancer. It was perhaps the greatest gift of my life to have been studying this and other Buddhist teachers when being faced with the possibility of a life limiting illness. Not only did I have the support of my family and loved ones, my teachers, but this and other of these books gave me access to not only contemporary teachers, but a lineage back to the Buddha himself. I no longer need a lineage chart; I have a blood line that connects me in a profound way. I will always be grateful for these teachings.

Buddhist Ethics

Buddhist ethics are based on the precepts. We take vows not to harm ourselves or others at the most basic level and practice in a way that helps us lead a wholesome life whether we go any further into the Buddha Dharma or not. Because the bottom line is to avoid harm, Buddhist ethics are situational. We are expected to use skillful means to the best of our ability as well. A classic example regards Anne Frank in the attic, and asking the question about the right thing to do and say when the Nazi's knock on the door to ask if any Jews are there. A presentation I do from time to time with new staff and with our Clinical Pastoral Education (CPE) students is about cultural diversity and understanding. I bring out two flip charts and on one, ask the students to list everything they can think of that is in alignment with their values and what they think of as good. Then on the other chart, to list the things they think are not good; not part of their values. Then I draw a line down the middle of each chart with the list of words on one side and we talk about when the good qualities are actually not so good and when the bad qualities actually are necessary or even good in a given situation. I want them to loosen up their idea of the shared values of one group and look at when values that they think are inferior or bad are understandable and logical.

Karma is the driving force of Buddhist ethics. The cause and effect of what we do helps us see what our actions produce. It can be a simple example that the Buddha used about anger: that anger is like gripping a hot coal in our hand. The only reasonable action is to drop the hot coal, not continue to grip it. The first level example makes sense to anyone; the analogy brings cause and effect to the next level. If we take an every day example, we could say that if we close our fingers in the door, our vow is to not do that again! We're going to give up closing our fingers in the door. We can take a simple, physical cause and effect and apply it emotionally, socially, and spiritually.

The four virtues for happiness are: confidence in the Dharma, following the precepts, generosity, and the development of wisdom. My favorite translation for Saddha, rather than faith or even confidence is "to place the heart upon." For me, this expresses the rest and comfort in taking refuge and implies that there is nothing more to worry or fret over. Forest Gump says something like "don't have to worry about money anymore... that's good! One less thing!" We can get down to the business of practice once we have placed our hearts upon the Dharma; that makes me happy, anyway. The precepts are a very tangible way to be happy. When we're tempted to do the wrong thing, we might do it anyway, but while it might feel good at the moment, we're only left with regret. The precepts give us some very basic guidelines when we only look at them superficially. When we look deeper, we find a wealth of the Buddha's teaching. The Buddha started his gradual method for teaching the Dharma with generosity. He knew that being generous makes people feel good and gives benefit to others. It's again a basic teaching that grows in depth as we look more deeply into it. The development of wisdom to help us end suffering cultivates true happiness and understanding. When we practice, we begin to taste the fruit of the practice in first simple ways like being more relaxed, sleeping better, and being more focused.

For me taking the precepts, first the five, then the 14 precepts of the Order of Interbeing and the 10 precepts of our order at Chua Bao An, were a very important step. In addition to giving a road map for this journey, I also felt a part of history. These precepts have been practiced for thousands of years and were created and continued because they have layers upon layers of meaning. There is a sense of community not only with my Sangha but with the larger Buddhist community through time. The precepts, I've found are a wonderful support for meditation as well, especially when practicing the four foundations of mindfulness. They become a walking meditation for every step I take. While I don't practice them perfectly, they help remind me of where I'm going and what I'm doing.

Renunciation

Renunciation is an important part of Buddhist ethics because it leads us in the direction of non-attachment. Renunciation is part of Right Intention, part of the Wisdom division of the Noble Eightfold Path. When the Buddha taught the Middle Way, he emphasized the balance between self-indulgence and asceticism, but we shouldn't confuse self-mortification with renunciation. Instead, we are resolved not to be attached to the emotions and feelings of the world while still being in the world. Sometimes you see the words pleasure or sensual associated with the concept of renunciation, that while that is true that we should learn not to be attached to the fun stuff, other habits need to be renounced as well. We can become just as attached to being critical of others, angry and disgruntled, or pissed off at the world. I have some relatives that bond by gossiping about the relatives that aren't around; my Dad used to say that they weren't happy unless they had something to complain about!

The three levels of vows are for laypeople, novices, and for Bhik-khus/Bhikshunis. The different schools have different numbers and word-ings for the Vinaya vows (as well as different colored robes, ceremonies, and rituals associated with taking these vows). Additional vows, like the Bo-dhisattva vows can also be taken by laypeople.

Pratimoksha vows were given by the Buddha to his followers. The parts of the word mean "toward liberation;" this is an important point to me, since it's so common in Western society to think of vows or lists of rules as self-sustaining – follow the rules and everything will be ok (or follow the rules blindly and you'll go to heaven!) But that kind of legalistic thinking is not what these vows are about. The Pratimoksha belongs to the Vinaya and is taken for the life, ending when the person who received it died or has broken one or more of the four root vows. We could even look at the vows as "things," in the sense of a "vessel." The term "break" connects to this idea.

Why is it necessary to formally take the precepts? Well, it isn't really necessary; in what I call my "California Zen" days, the teacher considered himself something of a Ronin and felt that we all should be responsible for ourselves in every way, including taking refuge and our vows. We designed our own ceremonies to be what was meaningful for us, even if that meant taking the vows privately. At the time, that was very helpful to me; leaving a rigid structure and family. On the other hand, as I became drawn to practice in a different way – I don't like to say "more serious," but in a deeper way, I began to see the value in the structure and ceremonies. When I took my "of-ficial" refuge and vows, including my Dharma name, the ceremony helped to solidify my commitment and helped me feel part of a larger community and tradition. I still keep my "California Zen" Dharma name close to my heart because it opened a world of creativity and spontaneity that helped me see the world with new eyes. The combination of the new and ancient eyes has deepened my understanding, creating yet a new vision.

Practicing the precepts is discussed so elegantly by Daido Loori. All of the practices reflect the precepts and give us an opportunity to look deeper to see things as they really are. I particularly like at the end of chapter 3 when he talks about that we are practicing all the time! But what is it that we're practicing? Are we practicing consumerism? Anger? Impatience? What we do on a daily basis is our practice. It's our choice to ask ourselves if our practice is benefitting ourselves and others or if we're actually punishing ourselves with how we talk, what we eat, what we buy and consume, how we escape our feelings, how we manage our work and home life. I really like that concept and found it very helpful. When I was tempted after reading this to be critical of a co-worker who was being discussed, I thought of this and asked myself what I should call this practice of mine. Ugh! I didn't care for that at all! Especially remembering that this is a family pattern of bonding through shared gossip. Time to renounce that habit energy once and for all.

Atonement

The reading I did this week was done mostly in hospital waiting rooms, unfortunately. My ex-husband and I are very close after all these years and he went into the hospital with kidney failure and had to not only start dialysis but have a cardiac catheterization for a blockage repair. It was a little strange to be sitting in the surgical waiting room in a religious hospital seeing all the inspirational pictures about "Hope" and "Faith" and "Jesus' Healing Touch" while reading about commitment to the Dharma. What an interesting juxtaposition.

One of the passages that stood out for me as I read (sometimes re-reading, realizing that I had drifted off, wondering and worrying about what was going on in that room) was "There is this causation, or Dharma, yet fundamental nature is empty." We have the three treasures to take refuge in, and Loori reminds us that we should also look at the manifested three treasures; the bodhi mind. That direct realization of the relative and ultimate dimensions is a personal experience. So here was this chain of causality happening before me; Greg's family history, his conviction that he would die young so why worry about taking care of himself, the doctor's appointments and decisions of how to treat his condition that brought us to this place. People in the waiting room; some praying, some doubting their faith, some asking why, and others just worried about their loved one. Then there was me, looking at how to be present to things just as they are; how to wrap my brain around how real the fragility of the body is, yet the ultimate reality that it is empty. What I did find was that when I could just take it all in and not pick and choose what I thought of as good/bad, ok/not ok, control/lack of control I had more "space" to be in. The highest level of faith that I had was in impermanence – that was very comforting really. I could just say, this is how it is now, things will change later.

I love Loori's explanation of atonement, "at-one-ment," creating a pure or blank slate. In a real way, we're not only atoning for our own transgressions, but all of those that lead us to where we are right now. We're all connected, so we can never really say that we're innocent of the evil or acts of ignorance that occur in the world. Being honest with ourselves is one of the hallmarks of Buddhism, I think – "honest" might even be the word I would choose if I were asked to describe Buddhism in one word. Just thinking through a given day we can come up with lots we need to atone for, all of those things gifts to help us unlock where our blocks of ignorance are; then open them up and sweep them away to create that open space where awareness lives.

These first three questions are really tightly integrated with each other. We can take refuge in the three jewels in a basic way and go through the motions of participation in Buddhist stuff, but it's only when we can take the leap into practice that is engaged by the rising of the bodhi mind that we can truly clear the slate through atonement and immerse ourselves in the reality of refuge. I loved Loori's example of his little kids leaping off the dresser into daddy's arms in that pure being-ness that little kids have. I used to love when my son would play so hard and so fully, then run back to me for a hug, his neck damp with sweat, his skin warm and pink, half crashing into me, then bouncing back for another dash around the yard. He was so fully engaged in the refuge of the sun and the grass and the joy of being alive.

The three treasures are very much like a gem that has many facets that we can explore and relate to as we practice toward the day that we can understand them as a whole. Loori talks about cause and effect not being linear and I think that this is a very important point. My teacher used to talk about healing past wounds, even if the parent who we didn't understand or who hurt us has died, we can still heal that karma and change the past. I used to chalk that up to that "cultural" stuff we Westerners tend to discount and didn't really take it seriously. But the more I study, the more it's dawning on me that he does know what he's talking about in a real, not metaphoric, way.

The five precepts seem pretty basic at first glance; after all how hard is it to understand that not killing, not stealing, not lying, no sexual misconduct, and not getting intoxicated. We can put these things in a positive way of speaking as well, talking about the concept that our subconscious doesn't understand a negative, so if I say "I will not eat donuts" over and over trying to convince myself to stay on my diet, my subconscious hears that as "I will eat donuts" and I have to agree I like that better, too! Framing each of them both ways is very helpful in understanding that the precepts aren't just about omitting some behaviors, but in cultivating the positive aspects as well. So if I have the start of not killing, then progress to nurturing life, and perhaps even to preventing others from taking life; then promoting peace I take my understanding from a small, personal point of view to a global view. As that view expands, I can see that the more I explore the cause and effect and interconnectedness, I can't just stop at "don't kill," the imperative grows to include all things.

Monastic Vows

The title of the monastic precepts is called the Pratimoksha (Sanskrit) or Patimokkha (Pali) and is contained in the Vinaya Pitaka. The Vinaya Pitaka is the "Basket of Discipline" that provides the framework on which the monastic community is built. This code contains a host of rules and the proper etiquette that governs the monastic community and the relationships with the lay community. The Vinaya presents a set a rules for the monastic to explore in depth but it also inspires the layperson toward what a life fully lived would be like.

Someone who has received the full monastic precepts is called a Bhikkhu or Bhikkhunis. Literally translated, it means "one who lives on alms" and is a person who strives to conduct themselves following the code of living set out by the Buddha and the first sanghas. The monk or nun takes vows to develop their minds in order to liberate themselves from suffering and to save all beings.

The three extant lineages are Theravada, Dharmaguptaka, and Mulasarvastivada. These three Vinaya are the three surviving lineages which all Buddhist schools and sects flow from. The texts that attempt to trace where each lineage came from and whence they go are challenging since a researcher must consider geographic dispersion, doctrinal differences, schisms, rivalries and political intrigue. The Theravadins currently practice in Southeast Asia, Sri Lanka, Indonesia, among other countries. The Dharmaguptaka played a prominent role in Central Asian and Chinese Buddhism. The Mulasarvastivada lineage has been preserved by the Tibetans and Mongolians largely because of political influence.

Reinterpreting some of the traditions can be a challenge. There is always a give and take about whether this is a good idea or not. On the one hand, times change and adapting to the current circumstances monks and nuns live in is important so that they have guidance for their lives. One the other hand, going too far afield with change can lose the important traditions that are timeless and give grounding in a world that is all too eager to abandon the past as it careens headlong into the future. Thich Nhat Hanh has re-written many of the precepts for modern times and while this is not without controversy, there are many of these rewrites that provide food for thought. He even covers cell phone use! Never one to dwell too solidly in tradition, he writes that he was the first monk in Vietnam to ride a bicycle; before that it wasn't considered proper – now monks and nuns drive cars and motorbikes to get around. I do enjoy reading the rules, although a bit sheepishly since I recognize lots of things that I do, say, or feel and would have a hard time with if someone called me on it on the spot. You've got to be pretty brave to take on monastic vows and be really willing to be honest with yourself, honest with others, and willing to make yourself open to scrutiny by the others in the monastic community.

Evil

The difference between a priest and a monastic seems to me to be largely cultural. Dependent on the school of Buddhism, of course, but the society where that school practices plays a part as well. Those who desire ordination make choices about what school makes the most sense to them doctrinally and culturally, so in one sense, there really is no true difference. Today, one of the advantages to Westerners is that we can go school shopping; we're not constrained to the school of Buddhism that is in our locale. We can look at our priorities and life to make the decision about what school to align with. In the Vietnamese Pure Land/Zen school that I practice in, the only option is to become an ordained nun, although there are unofficial additional vows that one can take for personal enrichment. I do wonder what it would be like to be an ordained nun with the dramatic change in my daily life and what the difference in experience would be like to be an ordained priest and in many ways not have much of a change in my daily life. Still, there seems to me to be case to be made for another option. There is something of a movement toward a Buddhist minister who would be neither a monastic nor a priest, yet could be of service to help his or her community.

We should conduct ourselves with respect toward ordained sangha. The way I was taught is that when meeting a monk, nun, or priest, one should stop and bow, saying "Nam Mô A Di Đà Phật" sometimes adding their title if known. When listening to a Dharma talk, we should sit upright and pay attention. When asked to do something by a monastic, we should strive to do it if we possibly can. We should help the monastic community by our contributions, participation in the sangha, and help with practical things like bringing food and other necessities and helping with the cooking, house-keeping, and grounds keeping of the temple. They give so much to us in the form of practice, ceremonies, and being good examples of how to practice that it is easy to want to give back to them. On the other hand, that doesn't mean that all monastics and priests are created equal or do all of the things expected with perfection. A good lesson I learned, though, was about a monk that was kind of a poor example of a monk and many of the people in the community didn't treat him very well because of it. An old lady there was very respectful to him, bowing deeply and being deferential towards him. Someone asked about her behavior and if she was aware that he wasn't a very good monk. She replied that she knew all about that, but that was his business and none of her affair. She continued to practice beautifully.

The three pure precepts are "not creating evil," "practicing good," and "actualizing good for others." Loori gives a number of helpful examples of these in our book and he goes on to explain that while the first two precepts give us the positive and negative side of things, the third helps us understand that there really isn't a good/bad duality. The point is to manifest awakening, transcending duality to seeing things just as they are. When we are fully present, we simply respond to others with deep understanding. Thich Nhat Hanh teaches that true love is only present through understanding. Understanding only comes through deep listening.

For me, I feel that I come closer to that when I can be more spontaneous with others. During my unit of CPE, I felt that I grew a lot in that direction. There would be visits with patients when I first started that my conversations with them were based more on what I thought might upset them or what I thought they expected from me. Later in the unit, I found myself asking questions or saying things that came more from what I was hearing from them, sometimes asking some tough questions about their spirituality or relationships. It felt like those interactions were getting closer to "actualizing good for others."

Oh that picking and choosing! It's so hard because it comes so naturally. A baby starts picking and choosing right away, or at least when you start to introduce solid food (not that you can blame any infant to spitting strained peas back at you!) I'm still working on this one, but for me, the Four Foundations of Mindfulness practice helps a great deal. When I find myself picking and choosing, I try to breathe in more space around how I feel. I like the analogy of the universe with infinite room for all the variations of matter. When I feel that my feelings are stuck in a tiny box, there's not much room for them, so they become overwhelming – and it's not just the big stuff, even those minor annoyances that drive me bonkers!

If you'll forgive a bit of Bible stories, I've always loved the story of the Garden of Eden and even as a young person I felt that the problem with the world was that realization of the duality of things that Adam and Eve experienced with they ate of the tree of the knowledge of good and evil. Now, we won't get started with why it was moral to punish people who didn't know the difference between right and wrong since that's another debate. But it always struck me that it was the Garden that turned into a dualistic world and that when we could learn to see the world in that non-dualistic way but this time at the level of awakening rather than naiveté, the Garden would be revealed to us.

Evil is confusion and ignorance. It seems like it should be easy not to create evil when we look at the evil that happens in the world. Because of mass media, we're exposed to so much evil and suffering. It's easy for me to have righteous indignation toward those who would harm others in such willful ways. It seems naïve to think that it's just "confusion and ignorance" when many of those people don't have any excuse for what they've done. Yet, when I'm honest and catch myself in that indignation, I see elements of that evil there. After all, I'm ready to judge them and harbor anger and even a wish for retribution toward them. For me, the best thing is to keep peeling the onion and keep reminding myself to be honest with myself. It might take a while to climb off my high horse, but it's important to get back on the ground to look at my own contribution to the culture of evil so that I can bring the space in to lighten it and transform it into understanding.

Good is a double edged sword in many ways. It's crafty because we can fool ourselves into believing that we're so lovely and sweet and making that into our identity. Then when unwholesome feelings come up, we can justify them because, after all, we're good, it's not our fault! There is value, though, in doing good through the actions of the precepts and being ethical. Doing the right thing because it is proscribed might not be ideal, but it does help us practice good; helps our mind develop habits that are wholesome for us and others. When we see the world clearly and have that perfect understanding, good flows from that naturally and without pretense or rule.

A fully realized person would simply act with clarity and understanding. The wisdom that flows from that place is filled with compassion and love. One of the teachings I've always loved is about the Pure Land. My teacher said that when we're in the Pure Land, we're surrounded by the most beautiful flowers and jewels. If someone were seated next to us in the Pure Land and needed our help, what would we give them? It would be pointless to give them a flower or jewel; they're sitting in the same field we are! What we could give them would be our full presence. We could listen with equanimity and compassion. That's the gift that is greater than all the jewels or advice we could ever come up with.

Ultimately, I think that actualizing good for others in a non-dualist reality is being there for the other person. Meeting them where they are, not, as our author mentions, at a distance. We need to empathize with the person without becoming overwhelmed by the suffering, yet fully understanding. In a sense it's about creating a space of true love and understanding so that they can see their own suffering clearly. Seeing our own suffering is the ability to see the gift within the suffering; exposing the rawness of the things we've stuffed down, peeling away the layers of picking and choosing that have buried our understanding. it's always about going deeper.

Saicho

Saicho was instrumental in reforming ordination of Buddhist clerics in Japanese Buddhism. He believed that the Vinaya was Hinayana in nature and taking the Pratimoksha vows would take a person's practice back rather than taking it toward awakening. He felt that the Bodhisattva Vows were superior and the vows he instituted in the Tendai sect. Doctrinally, it is important to note that the term monk would no longer be accurate, since in reality, this breaks with the teachings of the Buddha for ordination as a Bhikkhu.

Before this, ordination was determined by the state. The Buddhist religion and the monasteries were state authorized and served at the pleasure of the state to chant sutras, perform rituals, dedicate merit to assure prosperity and good fortune, and to satisfy the needs of the people in a way that could be controlled and directed.

Saicho was motivated by a variety of reasons personally, politically, and doctrinally. Saicho didn't want to be involved in the government positions, wanting to be independent of that system, yet he had to have permission of the Emperor and he worked hard to assure that he could teach his own curriculum based on the Chinese writings that he brought back from his travels, with an emphasis on the Lotus Sutra.

The effects of this break from tradition have had a ripple effect to this day with ordinations and lineages coming into question and being debated. The term "priest" has been taken on by many Zen schools and is preferred in the West to avoid confusion and to avoid the impression that the person is claiming Pratimoksha vows. As we learned in the book about the Platform Sutra, arguments and controversies about lineages and the validity of ordinations are nothing new and won't end as long as there are people around that have opinions.

I've always found the precepts to be very rich to come back to time and time again, exploring all of the layers they contain. It seems that just when I think I have one of them figured out, something happens to shake that up and go deeper. The fifth grave precept to avoid intoxication, to "proceed clearly, do not cloud the mind" seems like an easy one. With this precept, I've been taught to look closer at the other things that can cloud or intoxicate the mind. In fact, even teasing out the word "toxic" with that word "intoxi-cate" points toward many other ways that we bring toxins into our bodies and minds, clouding how we think and behave. Just because I'm not a drinker doesn't mean that this precept is one I can check off as "done" and not con-sider it. There are certainly times that I cloud my mind by spending too much time drinking in shows or political commentary or news that certainly gets my blood a boiling, and takes my thinking deep into picking and choosing territory.

The sixth and seventh grave precepts are very similar, one saying "See the perfection. Do not speak of others' errors or faults." This can be so diffi-cult when dealing with others, especially in the work environment. I like that Loori explains that this doesn't mean that we don't talk about another per-son's faults and errors when it's necessary. Being the quality and compliance manager, it's actually my job to discuss the faults and errors that I find! Where I do this well and with some skill is in bringing up these issues dip-lomatically and with a goal of providing better care for our patients and a better work life for the staff so that the quality care they provide brings sat-isfaction and pride in what they do. The fly in the ointment, though, is that in my family a bad habit was to bond over the criticism of others and despite some of my best intentions to keep my mouth shut, I've found myself sucked into a discussion of the failings of this or that person. Now, I've tried to con-vince myself that it's not gossip about trivial things but important issues that I'm involved in or some injustice and I'll do something to make the situation better or make things right.

This brings us to the 7th precept of "Realize self and other as one. Do not elevate the self and blame others." This precept cracks open the attempt to elevate the situation above into something if not noble, at least ok since things should be done better and if only this or that was fixed, things would be great. Luckily, I know what's best and it's not that I'm elevating myself;

I'm just speaking the truth! Right? Do I get to convince anyone of that? Anyone? Anyone? No – ok, that pesky honesty thing again! But I do think that this precept helps me look at my bad habits around boundaries as well. Part of me blames the other person for "sucking me in" to their bad behavior and part of me feels that I have to be part of these conversations, even if just passively, since I don't want to be "that person" who isn't part of the group or gets left out. Setting boundaries has always seemed so limiting to me, but what I'm discovering is that it's actually a way of being more genuine and true to myself. What I'm finding when I do that well, is that by not allowing the person to dump their negativity on me or by not giving myself permission to join them in their toxic conversation, I'm not only being true to myself I'm giving them a chance to make the choice to talk to me more honestly as well. I'm more than happy to listen to someone about how they feel and what their feelings mean to them; what I'm not happy to do is be a dumping ground for negativity when they get to walk away feeling much better, and I'm left down in the dumps.

The eighth grave precept: "Give generously. Do not be withholding" is one that has a lot of depth to it as well, since giving is not only of money but our time, talents, and attention as well. To leave on a positive note, the other day I went to the Asian market that is in kind of a rough neighborhood but because there are always a lot of people coming and going I don't feel unsafe going during the day. As I got in my car, a woman came up to the car and asked for directions. I rolled down the window and noticed that she looked really tired and run down. I gave her directions and she started to turn to head that direction, but she looked like the weight of the world was on her shoulder. I called her back and asked if everything was alright. She told me a little of her troubles and asked if I had any change I could spare to help her get downtown. I usually do give people a couple of dollars if I have money with me, but I really felt that I should help her more and was glad I had a twenty dollar bill to give her. She had tears in her eyes when she thanked me and started to assure me of how she would use it. I stopped her and said that the money had no strings attached; she could use it however she needed to. I reached out the window to give her a bit of a hug and wish her well. I can understand why the Buddha started his teaching with generosity. It's the thing that brings out the best in us and helps give us that glimmer of what true compassion is like.

The Buddha's Robe

"What are the dimensions of the Buddha's robe?" was the question that took me far afield for this assignment. I often find that one question or something I read in our assignment will lead to searching for this or that and becoming interested in tangents that take me deeper. Loori's description of the Buddha's robe is that it wraps us in liberation, protection, and keeps evil at bay. The form of the kesa is based on a rice field and symbolizes planting the seed of enlightenment, protecting the new sprouts that will nourish all of the world. During retreat yesterday, I spent a lot of the Dharma talk looking at the monk's robe (I couldn't understand much of what he said; he speaks a dialect that I don't know at all). I felt envious of that robe – I need a robe that will protect me from the perils to come, so I will have no fear when the thunderstorms shake the heavens or in my case when surgery and chemotherapy change everything. I read some interesting articles and websites that chronicle the making of the Buddha's robe; Joan Halifax writes eloquently about crafting hers and there are Zen stitchery groups who use sewing vestments as mindfulness practice. In Yampolsky's book, he recounts a legend of the monk who laid out his robe and it covered the whole region. For me, the Buddha's robe covers the whole universe. Learning to wrap myself in creation and seeing life as my protection is what I want to cultivate.

We've talked a lot about lineage from the other class, so I'll just talk a little about my own "Buddha name" as my Vietnamese friends say. My name, Tâm Bi Khai, means Compassionate Opening of the Heart. The "opening" word in Vietnamese references the blooming of a flower and "Tâm" is also the word for heart/mind or mindfulness. I love the name because I feel it's something I'm always striving for and even when I fail, I have a name that leads me back to my true home and my true nature. When fear or heartache make me feel I have to close or armor my heart, I can say my name and feel an opening to vulnerability and trust that it's ok to open. After all, my teacher entrusted me with that name and has confidence in me that I can open my heart to compassion.

I think that the symbolism of the phrase that sentient beings are numberless; I vow to save them all is a little different than "working to save a lot of people." For me, the idea of numberless beings goes much further, including the past, present, and future. I see a vast ocean of all of life when I hear that phrase. When I think of "saving them" in terms of running around fixing all their problems, then that really is impossible. When I stop my desire to fix; which is actually more about making things to my liking and choice, then I can open my idea of "saving" to seeing them in unity and emptiness. Things might not be the way they should be, but they are perfectly in the flow of life in all its phases and forms.

DES and the Buddha

Diethylstilbestrol. Abbreviated DES, it is a word that has haunted me since I was a young woman. About the time I needed to have regular check-ups with an OB/Gyn, I learned that the daughters of women who took DES during their pregnancies, termed DES progeny in the medical literature, had a higher than normal risk of developing vaginal cancer. As the years went on and we DES daughters grew older, more side effects became known and one by one, I had many of them mostly to a minor degree until I started trying to have babies. My mother, raised in a large family on a depression era farm by a distant mother and stern, verbally abusive father, was a people pleaser especially toward authority figure men. When her Dr. wanted to give her DES, marketed heavily by the pharmaceutical companies despite studies that showed it did nothing to prevent miscarriages, she was a good patient and took the drug.

When I found out about this, being far more independent and something of a know-it-all, I was indignant that she would just swallow whatever they handed her. Then I discovered that she had been desperate to have a baby, and I felt that tug within me too. When I had my first miscarriage, I was devastated and it was only then that I understood why my mother would do anything it took to keep her pregnancy. There was no longer anything to forgive her for. I went on to have a baby boy born prematurely because of a uterine malformation caused by DES exposure and a third pregnancy that ended in a late term miscarriage. We did not try again; grateful for a healthy son who grew up to be smart, strong, tall as his daddy, and creative.

And now, the next chapter is starting. Breast cancer is being found at more than double the normal rate in we DES daughters. When I first found the lump in my left breast, I was shocked at first but embarrassed as well. I had not done a self-exam in a while and had skipped my mammogram last year; I was upset with myself for not having found it sooner. When I got to work that morning, I started making calls to get a mammogram and exam and the whirlwind began. It has been a rollercoaster of emotions and a rollercoaster ride to pay attention to. Being terrified of dying, worry over who would take care of Matt, and just looking around my home wondering what would become of the life I have made, knocked the wind out of my sails. I didn't tell anyone what I was suspicious of for quite a while, but it became clear that there was no slender sliver of hope that this was not malignant. The other interesting thing that I found myself doing was wondering why this happened and if there was anything I could have done to prevent it. In some ways, knowing that my mother took DES and this is one of the chain of events from that makes it a bit easier. I do not feel that this is my fault and that lets me off the hook in my own mind.

Yet, am I really off the hook? Looking deeper at the way things are is not about sugar coating things or finding the final answer. Loori explains that we have to take responsibility for our lives; to make atonement – at-one-ment – to make a clean slate for the Dharma to move in our lives. Feeling the resistance within me when considering looking for my responsibility for what is happening is important to explore. Growing up in the era I have, I have heard all the pop psychology of "I'm ok, you're ok" and the effort to assure people that they are not at fault for what is happening; I guess in order for them to feel better and move on.

I have also heard the talks from those who believe in a personal form of rebirth or reincarnation that helps them cope with the bad things that happen. After all, if they cope with the bad things, maybe they will repay a karmic debt and better days will be ahead. Either of these approaches is too superficial. Rebirth, in my still limited understanding, is both personal and impersonal. Rebirth is happening every moment of every day and it is also the process of life that is me, yet not me as well. It is easy to make the big questions into abstract, soft focus, "God is love" kinds of things. If I let myself off the hook with karma and rebirth by saying that it is all just a process and I am made of the star dust of the Universe, so it is all One, I may be left feeling good, but what have I learned? Looking for some specific thing I have done in this lifetime to pin down as a reason why I now have cancer seems not only like an exercise in futility, but an unnecessary roughness.

So where does that leave me in looking at why this is happening? It seems that the question it boils down to is "why?" Who am I; a victim of cancer? Am I paying a karmic debt? Should I work to cultivate a positive attitude and "can do" spirit that the pink ribbon folks believe will cure them? Or should I find the koan in asking "why"? When Master Te-shan was confronted by the woman at the Inn who asked him: "if past mind, future mind, and present mind are ungraspable, with which mind will the venerable monk eat this cake?" Loori explains that this was the point for Te-shan that the question appeared. "The cup was turned upside down." This is the time that the thinking and the feeling and the perceiving are suddenly stopped and the direct experience appears. I remember seeing Salvador Dali's *Crucifixion* (the *Corpus Hypercubus*) for the very first time at the Dali museum in St. Petersburg. It is a huge painting and it stopped me in my tracks; the emotion of it flooded over me, the beauty of the painting overwhelmed me, and the experience of it was so direct.

I have worked with patients and their families as they have faced death. I have listened as they have asked "why?" and while I never felt that I had the answers, there was still some distance between what they were experiencing and my experience. I cared for them and had compassion as I could experience and understand it at the time, yet there was still an element of "thank goodness that is not happening to me." In those experiences, though, I have had times of realizing that it has always been thus; birth, death, and the full catastrophe that make up our lives. When my diagnosis was confirmed, I came home from the doctor's office and went out to the back yard. We are in the process of getting rid of the swimming pool to put in a walking meditation garden, but there is still some standing water in the bottom of the pool. I looked in and saw something strange floating; some sort of branch or what I thought was plant material. I used the pool brush to move it and discovered that it was a dead squirrel. I pushed its body up to the slope of the pool and just looked at it. I felt so connected to its little body; so sad, yet with an understanding that this was not the end either. I sat for a long time simply soaking in the blue sky, green plants, and the dead squirrel. When I reached up to brush a tear away, I pressed a bit on the bone of my cheek. A bone that one day will be bare of the flesh that now covers it; whitened and made like chalk in the earth.

Thich Nhat Hanh talks about his feelings when his mother died and expresses the importance of understanding our interconnectedness so that when a loved one dies, we will know to look to the flower petal and see our loved one there, or to look at our own hands and see the continuation of them within us. The past is now the present, and the present will become the future. When I look at my hands and know that I would have taken that drug had I thought it would save my baby, I can take responsibility for what is happening to me now. When I look deeply, I can heal the past.

> *"All evil karma ever committed by me since of old,*
> *because of my beginningless greed, anger, and ignorance,*
> *born of my body, mouth, and thought,*
> *Now I atone for it all."*

Loori goes on to explain that while every cause has an effect and every effect is the next cause, that we should understand that cause and effect are not separate things; they are one. Because they are one, they are not linear in nature. They permeate the ten directions. We can transform greed, anger, and ignorance into the three virtues. Each action, each thought, and each word I speak create who I am. Can I embrace the karma of what is happening right now in my life; experiencing the depth of the question "why?" Can I atone for it all? Or will I hold back; fearful not of taking responsibility, but of taking the leap into void? When I was being moved into the narrow tube of the MRI machine, a process that is mechanized so that the technicians can safely observe the process, I was face down with intravenous contrast going into my arm making me feel a bit dizzy. I was surprised to see that there was a mirror that I could look at that was reflecting the tree outside the window. The problem was that the tree's reflection was upside down. It made me feel that I was spinning and falling down Alice's rabbit hole! I closed my eyes and remembered to breathe more space into how I was feeling. Abandoning myself to the experience, I could allow myself to fall into the void. The loud thumping of the magnet becoming the Shaman's drum. Can I continue to allow myself to open to the whole of the Universe? Can I realize the dualities, yet not be stained by them as Loori describes? Can I prepare in this way to practice the precepts and experience the whole of the Dharma?

I love this poem by Antonio Machado:

Wanderer, the road is your
footsteps, nothing else;
wanderer, there is no path,
you lay down a path in walking.

In walking, you lay down a path
and when turning around
you see the road you'll
never step on again.

Wanderer, path there is none,
only tracks on the ocean foam.

Thich Nhat Hanh explains that we should use the precepts as a mirror, to see the truth within ourselves; that the whole of the Dharma is found there. As I look at where I stand – the path behind me impermanent, no path ahead – can I see the universe in the dust beneath my feet? Can I make a pure atonement so that I can enter through that door that the masters have so kindly pointed toward?

The question remains unanswered, but this quote from Rainer Maria Rilke holds great comfort for me: "Be patient toward all that is unsolved in your heart and try to love the questions themselves. Do not now seek the answers, which cannot be given you because you would not be able to live them. And the point is to live everything. Live the questions."

CHAPTER 6

The Doctrine of Mahayana

This is the most academic of the chapters, critiquing and analyzing Paul Williams' "Mahayana Buddhism: The Doctrinal Foundations." This text explores the variety of Buddhist thought in the Mahayana tradition, and not only explores, but celebrates the diversity found there. Mahayana Buddhists see this diversity as something to be proud of, and indicates a richness of thought that aides all sentient beings, who can inevitably find something for their spiritual quest - something for everyone.

The term "mahayana" is addressed, considering that perhaps there is no solitary "Mahayana" but, rather, "Mahayanas" or even "Bodhisattvayana" or the vehicle of the Bodhisattva. Several aspects of the Mahayana path are discussed in the book, including the misunderstanding that the Mahayana schools were prompted into existence by the laity. This was not the case, and even today, it would be a mistake to say that lay members of the Sangha are considered co-equals with the monastics. While some Mahayana doctrine would claim that lay practitioners are capable of attaining awakening, it is still recognized that this is a very difficult path given all of the demands on lay people, making the requisite study and meditative practice difficult to accomplish.

The other issue that deserves some consideration is the sutras themselves. The canon of Buddhism is both open and closed, meaning that in the Theravadin tradition, the canon - the Tripitaka - is closed. It is considered the whole and complete teachings of the Buddha. In the Mahayana sutras, there are texts that claim to have been found or uncovered, often claimed to be "when the time was right," or to have been heard directly from the Buddha supra-naturally. So, in the Mahayana schools, the canon is considered open, with works both from the Buddha himself and including commentaries and treatises that are seen as sacred.

The essays here, while occasionally dense and scholarly, continue to explore the personal practice even in the obscure sutras, treatises, and doctrinal positions. Buddhism, after all, emphasizes practice over intellectual prowess.

Doctrine

In the introduction to Mahayana Buddhism, Professor Williams begins by saying that "...every valley has its own language so every teacher has his own doctrine." While Williams admits that this is an exaggeration, we have to wonder what diverse doctrines means for Mahayana Buddhism. For the student, this can seem a daunting challenge since when a question is posed about what Mahayana teaches, we would have to ask "which teacher?" For the practitioner, it would seem an equally daunting challenge to answer the question "what do you believe?" or even to answer that question of ourselves. It seems counterintuitive that there would be so much diversity within a religion whose founder had such a long teaching career and left so many teachings behind. Why is that not enough? Toward the end of his life, the Buddha said that he had only taught two things: suffering and the release from suffering. Those simple things leave one thinking "Yes! I want my suffering gone, but how do I do that?"

The Buddha developed an effective program to lead a person to the doorway of that release, and in his sutras there were often illustrations and stories to illustrate what he meant. Hearing stories can spark a memory of a similar experience or feeling, bringing us close to the direct experience of that freedom. Each teacher continues this tradition of basically telling stories in a variety of ways that help the teacher reach the mind of the students who each have their own experiences and ways of thinking. While doctrines are many and ethics are (mostly) unified the deepest, most basic meaning of the teachings are the same, and most importantly, the outcome of liberation from suffering is the same with those who have walked through that door doing their best to communicate that ineffable state to the rest of us.

When there are numbers of different sects or sanghas, it is normal to wonder why, or even wonder what went wrong that the practitioners felt the need to separate from their monastery to form a new one. Williams explains that a schism in the sense of Christian history implies, for the most part, differences in doctrine and conflict. Samghabheda, meaning 'splitting of the sangha,' on the other hand, was, in the opinion of many scholars, less to do with doctrinal opinions than the behavior of the monks in following the monastic code. While Williams shares some of the research regarding whether doctrinal issues were ever grounds for a sangha to split, of interest is the quote from Joseph Walser's work discussing the *Mahasamghika Vinaya* and the disagreements over the changes promulgated by Devadetta. (Devadetta, was the Buddha's cousin who we learn wanted to take over the sangha when the Buddha died, but that the Buddha refused this request. Walser states that the disagreement was not just over monastic rules (Devadetta did this, as well, adding additional rules that he could then claim made him a more pure monk than the Buddha) but that it stemmed from "...a disturbance in the institutional mechanism for scriptural reproduction."

Completing the crimes of Devadetta were his failed attempts to assassinate the Buddha. While there may be other reasons for a monastic group to split, the sutras form the basis for understanding and following the Buddha's program to freedom. Intentionally corrupting this process is a far different thing than the development of doctrines individualized by teachers based on the sound foundation of the Dharma. When we look at the idea of lineage in Buddhism, we are looking at authenticity and validity. While the primordial, transmission, and institutional lineages have equal footing as parallels to the Buddha, the Dharma, and the Sangha, we cannot confuse the role of each of these types of lineage. A person with an honorary degree (or more cynically, a degree paid for by prestige and money; not earned) may have a title and certificate, but will not have the knowledge of someone who has taken the classes. Or as my teacher has said; the robe is like a library card, it gets you into the library where the books are, it does not mean that you have read them all. While the institutional authority can stand front and center in importance, the transmission lineage which connects the chain of wisdom from the Buddha through wonderful teachers to the student is, for most, indispensable, but the practitioner's direct experience is the only true lineage that each student strives for and that will transform one's life.

Once we understand the distinction between scriptural integrity and doctrine, we can go on to consider how important issues of doctrine are to Mahayana Buddhism. An ancient Japanese saying goes something like "there are many paths up the mountain, but the view of the moon is the same" perhaps mirroring the 84,000 Dharma doors concept, both illustrating that as individuals with different learning styles, cultures, experiences, family dynamics, and on and on, we have different ways of understanding. A teacher becomes a virtuoso at creating a learning space for the student and in crafting examples, illustrations, and analogies all referencing a very real truth. Sometimes these differences may seem as far apart as the North and South faces of a mountain, the terrain couldn't be more different the student might think, so how can the result possibly be the same?

Kierkegaard said "As you have lived, so have you believed." This helps us see that doctrinal differences are only important if they have as their basis the simple core of BuddhaDharma, suffering and liberation from suffering. While an individual may have to search for the doctrine that makes sense to them, ultimately, doctrinal differences do not matter. One can study one sutra or one of the Noble Eightfold Path for the rest of their lives and they will find the whole of the Dharma within it if it is true Dharma. Like a faceted gem, we start by focusing our attention on one facet that seems most beautiful to us, but as we look deeper, we not only perceive but experience the whole of the jewel.

To help us, the Buddha explains in the *Catuhpratisarana* Sutra that we can evaluate a doctrine for ourselves by using the Four Reliances which state: rely on the message of the teacher, not on his personality; rely on the meaning, not just the words; rely on the real meaning, not the provisional one; rely on your wisdom mind, not on your ordinary, judgmental mind. In each of these admonitions, the Buddha brings us back to what is important in simple wisdom. Much like pithy sayings we all learned at home like not judging a book by its cover, the Buddha helps us see clearly and cut through confusion. A teacher might be charismatic and exciting, we want to emulate him or her, or we love telling others that we are their student, yet we must listen to their teachings dispassionately. We need to listen, not eagerly nodding our heads in agreement, but allowing their words to penetrate our consciousness, truly listening. We can go to the amusement park and happily eat hot dogs and cotton candy, gobbling them down quickly because those first magical bites taste so good, but by the time we get home, our stomachs are upset. When we eat food mindfully, chewing each bite thirty times, it only takes a bite of an unwholesome food for our bodies to tell us that this is not nutritious and we should not eat any more. When we judge a teaching faulty based on the superficial meaning of the words, we miss the opportunity to understand that looking deeper into the meaning meant to be shared.

It can be difficult for some to learn lessons from other disciplines, yet even in the professional world, we can learn tools that we can use in our own field by using this reliance. NASA, for instance, pioneered the concept of doing a root cause analysis for discovering the true reasons for problems and failures. Because that language is based in mechanical engineering, it could be hard to see how that kind of analysis could be helpful in any other field. But looking past the superficial language and looking at the concepts and tools behind the work, many fields have adopted this technique. In healthcare, we use the root cause analysis to work to solve medical errors to try to prevent them, for instance. And finally, we are taught to rely on our inner knowing and experience, jhana, to understand rather than our typical thinking based on judgment. The *Bhikkhuvagga* says: "There is no jhana for one with no discernment, no discernment for one with no jhana. But one with both jhana & discernment: *he's* on the verge of Unbinding."

The origins of Mahayana are still being researched by a variety of scholars looking at the question from a variety of perspectives. While popularly, a simplistic view of the *vehicle* idea is to say that Mahayana is the vehicle that includes everyone and that lay people are equals to monastics. But this view leads one down a path to try to make the schools of thought into a vehicle metaphor which might not always be appropriate or accurate. Perhaps more accurate is the term *Bodhisattvayana* or Bodhisattva Vehicle. Rather than a movement developed as a lay-inspired, devotional school, the Mahayana appears to have existed more as a set of ideals and doctrines for the Bodhisattva path. Additionally, Williams notes that the Mahayana did not attempt to create a new Vinaya or ordination lineage from the early monastic orders.

Nattier references the *Ugrapariprccha Sutra* as an early Mahayana text, saying about it that "... the Mahayana is not a school, a sect, or a movement, but a particular spiritual vocation, to be pursued within the existing Buddhist community." Williams goes on to cite Schopen's work showing that the Mahayana was a minority interest within the early Buddhist framework as illustrated by inscriptional evidence in Buddhist art. According to Williams, Gombrich's research shows that the various councils that tradition teaches solidified the cannon at an early date are probably wrong. While the first council is considered to have established the non-Mahayana canon, this canon was not as closed and pristine as has been taught in the past. Context is important to consider with the society and cultural influences of the time as well as the geographic dispersion of the monastics who had no easy access to new and developing ideas. Williams cites Gombrich's work on the role of King Asoka in the spread of Buddhism and how that may have affected the rise of the Mahayana movement in relation to non-Mahayana sects.

Some of the Mahayana sutras are proven to be written many years after the death of Siddhartha Gautama, yet they are portrayed as the words of the Buddha. By standards, especially in Western societies, this is not defensible. Gautama literally could not have said the things they claim. For most people any fantastical claims of going down into snake pits or channeling the mystical man for revealed wisdom is not accepted as possible. So if we ask the question is it defensible that Gautama said those words; we have to say no; if we turn to the words being that of the Buddha, we can look at a larger context and deeper meaning. While many of the stories may have been written to lend credibility or create a fascinating air to attract people to believe the validity of the sutras, part of the mystique is also to understand that there are many deep symbols embedded in many of these stories which touch the subconscious as dreams do, showing us the treacherous path of new birth from a place of darkness into the light. The Buddha is not the man, and the Dharma is not the province of one man either. We have learned through the Four Reliances to use discernment and wisdom to evaluate teachings, the Buddha himself would listen to and approve of teachings spoken by his disciples, and the Three Dharma Seals of impermanence, non-self, and nirvana are delineated in the *Samyutta Nikaya* to help us recognize a teaching of the Buddha. We have the tools, it is up to us to use them to find our path and our responsibility to follow it to transformation and liberation.

Buddhahood

The Buddhist translator and historian Edward Conze describes four phases in the development of the Prajnaparamita literature, which stretches over more than a 1,000 years. When we look to understand the history and development of the Prajnaparamita literature, we must consider a number of factors: the geography of where the people who added to its' development lived, the time periods they lived and the impact of political, cultural, and societal factors, the literature itself, the archeological evidence, and the epigraphy of the documents themselves. Each of these aspects gives us clues to the placement of the sutras in history and helps to reveal the development and ripening of the conceptual framework for the Prajnaparamita. The four phases identified by Conze consist of: 1) the elaboration of the basic text, from about 100 BCE to 100 BCE that has the verse summary, and the oldest text, the *Astasahasrika Perfection of Wisdom*; during the following 200 years, the expansion of the text into the Satasahasrika, *Pancavimsatisahasrika*, and the *Astadasasahasrika Prajnaparamitas*; 200 later to about 500 CE, there was a restatement of the central ideas into shorter sutras including the *Vajracchedika* (the Diamond Sutra), and the work favored by the Tibetan school, the *Abhisamayalamkara*; finally, from 600 to 1200 CE, tantric elements find their way into the literature with the *Adhyardhasatika* Prajnaparamita being an example of the addition of *magical* elements. Williams goes on to explain that these phases are far from set in stone, and other researchers have some disagreements on the details, yet in understanding what the literature is all about and how it fits in context within Indian Buddhist history can help us understand the development of ideas, with the warning that we should be cautious of locking up this literature into to a set schema too tightly when additional research may shed new light on the details of its' development.

In Mahayana Buddhism, the aim is full Buddhahood for the benefit of all beings. Buddhists following other aspects of the path can be called Bodhisattvas, but when one is intent on returning as many times as it takes to achieve full Buddhahood, the term *mahasattva* (great being) is added – Bodhisattva-Mahasattva. Often a comparison is made to non-Mahayana traditions, considering the spiritual goals to be purely personal. Even in the early Prajnaparamita literature is found this admonition "They make up their minds that 'one single self we shall tame... one single self we shall lead to final Nirvana.' A Bodhisattva should certainly not in such a way train himself...." On the other hand, remembering that one who has attained Arhatship has also destroyed the 'I am' and is neither selfish nor uncaring.

Compassion is the very heart of awakening, whatever the level ascribed to it. We can also look at the Bodhisattva-Mahasattvas as legendary figures who, in their perfection, have amazing abilities and give anything and everything to sentient beings that need their help. In stories and legends many mythic tales are told of their deeds, yet we as individuals are encouraged to take on this aspiration and path ourselves. The idea of delaying enlightenment seems like a paradox; how can we strive to help all sentient beings by awaking up, yet delay awakening until all other beings have awakened – seems almost like a trick; the first one there is a rotten egg (lacking in compassion or breaking ones vows; and doesn't that make Bodhisattvas *better* than the Buddha himself?) According to Kensur Pema Gyaltsen, this postponement of Nirvana is not to be taken literally, instead we are to look at the idea of the Bodhisattva adopting a position of complete renunciation, renouncing even Buddhahood itself if there is even a glimmer of selfishness; thereby attaining the perfection of Buddhahood.

While prajna is translated wisdom, Williams explains that "Prajna is a mental event, a state of consciousness." This term has a subtlety of meaning with the context in which it is used. One may have a conventional prajna through the study and understanding of something in the world; the understanding that results from an intellectual analysis of the way things are, the correct discernment of the way things really are, and a perfection of prajna that is a gnosis that is beyond duality; a non-conceptual awareness. The development of prajna can take this path of understanding first through discursive reasoning, then experientially through meditative skill; moving knowledge from the head to the knowing of the heart. Practice traditions have emphasized different aspects of prajna, although they all have the goal of leading the practitioner to the perfection of wisdom, with traditions in

China and East Asia emphasizing the non-analytical aspects, perhaps with the influence of Taoist influence. Prajnaparamita also refers to a number of *paramitas* (perfections) that must be mastered by the Bodhisattva. These perfections include giving (dana), morality (sila), endurance (Ksanti), exertion (Virya), meditative concentration (dhyana), and wisdom (prajna) and are said to lead one to the perfection of wisdom. These concepts are rooted in the Buddha's gradual teaching method as illustrated in the *Uposatha Sutta* and others. So while there is so much to learn, and so many dharmas to penetrate, (and so little time) we can work hard and develop a great deal of knowledge and wisdom about how the world works, academic and historic knowledge, and many useful skills – all of which can be very valuable and helpful; the perfection of wisdom transcends these all because, at its' heart, it is filled with the compassion that eases the burden of suffering in all living beings. We strive to achieve full Buddhahood, but we also do not wait to help and follow our heart, so we practice ourselves to make ourselves capable of helping. Without inner peace and true compassion, there is just so far good intentions and sympathy can go.

Nagarjuna is so well regarded in Buddhist history; he is considered a second Buddha because of his grasp of the sutras and their ultimate meaning; developing or inspiring a large part of the Prajnaparamita literature. There may be more than one author by the name of Nagarjuna, and like a great deal of Buddhist history, this great monk has little written about him personally, but legends and mythology do play a part in understanding what his contribution to Buddhism is about. The word *naga* means snake (literally cobra), serpent-beings of the water realms, earth spirits, or dragon; Arjuna means *noble*, a person with a clear inner nature, free from impurities whose mind is ready to receive the highest understanding. Of the legendary accounts, it is said that Nagarjuna was sitting by a lake and the water serpents invited them to come into their realm to teach. When he emerged, he had the twelve volumes of the Prajnaparamita. Naga or Maha-naga (great dragon) is often used as a synonym for the Buddha or other sages who have attained Nirvana; they are also used in many Buddhist statues or other iconographic images to represent guardians of the Buddha, temples, or scripture. Legends say that the nagas guard the sutras placed in their care until humanity is ready to receive and understand them. Snakes, water, and underwater caves or grottos have strong symbology for birth, death, and rebirth. A snake, or its more powerful cousin the dragon, sheds its skin on a regular basis, during which time it is blind and lethargic, emerging with new vitality. Going deep into the water can also symbolize delving into the subconscious, the part of our mind that we cannot access through logic and reasoning, but through imagery and symbols. The name and the legend give us powerful symbols to set the stage for some of the most important lessons toward full understanding of the Buddhas teaching.

The Madhyamikas shifted the concept of intrinsic nature (*svabhava*) slightly to signify intrinsic or inherent existence in the evolution of how the dharmas are viewed in terms of ultimate nature and reality. Nagarjuna developed this *middle way* as the rejection of the two extremes of eternalism and annihilation. In working through the logic of the concept of an enduring essential nature, Nagarjuna found that this essential nature would prevent dependent origination since things would have always been and would always be. When we perceive of things as having an existence in their own right, we begin to believe that they are permanent; causing suffering because we are not perceiving things as they really are.

This is a particularly hard habit to break when it comes to our perception of our own self. All of our instincts are bent on self-preservation and certainly seem to back up our mind's insistence that we are indeed, at our core, enduring. Emptiness (shunyata) is not a doctrine or view, but as Nagarjuna says, it is a medicine to cure our sickness of seeing our ideas as having an essential nature; the antidote to all viewpoints. This development of emptiness expands on the not-self characteristic taught by the Buddha and discusses the differences between an intellectual understanding through reasoning and a gnosis of understanding. Williams talks about how disturbing these teachings must have been when they were fist taught; the idea of completely letting go of even the most subtle attachment would be, if taken seriously, very frightening. In one of his essays on the nature of the scientific process, Loren Eiseley talks about a colleague who was a scientist who spent large parts of his day looking into microscopes and delving into the microscopic world of the atomic structure of our physical world. What he saw on a daily basis was the large amounts of space within objects that we all take for granted as quite solid and impenetrable. There came a point in his life when he began to feel trepidations when walking across the floor for fear that he would fall through the gaps.

He had let go of the notion that things in the world are solid, but did not know what to do with that intellectual knowledge that had penetrated his understanding in a profound way. I read an article about a scientist who, in studying string theory, is convinced that everything that can happen does happen because a string is launched into a new dimension in space and our string selves go with the random occurrence. He said that he is extra careful because of his concern over what actions he may be setting into motion. These are people who, while not Buddhist or really having an experience of understanding emptiness, have found a gnosis that is profound and in an oblique way, touching the core of emptiness. They have moved their belief from an idea that does not affect their behavior to a core understand that informs everything they do. I have felt that feeling of being fearful of the lack of solid ground implied by the Heart Sutra, yet also the expansiveness of what the understanding of emptiness brings. Using this medicine to help me bridge that gap between understanding the facts of the way things are with the penetration of seeing things the way they really are is my heart's greatest desire.

The two truths further penetrate the understanding of emptiness. *Lo-kasamvrtisatya* is the relative or conventional truth and *paramarthasatya* is the ultimate truth. These two truths must be understood in relationship with each other, because as Williams states that these two do not oppose each other but imply each other. O'Donohue could well have been discussing these concepts when he said "The beautiful Gaelic phrase *fighte fuaighte*, 'woven into and through each other,' captures this." We live in a world of dust (*saha*) but we do not look to transcend this world to go to a dust-free world of Nirvana, since if we removed this world of dust, there could be no Nirvana. We are often tempted to want to do away with that opposite thing that we do not like. After all, wouldn't the world be better off if only the left existed and we could cut off the right? Without the right, there would be no left. We would love to do away with suffering, forgetting that in the relative world, suffering is subjective and without suffering there could be no joy. Without emptiness, there could be no impermanence, as Williams explains that emptiness and dependent origination mutually imply each other leading us to understand that that lack of intrinsic existence allows change.

I have a beautiful calligraphy of the Five Remembrances in our meditation room so that I can at least be reminded of them everyday even if I do not recite them. The Buddha recommends that we recite these daily: "1) I am of the nature to grow old. There is no way to escape growing old. 2) I am of the nature to have ill-health. There is no way to escape having ill health. 3) I am of the nature to die. There is no way to escape death. 4) All that is dear to me and everyone I love are of the nature to change. There is no way to escape being separated from them. 5) My actions are my only true belongings. I cannot escape the consequences of my actions. My actions are the ground on which I stand."

But in terms of the ultimate truth, there is no birth and no death; why would the Buddha want us to recite something that reminds us of the pain and suffering of the relative world? What comfort could any of that be to someone who has lost a loved one or who faces a terminal illness? Williams explains that acceptance of the relative world is crucial – without practice in the relative world, awakening cannot occur. When I was a little girl on the farm, I would help my aunt with her two milk cows. I loved going out early in the morning with her, the barn cats circling our feet, clanking the pails as we walked silently to the barn. We would take care of the cows and get them ready to be milked. We would milk the cows, the fresh warm smell of the grass fed milk was wonderful, and I loved the antics of the cats as they tried to get a lap or two of the milk (they liked me because I spilled more than my aunt). We would carry the milk back and I would help with pouring it into containers, then later separating the cream, making fresh butter, and the best was drinking the icy cold milk with the morning cinnamon rolls. When my cousins and I would lie in the grass watching the cows in the field, munching the grass, I remember thinking about that they were making that glass of milk I would enjoy the next morning. When Thich Nhat Hanh talks about seeing a cow on a hillside and realizing that the cow was making his morning yogurt which would enable him to give the daily Dharma talk and saying to his attendant that the cow will give today's Dharma talk, I was transported back to my youth and the simple way that the inter-being-ness of all things made perfect sense. So rather than transcending our suffering, we can transform it into the ultimate dimension of truth, beauty, and peace.

The Madhyamika teachings are the foundation of the Middle Way as a school of thought. Williams explains that Chandrakirti was a scholar who wrote commentaries including the *Madhyamikavatara* becoming the basis for study of the Madhyamika in Tibetan monastic universities. The Tibetan extensive analysis of the Self forms a nexus for understanding emptiness, delving into the logical explanations of the constituents of the self and explaining the limitations of identifying the whole with the constituent parts. It is not that we do not exist, but that "we do not exist in the way we think we do, as intrinsically existent, independent, monads." Armstrong discusses the dilemma that Christians face as well when attempting to define their God as possessing the psycho-physical components attributed to Him yet denying that He is subject to birth and death; to deny these components would then take those characteristics from Him, leaving an unchanging and meaningless thing. Christian scholars refer to God having a kind of emptiness of being, yet also being the "ultimate point of reference."

Chandrakirti further elaborates many forms of logical analysis to illustrate that one can search for ultimate truth through reasoning, only to find that nothing resists analysis, showing that in looking for the way things really are through reasoning, we find that nothing is really the way things are and this lack is the ultimate truth. He further shows that there is no such thing as something with an intrinsic nature on any level, even an everyday level, despite how hard it is to see things that way from a conventional point of view; that ultimate truth is not just a way of looking at things, but really true as well.

Yogacara

The *Three Turnings of the Wheel of Dharma* is an historical framework of the Yogacara tradition made to categorize the teachings in order of their understanding. Each of these turns of the wheel is considered necessary, because the first two turns were considered wonderful but they needed explanation and interpretation to avoid pitfalls so was not the final teachings. The first turning is considered the Buddha's talk on the Four Noble Truths, the *Dhammacakkappavattana*, turning the wheel of Dharma or setting the wheel of Dharma in motion. The second turning was the teachings on emptiness (sunyata) from the Prajnaparamita literature which, despite the stories of the first people hearing it either walked out, died on the spot of heart attacks, or were transformed on the spot, or perhaps because of those stories, more explanation was needed. The third turning was the teaching on the Avatamsaka realms, the Tathagatagarbha or Buddha-nature doctrines, and the Three Natures teachings from the *Samdhinirmocana Sutra* of the Yogacara.

On the one hand, we could be cynical and say that this concept is rather self-promoting in a "new and improved" kind of way. After all, "why go to any other school, this one has the last word in understanding!" might be the advertising slogan. But, as time has moved forward, so have the efforts of the monastics and teachers to continue to tradition of analyzing the first teachings and adding not only new commentaries to them, but to compose new material to help clarify and expand on the understanding of the teachings. The Buddha taught that there were many Dharma doors, and while at first blush we might ask why we need anymore, each of these teachers has developed ways to enhance our understanding. They have shared their thoughts, but more importantly their direct experience of the Dharma, and this clarification was a sincere effort to bring greater understanding, knowledge, and insight into the world.

The Three Natures of the Samdhinirmocana Sutra is considered by the Yogacara to be the definitive doctrine which needs no further interpretation and is the last word on the nature of emptiness. The first Nature is the constructed nature, the realm of words where the nature of objects is considered separate from ourselves and having an inherent existence. This is the world that the majority of us live in where we see things and others as being separate from ourselves. The second Nature is the dependent nature (*paratantrasvabhava*) which takes the flow of input from our senses and perceptions and concludes falsely that they exist, forming the basis for our suffering and pain based on our conclusions of what we perceive rather than the reality of how things really are. The third and final Nature is the Suchness or Thusness (*tathata*), the perfected nature in which things are seen correctly and has at its base the complete absence of objects meaning that the perceiver realizes that the perceptions construct the enduring objects and that flow of perception can stop to see things as they really are; it is the cessation of false constructs.

These natures enhance the understanding of emptiness showing that this perfected nature is what must be known for awakening and showing that emptiness is not a literal absence but the absence of an intrinsic meaning and existence. At first read of this material, I was puzzled how I would add any comment to it other than reporting the facts to answer the question. However, as I read further, I find that it is a logical and easy way to think about the steps toward perceiving the world correctly. While we will get to some of the problems in Yogacara thought in the questions of "whose consciousness is it?" this construct is an understandable progression which mirrors, perhaps, the developmental phases that we go through as children.

"There is neither subject nor object but only a single flow. It is also emptiness, explained for this tradition as meaning that one thing is empty of another. That is, the flow of perceptions – the dependent nature – is empty of enduring entities (i.e. the conceptualized nature)." Since the flow of perceptions, when viewed from the third Nature shows that each object we perceive is empty of its component parts, this flow of perceptions sets the stage for the realization of the relative and ultimate realities. Our nature is that of the flow of perception but our choice is to learn about and ultimately experience directly, is to stop making conclusions based on our instincts, culture, society, emotions, etc. that are erroneous, and to start seeing things as they really are, empty of an inherent existence. We see with our first nature that things are in the world that affect us and we assume that these things are permanent. We learn that we cannot really trust our eyes. Just as the example used in a commentary on the *Mahayanasamgraha*, when we see a mirage of water in the distance on a hot day, it is hard to believe that it is an illusion until we get close enough to find the water has disappeared. This image of water is the dependent nature and the absence of water in the image is the perfected nature. Williams goes on to explain that without the flow of perceptions there would be nothing at all because the true nature of the absence of inherent existence could not be there without it. The problem does not lie in the nature of things, but in our perception of their solidity and permanence. When we can see the fluid nature of reality, we begin to penetrate the true nature of things and to transform our perceptions.

"Both the Madhyamikas and the Yogacarins saw themselves as preserving the Buddhist Middle Way between the extremes of nihilism (everything is unreal) and substantialism (substantial entities exist)." The Yogacarins posit that only the mind is ultimately real; that consciousness is the basis for our flow of perceptions of external objects. The Madhyamikas believed that everything including the mind is a conceptual construct and that the goal of any discussion on the subject is to refute through reasoning any position that posits any sort of real existence. Williams cites conclusions made by other scholars who point to statements from the Yogacara school like "Thus if there is no object for consciousness then there cannot be the corresponding consciousness." showing that the Yogacara is ontologically the same as the Madhyamika. Williams states that he is unconvinced of this; however, it seems to me that if the Yogacara were truly looking for an essential, primordial mind, that would be tantamount to believing in an Essential Self which would be a step backward to the Samkhya-Yoga the Buddha studied with Alara Kalama prior to his awakening.

It seems more likely that these two lean toward one side or the other in the duality of eternalism and annihilationism in order to create a framework for study and examination rather than an experiential goal. Interestingly, Descartes thought through a very similar logic problem and in his meditations decided to strip away all of his beliefs, disbelieving everything that can be called into question. He reaches a very different conclusion than our friends in either the Yogacara or Madhyamika. "I have convinced myself that there is nothing in the world -- no sky, no earth, no minds, no bodies. Doesn't it follow that I don't exist? No, surely I must exist if it's me who is convinced of something. But there is a deceiver, supremely powerful and cunning whose aim is to see that I am always deceived. But surely I exist, if I am deceived. Let him deceive me all he can, he will never make it the case that I am nothing while I think that I am something. Thus having fully weighed every consideration, I must finally conclude that the statement "I am, I exist" must be true whenever I state it or mentally consider it." When Descartes said "I think, therefore I am" he had stopped short in his analysis, concluding that because we are thinking we are really existing. Nhat Hanh concludes the opposite "I think, therefore I am not."

If I can speculate, the other thought I have on this lean slightly to the left or right from the inexpressible Middle is where the discussions of the mind fit in when considering rebirth. The Yogacarins and Madhyamikas were both steeped in a tradition of reincarnation, even though the Buddha taught the more subtle concept of rebirth. How they embraced rebirth may well be a nudge in either direction to help the yet to be awakened one to reconcile this belief. A personal reincarnation is still a staple of what a lot of lay Buddhists believe, and this is a belief steeped in culture and tradition. Thich Nhat Hanh teaches, in keeping with classic teachings, that the rebirth of Buddhism is that everything manifests itself because of conditions.

He has said (I have looked for but cannot find the article) that it is far more accurate to look deeply at the not-self characteristic to understand the dynamic nature of life rather than looking to personal rebirth. On a personal note, I have always been fascinated with this seeming personification or obsession with consciousness that we humans, not just Buddhists, have. When we talk about that consciousness cannot come from nothing, I agree, but I do not see why a future consciousness would need to come from a past consciousness. All of the actions and circumstances, though, of the past create the future, but without a healthy brain, a consciousness cannot flourish.

Why have spiritual scholars not spend the same care, attention, and logic to our digestive systems? The way our bodies process food into energy is every bit as complex and remarkable as our nervous systems, perhaps more so; looking at the mitochondria alone is a wonder. If nature were to prioritize what spark should pass from life to life it would have to be the ability to synthesize food into energy rather than the thinking of silly thoughts. In a fetus, it takes weeks for the first synapses to start firing, but each cell is already busy processing nutrition within its cells from the mother. Maybe we should say "I digest, therefore I am!" (Or my favorite "if a man says something in a forest and there is no woman around to hear it, is he still wrong?")

According to Williams, certain objections were recognized that would need to be addressed in considering the perception-only perspective. These three major issues are: 1) spatio-temporal determination would be impossible, 2) many people experience x and not just one person, as in the case of a hallucination, and 3) hallucinations can be determined because they do not have pragmatic results. In neurology, we learn that our brains are actually what are receiving perceptions from our senses and analyzing those nervous impulses to make conclusions about what that input means. When we look at spatio-temporal determination in light of whether all perceptions have an external basis or not, Vasubandhu looks to dreams for his argument. As in dreams, we also have other forms of dreaming when we have flights of fancy or creative ideas that we allow to take flight in our minds as part of the creative process.

These perceptions are our private playground, perhaps a bit like when we were kids, lying back in a hillside watching fluffy clouds float by pointing out that this one looks like a buffalo, that one like a giraffe, and that one like a teddy bear. Someone else looking up might barely notice the clouds at all. When we consider the unique experience of a hallucination compared to what others observe, we can also look at a number of other neurological conditions which alter the way one person experiences certain external stimuli from other people. The hallucination example might be a bit problematic since one could argue, at least in this day and age, that the hallucination is the result of a malfunction of the brain and should not be considered in a philosophical argument. Synesthesia, for example, is not a hallucination, but a variant of perception, where a person may see a certain letter as a color or sounds will be a symphony of color which others do not see. One could very well be inspired to create an art work based on their experience with synesthetic input.

Consciousness can be divided into eight types in the Yogacara viewpoint. The first five apply to the senses: eye, ear, nose, tongue, and body – the Sense Consciousnesses. The sixth consciousness – the Mind Consciousness is the consciousness of ideation or the mind that analyzes the input from the senses together with the 'tainted' mind which takes consciousness as real and considers it a true Self. The seventh, the *klistamanas - Manas*, which is the consciousness that gathers karmic formations. The eighth consciousness is the *alayavijana*, the Store Consciousness which is the ground or basis for the other seven. Our sensory doorways, the eye, ear, nose, tongue, and body each has a consciousness or function of consciousness associated with each one. The Mind Consciousness (*manovijnana*) arises when our mind connects with an object of perception and is the every-day sense of mind, processing what is going on, being delighted by our child, deciding on what to have for dinner, jumping to conclusions, and making us say things we wish we could take back. This level might be considered an analogue to the Freudian Ego, the part of our consciousness that has the capacity to be trained and make choices and be trained to discriminate between ignorance and the whole-some seeds that can be watered.

We must be cautious because the Mind Consciousness is based on and influenced by the Manas and can be erroneous. The seventh level, Manas, is the part of consciousness that gives rise to and supports mind consciousness. Manas arises from store consciousness, takes hold of a portion of store con-sciousness and believes that this portion is a separate entity or self; wrong perception of manas creates much of our suffering because of this. Nhat Hanh goes on to explain that the nature of manas is delusion, and false per-ceptions born of the blocks of ignorance that are seeds in our store con-sciousness, grasping at ideas and always discriminating, working at this fool's errand ceaselessly. Manas fill our heads with ignorance, fueled by all that we consume in the forms of the nutriments of edible food, sense impres-sion food, food of volition, and consciousness food. This creates a vicious cycle of suffering; taking in perceptions that we misinterpret as being sepa-rate, permanent, or discriminating then causing us to consume more of the very things that harm us under the guise of dispersion, regret for the past, or worry about the future.

The eighth level, substratum consciousness, alaya-vijnana, or store con-sciousness has three functions: 1) to store and preserve the bija, seeds, of our experiences, 2) the bija themselves, and 3) function as a store for the attach-ment to a self because of the relationship between the manas, the seventh consciousness, and the store consciousness. The primary function of the store consciousness is to maintain all the seeds, keeping them viable so they can manifest. Nhat Hanh explains that there are both wholesome and un-wholesome seeds in the field of our consciousness and that when these seeds are watered; the result will be a manifestation of that seed. It is our choice which seeds will be watered, but this only comes as a result of practice since it is not enough to simply will our bad behaviors away by the force of our will, logic, or education, but rather, by having deep insight of the store con-sciousness. Prattis contends that the key to the spiritual path is the awareness of the nutriments we consume and that only by being mindful of our con-sumption on all levels can we create the fertile soil of wholesomeness so our store consciousness can flourish.

Basically, we can say that the mind creates the world only in the sense that we assign meaning to our observations or flow of perceptions, discriminating what is good or bad, what we like or dislike what we would kill or die for. In the Avatamsaka Sutra teaches that all things inter-are with all other things, that all principles enter one principle, one principle enters all principles so that inter-being-ness is emptiness. It is only in touching deeply inter-being-ness that we can our true nature. Or told through legend: "The wind was making the temple flag flutter. There were two monks arguing. One said that the flag was moving. One said that the wind was moving. They argued back and forth without reaching the truth. The Sixth Patriarch said to them, 'It is not the wind moving, and it is not the flag moving. It is your minds that are moving.' The two monks were startled." All karma created in the past and present life as well as the action and experiences of life is stored in the alaya vijnana. Karma means actions of body, speech, and mind. Every action and thought is of one of three natures, wholesome, unwholesome, and indeterminate. Store consciousness is unobstructed and indeterminate because it is neither wholesome or unwholesome though it contains all the seeds, both wholesome and unwholesome. Store consciousness never stops, yet is not permanent. Nhat Hanh (2001) explains that store consciousness is like a river, always the same river, but the water (the seeds) is continuously flowing and changing. The seeds are the basis of karma because they are capable of being manifested, creating the formations. In the *Mulamadhyamakakarika* we learn that "Seeds can produce seeds, seeds can produce formations. Formations can produce seeds, formations can produce formations."

When we have our seed of anger watered, it can manifest into the energy of anger in our mind consciousness as a formation. After manifesting for some time in our consciousness, it will return to the root having become a little stronger. Each time that seed is watered, it will be quicker to manifest causing us and the people around us much pain and suffering. It is with deep looking that we can touch the seed of anger and transform it. Awakening is said to extinguish karma, stopping the cycle of rebirth, therefore it follows that that alaya vijnana would cease upon awakening since its ground is karma. Implications of this are complicated as we consider the experience of being a Buddha: does a Buddha perceive *blue* with non-conceptual awareness free of duality, or is there a pure flow of content-less consciousness unstained by the image of objects? Williams goes on to consider that a Buddha might either enjoy the five types of direct jhana or may only be aware of his or her own nature, with the lifetimes old practice of compassion springing spontaneously helping without needing to be aware of the object of that compassion. Or perhaps, the awakened mind interleaves these two positions in the inexpressible middle, the razor's edge of awareness.

Buddha Nature

The Tathagatagarbha or Buddha-Nature doctrine is commonly held to state that all beings contain the potential to become a Buddha. Williams explains that the Lankavatara Sutra is the most influential of the literature that posits the Tathagatagarbha as the Buddha-nature within the alaya-vijnana, substratum consciousness. The term Tathagatagarbha is open to a number of nuances when translating the components of the word to understand its meaning. Zimmerman contends that the oldest and most natural meaning would be *containing a Tathagata*, containing a Buddha. The imagery of all sentient beings being compared to lotuses containing a fully formed Buddha homunculus sitting cross-legged in their center would then not be a metaphor, but a reality. The word garbha in Sanskrit also means womb/matrix, seed/embryo, or innermost part; the expression can also refer to all sentient beings having the innermost core of a Tathagata. Further, the Tathagatagarbha Sutra contains nine illustrations of how the Tathagata is hidden within sentient beings, proclaiming the true nature of the inner purity of all beings, encouraging them to have faith in the practice because of the ultimate truth of the Buddha within.

Perhaps the most important distinction in these two ways of defining *garbha*, either as containing a Tathagata or the seed of the Tathagata within, would be to look at the definition of containing a Tathagata as a separate thing other than the being containing it. To think of the Buddha of the lotus within as a metaphor, or potential, is to have confidence that with practice, honesty, and insight we can transform our suffering and experience liberation. To think of the Buddha within as a reality would be to expect a revelation from this divine being who could give us this transcendent knowledge. The *Lankavatara Sutra* states: "The Buddha said... now, Mahamati, what is perfect knowledge? It is realized when one castes aside the discriminating notions of form, name, reality, and character; it is the inner realization by noble wisdom. This perfect knowledge, Mahamati, is the essence of the Tathagatagarbha."

The oft quoted *Srimaladevisimhanada (Srimala) Sutra*, the Lion's Roar of Queen Srimala (great title!) we find: "This Dharmakaya of the Tathagata when not free from the *kleshas* (passions) is referred to as the Tathagatagarbha." The Dharmakaya or *Dharma/Truth Body* is none other than pure awareness itself. In the sutras we learn that the Tathagatagarbha cannot manifest itself because it is covered in defilements so when one awakens to the perfection of the Tathagata, the Tathagatagarbha is no more. The Srimala Sutra gives us the understanding that the Dharma body is empty of all defilement and the Tathagatagarbha is that pure *bindu* point contained within, hidden and un-manifest, yet rich with the potential of the Dharma. When the Buddha nature is manifested in full, the Tathagatagarbha is no more because there is no longer the potential, but the reality of the transformation of consciousness. This sutra also helps clarify the meaning of the word *garbha* in the Buddhist context as like a *seed* or *potential* as opposed to *containing*, since if we contained a Tathagata, that would not go away upon awakening nor could the Tathagatagarbha be subject to kleshas or rebirth nor be defiled in any way. This concept also dispels the notion that the Tathagatagarbha is a *true self* in the *soul/atman* sense, since when the Tathagata is manifested, it *goes away*. The iconography of the Dharmakaya is often represented by the sky, space, the mirror, and the Bodhisattva Samantabhadra who is portrayed as sky blue, unornamented, naked, and not possessing any divine attributes; beyond concept, form, ornament, or quality. The mirror is clear of defilements and reflects all that is without discrimination. "For now we see through a glass, darkly, but then face to face: now I know in part; but then shall I know even as also I am known." Corinthians 13:12 echoes this theme of not being able to penetrate this true nature, but having the confident faith that the true face is there despite its being concealed from us.

One of the constants of Buddhist thought is that Buddha-Nature is not a soul, self, or atman. Harder to explain is why this is true. Perhaps the simplest answer is to ask the question "who is it that is liberated?" But what does that mean? Going back in history might help. We can look at the mythology of the Buddha's life, using the term mythology not because the events are or are not true, but because they are so rich in symbolism where we see events of Gautama's life mirror or foreshadow what was to come. When Gautama studied with the great yogi Alara Kalama whose practice of Samkhya allowed him to achieve high levels of jhana (meditative experience or gnosis) and he claimed to achieve a plane of *nothingness*. The Buddha was able to recognize the truth of this experience: that this was not an ultimate experience of the Self; he had created this experience himself.

This state did not transform his life, it was temporary – impermanent. The Buddha realized that this version of "nothingness" was still not the Ultimate Dimension – Nirvana that he sought. He would realize later the perfect understanding of emptiness, sunyata, and find the uncreated perfection that would lead to liberation. Gautama was certainly influenced by this philosophy and practice, particularly its emphasis that nothing can be created from or dissolve into nothingness, but that everything is transformed. Samkhya held, though, that the highest liberation was moksha which is the realization of the soul (atman) with the highest Brahman, the source of all. Because Gautama saw this as limiting, we are pointed in the direction of what would become his ultimate liberation, but learn that in the Nirvana Sutra that only the eye of the Buddha can discern the Buddha-Nature fully and clearly. We can turn to the Lankavatara Sutra to learn more. When the Buddha is asked if Buddha-Nature is the same as the Self taught by other teachers and philosophers, he replies no, this teaching of the Tathagatagarbha is to "make the ignorant cast aside their fear when they listen to the teachings of egolessness and to have them realize the state of non-discrimination and imagelessness." This middle way of neither having a soul (eternalism); nor ceasing to be after we die (annihilism) is an inexpressible concept. We have seen the Yogacarins and Madhyamikas each take their position to either side of the middle in an attempt to point to that middle in a way that can be expressed and in a way that can, hopefully, help people find that which can only be experienced.

It might be a bit like looking at the optical illusion picture that can be seen as either the old woman or young lady, we shift our perception one way to see one and shift a bit the other way to see the other figure. We cannot see both as the same time, yet both are very much present in the same picture.

The difference between the Tathagatagarbha and Dharmakaya is that the

Tathagatagarbha is *like* a bija seed within the alaya-vijnana and the Dharma-kaya has the perfection of purity, self, pleasure, and permanence. Like a bija, but not quite that, since we cannot really say that the Tathagatagarbha dwells within us as though it is something separate from us or that we *own*. Nagarjuna wrote that Buddha Nature: "it's not physical, emotional, conceptual, impulsive, conscious – or anything else. It does not dwell in us, nor we in it. It does not own us." Yet, the Tathagatagarbha is also synonymous with the Dharmakaya. How can both be true? Williams explains that in the Yogacara tradition, the Tathagatagarbha is seen as the thing that makes us realize that we suffer, and so is the basis for aspiration toward Buddhahood. The Tathagatagarbha is seen to be reborn and to suffer, but because the Tathagatagarbha is hidden under our misperceptions, this idea of defilement is an error of perception. The Srimala Sutra helps us understand that the Tathagatagarbha is void of all defilement stores, but not void of the Buddha Dharmas. We also need to go back to the Avatamsaka Sutra to understand the alaya-vijnana to help us see the distinction between the two. When we water the wholesome seeds within us, those seeds grow stronger allowing us to look more deeply at the unwholesome seeds as they are watered by events in everyday life. When we look deeply, we can transform those negative feelings, inviting the unwholesome seeds not to grow. This practice helps us to bring delusion to an end. In the Fifty Verses on the Nature of Consciousness we read: "When delusion is overcome, understanding is there, and store consciousness is no longer subject to afflictions. Store consciousness becomes Great Mirror Wisdom, reflecting the cosmos in all directions. Its name is now Pure Consciousness."

On a personal note, because I spent many years as a neonatal intensive care nurse and am a mother, I have always liked the translation of Tathagatagarbha as embryo and as womb. Having worked with many women who have had premature babies and having had a premature baby myself, there is a special understanding of the delicate and profound nature of that embryo within. This so small thing, when we look deeply, contains what is nearly infinitely larger – the ancestral chain and the generations to come. There is such a feeling of deep and quiet waiting when a woman is pregnant. Far from the disdain of some writers when thinking of Briar Rose who is sleeping, waiting for her prince to come, we can instead touch an understanding of what it is to allow that seed to germinate. Looking deeply with the Buddha's eyes to see that seed which contains the whole.

When my mother first held my son, who had gained weight to be almost five pounds, she looked up and told me that she had thought we girls were wonderful when she first held us, but that was nothing compared to holding this little boy. Our own children are our personal connection, our grandchildren a connection and appreciation of the past generations and a connection to a future we will only see part of. The thread of continuity of life is clearly and tangibly being held in our arms. In those quiet moments, holding our baby, those bright eyes looking up at us perhaps asking "are you my mother?" we cannot help but ask "who are you, little one?" and realize that we are touching our own mother's hand when we stroke these precious little fingers.

The Rangtong (Rang sTong) and Shentong (sZhan sTong) are traditions within Tibetan Buddhism which have interpreted the Tathagatagarbha teachings differently. The Rangton traditions is represented by the dGe lugs pa school (the Yellow Hats) founded in the late fourteenth century and the lineage of His Holiness the Dalai Lama, while the Shentong, or *other empty,* tradition is associated with the Jo nag tradition. Characteristics of the Rangton tradition include: 1) draws on the Lankavatara Sutra, 2) understands the concept in the Madhyamika sense of emptiness, 3) the term Rang sTong means *self-empty* meaning that both Dharmakaya and emptiness itself are empty of intrinsic existence, and 4) looks at these teachings as having a specific purpose to help introduce Buddhism to non-Buddhists by teaching from their paradigm of belief in a Self. The Shentong tradition contains the following characteristics: 1) the teachings are taken literally, 2) they believe there is an absolute reality that intrinsically and inherently exists, 3) refers to its doctrines as the Great Madhyamika and the real teachings of Maitreya and Asanga, and Nagarjuna and Aryadeva, 4) believes that when one goes beyond reasoning and concepts, a real, intrinsically existing Absolute is understood.

The Rangtong teachings consider that the Tathagatagarbha is within all sentient beings and is why we are able to become awakened and it is emptiness that enables us to change; since change is a result of dependent origination and emptiness is the ground of dependent origination, it follows that the Tathagatagarbha is empty in the Madhyamika sense. The Shentong tradition considers that the Tathagatagarbha consciousness is obscured in the unawakened, but is identical to the Dharmakaya or *Essence Body* of the awakened mind. While these two traditions are new to me, I would have to say that my experience with Buddhism has been steeped in the teachings most closely related to the Rangtong. The reason why I would say that these Rangtong teachings seem most accurate to me is to go back to the two truths of the relative truth (*samvriti satya*) and absolute truth (*paramartha satya*) and look at how these two concepts work together. We have our own Crouching Tiger, Hidden Dragon story where we enter the path of Buddhism from a relative standpoint and we learn to notice our suffering and joy, learning more about how to see each of those states of being as subjective and temporary, yet they are an echo of what we understand when we transform our perceptions. The Buddha taught an Eightfold Path and Avalokiteshvara told us that there is no path; these two ideas seem to be in opposition to each other, but they are teaching the same thing from two different points of view.

Thich Nhat Hahn explains that "we do not have to transcend the 'world of dust' (saha) in order to go to some dust-free world called nirvana. Suffering and nirvana are of the same substance. If we throw away the world of dust, we will have no nirvana." We always have to look deeply into the inter-being-ness of all things, including the Two Truths, to see that they are not two separate things at all, but each contains the other fully. Transcending our lives toward an absolute reality is something much of humanity longs for, but, for me, Buddhism is not about transcending this life for a perfect heaven nor is it about self-improvement of exchanging bad habits for good ones (although that aspect of it has certainly been helpful to me and appreciated by the people around me), but about transforming how we perceive. The Diamond Sutra also shows us (kind of like a math problem) that a flower is not a flower; that is why we can say it is a flower. With these two concepts of the relative and absolute truths, if we make one literal, we break the equation and it leaves us adrift. If we see them as a tool, we can use the two points of view to penetrate that inexpressible middle way.

Madhyamika

I really do like all of the intellectual back and forth that characterizes Madh-yamika; there is a lot of meat on the bone to chew on here. We are challenged to think logically and really analyze what we believe and why we believe it. For me, it seems that far too many people who are religious take that religion on blind faith depending on their preacher or a televangelist to tell them what to believe. But we all do this – after all, the quintessential Zen question is "who are you?" We assume that we know or are searching to "find ourselves" like we did in the 60's and 70's looking for personal liberation or through to today looking for self-actualization through pop psychology and spirituality. If I explore the "who am I?" question, I open the rest of the universe up for that same examination. Kind of like redecorating, you start with the home office, then see how shabby the family room looks and pretty soon every weekend is filled with trips to the home improvement store toting supplies and color swatches.

When we are finished looking at all the philosophy and logic, or maybe before we even begin, we are within our rights to ask how this all will help; how can I apply this to my life? Will starting all this really be worth the inevitable trips to the store whether I start with the nature of the reality around me or my own true nature, working my way in or out? Brunnhölzl addresses this question in a logical way. We generally do not go looking for a solution unless we think we have a problem. The bigger the problem, the more strenuously we look and the further we are willing to go to solve it. On the other hand, the Buddha is telling us that we have a problem but we are pretty sure we do not. Unless we are really neurotic, we are pretty sure we know who we are, we might just want to fine tune our lives to be happier or more successful.

What the Centrists have at their disposal, according to Brunnhölzl is a well stocked medical cabinet with arguments and treatments to show us that we really do not know all we think we do, and to counter each of the diver-sions our minds come up with to protect our favored subjective view of re-ality. My personal favorite is how things *should* be. The biggest benefit of how things should be is that I get to paint a picture of the world, or my com-munity (or an industry like healthcare), or my workplace, or my home in the color palate that I like best. And after all, I am a very good judge about how things should be; I want the best for people, I want a clean environment, compassionate and competent care for patients, and a warm, nurturing home. What could possibly be wrong with that?

Calvin explains it very well to Hobbs when he says that he is completely serene knowing that it is his purpose in life is so that everyone will do what he wants. Hobbs rolls his eyes and says that it's nice to have that cleared up and Calvin goes on to explain that when everyone else accepts that, they will be serene, too. It's all so black and white; the absence of what I find to be unjust or unfair and the abundance of what I like and find good. However, there is a little problem – in the back of my mind, I know that this is not all there is to it, and a little Jiminy Cricket starts chirping that I am not being completely honest with myself.

Brunnhölzl explains that in Madhyamika, we are not to replace our so-lidified ideas about the world with more sophisticated ones about the two realities, but to see them as inextricable from each other; ultimate reality not being some idealistic mode of being opposed to relative reality as how things seem to be. Centrists use the tools at their disposal, speaking of each aspect of reality in order to offer a crutch or medicine to we who stubbornly cling to our views. Shantideva gives us a number of verses on preparing our minds for this study.

> "Wandering where it will, the elephant of mind,
> will bring us down to pains of deepest hell.
> No worldly beast, however wild,
> could bring upon us such calamities."

In trying to redecorate the world to my liking, the wild elephant of mind wreaks havoc on my peace of mind and equanimity, tramping around making up scenarios at three in the morning of what the meeting might bring or what calamities might befall. Worse yet are the times I have tried to use meditation, not to tame the wild elephant, but to fix it, too. The modern purveyors of mindfulness-based therapies do claim that I can fix my problems and meet my goals if I use mindfulness to become a better person. So instead of really looking deeply at a habit energy, I have found myself trying to pull out all of the bad seeds, hoping that only the good seeds would remain.

Our friends the Centrists are there to point out that ultimate reality is just a solution to the problem of relative reality, not meant "to substitute one thing for another, such as samsara with nirvana." Illness is not replaced with health, "rather, it is just the removal of the causes of illness that makes its symptoms disappear, and this absence of symptoms is what is called health."

It is important to remember that the object here is not to replace the self with Emptiness, either. "So consciousness can only ever be momentary, and such a momentary phenomenon would never qualify for the title of 'self.' Thus, the mind or awareness that seems to behind all our experience cannot be the self either." Rather than using the four foundations of mindfulness to redecorate my mind, the Madhyamika teachings are helping me to stop trying to replace the bad with the good; "Then the mind (when focused inwardly on the absence of self in the skandhas) can rest peacefully in empty space. Through meditation in this manner all subtle doubts are worn away and the mind can rest naturally in emptiness." Maybe I have become attached to emptiness as a concept and been as Nagarjuna says, hopelessly incurable. Just that simple statement "absence of the self in the skandhas" shifted me away from *Emptiness* toward *empty of.*

During my treatment for cancer, I had quite a few people tell me that they were amazed at how well I did, that I had a great attitude and all that; but the bottom line is that I was able, albeit imperfectly, to take each step at a time; to avoid clinging. I would go deeply into my feelings at each step, resting in the reality of how I felt. Each new morning was fresh; walking meditation was lovely seeing the clear blue sky, green grass, breathing with the pain and leaning into it – all of it was a meditation on impermanence. Now, shaking up my way of looking at emptiness will be an important process to work with.

With the Madhyamika teachings, there is nowhere to hide, no argument I can win, no one last project to finish first; time to surrender. Well, maybe after the guest room has been painted...

Avatamsaka Sutra

The *Avatamsaka Sutra* is a vast work that spans a number of works written independently and at different time frames. Also known as the Flower Ornament or Flower Garland Sutra, it is longer than the Bible and is composed of a number of topics which cover simple *gathas* for daily life, the progression on the Bodhisattva path, the interdependency of all phenomena, and a number of stories which paint vivid pictures of other realms and the mythic scope of individuals who journey there and their encounters with Maha-Bodhisattvas like Maitreya, Manjushri, Samantabhadra, and the Vairocana Buddha. While scholars might portray the Madhyamika and Yogacara as rival schools of thought, the Avatamsaka resolves any such conflict of seeing either annihilation or eternalism in the Dharma. In the Avatamsaka sutra, we are introduced to beautiful images that help us see the inter-being-ness of all things, exhorting us to touch each thing we see deeply to see the whole of the universe. We learn that the world is the collective manifestation of our minds; that the Samsara world of the deluded mind is filled with violence, mistrust, and hate but that in the world of the awakened mind, there is happiness, light, and space. In a beautiful analogy, Thich Nhat Hanh explains that the wave may believe that she is grand or beautiful, high or low, powerful or weak; all the while not realizing that she is made of water. In the world of relative truth, all of these qualities are there and make her feel superior or inferior, yet when the wave touches her true nature, all of those complexes will cease and she will transcend birth and death. We need the relative world but we also need to touch the absolute truth; relative and absolute truths inter-embrace; both have a value. The Buddha said that "this teaching is my true body" – the Dharmakaya, or Vairocana, the Buddha who has never stopped teaching. This is the universe as it really is:

> *"Clearly to know that all dharmas*
> *Are without any self-essence at all;*
> *To understand the nature of dharmas this way*
> *Is to see Vairocana."*

Williams goes on to explain that in this state that all things are perceived correctly, is the Buddha, is a penetrating awareness that is present in all beings and capable of helping others understand. In Vietnamese Buddhism, the Flower Ornament sutra is revered and often chanted in part during services.

One of the chants that is part of the liturgy after the incense offering and before chanting part of a sutra is this:

Nang le, so le tanh khong tich
Cam ung dao giao nan tu nghi
Nga thu dao trang nhu De chau
Thap Phuong chu Phat anh hien trung
Nga than anh hien chu Phat tien
Dau dien tiep tuc guy mang le.

This is translated:
"The one who bows and the one who is bowed to
Are both by nature, empty.
Therefore the communication between them
Is inexpressibly perfect.
Our practice center is the Net of Indra
Reflecting all Buddhas everywhere.
And my own person reflects in all the Buddhas
To whom with my whole life I go for refuge."

This world, the Dharmadatu, is one of infinite inter-penetration and inter-being-ness, and is seen, not from the perspective of trying to explain this world to us, but from the direct experience of the Buddha. This makes the themes of the Avatamsaka different from the philosophies of the Yogacara and Madhyamika. While the Yogacara attempted to explain the world in positive terms and the Madhyamika tried to refute all positions to illustrate emptiness, the Avatamsaka attempts to paint the picture of what it is like to see the two realms as they are and at the same time. Unlike us trying to puzzle an optical illusion, these stories show us that it is possible to look deeply into the nature of things and touch both the wave and the water. But lest we become dizzy contemplating the vision of the Buddha, those every-day gathas are there, too.

While Bathing:
Rinsing my body, my heart is cleansed.

The universe is perfumed with flowers.

Actions of body, speech, and mind are calmed.

In Fazang's *Treatise on the Golden Lion*, a work intended to help illustrate complex concepts like interpenetration in a simple, visual way, we are introduced to the *Li-Shi* model. *Li* stands for *principle* or *noumenon* (from the Greek, meaning something that is known without using the senses) and *Shi* for *phenomenon*, and Li-Shi for Buddha-nature. Fazang took for his example Empress Wu's gold lion statue to help illustrate the Huayan concepts that she was struggling to understand. To illustrate with a Chinese this-worldly outlook, Fazang was showing that the Li element, that earlier Chinese thinkers associated with the Tao, being an absolute, complete, and transcendent entity, was that the phenomenon is not an emanation from the absolute noumenon.

He used the example of the gold lion, showing that the gold stands for Li and the shape of the lion for Shi; the lion, therefore, *is* gold and there is no gold without the form that it takes on. Williams goes on to explain that this appealed to the Chinese appreciation of the harmony with nature as a quality of enlightenment since the Li, in this case gold, does not impede the shape being imposed upon it. Much as our illustration of the wave and the water above, this is an attempt to show the interpenetration of the Li and Shi with each other. Similar to the Madhyamika, phenomena lacks intrinsic existence and can only be spoken of in terms of the chain of causal relationships, and in these causal interrelationships, we see that taking any one element out of the equation, the other elements cease to exist; each entity must contain all of the others and inter-being-ness with each other.

Fazang held that sudden awakening is a necessary teaching because Suchness or Thusness is beyond the stages of practice because it is the noumenon and ground of all phenomena. In one sense the Bodhisattva must see him or herself as a Buddha already and behave accordingly. In another, the Buddha-nature is already present within the first and all stages on the Bodhisattva path. Since enlightenment is a perfected state, it cannot be said that practice affects or causes it, since it is the ground in which all cause and effects occur. In this view, it should not be implied that any practitioner sits and waits for enlightenment to occur, but that practice serves to bring out what is already there. Practice certainly opens our minds to other ways of thinking about life and gives us tools to learn to look deeply at the world. The idea that awakening has a timetable is probably not a real philosophical concept, despite the images of lifetimes and eons of practice it takes to reach full Buddhahood, likewise the idea that one can awaken in an instant is also likely to be a literary tool.

The Buddha warned his disciples that it could take at least seven years to awaken "Just as the ocean slopes gradually, falls away gradually, and shelves gradually with no sudden incline, so in this method, training, discipline and practice take effect by slow degree, with no sudden perception of the ultimate truth." And yet, in the story of the Buddha's life, we learn that he entered the first jhana spontaneously under the rose apple tree as a child. It has been said that the length of the spiritual journey is only about an inch long; the length of opening one's eyes. Yet, how long does that take? In logical thinking, we can certainly create a formula for the noumenon and phenomenal world and come up with all the potential permutations, but I think that we would have to take all of those as potentials and understand that the teachings are not about making us awake but about helping us realize that we are awake. Or, the way a former Zen teacher of mine would put it: "Why are you choosing not to wake up?"

Ekayana or One Vehicle is a concept from the Lotus Sutra explaining that the doctrines of the Three Vehicles was an example of the Buddha's Upaya or skill-in-means to help people on their path, but that ultimately there is only One Vehicle in the progress to perfect Buddhahood. The Ekayana teaches that the three Ways (*triyāna*)--the Śrāvakayāna, the Pratyekabuddhayāna, and the Bodhisattvayana all converge into one Buddhayana or Buddha body. So while the turnings of the wheel of Dharma showed a progression of understanding and evolution toward Buddhahood, the Lotus sutra is considered to be not merely a part or preliminary stage, but the final and complete teaching, therefore Ekayana. Other sutras point to this idea of Ekayana as well, since the philosophical provisions for any of the one-mind, the Tathagatagarbha concept, the Avatamsaka sutra, the Lankavatara Sutra, and Srimala sutras can be considered Ekayana sutras. These sutras could be said to be a synthesis of earlier work that strove to put these complex and deep topics into terms more likely to be understood by the people of that time. In the Lankavatara Sutra we read: "But in the Perfect Oneness of Noble Wisdom there is no gradation nor succession nor effort.

The tenth stage is the first, the first is the eighth, the eighth is the fifth, the fifth the seventh: what gradation can there be where perfect Imagelessness and Oneness prevail? And what is the reality of Noble Wisdom? It is the ineffable potency of the Dharmakaya; it has no bounds nor limits; it surpasses all the Buddha-lands, and pervades the Akanistha and the heavenly mansions of the Tushita." We have a vision of the ease by which the Buddha's mind can move through understanding and the absolute and relative realms, the singularity by which the awakened mind can perceive past the duality that we struggle to understand.

It might be like trying to explain what three dimensions are to a two dimensional being. I could draw a Necker cube for my new, flat friend, but he would still be baffled since he could find two valid interpretations but would not yet understand the whole. All is not lost, though (at least that is my hope!) and we are encouraged by the Buddha and many wonderful teachers that we can look deeply and transform our misperceptions and see clearly to transform our suffering.

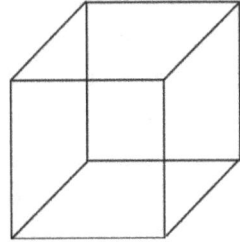

Upaya is a term that means skillful means, or skill-in-means, and is considered a key doctrine of the Lotus Sutra. In a famous analogy, the Buddha said that the teachings are like a raft to take us to the other shore, but would a wise man put the raft on his shoulder and take it along, or would he leave the raft behind after it served its purpose? The teaching transcends itself. The Buddha and many of the great teachers and sages have employed skillful means to help others see the truth, sometimes in paradoxical ways and this may be one of the most common complaints that new students and casual readers of Buddhism have – the "what the heck are they saying? First this idea is right, now it's wrong??" syndrome. The *Upayakausalya Sutra* is one devoted to questions and answers concerning events in the Buddha's life, relating them to his level of compassion and illustrating his deft use of skillful means to help. Buddhism can be held to be a pragmatic philosophy since the reliance on dogmatic or ideological views will limit the practitioner and prevent her or him from realizing anything further from that belief. Conze puts it very well: " 'Skill in means' is the ability to bring out the spiritual potentialities of different people by statements or actions which are adjusted to their needs and adapted to their capacity for comprehension." Each approach to teaching the Dharma has its own area of emphasis and those who advocate that method direct all their expedient teachings toward that method. In the analogy of the 84,000 Dharma Doors, we see that there are many methods that can be employed to help sentient beings become liberated. It is a testimony to the concept of Upaya that seemingly diverse practice methods like Pure Land compared to Zen can lead to the same goal. Part of the genius of the Buddha and the great teachers is the recognition that people have different learning styles and needs.

The Buddha put it as: "...the same water drunk by the cow and the cobra turns in one case to nourishing milk and in the other to deadly poison, and that medicine is to be given according to the disease. This is called the doctrine of skillful means..." Not all expedient means are positive in nature. Sometimes, at first, the event, words, or actions may seem unpleasant, frustrating, or upsetting. However, it may be that the seemingly adverse event may be what the person needs to jolt them out of complacency or bring about a temporary confusion that helps the person look at the events in a new way. In my job, I am called upon to teach a variety of topics, and one of the things I try to do is work in a variety of ways to bring the material to our staff knowing that they have a variety of learning needs. I happen to be a rather solitary, hands on learner. While it is great to hear a lecture, watch someone do a new skill, discuss the ideas, and other ways to convey new information; the bottom line is that I have to roll up my sleeves and do it myself to really get it. Maybe it comes from working on the farm and ploughing the fields – I like to get a handful of dirt, smell the soil, and feel the sunshine. Meditation is my version of being hands on; tending my inner garden.

Buddha Kaya

The Buddha Kayas, or bodies of the Buddha, are part of what is known as the *Trikaya*, a sort of Buddhist trinity. Made up of the Dharmakaya, truth body; the *Sambhogakaya*, the body of enjoyment; and the *Nirmanakaya*, the transformation bodies; these form *Svabhavikakaya*, the intrinsic body. In describing the bodies of the Buddha, Williams puts together a crazy quilt of definitions based on his model of physical, spiritual, and magical from the history of Buddhist writers and schools. The challenge is to put into perspective the aspects of the use of the term *kaya*, which means *body* in Pali and Sanskrit, yet because of its inherent ambiguity, the term lends itself to a range of uses in Buddhist thought. Kaya can refer to the actual body of the Buddha, and the literature is filled with glowing descriptions of his physical appearance and attributes; but also to groups of elements that pertain to the Buddha, including the qualities of awakening. In working through the thicket of definitions for Dharmakaya, Williams discusses the Dharmakaya as the Buddhas enlightenment or factors of that enlightenment, thus being the flow of Buddha qualities; the body of the Buddha's doctrine and teachings as the true body that remains after the death of the physical body to lead and teach us; and the body or collections of the ultimate truth (sunyata) or the understanding of ultimate truth (prajna).

The Sambhogakaya is the body of Communal Enjoyment and is a physical body (rupakaya) that actually appears, though not necessarily of matter. This is the body of the Buddha that sits in the Pure Land giving dharma talks to the Bodhisattvas who reside there. The enjoyment body is an impermanent body and can be considered the glorified body of the Buddha adorned with the many marks identifying him as such. Williams goes on to explain that it is this supra-mundane Buddha that is the object of devotion; a transcendent being animated by compassion, who appears in the enjoyment body for the benefit and experience of the Bodhisattvas and others. Historically, Williams seems to chalk this body up as the contrivance of Mahayana scholars to respond to the critiques of textual authenticity, but that it took centuries to develop this slant on the doctrine.

Williams states that little needs to be said of the Nirmanakaya, the Buddha's Transformation Bodies; that the actual body of the Buddha is merely a manifestation out of compassion from the Enjoyment Body. The Transformation Body can manifest in any way needed to help a being and provide a teaching. In the Tibetan dGe lugs model, the transformation bodies can appear in a variety of ways and perform deeds, including stories of artisans and craftsmen to illustrate aspects of the teachings. These manifestations might even be an animal or inanimate object that saves the day.

However, when we look at these three aspects in a different light, we see that far from being a hodge-podge of disparate thoughts, there is a cohesion that illuminates the way we see the world and ourselves. When we look at the Dharmakaya as the pure, unobstructed, and open awareness of the mind itself, we are seeing the perfection of emptiness. When we look at Sambhogakaya as thoughts arising within that awareness, we see the energy that the Buddha used to create the sutras and teachings, changing to fit the needs of the circumstances in the flow of existence. When we see the Nirmanakaya as the physical body, we see someone we can relate to, and can look with Buddha eyes at all the of the people we meet in a new way; after all, if the Buddha can transform into anything we need at the time to help us, is not everyone we meet the Buddha and every interaction, no matter how wonderful or horrible, a gift and a teaching?

Ray explains this type of framework as a way that we can see our own karmic proclivities, that is, that we tend to focus on one or another of these three kayas, wanting to create either a solid ground for ourselves, the drama of constant turmoil and change, or the desire to rise above it all into emptiness reluctant to connect to the other aspects of being. In an attempt to create an ego-identity out of any of these three without understanding and penetrating the inter-being-ness of all three, we find ourselves seeking permanence and security; only discover that we find that we cannot cling to an off balanced way of relating to our lives and ultimate nature.

So how do we reconcile these bodies which seem so different from each other? When we look at Svabhavikakaya, the Wisdom Body, as the union of all three, we see that these three cannot be separated from each other. Going back to taking refuge in the Buddha, the Dharma, and the Sangha, those three are interwoven with each other, interdependent, and one cannot exist without the others. The Trikaya is like that too, and as we learn in the Prajnaparamita literature, that without form there can be no emptiness and without emptiness, there can be no form. In form, we have a desire to help others out of our compassion, yet when we can rest in the ground of emptiness, we find that the compassion arising within that awareness brings appropriate actions when we do reach out to help.

We learned in the Avatamsaka Sutra that the Pure Land is a land filled with jewels, beautiful blossoms, and wonderful birds singing the Dharma. Williams makes the statement "There is no need for a Buddha to ponder the best way to help sentient beings." and we can realize that in a field of jewels and beautiful flowers, what could I possibly give to someone that they cannot simply reach down and pick up for themselves? By understanding the Trikaya, Ray explains that we can actually see this framework as our most intimate experience and the basis for our human existence. Helping us see that we can be in the world, but not of the world, and the very best gift we can give to others is to practice so that the fruits of our practice can allow us to be beautifully present for the other, to listen deeply to their suffering, and to let them know that we are here and we know they are here. Dwelling deeply in emptiness is to see the beauty of what is currently manifesting and moving peacefully and flexibly in the flow of life.

Bhumi

Kamalasila and Atisa came from India to Tibet to bring Buddhism and wrote intricate works developing in great detail the path of the Bodhisattva. The Bodhisattva path of the Lamrim teachings always starts with compassion as the root cause of all the Buddha qualities. The motivation of the practitioner in terms of his or her compassion or bodhichitta can be divided into three motivations. These motivations are: 1) people of modest aspiration who practice for the purpose of having a better rebirth or birth into some sort of heaven, 2) people of medium aspiration who wish to pursue enlightenment as an Arhat and eschew the pleasures of existence and lead moral lives, and 3) people of high or superior aspiration who have the desire to bring an end to all suffering for all beings. When bodhichitta has been awakened in an individual, we can also look at the qualities of bodhichitta as loving kindness (*maître* or *metta*), compassion (*karuna*), joy (*mudita*), and equanimity (*upekkha*). The cultivation of these is considered by Santideva, the author of the Bodhisattvacharyavatara, the guide to the bodhisattva's way of life, to be the most important thing we can do and a series of deep meditations can cultivate each aspect of bodhichitta. Williams explains that Santideva teaches that our bodhichitta transforms us, making us a son or daughter of the Buddha. When the practitioner practices meditations derived from Kamalasila and Atisa's work, bodhichitta will eventually arise. The first meditation is called the six causes and one effect which progressively lead us to the one effect of bodhichitta. These six causes are: 1) recognizing all beings as our mother, 2) being mindful of the kindness of our mother, 3) repaying these great kindnesses, 4) having a warm hearted love for these beings, 5) developing great compassion, and 6) taking on the commitment to help all sentient beings creating a firm intention.

The Bodhisattva stages are known as *bhumi*, as found in the *Dasabhumika Sutra*, the Sutra on the Ten Stages, which outlines the ten stages the practitioner passes through, progressively gaining greater wisdom and understanding. These stages are: 1) the Joyous stage where one develops generosity (dana), 2) the Stainless stage where one perfects virtue (Sila), 3) the Luminous stage where loving kindness and patience (Ksanti) is develops, 4) the Radiant stage perfects our vigor (Virya) due to increasing aspiration and compassion, 5) the Difficult to Cultivate stage focuses on the mastery of meditation (Dhyana), 6) the Manifest stage is the perfection of wisdom where the practitioner attains full insight into the conditioned arising, the not-self characteristic and emptiness, 7) the Gone Afar stage the practitioner becomes a Maha-sattva, Great Being, who has perfected skillful means, 8) the Immovable stage is the non-relapsing level and fully masters transference of merit granting grace, 9) the Good Intelligence stage is the perfection of power of insight to guide and teach others in the most precise ways, and 10) the Cloud of Doctrine stage is when the bodhisattva has the full perfection of knowledge (Jhana) and is ready to be consecrated as a full Buddha.

But why are these stages important? Atisa explains that we need to develop strong compassion and it is not enough to simply say that we wish to alleviate the suffering of others. By looking deeply into our own lives and using a gradually engage in the components of bodhichitta, we will be able to cultivate a true and fully realized bodhichitta. The framework of the three kinds of motivation or capacity helps us to see the intentions of our life and our mental state. We could also look at these stages as beginner, intermediate and advanced similar to the progressive of schooling we go through; we might also experience some of each of these capacities within ourselves at different times. By creating a systematic approach, Atisa gives us a map to explore our own feelings and experiences, then to relate with empathy to others, then to enter into the true meaning of the suffering of ourselves and others. By looking at the stages or scopes of motivation we can see how our motivations develop over time which also illuminates the basic concepts of

Buddhism; the fear of suffering, learning the reality of cause and effect and developing a defense against our afflictions by living a moral life, getting out of our own self interests and fears to be able to relate to the suffering of others and cultivating true compassion, and to dismantle all of our views so that we can bring about the full cessation of suffering for all sentient beings.

So, how long does all of this take? Amazingly enough, it takes three incalculable eons (asmakhyeya kalpas) to become a Buddha. That is a long time. When I first read superficially about these stages a few years ago, I just chalked it all up to culture and myth and just dismissed the idea as provincial; nothing I would bother with understanding. After all, would it not be better to just take as direct a line as possible to attain Buddhahood and get to work helping others? Yet, if I am honest with myself, it is important for me to recognize and accept the reality of what my motivations and understanding truly are. Additionally, since I naturally have an analytical way of thinking, it is important for me to understand the specifics of the concepts, but the practice is to have the experience of emptiness, not just an intellectual understanding of it as a concept.

Having spent my summers on the farm, I have a practical appreciation of a methodical approach; plowing a row in one direction, then plowing in the other is not a burden but an important part of the cultivation of our garden. Looking at the Progressive Stages of the Path can be considered a road map to awakening. Worrying about the time is takes is mistaking the path as a means to an ends. It is important for us to find a practice that enriches us and that we find joy in. If we are miserable in our practice, perhaps that is not the practice for us at this time. When we cultivate bodhichitta and develop a one-pointed desire to open our hearts and develop a heart of compassion that is as large as the ocean, there is a great deal of joy in the practice. Sitting in this joy is not a bad way to pass a few eons!

The concerns of the length of time it takes one to achieve Buddhahood in the Progressive Path are not new ones. Nagarjuna talks about this concern in the Precious Garland where he explains that the length of time is no grounds for discouragement; after all, time is a relative perception. When we experience something very painful, the time seems to pass very slowly, while when we experience something pleasurable, the time seems to fly by. Interestingly, this is a similar concept to Albert Einstein's famous quote:

"When a man sits with a pretty girl for an hour, it seems like a minute. But let him sit on a hot stove for a minute and it's longer than any hour. That's relativity!" Also when we first start the practice, we may find the first stages to be challenging and even painful, but that we can endure the hardships because when we transform our thinking, we become invulnerable to the pain. His Holiness the Dalai Lama also relates a story about himself when he was a teenager getting instruction on the progressive path he told his teacher that he felt that because the process takes so long it seems impossible and he felt that the Vajrayana path would be better suited to him. His teacher's response was to ask him rhetorically how can the Vajrayana (or any other Buddhist path) be viable without the practice and cultivation of bodhichitta.

Comparing the progressive stages of the path with the East Asian models like Chan seems to be a matter of perspective, not unlike the difference between a person who needs to learn methodically all of the history, background, and rationale of something before really understanding it or being ready to act upon it compared to the person who wants the most pertinent, bottom line, heart of the thing first. While the Progressive Path leaves nothing to chance, the East Asian models stress the direct experience of wisdom and emptiness as characterized by the Prajnaparamita literature. The Progressive Path further outlines the importance of morality and good behavior (maybe a *fake it 'til you make it* philosophy) which made it popular in the political climate of the times. Rulers are often fearful of anyone promoting too much self-reliance and independence in the people. As we look at the various schools, traditions, and writings, at their core they lead us to the same place – the task of the bodhisattva practitioner to help all sentient beings never changes.

Because of the political climate in Tibet, the introduction of Buddhism into Tibet was also fraught with division. The two forces which would come to be in opposition to each other were from India and China; the Bodhisattva Path was developed from the Indian schools and the Sudden Enlightenment tradition was from China with parallels to Zen. Sadly, history records that the presence of these two traditions led to challenge, debate, and perhaps even murder and suicide. Heshang Mahayana (the Chinese is Moheyan and this translation will be used in this paper to avoid confusion with the school) was a Chinese monk who was a follower of Chan. Moheyan testified that a person should enter deep contemplation and realize that there is no mind to engage or ponder; that discrimination is the enemy of awakening and one should therefore not cling to anything, even to the absence of thought.

He believed that this absence of thought led the practitioner to instantaneous enlightenment and that long lists of stages and things to do would not create enlightenment. Emptiness then, is the radiant pure Mind free of the obstacles of discrimination and concepts. During the debate, Moheyan summarized his position by saying: "He who has no thoughts and inclinations at all can be fully delivered from Phenomenal Life. The absence of any thought, search, or investigation brings about the non-perception of the reality of separate entities. In such a manner one can attain Buddhahood all at once, like a Bodhisattva who has attained the tenth stage."

While it is difficult to know all of the details of Moheyan's positions, it does seem that he did not ignore morality and felt that practitioners should, indeed, accumulate merit and practice the perfections of wisdom. Additionally, it seems that Moheyan believed that it would be through the enlightened mind from which moral and ethical behavior would spring flawlessly. However, in the history of the debates, it appears that Moheyan's position was purported to be an extreme of a blank meditation rather than stressing non-conceptual awareness. Kamalasila made the argument that if enlightenment cannot be cultivated through the progressive, moral path, then what is to be done? The approach, in this view, is that conceptual activity is divided into profitable and unprofitable which allows the practitioner to determine whether or not something exists intrinsically. The King agreed with Kamalasila and decreed that everyone should follow the teachings of Nagarjuna and cultivate morality and compassion in order to generate insight.

Unfortunately, while we will probably never know all of the details of Moheyan's teachings in order to give him a fair hearing, he was most likely doomed to failure given the political situation of a King who wished to promote moral behavior of the people and who was not likely to want to support a Chinese way of thinking.

Snake Symbolism in Buddhism

In the *Alagaddupama Sutta*, the Snake Simile, the Buddha admonishes the Bhikkhu Arittha for not wanting to give up a wrong view of the teaching.

Arittha believed that sense pleasures, or sense desires, are not an obstacle to practice and even though the other Bhikkhus asked him to abandon this wrong view three times, he refused. The Buddha called for Arittha to come to the assembly. The Buddha corrected Arittha's wrong view and continued to give a Dharma talk that included a number of similes. One of those similes included the warning that the student of the Dharma is like a man who finds a poisonous snake in the forest; he should use a forked stick to capture the snake's neck just below the head, then to grasp the snake's neck so that he won't be bitten. If the man simply grabs at the snake, the snake may strike at him and bite him causing much suffering.

The Buddha likened sense pleasure/desire to a list of obstacles like a pit of burning charcoal, a piece of raw meat, a dream, or a poisonous snake; he goes on to liken his own teachings to a poisonous snake that must be grasped appropriately. For many practitioners, both during the time of the Buddha and today, misunderstanding the intention of the sutras is common. Arittha confused the dangers of identifying with sense pleasures with the true joy and happiness of a peaceful mind. While some practitioners might hear of the dangers of sense pleasures and become fearful of appreciating the true joy and happiness in life, Arittha, it seems, went too far and believed that one could indulge in sense pleasures and not find it a hindrance on the path. The image of the snake serves as an excellent example of this important balance and discernment that a practitioner must exercise.

The snake represents a force that is powerful, valuable, dangerous, and mysterious. The symbolic role of the snake is among the most important and diverse in the majority of cultures throughout the world and throughout time. The snake as an animal always fascinates: the way it moves over the ground without legs, the slick scales that are beautiful to look at, even though it is cold blooded it is born from eggs, it sheds its skin from time to time (often blind during the process), it behaves in what seems to be a strategic since it does not win a fight with brute force but with guile, stealth, and cunning, and it's bite can be poisonous yet can also be used to make medicine. In many cultures the symbology of the snake has a dual nature as both a protector and adversary, masculine (because of its phallic shape) and feminine (because of its engulfing belly), and a symbol of power and renewal. The snake also carries with it the association with the spiral, potential energy, and the unknown of birth, death, and rebirth.

Perhaps one of the earliest evidences of yoga appears on a seal from the Indus Valley circa 2,000 B.C.E. showing a figure seated in what appears to be the lotus position with worshipers kneeling on either side being guarded by serpents. The ser-pent takes the role of guide and fierce pro-tector in many cul-tures from the ancient Greeks and Romans, the Aztecs and Ma-yans, Assyrians and the Egyptians. In cul-

Deity with worshipers and serpents, ca. 2,000 B.C.E., Indus Valley

tures as diverse as India and the North American indigenous people, and the religions from the Vedic to Christianity, the snake plays a role as guardian of the mysterious, the giver of life or death, and the transcendent. In Jung's Red Book, he painted a coiled serpent encapsulated in an energetic red swirl-ing mass, its head tilted up, mouth open, spewing forth light and creative energy, inscribed with the words: "For thou art the lord of sunrise, for though art the star of the East, for though art the flower that blooms above all, for though art the stag which bursts from the forest, for thou art the song which resounds far over the waters, for though art end and beginning."

In the *Samaññaphala Sutta*, we learn about the fruits of the contempla-tive life and the concept of rebirth, with our friend the snake making an ap-pearance. "With his mind thus concentrated, purified, and bright, unblemished, free from defects, pliant, malleable, steady, and attained to im-perturbability, he directs and inclines it to creating a mind-made body. From this body he creates another body, endowed with form, made of the mind, complete in all its parts, not inferior in its faculties.... Just as if a man were to pull a snake out from its slough. The thought would occur to him: 'This is the snake, this is the slough. The snake is one thing, the slough another, but the snake has been pulled out from the slough.' In the same way -- with his mind thus concentrated, purified, and bright, unblemished, free from defects, pliant, malleable, steady, and attained to imperturbability, the monk directs and inclines it to creating a mind-made body."

The Buddha is associated iconographically with the snake through a number of stories of the Buddha doing battle with the king of the serpents, Mucalinda, defeating him, and gaining the serpent king's protection and devotion. The Buddha also encountered a snake as a small child during the story of the ploughing festival, when little Siddhartha was left alone under the rose apple tree and was touched by compassion and mudita at the sight of seeing the ploughed fields cutting through the dirt, revealing the torn worms and insects which became food for the birds, lizards, and snakes, then seeing the hawk swoop down to capture the snake for its own feast. Seeing this cycle of life sparked bodhichitta in the young

Buddha sheltered by a Naga, Cambodia circa mid 11th century

boy, so he sat under the shade of the tree and entered the first level of jhana.

But the most famous snake story in Buddhism is the story of Nagarjuna and the Nagas, or serpent kings. Nagarjuna is so well regarded in Buddhist history; he is considered a second Buddha because of his grasp of the sutras and their ultimate meaning; developing or inspiring a large part of the Prajnaparamita literature. Little has been written about him personally, but the legends and mythology important in understanding what his contribution to Buddhism is in the way that myth informs us of truth in an experiential way. The word *naga* means snake (literally cobra), serpent-beings of the water realms, earth spirits, or dragon; Arjuna means *noble*, a person with a clear inner nature, free from impurities whose mind is ready to receive the highest understanding. Of the legendary accounts, it is said that Nagarjuna was sitting by a lake and the water serpents invited them to come into their realm to teach. When he emerged, he had the twelve volumes of the Prajnaparamita. Naga or Maha-naga (great dragon) is often used as a synonym for the Buddha or other sages who have attained Nirvana; they are also used in many Buddhist statues or other iconographic images to represent guardians of the Buddha, temples, or scripture.

Legends say that the nagas guard the sutras placed in their care until humanity is ready to receive and understand them. Snakes, water, and underwater caves or grottos have strong symbology for birth, death, and rebirth. A snake, or its more powerful cousin the dragon, sheds its skin on a regular basis, during which time it is blind and lethargic, emerging with new vitality. Going deep into the water can also symbolize delving into the subconscious, the part of our mind that we cannot access through logic and reasoning, but through imagery and symbols. The name and the legend give us powerful symbols to set the stage for some of the most important lessons toward full understanding of the Buddha's teaching.

Legend claims that when Nagarjuna was born, it was predicted that he would die as a child, despite a number of offerings to extend his life for a specific time frame. His parents sent him on a pilgrimage when he was nearing his seventh birthday because they could not bear to witness his death. Guided by a manifestation of Avalokiteshvara, the boys guardians found their way to the Nalanda Monastery where the boy could be taken under the care of the teacher Saraha. Under the protection of Manjushri, the boy was able to recite the Amitayus mantra without interruption and his death was averted. Sometime after growing up, studying the sutras, and becoming abbot of Nalanda, the Nagas invited Nagarjuna to visit them. After the Buddha died, Ananda was entrusted with sutras that the world was not yet ready for, and Ananda gave them to the Nagas to hold until the time was ripe and the correct teacher was found. Nagarjuna gained favor with the Naga by curing them of sicknesses with ritual prayer. Because of this, the Naga presented Nagarjuna with the Perfection of Wisdom Sutras so they could be shared with the world.

In the painting by Nicholas Roerich, we see Nagarjuna sitting at the edge of a lake in meditative repose, dressed in a red robe with a pointed hood, gazing at the home of the Naga King who is rising up from the depth of the water to present Nagarjuna with the sutras that were entrusted to him. The Naga King is wrapped around the mountain three and a half times, and has fully spread his hood in a show of power, with smaller nagas joining the King, their heads lining his hood. We see a source spring flowing into the lake from the cool blue mountains, contrasted to the reds, yellows, purples, and orange of the power welling up from the mountain, filled with potential energy, creativity, and potency.

Nagarjuna - Conqueror of the Serpent by Nicholas Roerich, 1925 (Russia)

Many symbols are present in the painting. Looking at the colors used, the red cloak of Nagarjuna stands out. Red is a color with a number of meanings: heat, fire, blood, warning, courage, power, lust, the masculine aspect, activity, danger, fruition, fertility, and anger; many fruits and flowers are various shades of red. The colors of the central mountain are a blend of red into blue and yellow to form shades of purple and orange, perhaps representing a volcano about to erupt, and taking on the qualities of both the core colors of red, yellow, and blue, blending them into a new color. Red is the color of the first, Muladhara or root chakra. The cloak has a pointed hood, representing a heightened spiritual sense.

Surrounding the central mountain are blue mountains and water. Blue signifies cooling, depth, breath, water, clarity, meditation, happiness, infinity, quietude, apathy, death, and stability; some fruits and flowers are blue, bird feathers and butterflies, and even some exotic frogs and lizards have blue skin. The color blue is the symbol of the Vishuddha chakra, representing the throat and our capability for speech and communication. The central mountain is rising from a lake of water. Water is representative of regeneration, purity and purifying, reflecting, restoration, fluidity, change, the feminine aspect, passivity, stagnation, the subconscious, life giving, birth, power, and the ability to carve or destroy forms yet not ever taking a shape of its own. The mountains surrounding the lake represent the link between heaven and earth, stability, transcendence, longevity, a sacred space, hard work, adventure, challenge, attainment, timelessness, and barriers. The mountain spring feeding the lake represents the flow of life, fluidity, passiveness, and a symbol of the not-self characteristic because the river is always changing and is both at its own source and end at the same time.

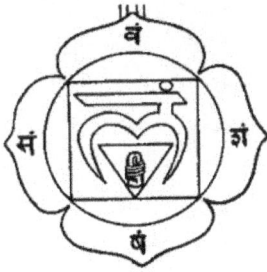

The Root Chakra
the Muladhara

The central mountain is representative of both the linga symbol and the world egg. Similar to the symbol of the female snake wrapped three and a half times around the linga in the Muladhara chakra, the specific number of coils represent energy expressed as purity, passion, and darkness with the half coil combining the three indicating the interplay between them all. The root chakra shows the linga surrounded by the white serpent goddess Kundalini, coiled three and a half times, asleep, covering the Brahma-door with her head. The spiral is a universal symbol that shows up from the leaves on a plant, our DNA, the vortex of a tornado, and the spiral galaxy we live in to the artistic representations of labyrinths, the often seen three and a half coils of a serpent, the dance of the dervishes, to the curls of the Buddha's hair topknots.

A mystical, mysterious symbol, the spiral represents the ebb and flow of life and consciousness, evolution, transformation, the cycles of life, the phases of the moon, growth, and the rising of the Kundalini (meaning *of a spiral nature*) force.

Whether the central mountain represents the world egg or the linga, both of these symbols would be appropriate for different reasons. The world egg would represent the totality of creative forces, perfection, rebirth, the feminine energy, potential, resurrection, fertility, nourishment, and the

The world egg
surrounded by a
female serpent

egg-shaped cosmos *Brahmanda* (Brahm means 'Cosmos' or 'expanding', Anda means 'Egg') The linga, a symbol of the male creative energy or of the phallus, the axis mundi, power, action in the world, light, protection, and pure energy. Interestingly, this symbol of the snake coiled three and a half times around a central object is found in a wide variety of cultures.

North American native sand paintings show coiled serpents emanating from central stalks of corn, in 880 B.C.E., the relief carvings of the Genies of Assyria showed rounded helmets, circled with a snake, Hygeia of 4th century Rome is shown with a serpent coiled around a staff, in 3rd century Mexico, feathered serpents, coiled around stone pillars are given offerings, representations of Eve and the serpent in the Garden of Eden, show the snake coiled around the tree of the knowledge of good and evil, and the basket of Isis in 1st century Rome shows a snake coiled around a basket of harvest with a moon and wheat icon are some of the many examples of this symbol. Additionally, the linga and yoni, representing the male and female are almost always shown together in Vedic and Hindu iconography. The two together represents balance, and just as importantly, by themselves they can only do so much, individually they represent more potential than true creative and transformative power. It is only when they are joined together as equal partners can the two powers rise, creating a lotus ladder or double helix, to bring the power of the physical and earthly (the root chakra) up through to the spiritual (the Sahasrara, or crown chakra) for transcendent understanding.

Before we leave the Naga of Buddhist tradition, I don't want to forget the feminine serpents, the Nagini. In the Lotus Sutra is a story of the daughter of Sagara (ocean) one of the Naga Kings, who was only eight years old when she learned it was possible for her to attain Buddha-Wisdom. She was told that as a female, she could not attain Buddhahood. In some translations, she transforms into a man and attains enlightenment on the spot in the Vimala world. But in other interpretations, her offering of a jewel was the sacrifice of her own life, which was accepted instantly, transporting her to the Pure Land.

❁

In the Reiki system of healing, there are three degrees of training that allow the Reiki practitioner to administer hands on healing touch, distance healing, and teaching the process through a series of attunements to the Reiki energy.

In the second degree class, the practitioner learns a symbol called the Chokurei. In the tradition of Reiki, the healing symbols have been kept secret. However, Stein published the symbols, to some controversy, with the intention of making Reiki and it's healing more accessible. The Chokurei, in Japanese meaning Imperial Edict, is a spiral around an axis and it represents the Kundalini energy, often called the power symbol. In Reiki classes, one usually learns the definition "The power of the Universe, 100%, come here now!"

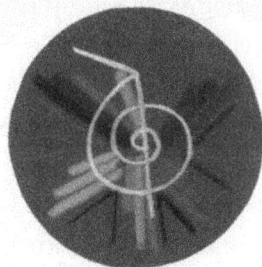

*Stylized Chokurei,
Cheryl Barnes-Neff,
1992*

This is a rather daunting vision of the power this symbol represents. While the term Imperial Edict is not greeted with much enthusiasm when I give classes to Westerners, the understanding of the term in Western mythology is in alignment of the story of the Holy Grail in the concept of the King being sick making the land sick. Only the knight who showed compassion and concern for the welfare of the King could save him, and therefore himself. The essence of the symbol is also found in the phrase "as above, so below." This symbol is drawn with the palm of the hand either in the air, in the mind's eye, or in some cases on the body. When I was working in a Neonatal Intensive Care Unit I would love to use Reiki on the newborns in my care. They were so open to the energy and it was nice to have a tool available to help them feel the healing energy. Most of the effects were subtle, many times a sense of relaxation and peace for a newborn having trouble adjusting to life outside the womb too early.

However, not long after becoming a Reiki Master (teacher of the technique), I was called to the delivery room for a delivery. It was supposed to be a normal delivery, but they saw some irregularities on the fetal monitor, so the delivery team wanted a neonatologist and NICU nurse there. When the baby was born, it was clear that the baby was struggling. He wasn't breathing well, and his one minute Apgar score was poor. We were concerned that the baby was not making the transition from antenatal circulation to the normal pattern, but nothing seemed to make total sense. We were working on the baby when a knowing came to me that I should use the Chokurei symbol. I cupped my hand and drew the symbol right at the cut of the umbilical cord then bringing my hand down to hold the energy there.

The baby took a loud gasp and started the vigorous, very welcome, crying and turned pink as a rose bud. The doctor looked up at me with a puzzled look and asked "what did you do?" We had work to do to get the baby back to the nursery, so I was off the hook to explain, but I have always wondered about that baby who did not seem to want to come into the world, how he did, and what his life is like. I rarely tell this story because I do not want anyone to get the idea that this kind of dramatic event is typical when doing Reiki or that I am some kind of super healer, but it is an interesting exploration of the power of symbols and how they can have literal as well as metaphoric effects.

No review of the symbology of the snake could be complete without a mention of the most famous story of Adam and Eve. We can look at this story with Buddhist eyes instead of Christian ones to discover a meaning that resonates with what the Buddha taught. In the history of looking at the Bible and analyzing how it was written, we discover that scholarship has uncovered that the book of Genesis was authored by a number of different people; then edited into a single book. The story of creation takes place in several parts and apparently, was written by different authors. The story of Adam and Eve in the Garden of Eden was authored by J (for Judah). This and other J stories are detailed with specific human characteristics and interesting relationships with God.

When God made Adam, he placed him in the Garden of Eden to work it and watch over it. God instructed Adam not to eat from the Tree of the Knowing of Good and Evil, telling Adam that if he did eat from it, he must die. After a time, God then saw that it was not good for Adam to be alone, and fashioned him a partner, Eve, from Adam's rib. They lived in the Garden uneventfully, hearing God walk in the Garden in the evening. Now, one day while Eve was walking by herself, the snake approached her and encouraged her to eat from the Tree of the Knowing of

Adam and Eve, Titian c. 1550

Good and Evil, telling her that it was good to eat. Eve told that snake that God had told Adam that they were not to eat of this fruit and if they did, they would die. "The snake said to the woman: Die? You will not die! Rather, God knows that on the day that you eat from it, your eyes will be opened and you will become like gods, knowing good and evil." (from the Schocken Bible) Eve saw that the fruit was good for eating and she took a fruit and ate. She then gave it to Adam as well.

Their eyes were opened and they realized that they were nude and fashioned loin cloths from leaves to cover themselves. God realized what had happened and banished them from the Garden and punished each of them: Adam – that his toil on the land will be hard, Eve – that childbirth will be painful, and the snake – that it would walk on its belly from then on. In the majority of conversations about this story, we hear an immediate indictment of Adam and Eve that they willfully disobeyed God's command. On the other hand, one of the questions I have always asked (and got into trouble for during a Bible study class when I was a kid) is how could they have really been responsible for their actions when they did not know the difference between right and wrong? The other interesting thing about the story is that Adam and Eve did not die from eating the fruit, so the snake was telling the truth.

This last point is an interesting one, though. We do not know how long Adam and Eve spent in the Garden before the apple incident, but when we look at the mythic story being told, we can consider that the knowledge of right and wrong, good and evil, is also opening the perception of Adam and Eve to the field of opposites, the understanding of duality. Before, they were innocent children without a mother; then they became adults in an instant with an angry father. We can come back to the spiral, considering that as they lived in the Garden nothing was happening; no movement, no change, they were vegetarians so there was no death or killing, no growth. It could be considered idyllic, but only from a distance; close up it had no life. When they have the realization of duality, they are in the same spot in their understanding, but at a new level.

It reminds me of the Zen story of the monk that said that before he studied Zen the mountains were mountains, waters were waters; as he was studying the mountains were not mountains and waters were not waters; and now that he had mastered Zen the mountains were really mountains and waters were really waters. Are the three understandings the same, or different? At first, we see the things in our world and do not look deeply at them. We would say that of course the mountain is a mountain and water is water, what else could they be? As we study, we learn intellectually and we leave our naive positions and promptly become very confused as we try to reconcile what we are learning with our perceptions; we are kicked out of the Garden because we cannot see reality as it really is. Once we can experience the non-dual nature of reality within the context of the world we live in, we are instantly transported to the Garden once again; now seeing that we had never left it in the first place.

The next thing that happens in Genesis is that God states that the reason he is banishing Adam and

Guardian statue outside the entrance of Chua Bao An, Orlando, FL

Eve is to guard against them eating from the Tree of Life and becoming immortal, guarding the tree with cherubim wielding fiery swords. In many Buddhist temples, there are Bodhisattva's, often fierce looking with swords, and they are said to guard the temple from evil spirits. Looking at them from a more mythological perspective, we might consider that they are preventing us from bring our inner evil, our misperceptions, into the temple. We need to come to the temple with an open heart and mind to be able to hear the Dharma with our Buddha ears. We need to walk into the Pure Land as we enter through the doors, leaving the muddy shoes that we wear when we tromp through the mud of our everyday, dualistic life at the door.

Why is it a valuable thing to look at these pictures and stories, from our own traditions and others? Campbell explains that myth and iconography have an important place in our understanding of our history and ourselves. What the mythic stories relay to us are examples, many times larger than life, of the hero's journey of striving to look past the local, cultural, religious, and societal expectations and break out from their limitations. Breaking free of these is to have a direct, undistorted experience and assimilation that Jung called the *archetypal images* and in Buddhism, *viveka*, discrimination. The other aspect that makes these stories and images important is that the artist is trying to communicate with us. Whether it is a song, a poem, dance, statue, painting, story, or photograph we humans understand that words alone cannot share an experience with another. And even though the art does not always get through to the viewer, nor can it replace the direct experience, the art can, in some wonderful cases, evoke the emotion that the artist was feeling at the time of the creation. We can share in the human experience and allow it to open a window into our own experience, helping us get nearer to that direct experience ourselves.

So even though my mother was terrified of snakes, when we spent our summers on the farm, I knew that when my pesky cousin came up to me with a handful of dirt, or bugs, a frog, or a snake that I would be best served not to act afraid. So when I first reached out and took the garter snake from him, intending just to get his goat, I was surprised to discover that the snake was fascinating, the scales smooth and beautiful, and the way he moved graceful. Sometimes we can trick ourselves out of our misperceptions, even though many times we allow our fears to get the best of us and we can trick ourselves into mistaking a rope for a snake. With patience and an open heart and mind, we can keep asking ourselves "Am I sure?" when we see those snakes that keep us from seeing the truth.

CHAPTER 7

The Myth of Freedom

The book "The Myth of Freedom and the Way of Meditation" is a collection of lectures by Chogyam Trungpa Rinpoche given over the course of three years. Many are short and pithy, and unafraid of approaching the teachings with modernity and his own unique teaching style. Yet, much of the book distills basic Buddhist teachings in an approachable way. Most of the work in this class was done through discussion forums, exploring and responding to our peers. A few essays came from this work dealing with Buddhist concepts and ways of thinking.

Five Skandhas

According to Chogyam Trungpa, the five skandhas (or aggregates) are a set of concepts that describe the ego. The first skandhas is form or basic ignorance. The second skandhas is "feeling," the third is "perception," the fourth is "mental formation," and finally "consciousness." In the Samyutta Nikaya, the Buddha described the skandhas as compared to the parts of a chariot. According to Bhikkhu Bodhi, the skandhas are an important part of Buddhist teaching because they help us understand the Four Nobel Truths, future suffering's cause, and release. In the Mahayana schools, the skandhas are seen as equally empty especially through the Heart Sutra, where they are listed specifically. When we grasp or cling to the aggregates, we cause ourselves to suffer.

Form is the *skandha* that is the most obvious. We see our body and all of the physical stuff around us and it certainly seems to be real. When we hurt ourselves, the pain makes sure we don't ignore what is happening to us. We want to avoid pain, so we deepen our idea of the body as who we are. Chogyam Trungpa also equates form with the birth of ego or basic ignorance. The idea that there is no solid self is a scary one, so we avoid looking at that.

Feelings are like a river within us, constantly moving and changing, yet they too lead us to believe that they are tangible and who we really are. Our feelings can sometimes over-power us prompting us to take action based on our feelings, sometimes leading to disaster. We tend to believe that feelings are caused by things outside of ourselves and not really under our control. We may develop strong beliefs about people based on our feelings about them, which may be completely wrong and unfair. Sometimes our feelings seem to over-power us and we feel we have to figure out some way to vent them or we'll explode!

Perceptions are crafty devils! We see things and our brains are hardwired to perceive and quickly draw conclusions. Primitive man might see the tall grasses move and hear a noise, quickly perceive a threat, and run away. He might not ever go back to check on his assumption but reinforce his idea perhaps even telling a friend about his close call. Our perceptions are conditioned by our past experiences, culture, and what we've learned. The Diamond Sutra says that where there are perceptions, there is deception. We practice to help us substitute perceptions with prajna, true vision or wisdom.

"Mental formations" is an important skandha, one that took me awhile to grasp. Anything made from other elements is a formation, and while this seems simple at first glance, it is one of the keys to understanding the not-self characteristic. These are enumerated as the bija seeds present in our store consciousness. These mental formations are impermanent, so we don't want to take refuge in them, yet we often delude ourselves into believing that certain seeds are actually who we are and are unchangeable.

Consciousness refers here to the store consciousness which is the base of everything we are. Our mental formations (bija seeds) reside here, dormant, until they are watered by something that happens. Our practice is crucial to our well being, because it is our practice that helps us water the wholesome seeds and invite the unwholesome seeds not to grow, ultimately transforming our consciousness at the base. According to Thich Nhat Hanh, consciousness is both individual and collective. The collective consciousness of a culture, nation, or other group can have profound effects on the people potentially causing a lot of harm or a lot of happiness.

Anatman

How do the skandhas support the idea of anatman? Using your understanding of anatman and the skandhas; write out an explanation and defense of the Buddhist teaching of non-self.

The skandhas are the very heart of the understanding of anatman. While it's tempting and quite common to assume that the way we feel and what we do is just natural or "who we are," when we take a closer look, we can see that our lives are made of component parts. When we have physical pain, we won't be able to do the things we had planned for the day, compounding our pain with frustration. If someone we care about isn't sympathetic to our situation, we might come to the conclusion that they are a bad person and allow that to color our interactions with them in the future. When we lash out at them, we may feel we can't help ourselves – after all, they treated us badly and we can't help our feelings. If that person is of another race or religion from us, somehow "other," we may feel justified to attribute their actions toward us as part of how all of the people of that race or religion act. When we make a harsh statement about that group, we see it as something we know to be true and may never break down the situation into its component parts for understanding.

The five skandhas show us that we are all made of a composite of elements and no element can be teased out as the element that is unique to us. A flower is only a flower because of all the things that came before, and just as science has illustrated, nothing can be created or destroyed, so all of the elements in the universe simply rearrange their manifestations depending on the ongoing flow of energy. When we take one cell of a living thing, be it a cat or sheep or human, we can now clone that body because the one cell contains the whole body. In Buddhist terms, this is the one in the all and the all in the one. I had always scratched my head when I heard people struggle with the question if a cloned person has a soul or not. It seemed to me to be such a strange question, but for those who do believe that each person has a soul that is something unique and other than the component parts and chain of causality, the idea that an identical body could be recreated might indeed bring a seed of doubt into their minds. Instead, the Buddhist concept of the five skandhas makes more sense to me. In being invited to look deeply into any one of the skandhas, we can see all of the others because the skandhas inter-are with each other.

Fascinating to me is Thich Nhat Hanh's teaching, pointing out when Avalokiteshvara looked deeply into the reality of the skandhas, she saw the emptiness of self and was liberated from suffering, and that when we meditate on the assembly of the five aggregates in ourselves we will see the oneness of our self and the universe. It seems to me that believing in a soul would stop that process from occurring, depending instead on contemplating on the soul which can't be connected to anything else.

Six Realms

In the psychological model, the six realms are thought of as states of mind that people experience or create as patterns of behavior. The hungry ghost realm is a feeling of craving that can never be satisfied. When we have a craving it is because there is a promise of relief or cure for the pain that we feel. While there may be an initial rush of excitement, there is no relief or cure for the pain. In this country, we are surrounded by hungry ghosts and there are times I certainly join them, too. We are bombarded with ads encouraging us to buy more, have more, and consume more. Yet, this is killing our society, our bodies, and our spirit.

In the animal realm, we are very rule oriented and we have to have things our own way – after all, our way is the right way, so why shouldn't we demand our way. Any deviation from our way is seen with great skepticism and fear, making it hard to trust anyone or anything. For me, I have to laugh at myself from my mom's comment to me asking if I want to be happy or right, and my answer that I want to be happy because I'm right! If everyone would just straighten up, the world would be great, and I'd be happy – what's wrong with that? In the animal realm, we don't see that we are responsible for our own feelings and place the blame on others when we are unhappy.

In the hell realm, there is nothing but anger. We can fly between these lower three realms without cravings sparking us to believe in rigid rules and then becoming furious when our rules are not followed to give us what we crave. In the hell realm, our psyche is on fire but nothing soothes the flames. Times when I get angry at something that I know is not that big a deal, I have to shake my head at myself, but it does help me have compassion for those who are really stuck in this state of mind. I have an opportunity to deal with the issues and tools to help calm the flames. For people who have a lifetime of bad experiences, who believe this is the way the world really is, and have not had an opportunity to practice, their hell is very real.

The jealous god realm seems like the narcissist; the person who feels the world revolves around them, but who is highly insecure. Any success of another makes them doubt themselves and want to prove that they are not only as good, but better. This is the person who feels that all eyes should always be on them and woe to anyone who speaks the truth to this person. Like the emperor's new clothes, they are actually naked, but no one has the courage to say so because of the rage that would ensue. This realm rises up in me when I'm confronted with arrogant or bigoted people who assume that I'm not as good because I'm female or older or whatever reason they come up with. I find myself angry with them and wanting to show that they are wrong.

In the god realm, we are above it all. We rise to new heights through spiritual practices, float along on cloud nine, and feel blissfully smug all the time. There is a preacher my sister likes to listen to that has a very funny story that she tells on herself about this realm (of course, in Christian terms) talking about spending the day reading her Bible, singing praise songs, and having a wonderful time in communion with God. Then the kids walk in and she starts yelling at them for their muddy shoes, noisy voices, and breaking into her bliss! Her experience is common to all of us when we confuse our spiritual "high" with the true purpose of looking deeply and honestly into ourselves. Our spiritual lives become more like a terrific movie that we get lost in, rather than a practice that will transform our suffering.

The human realm is the one that we are so lucky to be born in. it's the only realm where we can study the Dharma and practice with our Sangha the teachings of the Buddha. Yet, we often find ourselves confused about what being human even means. The very elements within us inform the other realms to us, yet can be tools to help us see the reality of the world and how to understand and move within it.

The more traditional way to learn about the six realms is the literal model of the realms is very colorful with glittering gods living in splendor, the powerful devas who accomplish spectacular things and fight fantastic battles, the scary ghosts who have pinhole mouths and tiny throats but huge stomachs, the angry and aggressive beings of hell, the frightened and ignorant beings, and the confused humans who find themselves on this wheel of samsara. In Vietnamese Buddhism, we are taught that we need to practice for ourselves, but also for the beings of these other realms because they listen to us and might be helped if we practice beautifully with stability. Because these realms are within all of us, this is very true! Those elements within us are benefitted when we can allow them to listen.

I do relate to the psychological model more, but I do find charm and value in the literal model. It's not that I feel there are beings and realms out there, but the mythic nature of the literal model helps me to bring the understandings of these realms into my consciousness in a way that analyzing and thinking about them can't. The colors and symbols bring a visual element that goes beyond thinking, and imagining the realms brings a kinetic element to understanding. Because I'm a kinetic and visual learner, this is important for me.

The Kleshas

The Kleshas can be seen as the root of suffering and our existence in samsara. There is a somewhat complicated taxonomy surrounding the idea of kleshas, including the "three poisons," "six defilements," "two obstructions," "round of defilements," and the like. Klesha means affliction, defilement, poison, negative emotions, etc. The emotions greed, hate, and delusion are considered the roots of suffering. Whatever the organization of the emotions and their effects, these strong emotions pretty reliably lead to suffering. We may feel overwhelmed by these feelings because that energy of "for" and "against," "right" and "wrong," can be compelling and we find ourselves taking action that is harmful for ourselves and others.

I've been working with the Shantideva "The Way of the Bodhisattva" for awhile now (I thought, well, if I want to take Bodhisattva vows and be a Bodhisattva, I wonder if there is a manual about how to do that – and it turns out that there is!). He talks a lot about anger and I really appreciate how personal his verses are about the feelings that come up with the kleshas.

For instance:

For it's as if by chance that I have gained
this state so hard to find, wherein to help myself.
And now, when freedom – power of choice – is mine,
if once again I'm led away to hell.

I am benumbed by sorcery,
my mind reduced to total impotence
with no perception of the madness overwhelming me.
O what is it that has me in its grip?

Anger, lust – these enemies of mine –
are limbless and devoid of faculties.
They have no bravery, no cleverness;
how then have they reduced me to such slavery?

I love these verses because I've felt that way on so many occasions from yelling at the TV during the news, to feeling on the edge of discontent and just waiting for the next annoying thing to happen so I can act cranky and feel justified for it, and the list goes on. When we can stop, on the spot if possible, and take that Shamatha breath, we can give ourselves just enough space to see that this klesha that is invading our consciousness really is not solid at all and it's our insight and wisdom that can stop our unwholesome action. It also gives us a chance to look deeply at the feeling to see the root of it.

One of the complaints a lot of men have about the way many women argue is that we girls get mad over you guys not taking the trash out then suddenly, a whole host of complaints that were stored up come spewing out. I've been guilty of doing that and it certainly doesn't seem fair! On the other hand, while not being done in a good way if we're spilling our guts over innocent by-standers, the chain of causality into the real reason for being upset is being revealed. When I've been angry over chores not being done, I learned to see that the torrent of angry accusations were more about the idea that doing the chores was, in my mind, a symbol of being taken care of, not just having a clean dish or trash at the curb. As a neglected child, a feeling of not being cared for can be terrifying, even when a dish in the sink isn't a threat to safety and wellbeing at all. When done through Shamatha and Vipashyana, we can have the opportunity to invite those negative seeds not to grow. We can also enlist the help of our loved ones not to water those seeds within us as we grow a healthier garden.

I have this verse from Chuang Tzu by my desk:

> *"Chaff from the winnowing fan can so blind the eye that heaven, earth, and the four directions all seem to shift place. A mosquito or a horse-fly stinging your skin can keep you awake a whole night. And when benevolence and righteousness in all their fearfulness come to muddle the mind, the confusion is unimaginable. If you want to keep the world from losing its simplicity, you must move with the freedom of the wind, stand in the perfection of Virtue. Why all this huffing and puffing, as though you were carrying a big drum and searching for a lost child."*

When I first read that I thought it said "when benevolence and righteousness in all their fear*less*ness..." but it says "fear*ful*ness" – what a difference! It was a koan of mine for awhile because I just couldn't get why he was calling these good qualities fearful. But it seems to me that this relates back to our kleshas; when we see ourselves as benevolent and righteous, we've set up an "us vs them" mentality that will lead us on that road to hell with the good intention paving stones.

Six Realms Mythology

The six realms are an aspect of Buddhism that can be looked at in different ways. We can look at the realms in the literal sense, which many Buddhists around the world do, or we can look at them in the psychological sense where we contemplate each realm as an aspect of our state of mind. In the psychological sense, we see the hungry ghost realm as a feeling of craving that can never be satisfied. When we have a craving it is because there is a promise of relief or cure for the pain that we feel. While there may be an initial rush of excitement, there is no relief or cure for the pain. In the animal realm, we are very rule oriented and we have to have things our own way –

after all, our way is the right way, so why shouldn't we demand our way.

Any deviation from our way is seen with great skepticism and fear, making it hard to trust anyone or anything. In the hell realm, there is nothing but anger. We can fly between these lower three realms without cravings sparking us to believe in rigid rules and then becoming furious when our rules are not followed to give us what we crave. In the hell realm, our psyche is on fire but nothing soothes the flames. The jealous god realm represents the narcissist; the person who feels the world revolves around them, but who is highly insecure. Any success of another makes them doubt themselves and want to prove that they are not only as good, but better. This is the person who feels that all eyes should always be on them and woe to anyone who speaks the truth to this person. Like the emperor's new clothes, they are actually naked, but no one has the courage to say so because of the rage that would ensue. In the god realm, we are above it all. We rise to new heights through spiritual practices, float along on cloud nine, and feel blissfully smug all the time. The human realm is the one we are born in and have the opportunity to study the Dharma to liberate ourselves from the other realms.

The more traditional way to learn about the six realms is the literal model of the realms is very colorful with glittering gods living in splendor, the powerful devas who accomplish spectacular things and fight fantastic battles, the scary ghosts who have pinhole mouths and tiny throats but huge stomachs, the angry and aggressive beings of hell, the frightened and ignorant beings, and the confused humans who find themselves on this wheel of samsara. In Vietnamese Buddhism, we are taught that we need to practice for ourselves, but also for the beings of these other realms because they listen to us and might be helped if we practice beautifully with stability. Because these realms are within all of us, this is very true! Those elements within us are benefitted when we can allow them to listen.

I believe that there is another way we can look at the six realms and that is in terms of mythology. Joseph Campbell identified a number of functions of myth, and I believe that the six realms can be seen in these functions. Campbell sees these functions as: the metaphysical, psychological, sociological, and cosmological. The metaphysical function assumes that the mysteries of life and being cannot be expressed in words, so must be pointed to through myth, song, art, poetry, dance, etc. We can only participate in the rituals, symbols; the expression of ineffable experience can only point obliquely to the experience. The cosmological function serves to help us understand the physical world and our relationship to it.

While many people believe that these stories were ancient man's attempt to understand the events of the natural world, my guess is that the ancient shamans were also using this aspect of taking a literal understanding and imbuing it with deeper meaning. In the sociological function, mythic stories bring relationships that are larger than life into the consciousness and invite the hearer to relate this big story to their own relationships, helping to further bond the individual to the social whole. The psychological function is to guide the person through the phases of their life. When we read these amazing stories with their universal themes, we can identify with the underlying emotions, desires, dreams, and inner strength of the character, bringing it to bear within our own lives.

To narrow the focus of the mythological way of looking at the six realms, hell will be the realm emphasized here. Hell is a concept that is found in many cultures over the ages. For some, it is a form of justice, a way to reconcile the calamities in life that seem in contradiction to a benevolent creator, or an allegory for the sinful nature of humans. From Dante's Inferno to modern movies, hell has been depicted as a literal, physical place with a wide variety of visual motifs to emphasize its punishing nature. When we look at the Buddhist representation of the hell realm, the Naraka-gati, we find a place informed entirely by anger, hatred, and aggression. The result of the three poisons of greed, anger, and stupidity. In this realm, the most terrible of the realms, the inhabitants would drive away anyone who showed them love and kindness because they can only relate to their anger and confusion.

From a metaphysical frame of reference, the anger and violence in the world brings an important question to mind – what are the causes and consequences of these actions and feelings? Having a construct of hell gives a context for these feelings which can be so overwhelming and powerful that they seem to have a life of their own. The Kleshas seem to be the very demons of hell when we are overcome with these violent emotions. The kleshas can be seen as the root of suffering and our existence in samsara. There is a somewhat complicated taxonomy surrounding the idea of kleshas, including the "three poisons," "six defilements," "two obstructions," "round of defilements," and the like. Klesha means affliction, defilement, poison, negative emotions, etc. The emotions greed, hate, and delusion are considered the roots of suffering. We may feel overwhelmed by these feelings because that energy of "for" and "against," "right" and "wrong," can be compelling and we find ourselves taking action that is harmful for ourselves and others.

In the cosmological aspect, hell as a place gives us a roadmap to help us identify where we are and where we want or do not want to be. The stories of the hell realms could bring a moral motivation for behavior. While the ideal is certainly moral maturity where we do the right thing because it is the right thing, not because of a fear of punishment or promise of reward, but before that level of maturity is attained, we must work through how to live our lives and what consequences there are for our actions.

Looking at hell from a sociological framework, the emphasis is on relationships and societies. Hearing stories of the behavior that comes from or leads to hell, or stories about the Bodhisattvas who return to hell to save the beings there through compassion, gives inspiration to those who read those stories whether it is a simplistic desire to avoid hell, a spark of interest in learning more about how to live a wholesome life, or the generation of bodhichitta through becoming immersed in the story.

From the psychological aspect of the mythological reference, we can hear the stories and apply them to our state of mind but also as a guide to how our lives progress through the phases of life. We might look at all six of the realms and think of it as a roadmap for how we would like to be reborn, or as cautionary tale of how to avoid the allure of these realms in order to focus our attention on our compassion and desire for awakening.

Anger is the hallmark of the hell realm and it certainly touches the personal and social aspects of human existence. We cannot turn on the television today without seeing examples of anger, often times a kind of righteous anger where a character in a show is abused or is trying to fight for justice and the culmination of that story is violence against the bad guy which is meant to have the audience cheer. In politics, politicians who blatantly know that they are distorting the truth or even outright lying, do so with the knowledge that the only thing that matters is rousing the emotions of the people they want to vote for or donate to them. And many people play their part very well, furiously screaming at their opponents, not letting the other side have a word. Understanding is not needed or wanted; only victory. Religion too, has its warriors wanting to fight off demons; believing that if only they can muster enough anger, they will be safe from the onslaught that may steal their very soul. Anyone who disagrees with their point of view is seen as in league with the devil and they must be stopped.

How do we work with anger, especially those of us for whom anger comes quickly to our emotions? Shantideva has many verses regarding anger, making us wonder if he struggled with his anger as well. In his verses, he recommends working with patience when we have angry feelings. He notes quite correctly that it would be foolish to be angry with a fire for being hot or angry with the sky when clouds cover it, so why do we get angry with people who, in their ignorance, do bad things? Why do we get angry with people who we believe should know better, do something foolish? It would be like spending your day screaming at a fire that it must change or huffing and puffing at the sky to clear the clouds away.

When we get upset with our friend or child who we know has a good heart and good intentions, but they have messed up, it would be like saying to them how angry we are with them for covering up their basic goodness, so they had better shape up. It is only partly a joke when I say that if only people would just follow the rules and get their acts together then my life would be perfect! But that really is not the case. As is true in the hell realm, there would be some other slight or new rule that I would create that others would fall short of because the unhappiness does not come from the other person not being perfect. Shantideva says: "the causes of happiness sometimes occur, but the causes of suffering are very many. Without suffering there is no renunciation. Therefore, mind, you should stand firm." And in a verse that I just hate: "Whatever wholesome deeds, such as venerating the Buddhas and generosity that have been amassed over a thousand eons will all be destroyed in one moment of anger." How unfair! Yet how typical of the hell realm to feel angry when confronted with how damaging this realm is to the mind and spirit. There is an old joke that seems the perfect hell realm answer to Shantideva's practice of patience: "Lord, grant me patience, and I want it right now!"

Thich Nhat Hanh also has advice for how to work with anger. Nhat Hanh is no stranger to the destruction that anger can cause. Living in Vietnam during the war, he witnessed firsthand a number of violent acts of war, both during fighting as well as the actions of soldiers on both sides. When he heard about the bombing of Ben Tre he also heard that a military officer had made the statement that "We had to destroy the town in order to save it." Nhat Hanh felt the rise of terrible anger within himself at such a horrific act and even more horrible statement and knew that he had to come back to himself to look deeply at this feeling and find his inner peace again. He wrote this poem:

For Warmth:
I hold my face in my two hands.
No, I am not crying.
I hold my face in my two hands
to keep the loneliness warm -
two hands protecting,
two hands nourishing,
two hands preventing
my soul from leaving me
in anger.

He talks about the dangers of stuffing our anger or venting it, even though it seems that venting is popular advice. A few years ago a friend of mine was our bereavement manager and she would do a number of support groups for newly bereaved caregivers. She was explaining to them how important it is to vent their feelings in an appropriate way. To illustrate, she picked up a tissue box and threw it across the room meaning to hit the opposite wall. Instead, she missed and hit one of the participants. The person was not hurt and took the incident in stride, but she was very upset with herself and came to talk with me about it. I mentioned that there really is a third way, a middle way, to look at dealing with our anger. The idea is that we can hold our anger like a crying baby and be with our anger.

The analogy can also be that we cannot eat too much raw potato without feeling sick so we have to boil the potatoes for at least twenty minutes so that they are soft and ready to eat. If we can sit with our anger like a boiling potato for twenty minutes, we may be able to actually see it for the first time. When we try to settle down and push it away, stuff it down in frustration, or vent it by punching a pillow or screaming we never give ourselves the opportunity to see what the anger is really trying to tell us. My opinion and in my experience, anger is a wrap around emotion.

When I feel myself enraged at what I see as injustice in the world, to my family, or to myself I sometimes have a hard time understanding what is making me so mad. My blood is boiling and breaking the crockery out on the driveway seems like such a great release, but when I start trying to analyze what is really going on with me it is very hard to think it through intellectually. Anger becomes like a protective shield, preventing me from really looking at the wounded seeds that are being watered by the thing that I believe has gone so terribly wrong.

In Nhat Hanh's Fourteen Mindfulness Training, which are the vows that one takes to become ordained in the Order of Interbeing, there is a specific vow regarding anger: "6) Dealing with Anger: Aware that anger blocks communication and creates suffering, I am determined to take care of the energy of anger when it arises and to recognize and transform the seeds of anger that lie deep in my consciousness. When anger comes up, I am determined not to do or say anything, but to practice mindful breathing or mindful walking and acknowledge, embrace, and look deeply into my anger. I will learn to look with the eyes of compassion on those I think are the cause of my anger." This is a powerful vow for me to take. Because my father suffered with mental illness and one of the manifestations of his disorder was out-of-control anger, I find that habit energy within me as well. Even though I am generally very calm and take the ups and downs of life easily, I do let the irritations build up and often feel very angry especially at things I feel justified to be angry about.

Working with those feeling is a very important part of my practice. Identifying how I really feel is an important step. Instead of feeling angry about a stupid decision my company made, for instance, I can explore that in that circumstance what was really going on with me was a feeling of ambivalence with my career and what I should be doing with my life. I want to jump up and fix the problem, but my role is not about fixing that specific problem. I might passionately defend my point of view when that might be my way of venting anger and better might be to allow the people involved deal with the situation either to my liking or not. Living in the hell and animal realms is tough – an angry control freak! Luckily, I get to visit the other realms as well.

Instead, we can learn to deal with our anger more effectively. When working with anger in our closest relationships, Nhat Hanh recommends expressing our anger wisely. We can develop good communication skills with our loved ones to let them know that we are suffering in our anger, that we are doing our best to take care of our anger, and we need their help and support. You are being truthful with each other and being mindful of the way you express your feelings. Hearing someone out is a wonderful way to be fully present with them, but being on the receiving end of someone spilling their guts all over you is rarely fun or fruitful. When my partner, Matt, and I have a problem that we need to talk over, especially is one or both of us in angry, we have agreed not to talk until we have gone into the meditation room and sat for the length of an incense stick. This gives us a chance to sit with our feelings and look deeply at them. It also gives us a chance to remember that we can be Bodhisattvas to each other, going into hell to save ourselves from our anger.

While hell seems the most forbidding and worst of the realms, there has been a Bodhisattva who went into hell to save beings there. There are a number of variations of this story, and the story is an excellent example of a mythic journey. The Bodhisattva Ksitigarbha (Skt) or Dia Tang Voung in Vietnamese is the story of a monk who was troubled when his mother died, fearing that she was in hell because of her past deeds. He passes through hell and finds his mother, freeing her through offering merit on her behalf. Traditionally, he is portrayed in a simple monk's robe, holding an orb of light, and carrying a staff with rings to warn small animals of his approach so they will not be accidentally harmed. He feels great compassion for the beings he sees in hell and vows to relieve their suffering and liberate them. Because of his filial piety, he is revered in many Mahayana schools, and in Vietnamese Buddhist temples, his name is praised alongside Quan The Am, Manjushri, and Samantabhadra. He is not the only one to attempt to penetrate the fires of hell, of course. In Greek mythology, Orpheus goes into hell to find his wife Eurydice and bring her back to Earth, but he is unsuccessful.

I have been fascinated by this story for some time now because I find anger to be a potent emotion in me and have looked for ways to cool those flames. It seems not only comforting to think of a compassionate being with a light to illuminate the way out of hell, but also the inspiration to help others. One of the characteristics of hell is that the feeling of anger is so overwhelming that the beings push away any attempt to give love, kindness, or the cool relief of compassion. For the angry, the tendency is to kill the offenders whether figuratively or literally in an overpowering feeling of righteousness and judgment. Chögyam Trungpa explains that the more you kill, the more you strengthen the killer who will create new things to be killed. The irony is lost on those of us in anger's grip. So what would a modern story of Dia Tang Voung be like?

The movie adaptation of the book "What Dreams May Come," may not have been inspired by the story of Dia Tang Voung, but the film can be watched with Buddhist eyes bringing the story to life in a modern way. The title of the film is from Hamlet's soliloquy "For in that sleep of death what dreams may come When we have shuffled off this mortal coil..." (Hamlet, Act III, Sc. I) when Hamlet is contemplating the choice between life and death.

In the story, a shy young man named Chris falls in love with a beautiful young woman named Annie who is a spontaneous, lively, and talented artist. They make a life together and have two children who help provide life's ups and downs. Tragedy strikes when the children are killed in a car crash, and Annie blames herself because she sent them to school with the nanny driving so she would have more time to finish some work. She has to be institutionalized because she attempts suicide, and struggles with a deep depression. Chris tries to be strong for her, but she instead desperately wants him to join her in the depth of her feelings, saying "sometimes when you win, you lose." He had begun to lose hope that she would ever recover and goes to the hospital with a one way plane ticket and divorce papers, but they reconcile after committing to each other that they would never give up.

Annie recovers and goes back to work, but is still emotionally fragile. Chris often uses his knowledge of art and his love of her art to reach and calm her. They have plans to meet for dinner, but Annie calls in a panic over an art installation at the gallery and needs Chris to run home to retrieve a painting for her. On the way to the gallery, Chris is killed in a car crash. From Chris's point of view, he is still living on earth and is confused why people cannot see him and why time seems to be jumping erratically. He is beginning to see a person that he thinks he might know and is trying to communicate with him, but who seems to be made of light and is difficult for him to make out or understand. In Pure Land Buddhism, we are taught that in the levels of attaining Buddhahood, we have a step after the Arhat phase where we are born into a lotus of light. This is a circle of light of the Amitabha Buddha to protect us as we continue to practice so we will be able to see in the rarified light of the Pure Land.

Chris is having trouble learning to see with new eyes. He finally realizes that he is not doing himself or her any good and wakes up to a new plane of existence – one where his favorite paintings have come literally to life! He squeezes a flower and finds a handful of bright blue paint, he watches a bird swim through a sea of sky, and makes new vistas with a wave of his hand. The Pure Land with its glowing flowers, singing birds, and magical lands is there in all its splendor. Replacing the Bodhisattvas walking mindfully and teaching the Dharma is his old mentor and friend, now young and vibrant again. This friend, Albert, is there to help the transition and explain what is happening to him. He tells Chris that where they are now, there is plenty of room for each person to have their own universe; that "thought is real, the physical is the illusion, ironic, huh?" This motif of their minds creating a universe is similar to teachings about the Pure Land and Amitabha Buddha being the whole universe; the Buddhakaya or Buddha nature. The Amitabha is the source of everything and the whole universe is our mind; the Amitabha is each of us.

Chris's Pure Land is based on his favorite paintings, but also the painting that Annie had done for him with their dream home and landscape. His thoughts drift to her and how lonely he feels without her. As he and Albert look on, a beautiful flowering tree appears. Albert believes that Chris and Annie still have a connection even beyond the barrier of life and death. But the tree begins to fade and streaks of paint obscure its form: Annie has destroyed the painting in her desperation that Chris can never see her work again.

Annie cannot cope with what her life has become and kills herself. Albert tells Chris about this, and Chris assumes that he and Annie can now be together again. Albert explains that this is not possible because Annie is now in hell. This enrages Chris; how can this be just or compassionate? Albert tells Chris that it is not a judgment but a state of mind that Annie has created and cannot escape. There may be a person who can help, though: a tracker. They meet the tracker who agrees to take Chris on a boat ride through the canals bordering the lands to hell and explains along the way that Annie has created a hell for herself and because she cannot imagine anything else, she cannot see the reality of her death. He explains that Annie will not recognize Chris because "her denial is stronger than her love, in fact, it's reinforced by it."

This illustrates the hell realm where everything is seen as a cause of anger. The denial we are in when we are enraged is very strong, so strong that often we cannot see that the person we believe is so strong and ready to hurt us is filled with suffering themselves. Even when someone tries to help us, we push them away because we feel it is "too little, too late!" We feel that we were abandoned and neglected, so any attempt to reach out is seen as an affront. We are doing just fine, thank you, and do not need anyone. This feeling of both isolation and bombardment leaves the nerves raw. Like burned skin, even a cool breeze is painful. When anger becomes too powerful, we may plunge into depression where the anger can be buried deeply.

Chris finally finds Annie, but as predicted, she does not recognize her husband, instead she apologizes for the mess in her house, confused because her things seem to be fading away and only debris and spiders, which she fears, remain. Chris attempts to keep talking to Annie, but she tells him to go away, after all, she is the one who killed her wonderful children and sweet husband and that is unforgivable. Instead of trying to talk her out of her point of view, he tells her their story as though it was the story of two strangers. She agrees that the story was romantic, but since the woman committed suicide, she "gave up;" something that her husband would not approve. Chris realizes then that he had not dealt with the deaths of his children and the suffering of his wife and says to her "He was a coward! Being strong, not giving up, it was just his place to hide.

He pushed away the pain so hard he disconnected himself from the person he loved most. Sometimes when you win, you lose." When we approach our suffering and our anger from a Buddhist point of view, we learn that we should neither suppress nor express our anger. As Thich Nhat Hanh so eloquently explains, we need to treat our anger as an emergency. Like a loving mother who comes to the side of her crying baby, holding it tenderly, to be with it without judgment. We hold the feeling to allow it to soften so we can look deeply at our pain. Then we can look at the causes of our intense feeling. Only then can we have insight into the roots of our suffering and transform the pain.

At that point, Chris decides to join Annie in her hell, surrendering his sanity. Like the romanticized story of Nietzsche choosing to go mad; to dive into the abyss, when he saw the horse being flogged and rushed to save it mirroring the story of Zarathustra in Zoroastrianism. Annie awakens then to the truth of who he is and calls out to him. They flash to their "heaven" and are sitting on the porch of their dream home. The smile at each other and she says "sometimes when you lose, you win." By surrendering to their suffering and pain, they were able to see it for what it really was and awaken to the reality of their true nature. They were able to be bodhisattvas to each other, saving each other and themselves.

At the end of the movie, they make the decision to return for a human rebirth so they can both work through their mistakes and have the joy of finding each other again. They have a reunion with their children who bid them well on their new adventure, their return just a blink of an eye in time. The final scene is of a boy and a girl meeting beside a fountain laughing as he offers to share a toy boat with her.

While not a perfect representation of the Buddha Dharma, the movie is filled with similar motifs and certainly stunning visuals that we can imagine might be what some of these realms would look like if we had the eyes to see them.

Nam Mo Dia Tang Voung Bo Tat!

CHAPTER 8

Immeasurables & Paramitas

The Foundation of Buddhist Thought is a series of six books by Geshe Tashi Tsering. All of the volumes are excellent, and highly recommended for one's personal library. This class focused on volume three of that series "Buddhist Psychology." While it is certainly a strength of Western Psychology and thinking to rely on logic and reasoning, Geshe Tashi Tsering emphasizes that Buddhism approaches reality with reason hand-in-hand with compassion. So, while we must have a knowledge perspective, there must be a practice parallel - a process for developing a good heart.

The Four Immeasurables

The Four Immeasurable Minds are my favorite teaching - I've really been looking forward to this course! The practices of the 4IMs have made a big difference in my life. When I first read about them, I thought they were more like the Greek philosopher's ideas on the kinds of love, and I guess they are like that a bit. But I see the Buddhist way of looking at the aspects of love to be less emotionally driven and more about the deep potential we have for realizing that our nature is love. To be love, not just to feel love.

The 4 are love, compassion, joy, and equanimity. Joy was the one that I have had the most trouble with and yet has been the most helpful to me as I've studied and practiced. To look for or cultivate joy seems like a selfish thing to do. Having difficulties in life made it tough to believe that joy is anything but a fleeting thing, and emotion that comes and goes. Yet, through these practices I've been able to see that cultivating true joy is a very valuable thing. My Dharma name is translated True Joy in Peace and my teachers Dharma talk for me was about finding true joy in inner peace.

What I also found so helpful is seeing the sympathetic aspect to joy, meaning that finding joy in the happiness of others is a valuable practice. Because I didn't have the best relationship with my parents, I felt envious of others that did have a great relationship and very sad with a sense of emptiness because that kind of love wasn't there for me. It seemed that there was a wound there that I could never heal. How could I heal it when my parents were too damaged to be able to help me? What I learned through cultivating sympathetic joy was, perhaps a bit of living vicariously at first, then listening and empathizing with their happiness, but finally realizing that the appreciation and gratitude that there is that kind of love and connection in the world helps me see that emptiness removes the barriers - not only am I "empty" of everything, I'm also "full" of everything.

I can have it all because all is within me.

These are practices that the Buddha taught in the Metta Sutta (discourse on love) and we learn that by practicing the 4IMs in ourselves, love grows and begins to spread out to our family and loved ones, to our friends and acquaintances, to our culture, to our enemies, to the whole world. Many lineages of Buddhism practice chanting a variety of themes on "may all beings be happy and safe, may their hearts be filled with joy" as a practice to cultivate love. When our hearts fill with love, we can't help but feel love for others. Love and reaching out to help others is the fruit of the practice.

The fruit of the practice is an important point since if we simply sit and imagine sending love to the world it's like imagining that our love is a cloud floating over the whole world. A real cloud produces rain, so we need to recognize the fruit of our practice by seeing if our mind of love is there when we're around others.

I'm working with the Shantideva instructions right now looking toward taking Bodhisattva vows and he talks a lot about looking deeply at our anger and the suffering that prevents true love from flowering and bearing fruit. When bodhichitta is generated in us, the desire to help others, the energy of love arises. Our consciousness is permeated by love. As we practice, we become love - not an ideal or concept, but our true being.

The Pure Land teacher that I'm working with always laughs when I talk about my desire to help others. He talks about being surrounded by jewels and brilliant flowers and the most beautiful animals and birds. We're all surrounded by this beauty, so what good is it to help - as though I am offering a jewel to someone sitting on a mountain of them. To really help, I need to do nothing - to cultivate the equanimity to sit with stability and deeply listen. My presence is the gift, giving the other person the opportunity to see the jewels they're already surrounded by.

Oh, and on a more practical note, the *Anguttaa Nikaya* claims that there are a list of eleven advantages to practicing the 4IMs and the first one is that the practitioner sleeps well! If I had fewer cats, I'd probably sleep better too, but it is one of those things that remind me that if I'm waking up thinking or worrying that I need to work on metta meditation.

Rejoicing

Rejoicing could be considered the principle practice of the Bodhisattva. We cultivate those things that we rejoice - in quality circles, we say "celebrate what you want to see more of" - and this is really the key to understanding merit, in my way of thinking. When we gain merit, it's that we're practicing a way of being and thinking as opposed to some cosmic bank account. We share in the energy of someone who has cultivated their wholesome seeds, we're watering our own wholesome seeds. When we, for instance, invite the seed of jealousy not to grow by looking deeply at its cause, we can then turn our gaze to others who are successful and allow their energy to support us. This can be challenging some (a lot!) of the time, since we have so many issues to deal with when we look at society comparing people to some ideal, advertising telling us we're not good enough unless we buy this or that, and our own insecurities telling us we don't measure up. We may have grief at the losses in our life and when we see others who don't seem to have those same losses, we may feel despondent. When we see the virtues of others as something that we all share and as a help to us, we can turn those feelings of loss into the feelings of support we actually long for. At least that's how I've felt about that at many points in my life.

Dedication of merit was something that I thought for many years was just part of the superstitions and cultural trappings of Buddhism and nothing I would be interested in. But especially in attending a Vietnamese Buddhist temple, I've discovered that there is more to it than that. I look at merit as the fruits of cultivating my inner garden. I've mentioned before that while I can't make a strawberry, I can grow a strawberry plant. It's the practice that grows the plant, and the practice produces the fruit. The quality of the practice produces the quality of the fruit. So if I'm cultivating a beautiful garden, I'll have plenty of fruit to share with my friends and neighbors. If you've ever grown zucchini, you'll know that you want lots of friends, neighbors, passersby, and co-workers to give them to! There's just so many loaves of zucchini bread and so much ratatouille that one person can eat!

When we take refuge in the triple gem at temple, it is always followed by a dedication of merit to all beings. One of the most wonderful teachings I've ever heard was about that. The teaching was that we're all sitting in a beautiful field of gems, brilliant flowers, lovely birds, and wonderful foods. What do I need to give you if you too are sitting in this Pure Land? I can give you the one true thing; my presence. That, in all its component parts to help us learn, is the merit I can give.

The Paramitas

Paramita means "perfection" and they are practice instructions in different aspects of our lives. According to Thich Nhat Hanh, the Chinese character for paramita means "crossing over to the other shore" reminding us that we can use these practices to overcome our suffering and become liberated. We use the paramitas to plant seeds within us and to cultivate our inner garden. A quote from the Buddha in Thich Nhat Hahn's book "Heart of the Buddha's Teachings" that I really like is: "Don't just hope for the other shore to come to you. If you want to cross over to the other shore, the shore of safety, well-being, non-fear, and non-anger, you have to swim or row across. You have to make an effort." It's a good reminder that no one can give us the paramitas or awakening, we must take the journey ourselves, grateful for the wisdom and guidance of wonderful teachers, but it is our own choice and our own effort that we open our eyes.

Dana Paramita is the first teaching in the Buddha's gradual teaching method. When the Buddha went to a new area, he usually taught about the merits of Dana before talking about the Four Noble Truths. He told people that they should be generous and it was a good thing to feel good about help-ing others. Feeling good about being generous leads a person to have a pos-itive association with a wholesome way of living. As we develop these wholesome habits, we want to learn more about the path, and even if we just stop there, it makes the world we live in a better place. Awakening is the culmination of a gradual progression of training; the mind must make this progress to become ripe for the moment of awakening. Access to Insight has a very good section talking about the Buddha's six step teaching method. Dana is the first step. The sutras talk about the benefits of Dana and the aspects of being selfish that harm us. But the bottom line of giving is that we receive what we give. Most important is to see that the true gifts we have to give are our stability, presence, understanding, compassion, and love.

The sutras describe many different aspects of giving and receiving, dis-cussing the types of offerings (possessions, sharing the Dharma, and shelter), the types of consciousness of the giver and the people we give to, and the types of motivation we have when we give. The types of Dana can also be divided into what we give to a deserving person, an emotional or passionate gift, and giving that is forced or mandated in some way.

Most importantly, we should give without expectation of reward; that we should give with no strings attached. We're giving for the sake of doing well for someone else, not for our own sake. We can also look at the factors for the amount of merit gained from Dana, namely the motivation we have when we give, the consciousness or deservedness of the recipient (I always think of the phrase "don't caste pearls before swine" when I read about this aspect), and the kind and size of the gift.

Now, if we read this superficially it might seem like just another charity event from the society pages of the newspaper where people find pathetic children to gift large gifts to more to show how rich and noble they are than to really help. But when we look closer at what the Buddha is showing us to cultivate, we see that we need to cultivate a motivation that is "pure" mean-ing that we're listening deeply to what the person wants and needs not giving from our own agenda. We might see someone crying and in distress and try to comfort them, wanting to hug them or give them something. But if what we're trying to offer isn't what is needed to help, we're just doing something that is helping ourselves avoid the discomfort we feel at their pain. When we listen deeply, we find what will help the person most and do that. It seem cold hearted to consider if the person we're trying to help deserves our help, but I think the Buddha is really talking about looking deeply again.

Of course if someone is bleeding in the street, we offer aide and get them to the hospital without any regard to how or why they get into that situation. On the other hand, if a person is having a hard time coping with some problem and we try to help them by listening and sharing the teachings with them, but they won't listen or reject our help, then we really need to find the stability to leave them alone. Continuing to push will only do more harm. I used to think that to listen deeply I had to be a doormat and listen and listen and listen to the same story over and over and over.

But then I realized that listening and talking mindfully is a two way street. Part of the problem in my first marriage was that we did a lot of talking and I felt I did a lot of listening, but it was the talking part that was the problem. We weren't deeply looking at our own issues and problems and talking from that insight, only saying the same things over and over. When we look at the aspect of the size of the offering, I think it's more about proportionality. To me, when I've received a small gift that was clearly something that the person thought about and was very much from the heart, it was far more meaningful and precious than a large gift that seemed more about making an impression or by obligation than a symbol of caring and love. I think that the same can be said for donations, charity work, volunteering, or interactions with friends and family. When we know someone is in need or hurting, bringing the paper and taking over a meal might be a pure offering while making a big donation to however worthy a cause to get our picture in the paper could ever be.

There are so many things that hold us back from giving. Sometimes we're so wrapped up in our own pain that it's hard to cut through all the layers to see what someone else might need. Giving and receiving is really the same thing when done in the way the Buddha teaches, but when often times giving and receiving becomes a game of one-ups-man-ship and the receiver becomes "less than" the giver. When there is inequality between the two, the gift is not really a gift, but a move in the game. And sometimes our insecurities prevent us from reaching out for fear of looking silly or getting trapped in a cycle that is unhealthy.

Loving-kindness really is the key, isn't it? Learning to be still and listen is hard work, yet it's the only way to really help - often it's simply the act of listening that helps the most. I also like that you recognize that aspect of putting our aspirations into action. I'm working to put my money where my mouth is, too and finding it challenging and a wonderful instruction for where I need work. One of my patients that I'm visiting in my chaplain training has dementia, so she can't talk too much and what she says doesn't make a lot of sense, but she really wants company. She's become such a good teacher in sitting with someone in stability. Now when I sit every day, I think about that I'm working on a skill that will help her and I find the practice infused with more focus. After all, if it was just for me, what difference does it make if my mind wanders or if I'm thinking about what to have for dinner – I can kind of kid myself that what I'm doing is worthwhile.

Patience

Kshanti paramita is commonly referred to as the perfection of patience. Kshanti can also be translated as forbearance or inclusiveness. Like the old saying "Lord grant me patience and I want it right now!" patience is something that we know is a good thing, but it can be a challenge to cultivate. After all, we need to be patient with ourselves as we develop patience. When we start looking at what the Buddha meant by patience, we find that we're looking at the concept of non-discrimination and developing a big heart. One of the images I really like is the example the Buddha gave of pouring a handful of salt into a glass of water making the water in the glass too salty to drink. But if we pour the same amount of salt into the river, the water can take the salt and the river has the capacity to receive that salt and we can still drink from it (ok, we're talking 2,600 years ago here – rivers were safe to drink from back then!). When we can cultivate a big heart, those slings and arrows don't make us suffer because we have the capacity to include even those hurts with understanding and love.

The three types of Kshanti are to practice patience toward those who would do us harm, those unavoidable day-to-day issues that can be such a fly in the ointment of life, and the acceptance of the teachings. All three of these are very important to cultivate.

In working with these in daily life, the most obvious one is about the harms inflicted; kind of the big ticket item. When we have been harmed by someone or suffer an injustice, we initially want to figure out how to retaliate or get even. Or if we feel powerless, we might feel that we're a doormat to others who are more powerful and dominant so we tolerate the behavior, thinking that it's the only way to get along. Instead, we're encouraged to develop equanimity and love so that we have a heart that can include even the things that we disagree with, understanding the suffering of the other person. We learn not to take the bad things personally, but we also need to remember to watch out for taking the compliments too personally either.

We can be lead astray in our practice of patience when we take to heart those comments that we agree with and go down the garden path of building up our own ego. In developing equanimity, it may seem that we're becoming more aloof, but in reality, we're bringing people closer to our hearts. When we get angry because someone is doing something we don't like or that hinders us, we kind of objectifying that person, thinking of them as a roadblock to what we want. Likewise if the person is complimentary or blowing smoke up our skirts, we like them because they're inflating our sense of worth. If we can begin to see people for who they really are instead of cogs in the machinery of making me happy, we can realize others have the same desire for happiness although they may not realize that their unwholesome actions are making matters worse for themselves, not better. So when we, who have access to these tools and instructions, put them to good use, we learn that we can not only tolerate the other person's actions, we can actually, as Geshe Tashi Tsering says in his book "Buddhist Psychology," offer the other person victory in the sense that we can help that person, helping them to become happy. Shantideva writes: "The victorious warriors are those who, having disregarded all suffering, vanquish the foes of hatred and so forth; common warriors slay only corpses."

The day to day annoyances are also important to work with and they're actually very handy as a practice tool since they are right at hand. We often hear that the reason we are encouraged to come back to the breath in meditation is because it's so omnipresent, it's right there at the tip of our nose. Those petty annoyances are just as omnipresent, aren't they? Sometimes I think those little flies buzzing around are Quan Yin herself teasing us "does this bug you? Does this bug you? Does this bug you? I'm not touching you.."

I've found that when I find myself bugged by the buzzing flies, the long line in the market, the crazy drivers it's actually because I'm lost in thought or distracted by my ideas, plans, to-do lists, and the rest. I'm not being mindful of what I'm doing and what is going on around me and I don't like being taken out of my "more important" thoughts. Working with those annoyances is less about being patient with them and more about being in the present and not judging how they will affect what I want, where I want to be (instead of where I actually am), or what my fantasy is about the future.

Acceptance of the teachings is a very important factor here since there are times that we're tempted to set aside a teaching as maybe provincial or not really relevant or that we just don't agree with. It's a good practice to listen to Dharma talks with this level of patience that we're listening to the words without looking to figure them out, to agree or disagree with them, or figuring out how to use them to our advantage. A common way of expressing this is allowing the Dharma to be like rain that falls on our heart, our inner garden. We allow the words to fall gently, soaking in, and patiently waiting for the fruits of the wisdom and our practice to bloom.

This one is a tough one in my daily life – and I'm actually pretty patient! The issue I wind up getting stuck on is that issue of justice. I tend to look at the right and wrong of a situation, often frustrated with how simple things would be if people just followed the rules of the road – they're not hard or oppressive rules – just do it, dammit! Karma can be a sticking point here since it's easy to want to figure out the victim and the perpetrator and feel that it's unfair to look for my role in what is happening. But to think of karma as being some kind of divine justice is to have the misperception that there is some kind of divine guidance to it instead of the cause and effect that we're all subject to. We always have a role to play in the circumstances we find ourselves in, and being honest with ourselves helps us to penetrate the reasons why we find ourselves in situations, sometimes over and over until we (ok, until I) get the lesson through my thick skull. When I'm busy tallying the points of right and wrong, I'm not cultivating patience or equanimity, I'm fueling my own ego and sense of self righteousness. Going back to the breath is a great help when I'm sizing up a situation or other people; asking myself "Are you sure?" – advice from a Zen teacher of mine many years ago.

For me, the most specific practice around this paramita is looking deeply at the emotions that arise when I feel I've been wronged or insulted or judged unfairly. Shantideva talks about asking ourselves why would we be angry at fire for burning us since that is fire's nature, yet I stick my finger into the flame then curse that I got burned. When people treat us poorly or try to manipulate us, they are acting out of their ignorance. When I get angry or fall for their ploy then feel betrayed, I am acting out of ignorance too; so why do I think I'm so innocent and righteous? I'm being just as ignorant in my response. So, for me, patience is about sitting still while I look deeply at my feelings, discovering the roots of where that feeling comes from (it's never about what was said or done, but always some underlying issue) and penetrating that seed, inviting it not to grow even when watered. By cultivating this type of practice, my inner garden is healthier, helping those wholesome reactions to blossom and having less space for the weeds to grown.

Effort

Virya can be translated a few ways and the Virya paramita is often called the perfection of effort, but it can also be called the perfection of joyous effort or enthusiastic perseverance. Having grown up spending summers on the farm, this one has always made sense to me since I have something of a farmer personality. I can plow the rows all day long, unlike the folks with more of a hunter personality who flit from potential opportunity to the next wanting to find the elusive prey. Lots of people consider the fate of *Sisyphus* to be the worst possible fate. I look at the sun coming up every morning and the chores to be done and the grass growing despite being mowed as something comforting and good. On the other hand, the danger for someone like me is to turn practice into something rote. It's kind of like wondering on your way to work if you've remembered to turn off the coffee maker. You most likely did it, but because of thinking about other things while doing the morning routine, you didn't actually experience pushing the button. We also need this paramita to help us keep plowing the rows even when we don't feel like it. When the grass is cut over and over all summer long, it doesn't say "oh, what's the use!" and stop growing. We humans aren't so persistent; we tend to give up when we run into roadblocks. Working with this perfection helps keep us going.

One aspect can be translated as zeal, courage, or even joyfulness. I like all three words to compliment the second aspect of effort or perseverance. It's important to cultivate the inner energy to practice. One of the biggest misconceptions I had about this when I first started studying about it was that I would have to create this energy. Instead, I learned that this isn't something that we can create; it's something that we already have. We all have plenty of energy; it's how we direct that energy that this paramita asks us to consider.

I think about how much time and effort I put into something that I'm upset about, even to the point of being awake in the middle of the night and thinking about it with such passion and intensity for hours and hours. Then I have to ask myself why I don't bring the same level of intensity to practice. I'll sit and be distracted by every little noise or itch, sneak peeks at the clock, and think of excuses why I need to get up and do something else – that doesn't happen at all when I'm stewing over some issue. Instead what I need to do is work on redirecting this abundance of zeal to cultivating the wholesome seeds, strengthening those qualities so that even when the unwholesome, painful bija seeds are watered, my seeds of equanimity and compassion are stronger than the seeds of anger and instability.

We can question a couple of different issues – practice lethargy and the availability for practice. I think those are both important issues to address since they are things that come up for everyone.

It's interesting that sometimes when my practice seems to be in good shape that I think I'm actually in a kind of practice lethargy. Because I am a good farmer, I do have a good routine for practice and for awhile there, practice was nice and pleasant, but when I was being honest with myself I was just goofing off. That was a good hint that I was in a rut – it was a nice rut, but a rut none-the-less. I was kind of treating practice like a pleasant part of my routine instead of really being present with myself. In a sense, I had turned it into more of a little Disney film to enjoy as I started my day. The major thing that helped kick me in the pants was working with one of our hospice patients. His need for having someone who had a stable practice generated bodhichitta in me and helped re-energize my zeal for practice. The other thing that works in my favor is having a temple to go to. Even though there too can be a hazard of drifting off or just watching as though it was a nice TV program, having a practice center is a good reminder that helps me prevent too many days going by without a reminder to practice diligently.

Part two of the question is about finding time. This quarter has been a bear for me with time. I have a fairly demanding job, but one that I've done for a number of years now so it's not that stressful. However, I've found myself with additional responsibilities so that has added to the stress of learning how to manage and organize all that. I'm taking on the unit of CPE which turned out to be more work that I had imagined and I'm learning lots of new stuff there. There is our courses here and responsibilities at home and sometimes I wonder when I'll find the time to brush my teeth, let alone practice! I've found that being creative has helped bring practice into some unlikely places and helped with doing a better job with all of these things to do. Making an effort to focus on each task at hand is a good practice in mindfulness and it helps me learn better. Bringing chanting CDs and Dharma talks on the road with me help to realize that practice is life; that the flow of life is practice. My teacher teased me when during our time together I was explaining about all the hats I have to wear – "No hats! No hats! And in my case, no hair!" Rather than compartmentalize my life and who I'm showing up as, I'm working on taking the hats off and being my practice.

Meditation

Dhyana paramita is the perfection of meditation. This can also be translated as perfection of concentration. That's not a bad way to think of it really, but concentration is one part of it, not all of it. It's important for us to be able to explore our minds in a variety of ways. Because we're always distracted and restless, it's tough to concentrate. Because we become passionate and immersed in things, it's tough to stay focused on what is happening now. It's probably hard wired into us, whether farmer or hunter, to look for the new; to search for the next morsel of food; to jump at every noise wondering if it's a danger. The Buddha asks us to counter our instincts many times through the Dharma, and this is no different. Meditation is a challenge, but it is also a comfort to us and can help us through the troubled waters of life. I had to laugh when Jim talked about times on the cushion when you're feeling all comfy cozy and kind of ready to doze off as a kind of subtle torpor that we have to work through. Last assignment I mentioned that very habit that I've had; my meditation room is like my secret garden and I have to guard against using it like a warm blanket too often. Meditation really is work; it's the homework given to us by the Buddha himself. It's the best kind of work though; work that has the potential to be joyous as we do it and it cultivates our minds to bear the fruit of awakening.

The two kinds of meditation are shamatha and vipashyana and there are many different types, techniques, and varieties of these available to help us learn these two.

Shamatha is about stopping the mind. Here we learn to stabilize our minds and become mindful. We need this aspect of meditation not only to ready us for the insight of vipashyana, but to give our mind rest. When we chase our regrets of the past, chase the diversions of the present, and the worries and anticipation of the future, our minds sometimes feel like they are in a blender. Sometimes we delude ourselves, believing that we can't stop – after all, I have to keep the world spinning by being awake at 3 am worrying about all of the problems in the world! Shamatha lets us off the hook by showing us that we can stop, we can rest. A Dharma talk given at the last mini retreat I attended a couple of weeks ago was about "healing is possible through resting." What a wonderful permission to truly rest! So, while I had the idea that concentration was this serious effort that I would have to furrow my brow and concentrate until my head hurt, the reality is that the focus of mindfulness actually calms our minds, allowing us to live each moment of our lives deeply.

Vipashyana is about the insight which leads to wisdom. When we practice vipashyana, we look deeply into things to understand their true nature. When we've developed the calm abiding of shamatha meditation, we have far more space to look deeply into how we feel, why we suffer, and the development of those wholesome bija seeds that we aspire to. In some respects insight is about thinking through what is happening to us or what is bothering us; using our intellect to analyze things, but if we're merely problem solving we can only go so far. More important is learning to look deeply at those seeds and aspect of ourselves whether wholesome or unwholesome – after all, we want not only to invite the unwholesome seeds not to grow but to cultivate the wholesome seeds to produce a beautiful inner garden. A very important teaching for me is the understanding of what looking deeply is about. I still struggle with this since I'm something of a natural problem solver, but it was so helpful when it was explained to me that we can use the three dharma seals to look deeply at things. When we use the keys of impermanence and no-self in all things, we can begin to unlock the true nature of our thoughts, the things that happen, and our suffering. When we look deeply into ourselves with the eyes of Nirvana – emptiness – that understanding generates deep love and compassion.

Prajna Paramita is the perfection of wisdom. There is a huge body of work dealing with the Prajna Paramita; the Diamond Sutra, the Heart Sutra, and numerous discourses and other sutras that help us understand prajna paramita. We can also look at prajna paramita as "Right View." This is the paramita that helps us to let go of our discriminating mind, our concepts, and our attachments. When we have right view and see the world through the eyes of prajna paramita, everything is "nirvanized;" we look deeply and see that the true nature of all things is emptiness and we can touch the Suchness of reality. This is a core teaching of the Heart Sutra that we don't have to attain Nirvana; we are always dwelling in Nirvana. When we have touched the ground of our being, our fear vanishes. When fear vanishes, there is no more room for suffering.

The two aspects of Prajna are relative and ultimate prajna. In relative wisdom, we have knowledge of the world and that's a good thing. We can learn a lot of valuable things and live a very good life through our worldly wisdom. We learn about the dharma through relative wisdom and that can help us set the stage for the deeper wisdom of the ultimate dimension. We can separate ultimate wisdom into stages of transcendence; "lesser" and the highest transcendent wisdom. In the lesser stage, we have a gnosis or knowing of the reality of the three Dharma seals and practice all six paramitas as an integrated whole. We are still operating, however, from duality. Granted it is from a positive point of view and we're working to ease the burden of suffering from all beings.

When we perfect wisdom to the highest transcendent wisdom, we transcend duality; the pure essence of Madhyamika. At this point, we transcend our desire to help. The image I love in understanding this is from the Pure Land tradition. In the Pure Land, we are surrounded by beautiful flowers, glowing gems, lovely birds flying through the air singing their songs, and

Dharma teachers walking mindfully to give their talks. Imagine being in this amazing place and seeing everyone else there equally at peace and surrounded by everything they could ever need. If you saw someone sitting in a pile of gems, what use would they have of you handing them a gem? So what can you give that person? You can give your full presence with stability, compassion, and love – your authentic, transcendent nature – the only true gift. When we see that truth, it puts our helping into a new perspective because we're seeing reality as it truly is.

Wisdom

The six Paramitas are a teaching that provides guidance to us for how to live our lives and, on a deeper level, demonstrates the awakened mind. The definition of the word paramita is "perfection" or "perfect realization." The Chinese character for paramita is translated as "crossing over to the other shore." While this sounds daunting and not something a normal person can achieve, when we feel suffering, we cannot help but turn toward the paramitas and wonder if it might help. When we have that spark of curiosity and desire, we have a roadmap that the Buddha gives us, but does not carry us on. The Buddha said: "Don't just hope for the other shore to come to you. If you want to cross over to the other shore, the shore of safety, well-being, non-fear, and non-anger, you have to swim or row across. You have to make an effort." This effort is the practice of the six paramitas.

When the Buddha taught to a new community, he used a gradual teaching method (anupubbi-katha) that started with dana (generosity) and sila (virtue). Practicing giving, offering, and generosity benefits us in a practical way first by enhancing the way people view us, in gaining merit, and giving us a sense of self-satisfaction. It feels good to help others, and when we feel good about what we have done, we tend to repeat that. When the Buddha taught about dana, he taught specifically about what prevents us from giving freely. The source of miserliness is fear; we cling to things that are impermanent out of fear of lack, fear of being treated unfairly, and the ignorance of the inter-connectedness of all things. We are also given five precepts to practice for our cultivation of ethical behavior. While on one hand it would seem not to be such a great accomplishment to do good when you are required to do good, living an ethical life in alignment with the precepts gives a basis to a community that makes life for all of the members better, and would certainly make the world a better place, even if we went no further than that.

On a day to day level, the practice of generosity is one that we can participate in quite easily. We might think we have to make donations of money or volunteer in some big way to be generous, but we can actually be generous in simple ways as well. When a friend at work died after a short illness, we held a memorial to her at work. A few people spoke to remember her and one of the women there made a comment that really stuck with me. She talked about how much she wished she had said all the complimentary things she had just shared with us, with her, but now it was too late. One of the habits I developed after that was to compliment people when things happened, even if it was a simple as telling someone that it was great to see their smile this morning. It's not something that I have to cook up; it's just that I now say what I was already thinking.

Practicing the five precepts is something that everyone can do, even if imperfectly. The precepts can be a north star to guide us through the dark. Even if a precept does not seem to be that important, after all, what difference does it really make if I take a drink from time to time? I'm not an alcoholic and do not drink to intoxication, so why not. Yet, when I practice, I am not just practicing for myself, but practicing for everyone else as well. I can see the suffering caused by drinking alcohol, so my decision not to participate in that supports those who are trying to get out of alcohol's grip. When I was in grad school, I went to a cocktail party but I had taken the vows to uphold the five precepts, and our teacher instructed that we should not drink at all. So I had a glass of sparkling water with a slice of lime and that was that. I did not really think at that time that not drinking for anyone else was more than just a nice abstract idea. But a man I knew that had attended the party came up to me a day or two later and let me know that he had a drinking problem and had been very tempted at the party. When he saw me drinking water yet having a good time, he stopped himself from taking a drink and thought "if she can do it, I can do it." He wanted to thank me for support that I did not even realize I was giving. What a great gift he gave me that day.

When we have practiced this way for awhile, though, there is the potential to begin to get a glimpse of something deeper. When we think about the precepts, we might see that they have more to offer us than a set of rules.

When we explore the third paramita of patience, we begin to cultivate our capacity to receive, bear, and transform the pain we feel is inflicted upon us by others. As we practice patience, which is a good quality to have and certainly has its practical applications, we feel calmer and have more capacity for not only bearing our suffering but also to have patience for ourselves. We are not just being well suffered, but we begin to develop a quality of equanimity that we can apply to our own impatience with ourselves and also for others. We might just consider cutting the other person some slack, recognizing how hard it can be to do the right thing despite our best intentions.

Opportunities to practice patience happen lots of times every day. Just this past week, my computer at work got a particularly nasty malware virus and had to be wiped and reformatted. I had a lot to get done but I was determined to practice patience and worked on some projects that I had been putting off. I cleaned out filing cabinets, filling three wastebaskets with old stuff; scanned papers that I need to keep but do not want to store, and breathing and reminding myself to relax when I would start to get anxious about what was not getting done. The cleaning was nice, but not the priority for the day. Finally, the computer was done and back, but it was time for the NSE to go home.

As I was diving in to at least get one project done, I realized that I had the wrong software installed! I called home and vented about how upset I was, then admonished myself for not being patient, and considered how to break the glass of my office window to toss the computer out. Everyone else in the office had left for the day, so rather than continue to rant and rave, I turned off the computer, put my papers away, and walked mindfully around the office halls. I thought about the Shantideva instructions on anger and patience, and felt a kinship with so many people who suffer with having our sense of happiness shattered even by something that seems like it should be no big deal. I felt much better when I got back to my office so, rather than continuing to fight with the computer and try to make it do what I wanted, I closed up shop, got my things, and drove home. The next day, I got everything sorted and had a productive day.

Interestingly, those first three paramitas begin to feel connected; after all, feeling generous can also be to feel generous of spirit in forgiving someone for hurting us. As we practice the precepts and see that it can take a lot of patience to keep the precept on, say, right speech and in refraining from being critical or cruel back to someone when we give ourselves enough space to see that there is another side to the story. Within the third paramita are the tools for developing this patient inclusiveness in the form of the Four Immeasurable Minds. By practicing maître (love), karuna (compassion), mudita (joy), and upekkha (equanimity) we will cultivate a huge heart, one that has room for all of the ups and downs of life. We learn to be patient not only with people who are mean to us or treat us unfairly, but also with people who praise us. This one can be puzzling at first since we all like to be praised or agreed with, but sometimes we can find ourselves more rooted in our opinion and belief in self when we feel it is not just us who perceives a personal Self, but a supporting cast of characters who agree with how wonderful we are. The teachings can get really challenging when it comes to our desire to help, especially when the person we help may not appreciate what we have done for them or even return our kindness with harm. Shantideva teaches that we should practice treating that person as our holy guru, one who is helping us practice patience and humility.

At this point in our practice, it is a good idea to work with Virya, diligence. The energy that we put into the many pursuits of our life can be seen as a potential of energy that we can use in our practice. Instead of seeing practice as a warm blanket to sit with and daydream or a chore that we have to do, we can bring our energies to cultivating our inner garden by developing the wholesome mental factors. As we practice with diligence, we are developing not only our aspiration to give rise to the Four Immeasurables in our minds, but to bring them into the world through our words and actions. We must continue to practice until we are able to offer peace and love to others, not just as a thought experiment sending love through the ethers, but to offer true love to others even those who have harmed us or who do not understand us. We can develop the capacity to understand them and see them with the eyes of compassion.

Interestingly, I have heard people say that they skipped going to a meditation or other mindful event because they just did not feel they were in the right place for it, they were too upset, or just out of sorts so they would not benefit from the session. Those are the times we need to practice the most!

During times when I have felt anxious or worried about things I will sometimes find myself awake at three in the morning and beginning a litany of
worry that I will realize has looped itself and I have started again from the
beginning. There have been lots of nights when I just fight myself instead of
doing the sensible thing and getting up and getting on the cushion. The past
couple of years I have found it easier to do just that, though. A number of
years ago, I took the advice to make a small bedroom in my house into a
meditation room. It has been one of the best decisions I have made. Practice
has become something I look forward to and it feels that a safe space has
been created for my family in the meditation room. Each of us uses the room
and it is such a pleasure to hear the bell ring or smell a stick of incense during
the day; sometimes joining that person on my cushion. Even in the middle
of the night, there is a feeling that the energy of my family, the energy of the
Sangha, and the energy and support of the Buddha is there. It gives me the
courage to use that energy of worry, anxiety, or whatever other thing I give
my energy to is transformed into the energy of practice.

Each of the previous paramitas has specific instructions for what we
should do and the practice of them deepens our understanding. However, it
is with the fifth paramita, Dhyana (meditation) that gives us a way to look
deeply at each of them. We learn to focus and concentrate our minds in order
to have the capacity to look deeply at the nature of things to gain insight.
The other paramitas dovetail with dhyana in the direct practice and in giving
us the capacity to fulfill our aspiration to act on the instructions of the paramitas.

In our daily lives, it is important to practice and find a community of
practice to support us. On a day to day basis, we can develop a habit of
practice that can take a variety of forms; using the discipline of Virya we
can cultivate Dhyana through our practice. When I first started to meditate
and study Buddhism, I did not have a sangha to go to and did not even know
such a thing was possible anywhere near me. It was more difficult to keep
up a practice. When I found a teacher and had regular time to sit with others,
I realized how important a community of practice was. I moved away,
though, and thought it was a distant memory, until I started writing to a
friend and we agreed to practice at the same time each day, lighting a candle

to remember that shared energy and to help each other. Even when we practice by ourselves, we can discover that we are actually practicing with our friends, our larger community of practice, our ancestral teachers, and a wide world of people looking to find peace. Their support can bring a lot of energy into our efforts at focus and concentration. Each time we bring our best effort to our practice, we are supporting all of them, too.

In the Prajna (wisdom) Paramita, all of the others is brought together into a unified whole. This understanding is the fruit of our practice. When the Buddha taught that our miserliness is caused by fear and then toward the perfection of wisdom, we find that we cross over to shore of no birth and no death, receiving the gift of non-fear. As with all of the Buddha's teachings, there is a relative level that yields practical benefits to each of the paramitas. When we practice generosity on the relative level, we create an environment that is fulfilling for ourselves and others. When we practice ethics on the relative level, we create an environment that is just and fair for people and ourselves. When we practice patience on the relative level, we create a life that is kind and nurturing.

When we practice joyous effort on the relative level, we create an environment that is encouraging and positive for ourselves and others. When we practice meditation on the relative level, we create an environment that is calm and insightful. When we practice wisdom on the relative level, we interact with the world in a rational, thoughtful way. When we practice any of these or all of these paramitas with sincerity on the relative level, we begin to appreciate how rich we are inside.

We are cultivating a garden that is wholesome and positive on its face, but is also developing the fruit of wisdom. This fruit is not something we can make for ourselves, but something that is born of practice. When we perfect wisdom to the highest transcendent wisdom, we transcend duality; the pure essence of Madhyamika. As the paramitas become integrated into us, we see that there are no obstacles to our minds, everything is "Nirvanized" and we can touch the Suchness of reality.

CHAPTER 9

Agnostic Buddhism

The work of Stephen Batchelor is important for all students of Buddhism. For the student wishing to become a monk, nun, or chaplain, if they are Westerners, they will very likely have many of the same questions, doubts, and skepticism as Batchelor. Working through these questions is important for one's own spiritual formation, and equally important when working with students. Lay members of the Sangha may have read these books and want to discuss them, or even feel a crisis of faith when confronted with these questions and doubts.

Batchelor's books: "The Faith to Doubt: Glimpses of Buddhist Uncertainty," "The Agnostic Buddhist: A Secular View of Dharma Practice," and "Buddhism Without Beliefs: A Contemporary Guide to Awakening" were discussed in this course. In them, Batchelor is beginning a process of producing a kind of Jeffersonian Bible for Buddhism; and attempt at being able to identify and uncover Source Buddhism, unencumbered of cultural accretions and legends. What if we could jump into a time machine and hear the Buddha's words for ourselves? How much more valuable would a Dharma and practice be if it were pure and clear? Seem to be the questions Batchelor is asking. Asking ourselves these questions and exploring them in the context of our own world view is important for our own development, and even more important when working with others.

A Teacher's Death

For me, the most interesting in these chapters was the beautiful essay on his teacher's death and the experience of being there and witnessing the ritual of the cremation and everything that went along with it. I was envious of that experience, but grateful that he wrote about it in such detail that reading about it late at night, I felt I was there.

When my mother died, we drove up to Michigan from Florida. She had had a stroke and I didn't know what we would find when we got there; would she be in the hospital still, would she have begun to recover and be transferred back to the nursing home, or would she die before we arrived? It was late April; the weather in Florida was that of late spring/early summer. There were flowers in full bloom, but some had already started to fade. As we travelled, it was like we were going back in time – the flowers in the south were the light pinks and purples of spring with cooler breezes and bright blue skies. By the time we reached the Ohio valley, it was early spring with little redbuds starting to show on the trees; the sky paler and more grey. In Michigan, there were clumps of snow on the ground, only crocus and snowdrops starting to emerge and bloom.

At the hotel about half way there, my sister called to say Mom had died. In the car on the trip the next day, we played a CD I had brought that had the components of a Buddhist service, especially an offering of merit chant in English that I love. Driving through the hills the chant filled the car and brought an infinity of space into and around our grief. The morning we arrived we went straight to the funeral home to the viewing. My sister was feeling that it was all happening too fast, yet she was doing her best to follow mom's instructions, having the viewing right away and having the cremation as soon as possible. I brought a small rin gong with me and asked her if it was ok to ring it. The sound of the bell filled the funeral home and we all found a way to slow down as we followed the sound. We just sat quietly, holding hands for a few minutes.

Rather than a funeral pyre for a cremation, the process was more about there not being any fuss. When it was time for my sister and I to pick up the cremains, it was hard to find the address. We went to an industrial looking area of the town, but there weren't any signs to identify the building. When we did find it, it was like a big box of a building, with a huge open garage like area on one side. We picked up the box and drove to a nature park that mom had loved. We had to concoct our own ceremony, but scattering her ashes into the wind at a waterfall was beautiful and profound. The bell rang and the ashes sparkled as some of them blew off with the wind and some fell to the ground. I looked at the ground and wished I would be able to come back to see what would grow there by the end of the summer.

What a difference the utilitarian experience of cremation was and usually is here with the richness of the ritual in Korea. We did a pretty good job creating a space for our grief and to honor the time, but it would have been wonderful to have had a guide to bring it all together for us so we could have simply been with the mystery. And what a mystery it is. Taking a question like "Who am I?" when we think that all is well in the world and tragedies and problems are for tomorrow, then experiencing death in such a personal way then asking that question again. Sitting with it is never the same.

Critiques

In reading the books, listening to the media selections, and reading other articles about Stephen Batchelor including critiques of his ideas I found myself caught up in the drama of whether or not I agree with his concepts and approach or not. The more I think about this work, both the pros and the cons, the less I find myself interested in whether or not I agree or disagree or even what Batchelor appears to be trying to do. I am far more interested in his process and journey. One of Batchelor's aims appears to be to make Buddhism accessible and viable to Western audiences. This is an aim that many teachers have, whether they have come to the West or have been born in the West. Certainly, Batchelor is contributing to the formation of a Western Buddhism that is evolving however speedily or slowly as the proponents or critics of that contend.

When I took my first unit of Clinical Pastoral Education (CPE), our supervisor asked us to send him a bi-weekly reflection that would cover a list of topics that included how we were relating to our patients, our co-workers, fellow students, our supervisor, and with God. I changed that to "Triple Gem" on my template and my supervisor and I developed a valuable dialogue about how someone can have a relationship with Buddhism in general and how it was for me specifically. I grew to enjoy writing the reflections because I saw them as a journal of sorts for the development of how I was learning to relate to my patients, but it was also a useful spiritual journaling for how I saw my understanding of my journey in Buddhism to be developing. Taking classes at Prajna Institute of Buddhist Studies (PIBS) and participating in short retreats during the CPE unit factored in as I explored and worked at how I could become a Buddhist chaplain. Classes, retreats at Chua Bao An, intensive work with CPE, and interactions with patients who are dying and the family members grieving them became a crucible for my growth. My biggest concern was that I not mess up too badly for the sake of the patients I saw. Over the nine months, I saw personal growth as I confronted old habits, got more comfortable with being out of my comfort zone, deepened my appreciation for the Dharma, and realized that I want to be a chaplain who happens to be Buddhist rather than a Buddhist chaplain.

The reason I go into all that is that I would like to look at my own journey in Buddhism in the context of the personal journey that Mr. Batchelor shares with the people who read his books or attend his lectures. I do love to read or listen to material even when I am very familiar with the topic because I always find something new or a detail that I did not know before, making it always worthwhile. In this context, though, I am not as interested in what Mr. Batchelor has to teach about the Dharma (I have my root teacher who I always go back to as the touchstone, wonderful monks and nuns from my lineage who I learn from, and the most excellent teachers at PIBS for that) but rather, what he is teaching indirectly by looking at how he has come to his ideas. In one of the audio lectures he talks about deconstructing Buddhism, taking away all of the layers that have been placed on the basic teachings of the Tagathata and getting back to the root teachings. Rather than heading off to a Theravada temple, Batchelor decides to do the peeling back himself. Like doing a root cause analysis, he continues to ask why to get to the first cause of what Buddhism is trying to convey. One of my favorite sayings is that when we peel back all the layers of the onion, we are left with nothing and we are in tears – seems very Zen.

When I was doing my reflection notes, I found myself with a lot of information to funnel into these reflections. How did the relationships with co-workers as we planned the care for our patients, the interactions with the patients themselves, the work done in class or on the cushion relate to the most important work that I should be doing; that of waking up? I would write last about my relationship with the triple gem, and usually would end my reflection note with a quote that related or summed up the previous two weeks or what I was mulling over. My supervisor noted at one point that it was different for him to see the quotes at the end of the reflection. He said that usually, preachers would start with a quote or scripture and build from there. It occurred to me that my approach to Buddhism has been inductive as well. I realize that this drives bottom-liners crazy and my favorite illustration of this is explaining that if I were a restorer of find tapestries, I would not start work until I had examined the art of the tapestry, considered the construction, looked that the patterns in the reverse side of the work, the materials included, the history of who had created the work and who had worked on any previous restorations. The punch line is that bosses I have worked with would say "Cheryl, just repair the yellow beak on that little bird in the corner and get on with it!"

I was still a kid when I began deconstructing the Christianity I was introduced to and only expected to practice after I was about twelve years old. In my own version of a root cause analysis, I kept asking how people knew about the teachings of the Bible and Jesus; where did the information come from in the first place? The fine point on the analysis for me was that belief in God was no more credible than a fantasy character in any other kind of book. I had no falling out with Christianity, no beef with a god that was not fulfilling my needs; no upset at the knowledge of the evils people commit in the name of religion even. I was not angry with God and I did not believe that there was no God, I simply did not believe in God. I was always amazed that when I asked others to go through that straightforward process with me that they usually had no desire to go through all the steps; they put on the brakes much too early. Yet, I still had a desire to learn about what I could only call "spirituality" even though I knew that was not the right term. I would spend long hours in the library reading about lots of different topics; I wonder what my favorite librarian thought when I announced to her that I wanted to pick a religion, so I needed to research which one was the best. She always talked with me as though I was an adult and helped me learn how to find what I wanted to read, making suggestions that I always found helpful. Reading about Buddhism at that point planted a seed, even if it did not seem like the definitive answer yet.

I appreciate when Batchelor talks in the video about his quest to find answers to his questions and heads off to other countries and eventually finds himself as a monk without a sangha to support him. While not as dramatic, when I found a Zen teacher during college, I was convinced that Buddhist practice was the way I needed to follow. In the following years, I was sure that being a solo practitioner was not only good enough, but with books and workshops to attend I believed that my understanding was just as valid as the people who looked at Buddhism as a religion and simply went through what I saw as ritualistic motions. I was certain that they were deluding themselves and felt that it was far better to look at all of the great religions and Buddhist schools and find the right mixture of ideas that would crystallize into a new framework, free of the mythology of the past. I had all sorts of in-the-know words, went to New Agey workshops, took courses, made mandalas, and drank green tea. Even though I was totally wrong, it was a lot of fun and a good experience along the path. I learned a lot about myself. I also realized that I needed to get back to basics.

Batchelor talks about the simple fact that you do not have to be religious to practice the dharma – that is true and perfectly fine. However, I do not agree with him that supernatural or paranormal phenomena are the hallmarks of religion and that the only way to avoid that is the agnostic point of view. At the heart of agnosticism is acceptance of what we do not know and that is true of Buddhism as well. However, agnosticism posits that ultimate truths are not only not known to the person at this time, but that they are unknowable; that our ability to know is limited and we will always have an element of doubt. Buddhism takes a similar stance, then takes it deeper by exploring emptiness but deconstructing even that concept in the Diamond Sutra and then further explored in the rest of the Prajnaparamita Sutras which point to the reality that emptiness is not a concept at all.

To go back to basics, I did not really have the option of the Christian church because I did not have true roots there and I knew deep down that Buddhism was the right path for me. I decided that I needed to suspend all my skepticism and agnosticism and retrace my steps. I went on a twenty-one day retreat with the monk who would become my teacher and went with the intention of having an open mind, open ears, and an open heart. I took formal refuge at that retreat and realized that it was the element of refuge that was missing for me. When I learned that a way to translate saddha, conviction or faith, is "to place the heart upon," I realized that was how I felt. I was placing my heart upon this path and taking refuge in the three jewels. I began experiencing the rituals and ceremonies with much more openness and found myself feeling centered and peaceful in a more organic and natural way. I made more of a point to find at least sitting groups to keep a connection with the shared energy of sangha. It was still a few years before we moved to an area where I could practice with a temple and follow the Buddha's advice to keep company with monks and nuns.

When I read the critique of the book *Buddhism Without Beliefs*, I came upon the comment that taking refuge was "notably absent" as was any discussion of the precepts or moral code in the book. That took me by surprise and I went back to the book to check if that was correct. In the early days of my exploration of Buddhism, even calling myself a Buddhist, I was without a need for the formal rites. In fact, the early readings and classes/workshops I took there was no discussion of these things. The Four Noble Truths were barely, if ever, mentioned.

Those things were considered terribly conventional, perhaps cultural accretions, and certainly not in keeping with the "truth" of what the Buddha taught as liberation. The idea was not just to leave the raft at the shore of the other side, but to skip the raft all together. After all, if all is one, in unity, then all are equal; each of us on the same footing as Jesus, the Buddha, and all of the great teachers. I still do fully embrace the idea of moral maturity; that humans do not need religion or God/god(s) to be moral. On the other hand, I also recognize the superb ability of the ego to convince us that we are justified in our actions when they deviate from what we believe is right, ethical, or moral. Having a code of conduct, especially one developed by a great teacher who has no interest in punishing us for bad behavior, gives us further instruction on the path and illustrates larger truths when we look deeply at each precept.

The bottom line for me is that I do agree with many of Batchelor's positions, enjoy his examples and creative illustrations and analogies, and really like his writing style (which in re-reading this, some of which has rubbed off on me – that will wear off, I am sure). I especially appreciate what he says about the future of Buddhism in the West that "we may have a great deal of scientific understanding about oak trees, but that knowledge in itself, and our access to that information, is not going to speed up the growth of oak trees." Buddhism, like the oak tree is an organic thing. A Western Buddhism is being created whether it will fully flower in our lifetimes or not is yet to be seen, but with a little humility and trust in the practice, we are part of that creation.

Three Themes

The books *Confessions of a Buddhist Atheist* and *Buddhism Without Beliefs* are controversial because they attempt to reframe Buddhist doctrine to a more secular, Western way of thinking; Batchelor might claim them to be more accurate. While the assignment is to write about three things that I learned in taking this course that I did not know beforehand, I will be taking liberties with the assignment as written by looking at some of the Batchelor's thematic ideas and assertions. Technically, I will spin my decision to "I did not know that Batchelor had these ideas," so I will hope I will be forgiven for not taking the assignment more literally. I do feel that it is helpful to take a more in-depth look at what I learned when I engaged this material. What I would like to do in this paper is to look at: 1) the ideas presented in *Confessions of a Buddhist Atheist* regarding what happened to the Sangha after the Buddha's death and Batchelor's analysis of those events, 2) what I see as the over-arching theme of the two books; the attempt to create a "Jefferson Bible" or a form of "Source Buddhism" from the Buddha Dharma, and 3) Batchelor's attempt to reduce core Buddhist theological concepts like rebirth, karma, and emptiness to "conceptual and linguistic abstractions."

In the first point, the views about what happened to the Sangha after the Buddha's death, I really enjoyed reading Batchelor's reconstruction and dramatic portrayal of the Buddha's last days and the events that occurred after that. He drew from a number of different sources to put this version of events together, and he was especially cognizant of the implications of what would happen if the Buddha *had* named a successor and what might have happened had the community of monastics stayed true to his not naming a successor. In most versions of the story, the Buddha did not name a successor; his most senior monks having died before him, he makes the statement that "It may be that you will think that after my death you will have no teacher. Is should not be seen like this, Ananda, for what I have taught and explained to you as the Dhamma and training will, at my passing, be your teacher." Interestingly, Thich Thien-An makes the statement that the Buddha did, in fact, name Mahakasyapa (or Maha Kassapa) as successor, making the connection between him being the leader of the First Council as proof enough. Batchelor speculates about this turn of events.

He considers that while the Buddha may have indeed wanted the Sangha to continue to go as a Sangha without a catholic leader or "Pope," Batchelor wonders if that had happened, would Buddhism have continued? When we look at the history of Buddhism, we find that there have been a number of leaders in the various schools. They have often taken on the political and cultural influences of their days; sometimes fighting against the influences, and sometimes making strange bedfellows with royal benefactors. When I consider my own introduction to Buddhism, and how grateful I feel to the many teachers who risked and sometimes lost their lives to assure the continuation of Buddhism, I have to ask that question, too. Are some of the events that we might disagree with or worry if some of the royal patronage may have swayed monastic leaders from the truth of Buddhism, enough to discount what has come down the river of time to us, or can we have confidence that the over-arching themes and ideas of the Buddha are safe?

The second aspect of Batchelor's is his effort to find a "Source Buddhism" or, at least, create a Jeffersonian Bible of sutras that can be attributed directly to the Buddha. A cynical reading of his efforts might be that he simply wants to clip out the parts of the Dharma that he disagrees with and attribute to the Buddha the concepts and ideas he agrees with. Much of what Batchelor writes is compelling and gels nicely with the Sutras themselves and other commentaries, but in other aspects, Batchelor seems to bring to his translations and analysis a retrojection; he attributes his own values, beliefs, and assumptions back to the teachings of the Buddha. What Batchelor fails to consider in his attempt to find modern sensibilities and ideas in writings that have their source over 2,500 years ago, is that both he and the Buddha can only be viewed in their own *umwelt* or "situatedness" – we all view the world from where we are; a complex world view of culture, religion, artistic expression, politics, social mores, education, family, heritage, and the list goes on and on. We must be cautious when we claim objectivity, since we often fall for what Donna Haraway calls the "God trick" of "seeing everything from nowhere."

Batchelor also complains about the culture imbedded in Asian Buddhism, asserting that these cultural departures damage the message that the Buddha was actually making. It seems a bit unseemly for a British man to make this assertion in light of the damage colonialism has wrought throughout many primarily Buddhist countries, since it smacks of the contention that the Western values and ways of looking at things is inherently superior and should be adopted, or even considered what the Buddha himself had in mind. This co-opting of the Buddha's words to support Western culture, is distasteful at best. However, this analysis is not making a claim that this is Batchelor's intent, even as he approaches perilously close.

Instead, Batchelor argues that there is a risk in trying to preserve and crystalize Buddhist practice that it may well lose its "inner integrity and critical edge, it could end up being swallowed by something else, such as psychotherapy..." Batchelor's vision is an admirable one: to create the philosophy, or culture of awakening, that promotes a freedom *from* suffering, and simultaneously, a "freedom to realize his or her capacity for personal and social fulfillment." The way Batchelor proposes that this happen is to individuate practice and to become more socially engaged. He places the highest value on individuality and autonomy. These values are the highest of Western thought as well. Joseph Campbell talks about the sea change that happened in Western ideas of love as the manifestation of individuality; we changed our notions in the 12th century about romantic love to being two individuals finding completion in each other rather than a social notion of the tribe or community being more important that the individuals that make it up. This premise does not always translate into an Eastern culture, so it may always remain something of a stumbling block to communication between the two paradigms.

The third point, is Batchelor's attempt to reduce core Buddhist concepts such as rebirth, karma, and emptiness to "conceptual and linguistic abstractions." When discussing especially the concepts of rebirth and karma, Batchelor has written a great deal and encouraged readers to see these concepts agnostically; to reserve judgement about them and continue to learn with the idea of someday integrating them into ones mature view of the Buddha Dharma. However, Batchelor has moved past agnosticism to his more atheistic point of view (using atheistic here in terms of denying the concepts of rebirth and karma, as opposed to the atheism of many Buddhists, not believing in a personal God). Batchelor has also made the logical leap to regarding emptiness, too, as an abstraction or teaching device which he views as disconnecting the practitioner from the world, providing a hollow sense of security in an impermanent world.

He even goes so far to state that "the aim of meditation, for Dharmakirti, was not to gain mystical insight into emptiness, but to arrive at an unfiltered experience of the fluctuating, contingent, and suffering world." However, what Batchelor claims is the true aim of meditation, sounds very similar to a good definition of śūnyatā, that "All things are in a state of constant flux where energy and information are constantly flowing throughout the natural world giving rise to and themselves undergoing major transformations with the passage of time." Where Batchelor has accepted a Western translation of śūnyatā as *emptiness*, and been led to believe it connotes a sense of nihilism, suggesting that personal lack of meaning that he seems to give it. Instead, we can look deeper at the meaning of śūnyatā as "the realization of the 'boundlessness' or 'transparency' of phenomena, at basic level, [which] enables us to realize that all things which ultimately have no substance are trivial and not what we think they are, as our thinking is merely an overlay on top of experience. The fundamental nature of śūnyatā is before thought." It is in our clinging to the illusion of a separate, individual nature that causes us to suffer. When we bring the integral nature of karma, rebirth, and śūnyatā together in our practice and realize them on this fundamental level, that we are liberated from the limitations of our perceptions and assumptions.

When reading Batchelor's work, he makes a number of assertions and arguments that we must evaluate. We can ask: are his arguments compelling, are there more questions than answers, and where will these assertions take us? There is a great deal of value in Batchelor's work, and it would benefit any Buddhist practitioner and certainly any Buddhist teacher to be familiar with his work and ideas. In many cases, when we work with Western students who have been steeped in Western philosophy, culture, and religions, we will find that they have many of the same questions, resistance to seemingly exotic ideas, and arguments raised by Batchelor in his books. To his credit, Batchelor is painstakingly honest in recording his thoughts, feelings, questions, and mistakes and missteps.

Many times students feel that the spiritual path should be a linear journey, and that meditation and the other practices should make them feel better pretty immediately, and led them ever on to the perfection of human achievement. When they stumble and fall, they feel that it is the teachings that have let them down. In Batchelor's case, it seems to me that he understood this aspect of spiritual life, but when he was offered an open door into the Buddha Dharma, he choose not to step through.

While in Korea, Kusan Sunim, his Zen teacher explained where the practice was taking him, "Finally, when this mass of questioning enlarges to a critical point, it will suddenly burst. The entire universe will be shattered and only your original nature will appear before you. In this the way you will awaken." Instead of trusting his teacher, he turned away from the teachings, "Once again, I found myself confronted by the specter of a disembodied spirit. The logic of Kusan Sunim's argument failed to convince me. It rested on the assumption that there was 'something' (i.e. Mind) that rules the body, which was beyond the reach of concepts and language. At the same time, this 'something' was also my true nature, my face before I was born, which somehow animated me. This sounded suspiciously like the Atman (Self/God) of Indian tradition that the Buddha had rejected. I could not reconcile the Zen Buddhist love of snow on bamboo, cypress trees in the courtyard, or the plop! of a frog jumping into the pond with the mystical experience of a transcendent Mind revealed once the universe of bamboo, cypresses, and frogs was 'shattered'." This statement broke my heart. It seems to me that the deepest agnosticism is when we fully embrace the "only don't know," and fully live our conditioned lives within a conditioned existence, saying "yes!" to everything. It is when the illusion of control and separateness is shattered, that we have a direct experience of everything just as it is. I do sympathize and relate to Batchelor's holding back; I feel that I do that, too. It's like I get to the edge and get scared.

We just watched the movie *The Good Dinosaur*, and it may seem silly, but it struck me that it had a Buddhist theme. The tiny dinosaur Arlo, was afraid of everything, and his father worked hard to try to convince him to jump into life and not be afraid. We really cannot be "convinced" of not being afraid, and so Arlo learned as well. He was separated from his family and went on adventures he could hardly believe he was able to do. It was making friends with a little proto-human boy, Spot, that he learned it was love that would allow him to overcome his fear; caring more about his friend than what might happen to him.

I learned a lot reading these two books, many things that I agreed with, much food for thought, and some important cautionary tales. Much of what Batchelor has written is really wonderful, and some of it is a good to approach critically. Batchelor is eighteen days older than me, and while his life diverged pretty dramatically from mine, we have been on each our own journey with Buddhism for nearly the same amount of time, with some of the same background and baggage along the way. These books have given me a lot to think about, especially the places that I hold back and withdraw instead of making the leap that the many wonderful teachers and the Buddha himself are inviting me into.

CHAPTER 10

Japanese Buddhism

This is the final essay for the course that included Groner's book, "Saicho: The Establishment of the Japanese Tendai School." The history of Buddhism, in any region has the challenge of finding a balance between the religious and the secular. Saicho was a monk that understood that better than most. Rather than being remembered as a deeply religious or philosophical thinker, he was most adept at finding ways to frame Buddhism to fit with the external, and even political world.

History

The history of Japanese Buddhism is diverse in its scope and range. We find that a number of Buddhist schools arrived in Japan and the leaders of these schools cultivated their teachings and practice, but the interests of their leaders were not limited to religious and doctrinal concerns. They had to show the government how their school could benefit society and promote the powers in the political realm. They had to integrate their school into the culture of the people and show how their school could benefit the people. And most importantly, they had to attract and keep followers by promoting their schools ideas and doctrines and, often times, debating with other schools to prove the superiority of one over the other. While the political and societal concerns might seem just a necessary evil, they do help to illustrate the inclusion of Buddhism into the fabric of Japan during the era of Saicho and the competing schools of his day. But it is not that different from today; while in the United States there is separation of church and state, the role of

Buddhist leaders continues to be one that is developing and not without its own controversies. People who are interested in Buddhism not only want to learn how Buddhism can benefit them, but how it will fit in their everyday lives spiritually, intellectually, culturally, politically, and socially.

The debates among the schools in Japan and Saicho's work, both developing Tendai principles and in refuting the other schools made Saicho a major figure in Japanese Buddhist history and were a high point in Japanese intellectual development. A major area of dispute in Saicho's debates was his dispute with Tokuitsu of the Hosso (Yogacara) School on the nature of man and on the potential for attaining Buddhahood. Each of these masters agreed with the concept of "Buddha-nature," but they diverge when discussing whether or not all sentient beings have a Buddha-nature. In essays and fascicles, Saicho used sutras and his interpretations of the Lotus sutra in particular, to argue against the idea that not all people contained the proper seeds to attain Buddhahood.

The Hosso scholars took the concept of the two truths of relative and absolute realities in the Avatamsaka sutra and the bija seeds stored in the alaya consciousness and created an elaborate structure concerning tainted and untainted seeds and correlating the various levels of attainment (arhats, pratyekabuddhas, etc.) in a literal and rather rigid way. On the other hand, the Tendai School took the more egalitarian view that all beings had the potential for Buddhahood and Saicho argued that it was only provisional teachings that claimed that not all people could attain Buddhahood, so these teachings should be considered simply encouragement for those with lesser facilities toward the ultimate goal of Buddhahood, not as an admonition that some people cannot attain Buddhahood.

Saicho made good use of a number of interpretations by scholars within the Yogacara school and other schools that had adopted Yogacara principles, yet also agreed with his position of universal salvation. Most notably, Paramartha's translation of the Mahayanasamgraha sutra, the Hua-yen texts and Fa-tsang's writings, and works by monks who had studied under Hsuan-tsang who was a renowned translator of the Yogacara texts but who disagreed with his interpretation that not all sentient beings could attain Buddhahood. Saicho was convinced and argued persuasively that the Hosso interpretation of the Yogacara texts of classifying Buddha-nature into relative and absolute was an incorrect extrapolation of the relative and ultimate dimensions of understanding and "simply not true."

When considering the reasons behind how these differences of interpretation occurred, it is interesting to look at what some of these concepts mean. Tathagatagarbha or Buddha-Nature doctrine states that all beings contain the potential to become a Buddha. Williams explains that the Lankavatara Sutra is the most influential of the literature that posits the Tathagatagarbha as the Buddha-nature within the alaya-vijnana, substratum consciousness. The term Tathagatagarbha is open to a number of nuances when translating the components of the word to understand its meaning. The oldest and most natural meaning would be *containing a Tathagata*, containing a Buddha. The imagery of all sentient beings being compared to lotuses containing a fully formed Buddha homunculus sitting cross-legged in their center would then not be a metaphor, but a reality.

In the Yogacara school, literal translations of the sutras are common and often the source of criticism of their ideas when considering the richness of metaphor to explain concepts that are ineffable. The word garbha in Sanskrit also means womb/matrix, seed/embryo, or innermost part; the expression can also refer to all sentient beings having the innermost core of a Tathagata. Further, the Tathagatagarbha Sutra contains nine illustrations of how the Tathagata is hidden within sentient beings, proclaiming the true nature of the inner purity of all beings, encouraging them to have faith in the practice because of the ultimate truth of the Buddha within. Perhaps the most important distinction in these two ways of defining garbha, either as containing a Tathagata or the seed of the Tathagata within, would be to look at the definition of containing a Tathagata as a separate thing other than the being containing it.

To think of the Buddha of the lotus within as a metaphor, or potential, is to have confidence that with practice, honesty, and insight we can transform our suffering and experience liberation. To think of the Buddha within as a reality would be to expect a revelation from this divine being who could give us this transcendent knowledge. The Lankavatara Sutra states: "The Buddha said... now, Mahamati, what is perfect knowledge? It is realized when one castes aside the discriminating notions of form, name, reality, and character;

it is the inner realization by noble wisdom. This perfect knowledge, Mahamati, is the essence of the Tathagatagarbha."

While the Hosso scholars argued that the absolute dimension was static and unchanging, it could not produce phenomenon or untainted seeds, so that if one did not have untainted seeds from the beginningless past, he could not obtain them in the present. However, in reading the Lankavatara Sutra, it is clear that the Tathagatagarbha is not meant to be seen as a self, that it needs no cultivation, only an uncovering or re-discovery as already present and perfect within each being. If I were going to debate the Hosso position, I would want to compare the Tathagatagarbha and the Dharmakaya; that the Tathagatagarbha is *like* a bija seed within the alaya-vijnana and the Dharmakaya has the perfection of purity, self, pleasure, and permanence.

Like a bija, but not quite that, since we cannot really say that the Tathagatagarbha dwells within us as though it is something separate from us or that we *own*. Nagarjuna wrote that Buddha Nature: "it's not physical, emotional, conceptual, impulsive, conscious – or anything else. It does not dwell in us, nor we in it. It does not own us." Yet, the Tathagatagarbha is also synonymous with the Dharmakaya. How can both be true? Williams explains that in the Yogacara tradition, the Tathagatagarbha is seen as the thing that makes us realize that we suffer, and so is the basis for aspiration toward Buddhahood. The Tathagatagarbha is seen to be reborn and to suffer, but because the Tathagatagarbha is hidden under our misperceptions, this idea of defilement is an error of perception.

The *Srimala Sutra* helps us understand that the Tathagatagarbha is void of all defilement stores, but not void of the Buddha Dharmas. We also need to go back to the Avatamsaka Sutra to understand the alaya-vijnana to help us see the distinction between the two. When we water the wholesome seeds within us, those seeds grow stronger allowing us to look more deeply at the unwholesome seeds as they are watered by events in everyday life. When we look deeply, we can transform those negative feelings, inviting the unwholesome seeds not to grow. This practice helps us to bring delusion to an end. In the Fifty Verses on the Nature of Consciousness we read: "When delusion is overcome, understanding is there, and store consciousness is no longer subject to afflictions. Store consciousness becomes Great Mirror

Wisdom, reflecting the cosmos in all directions. Its name is now Pure Consciousness."

On a personal note, because I spent many years as a neonatal intensive care nurse and am a mother, I have always liked the translation of Tathagatagarbha as embryo and as womb. Having worked with many women who have had premature babies and having had a premature baby myself, there is a special understanding of the delicate and profound nature of that embryo within. This so small thing, when we look deeply, contains what is nearly infinitely larger – the ancestral chain and the generations to come. There is such a feeling of deep and quiet waiting when a woman is pregnant. Far from the disdain of some writers when thinking of Briar Rose who is sleeping, waiting for her prince to come, we can instead touch an understanding of what it is to allow that seed to germinate; instead, looking deeply with the Buddha's eyes to see that seed which contains the whole.

When my mother first held my son, who had gained weight to be almost five pounds, she looked up and told me that she had thought we girls were wonderful when she first held us, but that was nothing compared to holding this little boy. Our own children are our personal connection, our grandchildren a connection and appreciation of the past generations and a connection to a future we will only see part of. The thread of continuity of life is clearly and tangibly being held in our arms. In those quiet moments, holding our baby, those bright eyes looking up at us perhaps asking "are you my mother?" we cannot help but ask "who are you, little one?" and realize that we are touching our own mother's hand when we stroke these precious little fingers.

According to Buddhism, there are two kinds of truth, relative or worldly truth (*samvriti satya*) and absolute or ultimate truth (*paramartha satya*). When we look at the conventional world around us, we cling to the reality of things and phenomenon to give us confidence in our world. Things certainly appear to be real. I can knock on the desk and the sound tells me it is sturdy and will hold my monitor and books as I work. But when something happens that takes what I consider permanent and my own, I suffer and feel distress. I may only feel annoyed when I need to replace my pen, but feel pain and anguish when a loved one dies or I become ill and must confront my own mortality. Suffering, though, is not objective; it depends on our perception. When we look more deeply, we begin to see and understand the ultimate dimension or emptiness in things and phenomenon. Near the time of his death, the Buddha said:

> *"All conditioned things are impermanent.*
> *They are phenomena, subject to birth and death.*
> *When birth and death no longer are,*
> *the complete silencing is joy."*

We have our own Crouching Tiger, Hidden Dragon story where we enter the path of Buddhism from a relative standpoint and we learn to notice our suffering and joy, learning more about how to see each of those states of being as subjective and temporary, yet they are an echo of what we understand when we transform our perceptions. The Buddha taught an Eightfold Path and Avalokiteshvara told us that there is no path; these two ideas seem to be in opposition to each other, but they are teaching the same thing from two different points of view. Thich Nhat Hahn explains that "we do not have to transcend the 'world of dust' (*saha*) in order to go to some dust-free world called nirvana. Suffering and nirvana are of the same substance. If we throw away the world of dust, we will have no nirvana."

Nhat Hanh explains the Madhyamika concept of emptiness through the related concept of interdependence. In this analogy, there is no first or ultimate cause for anything that occurs. Instead, all things are dependent on innumerable causes and conditions that are themselves dependent on innumerable causes and conditions. The interdependence of all phenomena, including the self, is a helpful way to undermine mistaken views about inherence, or that one's self is inherently existent. It is also a helpful way to discuss Mahayana teachings on motivation, compassion, and ethics.

Further detailing this idea of emptiness, the Madhyamika philosophy divides into two trains of thought: *Rangtong* or "empty of self," and *Shentong* or "empty of other." In Tibetan *rang* means "self," and *tong* means "empty," literally "self-empty." *Zhen* means "other," so *Zhentong*, or *Shentong*, means "other empty." Because it can be difficult to understand and explain the nature of emptiness, these two branches attempt to apply logic to the nature of objects and phenomenon through their major arguments into the nature of reality and our perception of it. These two systems "...do not differ in the way they determine all conventional phenomena to be empty, nor do they disagree that the extremes of conceptual elaborations cease during meditative equipoise.

Nevertheless, they do differ in terms of the way they use conventional cognitive and verbal expressions during the subsequent state of attainment." The Rangtong teachings consider that the Tathagatagarbha is within all sentient beings and is why we are able to become awakened and it is emptiness that enables us to change; since change is a result of dependent origination and emptiness is the ground of dependent origination, it follows that the Tathagatagarbha is empty in the Madhyamika sense. The Shentong tradition considers that the Tathagatagarbha consciousness is obscured in the unawakened, but is identical to the Dharmakaya or "Essence Body" of the awakened mind.

"The wind was making the temple flag flutter. There were two monks arguing. One said that the flag was moving; one said that the wind was moving. They argued back and forth without reaching the truth. The Sixth Patriarch said to them, 'It is not the wind moving and it is not the flag moving. It is your minds that are moving.' The two monks were startled." There is an old saying that there are two sides to every story, yet it might be more accurate to say that to the deluded mind, there are an infinite number of sides to every story. Saicho was eager to bring the teachings of the Lotus Sutra to the people of Japan. He was convinced of the superiority of the teachings and he was convinced of the exceptional nature of the people of Japan that made them ready to hear the teachings. His culture, upbringing, and society all influenced this conviction as much as a spiritual understanding of the sutra. Today we are no different in that we bring our cultural and political beliefs to our understanding of Buddhism. Fundamentalists are looked at by more liberal thinkers as shortsighted and narrow minded. Saicho was quite blunt in calling the Hosso School's position on Buddha-nature "simply not true." I agree with him, as I agree that modern day fundamentalists are often simplistic and wrong in their interpretations of Christianity using morality, spirituality, and ethics as a lens. When I was younger and more willing to debate or confront aspects of Christianity I found problematic, it seemed clear that modern man has superior ethics than God himself. After all, it seemed to me that God's insistence that everyone love him or be sent to hell seemed more like the morals of a controlling, abusive boyfriend or selfish, spoiled girl-friend than that of a being infinitely wise and loving.

The Bible is packed with morally questionable passages and rules. Yet, early Christians had a similar type of debate going on with the Jewish lead-ers. Christianity was a Jewish movement and in the epistles of Paul, he cast the two as pairs of opposites talking about the Jews as being the ones reading the scriptures to the letter, while they Christians read it to the spirit. Paul felt that the Jews were living the error of perception and cognition more than theological error; that they were a prisoner of the world and its laws. Chris-tians, therefore, were liberated from legalism through their faith in Jesus. Yet this is an error that Christians of today are highly prone; binding them-selves to the rule of law and ignoring its spirit.

In exploring the reasons for taking a less fundamental and more meta-phoric view of Buddha-nature, it was interesting to explore some of the cul-tural, societal, political, and moral reasons that I was bringing to the table as well. It is easy for me to believe that all sentient beings have Buddha-nature, in fact, as soon as even a hint at a class structure in which any type of person might be considered above another would raise serious skepticism in me. (You might even call it raised hackles.)

Yet, the Mind-Only School and Yogacara ideas have contributed a great deal to my understanding of Buddhism and myself. They are simply taking literally some direct teachings. My sense of fairness and justice demands that I be considered an equal with all other people so, because I consider myself a Buddhist and want to follow Buddhist teachings, when sexist or other discriminatory concepts raise their ugly heads, I look for ways to fix what I consider the cognitive dissonance. Now, I did not have to look far to agree with Saicho's work on Buddha-nature even while considering that not all of his motives might have been doctrinal or practice oriented.

On the other hand, the Tathagatagarbha concept is one that I tread lightly on as well. It is terribly close to the concept of a soul and seems only a whis-per width away from being an outside influence ready to save us from our-selves. There are clear reasons why neither of these concerns are valid, but I do think it is wise to be cautious when looking at these concepts. I take a lot of Buddhism as metaphor because first and foremost, I consider myself a materialist and believe that everything in the universe can be explained in the dynamic flow between matter and energy. When the ideas of "seeds" and levels of consciousness is posited, I always want to ask if the intention is to consider these things "real" in the sense of something that should be measurable or otherwise "findable" by assessment and observation. In the Avatamsaka Sutra, we learn:

"If one wishes to understand fully
All Buddhas of all time,
He should contemplate the nature of the Dharma Realm
Everything is made from Mind alone."

The sutra goes on to express that:
"One wholesome thought is the condition
for the creation of the Buddha-lands;
One errant thought
is the very cause of the nine realms of Samsara."

Cleary explains that "this does not mean creation in the sense of creating something out of nothing. This doctrine means that, practically speaking, the world only 'exists' as such because of our awareness, and that what we take to be the world in itself is our experience and inference based thereon. The conceptual order which is taken to be characteristic of objective reality is, according to this doctrine, a projection of the mind, a description that filters and shapes experience in accord with mental habits developed throughout the history of the species, the civilization, and the individual." Thich Nhat Hanh continues the thread of the explanation by explaining the teachings of Master Lin-Chi that the mind *creates* the world in the sense that it invests the phenomenal world with value and meaning. The remedy to this is to calm the mind and stop it from making discriminations; nurturing certain attachments, and feeling aversion toward others. Matt and I have been watching Deep Space Nine the past couple of weeks, and the pilot episode shows the human commander and Trill first officer encountering non-corporeal life forms. They seem to be taking the commander to different places where the memories of wonderful times in his life or the most terrifying times in order to communicate and understand. When he asks "why do you keep bringing me back here?" in reference to being back in the time of his wife being killed, they reply "you exist here – we're not bringing you here, you're bringing us here."

Good Buddhism that; how many middle of the night sessions of worry or battles with unfair bosses or rage against the injustices of the world could be calmed if we realized that we don't "exist here"? When walking through the corridors of the worm hole, the commander sees a terrifying landscape of rock and storms; the three hundred year old Trill sees a pastoral setting with birds and flowers. What would a Buddha see?

What happens to us when we achieve the state of calmness that Master Lin-Chi guides us to? It is then that the darkness of ignorance and passion will be dispelled and the mind can perceive the underlying unity of the absolute. "The individual will then have achieved the state of enlightenment and will be freed from the cycle of birth and death, because such a person is now totally above them both." The message here, it seems to me, is that while my personal preference is to trust and depend on my brain, that to do this work and be liberated from suffering, it will require cultivating a different kind of energy. "The flowers and fruits of awakening will arise from our store consciousness. Mind consciousness has to trust store consciousness, just as a gardener has to trust the land. Both roles are important. Remember, though, that enlightenment, insight, will be brought to you not by mind consciousness, not through your intellectual understanding, but through the deeper wisdom of your store consciousness. After transformation, store consciousness becomes the Great Mirror Wisdom, shining forth and illuminating everything."

Thich Nhat Hanh relates a story the Buddha told his monks of a king whose guards have captured a dangerous bandit and bring the criminal to the king for judgment. The king orders that the bandit be taken outside and the guards are to thrust three hundred swords into the bandit's body. They do as they are ordered, but find in a few hours that the bandit is still alive. They report back to the king who orders an additional three hundred sword thrusts be delivered. By the end of the day, the king asks how the bandit is, assuming that this time the answer would be that he was dead. But no, the bandit continues to live through these wounds. The Buddha then told his monks that this is what we do to our consciousness every day! We thrust unwholesome nutriments into our consciousness and wonder why we do not experience peace. Cultivating awareness and being mindful of what we consume is the best way of transforming our seeds and providing fertile soil for our store consciousness to flourish.

So, do I have Buddha-nature? Honestly, I don't know. What I am willing to do is, at the very least, cultivate a store consciousness that is fertile and wholesome so that even if the Pure Land isn't for me, I've contributed to the day that we all will walk in the Garden of Eden again.

CHAPTER 11

The Compass of Zen

"Compass of Zen" by Korean Zen Master Seung Sahn is a series of talks that help cut through the esoteric and even academic language of Buddhism. Master Seung Sahn made his teaching accessible to his students with practical examples, and humor. Perhaps most notable is the reliance on story telling and personal experiences that characterize his teaching style, making the meaning of Buddhism relatable to his students.

Books

Growing up, I did not have any religious training. Our family didn't go to church, and I only knew about the Christian tradition from spending summers with our relatives and saying grace at meals at their house. I must have been 10 or 11 when we started going to the Presbyterian Church in town. I didn't mind going and despite getting the feeling that my many questions weren't exactly welcomed, I didn't have any bad experiences there. On the other hand, I knew that Christianity wasn't for me. We lived within biking distance of the library and I approached my favorite librarian one day with the request that she help me find books about different religions because I needed a religion and I wanted to figure out which one was right for me. She gave me a variety of books to check out, including The Gospel of Buddha by Paul Carus. I was very interested in all of the books she gave me and weighed the various texts in the best way I could at such a tender age.

Because my sister and I had a challenging childhood – our mother was very insecure and our father was diagnosed with paranoid schizophrenia – we had to lean on each other. While I was very independent, my sister was very sensitive to the drama and conflict in our upbringing. One night when she woke up crying in the middle of the night, I sang her back to sleep and when she fell asleep, I was overwhelmed with a feeling of connectedness and compassion for her and for my whole family. It was a bitter sweet feeling of love and sadness and feeling that because I could do nothing to change things; acceptance. I went out to our back yard and climbed my favorite tree to look up at the stars and had what I guess would be considered a religious experience. I saw a shadowy figure sitting cross-legged in the night sky, serene and still, with great strength and stability. I saw the night sky in a whole new way and sat for a long time, simply looking at the sky. I "meditated" for a number of years like that, just sitting.

When I went off to college, I finally found resources for learning from Buddhist teachers, but was still far from a true sangha. Because I've lived in a wide variety of places, I was able to find teachers of a number of different schools, and always took workshops and other retreats to learn more. In the 80's I discovered the work of Thich Nhat Hanh and kept coming back to his work, finally going on a retreat with him and his monastics. I considered him my teacher and took refuge vows a few years later, and became ordained into the Order of Interbeing (OI) in 2005.

Because I took the Buddha's advice (from the Mahamangala Sutta; Discourse on Happiness) to spend time with monastics seriously, I wanted to find a way to do that. In 2003 living in Florida, I didn't think I would have much luck, but learned that there was a Vietnamese Buddhist center across town. I started attending and have since formally joined the sangha there. Practicing Buddhism for me has always been something of a crazy quilt, finding sources in English, yet being careful to find authentic teachings and not focus solely on Western writers. So at this point in my life, my practice centers around the services at our church, consisting of a Pure Land focus on chanting, sutra recitation, and meditation. We have Sunday services, evening chanting, weekend retreats once a month, four day retreats twice a year, and I'm often invited to attend the novice nun training that we hold once a year for our Order's region. We have festivals during the year, too, and hosted the Jade Buddha for Universal Peace last year. While that in other circumstances be quite perfect, the problem is that everything is in Vietnamese. I'm learning, but that still brings me back to the "crazy quilt" part of my practice. I feel so fortunate, though, that there are many recorded Dharma talks out there to add to my practice schedule. Meditation is important to me, so we converted the smallest bedroom in our home into a meditation room about six years ago. I'm so happy we did – my partner Matt and my son Chris and I all use it. Reiki, an energy healing practice, is also an integral part of my practice. I find that self-treatments and sending Reiki to loved ones and the world helps me center when the world throws me off kilter.

What keeps me practicing is that the practice helps. I've certainly had my ups and downs with practice, thinking that it was an exercise in futility, taking it for granted and not very seriously, to getting serious about my practice. Because I felt like a neglected child, I've spent many years feeling unloved. I had thought that it was my fate not to have true love in my life, yet had great longing for love. I can remember being incredulous when it came out that in 2000 there were over 6 billion people on the planet – how could there be 6 billion people on this planet and not one of them loves me? It was hard to fathom. I spent a lot of time ignoring that feeling or figuring out ways to explain it away, yet the pain was still there.

During a retreat and a lot of one on one work, I was finally able to understand how to look deeply at my feelings; partly because I was finally able to admit that I had no clue what "look deeply" meant. But over time, finally looking deeply, I understood that seed of longing. My prescription worked and that little seed rests quietly now. I attend to it from time to time to let it know that I won't neglect it, but it's been one seed "cured" that helps me understand that this process works and I have access to use it with the other seeds that want to grow wild from time to time. While I've always been a caring and compassionate person, until this seed – a gift of pain that I fought for a long time – taught me the power of looking deeply, I really didn't see what the potential of true compassion could be. Lots of things inspire me to continue to practice, sometimes giving me a push to remember not to fall back into complacency.

Recently, I've visited patients at our hospice who wanted to learn more about Buddhism, and one patient in particular has inspired the bodhichitta in me to learn as much as I can and to practice as well as I'm capable of so that I can bring these teachings to people who need the peace and stability the practice can give.

According to Master Seung Sahn, the purpose of Buddhism is to attain enlightenment and instruct all creatures. Seems simple enough. One of my first Zen teachers would simply ask, when I would be frustrated about something or ask a foolish question, "Why are you choosing not to wake up?" I love that question (well, I didn't love it at the time) because within the question is not only an admonition to get back to work, but also the implication that waking up is available to me right here and right now. Practice gives us tools to help us experience reality as it really is. Structure is a liberating thing; when we don't have to reinvent the wheel every day, we can spend our energies on the creative work of practice. Unfortunately, we tend (at least I do!) to reinvent the wheel all the time. Instead of taking the medicine, we want to turn it this way or that hoping to change it into something we approve of, make excuses (since, after all, if those other guys would just shape up, I'd be happy as a clam), and going off in all sorts of directions chasing butterflies that catch our attention. The Buddha put together a program for us to follow, a prescription for healing our inner hurts to see the world as it really is, freed from the baggage of our physical, emotional, social, and spiritual preconceptions. As Master Seung Sahn says, it frees us to do our job, to function as full human being.

Master Seung Sahn teaches that pre-sectarian Buddhism teaches the basics; the Four Noble Truths, dependent origination, and the practice of various insights. This division of Buddhism is characterized by the concept of duality, that when thinking appears, "I" appear. This creates a false sense of the world informed by discrimination rather than reality. We think that birth and death, right and wrong, up and down, chocolate and vanilla, are real things; things so solid that we have to defend them even to the point of killing and dying for them. It also teaches about the suffering the belief in permanence causes. The reality is that everything changes, yet this fact is hard to swallow and we pretend that it isn't true. This causes us much fear and suffering. My patient who wanted to learn about Buddhism was afraid of dying and hoped that there would be some insight in Buddhism that could help him die in peace. He was raised Catholic and wanted to somehow reconcile the two ways of thinking.

One of the things we talked about was looking at Bible passages with Buddhist eyes. We talked about the story of Adam and Eve in the Bible, and how interesting it was that the fruit that they ate from was from the tree of the Knowledge of Good and Evil, and that if they ate from the tree, they would surely die. Now the snake scoffed at this idea, and Eve believed him. But when they ate the fruit, they didn't die, but they were no longer in the Garden of Eden, a land with no discrimination, pain, death, or judgment. But because they had never been conscious of where they were, they simply existed within this space. Once they could perceive the pairs of opposites, they were no longer in the Garden. When we can penetrate the duality, we would find ourselves once again in the Garden, but this time in awareness. Master Seung Sahn explains that the Buddha showed us this suffering world, *samsara*, and taught us how we can get out of it, a world of suffering created by our own thinking. Attaining Nirvana, as Thich Nhat Hanh explains is the extinction of all concepts and notions because it is our concepts about things that prevent us from really touching them.

The three jewels are an interdependent way of looking at the Buddha Dharma. The Buddha, the awakened one; the Dharma, the way of understanding; and the Sangha, the community of understanding, are all equally important because you can't really have one without the others. These three give structure to the process toward liberation. We take refuge in all three, promising to look deeply into each aspect of the teachings and take advantage of all they have to offer so that we can wake up and help others see as well. The superficial forms of the three jewels vary from country to country, temple to temple, as Master Seung Sahn observes, yet the three are still the path to liberation. In Vietnamese Buddhism, we take each refuge vow by taking refuge in each of the three jewels and add taking refuge in the Buddha, the Dharma, and the Sangha within myself. Thich Nhat Hanh teaches that when we hear "I take refuge in the Buddha," we should also hear "The Buddha takes refuge in me." Otherwise, the refuge vow is not complete. Refuge is also about finding the help and support that we need on the path – and I can use all the help I can get! I am so happy to know monastics that I know are practicing beautifully, sharing their energy with me.

When we have a ceremonial meal during retreat, sometimes during holiday seasons, there will be people there who don't practice very often and haven't learned to eat mindfully. They might eat their food too fast, or reach across the table, or whisper to each other; rather than getting annoyed, or more likely, when I start feeling annoyed, I can look over to the table where the monks and nuns are sitting and watch them take a mindful bite, serene and fully present. I can breathe, come back to the present moment, and continue eating my meal mindfully and happily. When I'm at work and feeling pressure to get everything done and feel like I have to bolt my lunch, I can stop and remember that energy of mindfulness and come back to myself. It might only be for a bite or two, but it helps me to renew myself.

Mutual Causality

Mutual causality, or inter-dependent co-arising, elaborates on the Second Noble Truth by explaining that everything has a sustaining cause, not a first cause like God or Brahman. In the Samyutta Nikaya, we learn "When this exists, that comes to be. With the arising of this, that arises. When this does not exist, that does not come to be. With the cessation of this, that ceases." This helps us to see that we are made of non-self elements and we are manifesting in our current form because of all of the causalities that have led to this moment in time. When we take some time to think about the chain of causality that led to ourselves at this moment, we can have a reverie that would read like the Thorn Birds novel, or one of those websites that show the genealogy of our family.

My ex-husband and his mother love to trace their family tree, and can go all the way back to Charlemagne, yet all along the way, one change would have changed their fate or even their existence. We're very attached to the idea that we are born and we die, yet we can't really point to the real "start" of our existence. Knowing this, we should have a great deal of confidence that since we know that the stuff of the past created the present; that the stuff of the present will create the future. Reasonably, we should take that knowledge and practice to wake up from delusion and not worry or fear death or the future. Logic and knowledge are just not enough. When I teach classes for managers at my work, I always say that the shocking statement for the day is that education does not change behavior. After all, does any healthcare professional who smokes really need more knowledge about that it's not good for them to smoke? Probably not; yet it's frustrating – we should just change when we learn this very reasonable stuff! It makes sense, yet I still worry about what might happen to me. We need the knowledge to understand and start the process, but it's moving the knowledge from our heads to our hearts that makes the rather scientific information about mutual causality meaningful on our path to awakening.

Making a case that any of the links in the chain of dependent origination is fundamental is a trick question. Each of the links is empty, because each of them would not exist without the others. On the other hand, when we solve the problem of any one of the twelve, understanding can arise. Each of the twelve actually has a good side and a bad side. If we called "Life" the fundamental link, we could say that the whole chain would stop if there was no life. That would be true, but not much fun. And if we pick ignorance, it is ignorance that leads to volitional actions (mental formations) and the clinging to life, but it's really not accurate to say that the end of ignorance would lead us to want to die. It could very well lead us to want to stay and help others. If we say that consciousness is the fundamental link, then we would have to consider where consciousness came from which would lead us to look at mental formations and the karma of our habit energies and the history of our ancestors. It is certainly true that consciousness leads us to suffer, especially when we allow our unwholesome seeds to be watered and have aggression, jealousy, hurt feelings, or anxiety. It can also lead to others suffering when we act on those unwholesome feelings, thinking that the other person deserves our negative words or actions; only perpetuates the chain. On the other hand, it is with our consciousness that we can reach out to others with compassion, plan for a positive future, appreciate the present moment, and bring the wisdom that is within us out into the open. The interdependence is really the important part, despite that it might make our heads hurt to follow the links and all of the possible permutations.

In retreats I have attended, some of the elements included keeping Noble Silence, sutra recitation, chanting, meditation, a mindful or ceremonial meal, walking meditation, listening to a Dharma talk, and sometimes a Dharma

discussion, question and answer session, individual interviews, or a tea ceremony. The different elements give us examples of different ways to practice, helping to mirror our normal daily activities, showing that all of those
things can be done in mindfulness and with peace. I always feel a real connection to the past when we do sutra recitation together. For hundreds of
years, Buddhism was a solely oral tradition, and it's really touching to think
that the tradition of reciting these sutras is something that has been done for
hundreds of years by the wonderful teachers who have brought Buddhism
down through the ages to us. For a long time, I bought into the idea that
reciting sutras without having them written down would lead to errors and
mistakes like playing a game of telephone; so could we really be sure that
the sutras are actually what the Buddha spoke or taught? Then I started attending a Buddhist center regularly and realize that the most important people who keep the sutra's accuracy are the Vietnamese grandmothers.
Mistakes are caught right away! I can't really say that I have a favorite one
of any of the elements, although I do love having our ceremonial / mindful
lunch, doing kinhin around the sanctuary, often chanting Nam Mô A Mi Đà
Phật, having a brief recitation, then we all relax and take a nap! The after-
noon time when we have question and answer sessions together or interviews with either the visiting monk or our teacher is very helpful, especially
when we've had time during the morning to come into a proper frame of
mind, to center ourselves, and to have spent time in silence. I find that I'm
much more able to peacefully ask a question or ask for advice in my practice
and listen to the answer with stability after spending time setting the stage,
so to speak.

I've been to a number of Buddhist ceremonies over the years in a variety
of schools. Most near and dear to my heart, are the ceremonies at my church,
Chua Bao An. When I first attended, I wasn't sure that I liked it. The altar is
very ornate and even had these rather gaudy fiber optic lotus flowers on it.
The large gold Amitabha Buddha above the alter has a halo disk behind his
head that has a light behind it that rotates, giving off little sparks of light. So
different from the Japanese aesthetic that I personally prefer! The service is
given in Vietnamese, so looking at the chanting book and hearing the chants
didn't seem to match at all. The people were remarkably friendly and the
gentleman assigned as librarian gave me an English translation booklet to

help me. I kept coming back and as I read more about the Pure Land, the more beautiful the church began to look to me. I was seeing it as a representation of the Pure Land itself, realizing that just as I was confused and not appreciative of what I was seeing when I walked into the church for the first time, if I was suddenly transported to the Pure Land I wouldn't know what I was seeing either. When I looked at the detail of the carving on the altar, I saw a lotus blossom, its long stem leading through the water to the roots anchored in the mud. I could ask myself where I was in my lotus existence. Was I the lotus blossom, or still at the roots clinging to the mud, thinking that I still need to rearrange the mud and other roots? During ceremonies, I often feel that I might be a lotus bud starting to enter the Pure Land, maybe a little mud on the sepal still on my head, but able to peek in a little bit.

Elements that are common to Mahayana Buddhist ceremonies that I've been to would be an incense offering, reciting the three jewels, sutra recitation, bowing to the bodhisattvas, reciting the Heart Sutra, taking the refuge vows, and a Dharma talk. Special ceremonies would include additional elements depending on the holiday or for celebrations, like someone taking refuge vows and precepts, ordinations, weddings, funerals or honoring ancestors, and the like. I've never been to a Theravada ceremony, but I believe that they have specific chanting, meditation, special ceremonies for occasions, and Dharma talks as well. In Order of Interbeing and Vietnamese Buddhist ceremonies, the ceremony starts with sounding a large temple rin gong and the large temple drum, perhaps ceremonially banishing evil spirits, but for me the sound that fills the space is very cleansing. The bell and the drum fill the space with the vibration of sound, penetrating the body and filling the mind with their powerful and beautiful call to mindfulness. I feel like I'm instantly snapped back into being centered. As the monks and nuns enter the sanctuary, their slow, mindful walking represents the chain of wonderful teachers going all the way back to the historical Buddha and giving a promise of taking their inner peace into the future. I feel so fortunate to be so welcomed by our church; it's so helpful to have such a clear image of what stability and peace of mind feel like and to have a spiritual home to go to emotionally in times when I don't feel so stable or peaceful.

Diamond Sutra

Master Seung Sahn seems to be a "bottom line" kind of person. He teaches that the correct translation of important lines in the Diamond Sutra reveal our true nature. His central teaching is based around this line: "Do not become attached to any thoughts that arise in the mind." He goes on to explain that when we think that we perceive something, we have already created a subject and an object. He asks how impermanence can perceive impermanence; who is doing the seeing? Instead, it is the perception itself that is our true nature. He gives examples of "just think" meaning that there is no "I" and when we observe the sky, there is only blue. I've done some classes on relaxation techniques at our hospice both for the staff to use for themselves and to use with their patients. To start the class, and during some basic guided imagery exercises, I ring a small rin gong. I simply invite them to follow the sound of the bell; nothing fancy, nothing particularly "Buddhist." So many times, people will come up to me afterward, and say "there is something about that bell!" They can't put their finger on it, but they felt they could just follow that sound. Many of them will say that the exercises are nice and all, but it would be wonderful to have just the bell sound when they need to stop. There is a profound simplicity when we find ourselves in that moment of just perceiving, only to have it shattered when we begin to think about it, analyze it, explain it, or even try to share it.

The concept of emptiness is first introduced in the *Anatta-lakkhana Sutta: The Discourse on the Not-self Characteristic* and the sutra, the *Adittapariyaya Sutta: The Fire Sermon.* We learn early on that what we have come to believe is who we are, doesn't belong to us at all, and is in fact, on fire causing us great suffering. In the Mahayana sutras, this idea is expanded upon especially in the Prajnaparamita literature, most famously in the Heart Sutra. The Heart Sutra makes it crystal clear that what we are made up of, the skandhas, are empty – our mind is empty, all form is empty; so what vessel can contain our suffering? Master Seung Sahn gives the example of a cup of orange juice; it's only the cup that keeps the orange juice here, if the cup breaks, the juice is gone. So it is our attachment to form, feelings, perceptions, and consciousness that creates a vessel for our suffering. When we can break that attachment, our suffering has no place to stay. In the Vietnamese translation of the Heart Sutra, we go through the list of what is not there in emptiness, including no understanding and no attainment, and "because there is no attainment, the bodhisattvas, grounded in perfect understanding, find no obstacles for their minds. Having no obstacles, they overcome fear..." that last phrase was a real eye opener to me. I've always found the Heart Sutra to be a little bit scary, after all, where was I going to find the ground under my feet when times get rough? This sutra is telling me that there is no ground! Yet, that last line "having no obstacles, they overcome fear..." helps me see that the obstacles I think I'm having such a problem with aren't really there at all, the obstacle is my way of thinking.

Impermanence and non-self are taught to help us understand emptiness. We have to look at emptiness obliquely, because it's a bit like trying to explain three dimensions to a two dimensional being. Even if we draw a cube, like the famous optical illusion Necker cube, the two dimensional being will still see lines arranged on a two dimensional plane. By looking at impermanence and the not-self characteristic, we begin to penetrate what emptiness is. Impermanence may be something we don't like a lot of times, but nearly everyone understands the reality of it, however grudgingly. We hear lots of clichés like "the only thing that doesn't change is change" or "the only constant is change" so, despite the fact that we fight it, we know about impermanence. The not-self characteristic is actually a scientific fact, revealed in the last century. This one is trickier, since so many religions believe in a soul or spirit of some sort. Hand in hand with an unchanging deity is a permanent essence that is created for the person and has eternal existence with the deity. Instead, Buddhism shows us that we are made up of non-self elements, as is everything else in the universe. Thich Nhat Hanh's favorite example is looking at a rose, and imagining going back in time for the rose's origins: it was a partially open flower, a bud, a stem, a seedling, a seed, part of the parent rose; and interwoven with that the person who cultivated the flower, the rain, the sun, the soil, the people who brought the flowers to the store for me to buy. Then I know the rose will wilt and I'll throw it onto the compost heap for it to become soil. No where can I find an element that is uniquely and only "rose." The rose is made up entirely of non-rose elements and it is the conditions that allow it to manifest at the present time. The point then is to see ourselves and every other thing within this matrix of being, and to be able to see the sun in the rose, the rose in the garbage, and myself in inter-being with all other things. When we can see this, that is to penetrate this reality with more than just knowledge, we touch emptiness.

The common themes of the Mahayana sutras can be characterized by the Dharma Seals. The three Dharma Seals are explained by Thich Nhat Hanh as impermanence (anitya), non-self (anatman), and nirvana. When we look deeply at either non-self or impermanence, we can see the other; they are integral to each other. These point to the true nature of reality, the extinction of concepts, duality, discrimination, and subject/object helping us see things as they truly are. Nirvana could also be called the Ultimate reality or dimension, with our day to day ideas of like and dislike, good and bad, up and down, the Relative reality.

But these two dimensions, even though they are as hard for us to see as it is for our two dimensional friends trying to see a cube, inter-are with each other as well. My friend Matt likes to explain these concepts with the help of a cookie – that the cookie might think it is separate, but when we see the bowl of cookie dough that the cookie came from, we know we can touch both the dough and the cookie – they share inter-being-ness with each other. The cookie is made up of non-cookie elements like butter and flour, peanut butter and sugar, and is delightfully impermanent since it would be a shame to let the cookie go stale instead of eating it. And the best part is that you cannot truly understand the cookie until you eat it! Nirvana!

In Sir Edwin Arnold's wonderful work "The Light of Asia," we hear an extended version of the life of the Buddha. As Siddhartha was growing up, the young prince attended the ploughing ceremony which included plough-ing the fields and readings of the scriptures. When he was left unattended, he noticed the worms and shoots that had been cut apart by the ploughs, and the birds and snakes that came to feed on the little bugs and worms, and an eagle that swooped down to capture the snake for it's own feast. He had in-sight into the unity of all things and great compassion for all the creatures and people that he saw; he sat and entered the first jhana under a rose apple tree. When the queen came to find him, and saw him sitting in such stability, she was astonished.

His first comment to her was "Mother, reciting the Vedic scriptures does nothing to help the worms and the birds." Perhaps this was the first Zen teaching. In stories that the Zen teachers are shown to be better than the foolish sutra teachers, the point really is about remembering to eat the cookie, not just read the cookbook. On the other hand, the cookies I bake won't turn out very well unless I learn how to make them. It seems better to me to think about it in terms of stages. When I'm first learning to cook (or play the piano or learn to ice skate) I need to read and practice. Once I learn the concepts, I can be more creative and put together my own combinations using the basics. Ultimately, though, I must not only be an expert at my craft, but I must deeply experience the thing and deeply penetrate it to become it. Master Seung Sahn gives an example that helps put the knowledge part of our learning into perspective telling of the monk Sok Du who thought that the Master said "Buddha is grass shoes." It didn't really matter that the statement was wrong, it only mattered that he put all of himself into one-pointed determination on this question. When he could finally break his grass shoes, his mind became one with the universe and he understood.

Avatamsaka Sutra

The Hua-yen school is based on the Avatamsaka sutra and presents us with some interesting ideas to work with. We learn that the mind creates everything, and so this is called mind only or consciousness only. Master Seung Sahn explains that everything we think and believe is created by our minds and is truth. This seems like a shocking statement; we know that there is a difference between false and true, yet this teaching seems to be telling us that our good sense is wrong. Yet, Master Seung Sahn goes on to tell stories that illustrate our mistake in believing that we know the truth based on our judgment of circumstances and limited information. Attachment to concepts, words, ideas, or philosophies only further concretize our minds. Allowing the "only don't know" or Great Question; try mind, to be present opens us up to seeing. This idea could also be controversial if we don't understand what it really means. There is already a great deal of apathy in the world, and this kind of teaching might be misunderstood by someone to mean that we should just live and let live; just do whatever we please; not speak up against injustice since it's all just an illusion – not much of a bodhisattva way of living.

The Avatamsaka Sutra identifies the Buddha's body with the universe. This seems very esoteric and remote; not something we can relate to or do anything about. We think of ourselves as having ground beneath our feet when we live a good life and try to do the right thing. Yet, when we learn about the universal nature of the bodies of enlightenment, we get the rug pulled out from under us and find there is no birth no death, no coming no going, and an openness that knows no bounds and gives us no ground to stand on. It's shocking and scary! But when we take a breath and think of the component parts: impermanence, (ok, I get that, I can understand that everything changes); the not-self characteristic, (ok, that's ok that I'm made up of parts and there is no intrinsic "I" – well, maybe I understand that, but don't like that too much since I like being "me," warts and all) it can help us connect those things with the groundless ground of emptiness. I was reading an article the other day talking about the meaning of Easter, the author ended the article that in Christianity, people go to heaven and unlike Buddhism, we remain ourselves.

I was so taken by that statement, and wondered what version of himself the author imagines will be in heaven or who he thinks Buddhists turn into? Our infant self is very different from our child self, from our young adult self, our mature self, our elderly self. What about illness and infirmity? Does the person who has Alzheimer's go to heaven in that state of being? So, while I may cling to myself because I want to experience, be curious, and know about life, I also understand that this "self" has undergone a whole lot of rebirths already. Are they all me? sure – are they all not me? yes – are they in inter-being with everything? that gets us closer to the integral nature of the relative and ultimate dimensions.

Master Seung Sahn finds it funny that people think that space and time actually exist, and he explains that because of the inter-being-ness of all things, the one in the many, the many within the one, that it is only our thinking that makes us believe that time and space are real. It's interesting that in science, there are hypotheses about the nature of time and space that defy our common sense understanding of how the world works. I think it was Einstein who remarked that relativity is easy to understand: when you have your hand on a hot stove, a moment feels like an hour, but when we have a conversation with a wonderful companion, an hour flies by in a moment. In physics, the term is more accurately put as the space/time continuum, and a few theoretical physicists even consider that time might actually be contained in packets that we merely perceive as being fluid and moving, like the still pictures on the movie film. It's only an optical illusion that makes us see them as moving through time. (Now, if only we could get time to slow down and wait while we finish all the things we need to do!) In Buddhism, Master Seung Sahn explains that these issues aren't simply academic exercises, but the most important thing we can experience is to attain our true wisdom of coming from that one still point. In fact, he explains that an intellectual understanding of these ideas will not help us. Nagarjuna spoke about emptiness as the medicine for helping us to stop concretizing concepts, but if we turn emptiness into a concept, we're incurable! We must experience this directly through meditation and looking deeply.

In the Wheel of Life, we find ourselves going around and around in these six states of being called the six ways of samsara. We find ourselves part of heaven and hell, fighting realms, human realms, and animal and hungry ghost realms. These are not places, but states of mind that are made by our karma and thinking. We go through so many states of mind even in a single day that we can feel dizzy. We feel that we're buffeted by the winds of change and the whims of fortune, yet our reaction to these changes in our circumstances is actually under our control. When something bad happens to us, it feels normal to fight or get angry but that puts us in that *asura* state – even when we feel we have righteous indignation over the ills of the world. For those things that we do that we know aren't really good for us, but seem to promise comfort, we enter the realm of the hungry ghosts – always starving, yet the more we take in, our very narrow throats prevents us from being satisfied. It's interesting, too, that we can visit places where it certainly seems like hell on earth, yet we can find people there who are not in hell at all. When I was a young nurse, I spent part of a summer in Panama helping at a free clinic there. I was shocked at the poverty I saw, yet the family I stayed with didn't feel poor at all. They lived in a cinder block house and we would move all the furniture out to the patio and literally use a hose to wash the inside of the house. We slept in hammocks that hung from hooks built into the walls, and we used room dividers to make the rooms as needed. The family felt quite well off because they had a record player and a phone. And comparatively, they were right – the poverty of many of the people there was relentless. I remember coming back to the states and going to the grocery store with my mom and starting to cry when I saw the displays of fresh produce. All that food that we could just pick and choose from, yet I had just come from a place where food was scarce and it seemed so unfair. Yet, I know many people who live such privileged lives, but they feel they are in hell because of their troubles and their mental torments.

Karma and rebirth are inter-related, perhaps even inter-changeable with each other. Master Seung Sahn tells some pretty fantastic stories about rebirth in his teachings on karma. I realize that there are many people who believe in a personal reincarnation. I tend to both not take it personally, and to take it personally in a somewhat different way. It seems to me that the idea of a personal rebirth is based on the idea that consciousness continues, rather than a notion of a soul that transmigrates from body to body over time. But when we look at consciousness, it seems like there may be some attachment to it going on.

I have heard arguments that consciousness can't be only the result of the biological processes of the brain and body. That's an interesting argument, but once we visit a brain injury rehab center, we might need to rethink that a bit. Other biological processes are just as complex as our thinking. I would venture to say that the energy factory of the mitochondria in the cell is every bit as complex and more vital to the continuation of life than our thinking ever could be, for instance. Yet we don't talk about the rebirth of our digestion! Karma, too, can be a controversial topic, especially as Master Seung Sahn describes it. It's difficult to reconcile the suffering of the world with a seemingly "blame the victim" mentality.

It seems like that could lead to abuse if Buddhist leaders counseled victims of abuse that this is their karma and perhaps they should endure the abuse to burn up their karmic debt, or blame themselves for their actions. I do think that cause and effect happen on a variety of levels – after all, the path of a hurricane is based on physics, and it's hard to believe that the destruction has anything to do with whether or not the people in its path did good things or bad. On the other hand, I do think that we all need to consider our role in our circumstances when bad things happen. We also need to consider our role in the state of the world and not just blame the bad behavior on those bad other people. The bottom line of karma is that the stuff of the past makes the present manifest, and we part of both the past and the present. It is ultimately logical to believe that the future will be made up of the stuff of the present. So living in a way that promotes peace, harmony, and compassion can only contribute to making the future better.

The Six Paramitas

The six paramitas are described by Master Seung Sahn as practical guides for our understanding of Mahayana Buddhism. These six are Generosity (Dana paramita), Precepts (Shila paramita), Perseverance (Kshanti paramita), Effort (Virya paramita), Samadhi (Dhyana paramita/meditation), and Wisdom (prajna paramita). These six give us a way to live our lives and a guidebook for our practice. Generosity is a very important and is the first of the Buddha's gradual teaching method. The Anguttara Nikaya gives specifics about what our motivations might be for giving and how to learn generosity that will benefit our practice and benefit others. The precepts help us to live a good life, but when we look deeper at them, we see the whole of the dharma with each of them. Meditation is a skill that we learn and it is something that evolves as we practice to produce a mind that is not moving in any situation, but dwells in the experience of reality.

The paramitas of perseverance and effort seem to be blended together in this talk by Master Seung Sahn, or I'm not seeing a distinction. However, these paramitas seem to point to what Master Seung Sahn calls "try-mind." Perhaps the distinction here is that we need perseverance since our job of saving all beings never ends because "sentient beings are numberless; we vow to save them all." And our effort is done moment to moment, not just in the practice methods that are taught. We can practice by doing all sorts of things during our day if we have true Samadhi. These paramitas produce wisdom, which Master Seung Sahn calls the medicine that cures ignorance.

In the Vietnamese Buddhist school that I practice in, the paramitas (perfect realization) are taught and practiced in a very similar way. The idea is that when we practice these aspects of wisdom perfectly, we step into the Pure Land, crossing to the other shore of well-being. We're taught that we have to make an effort to practice, but that these paramitas will be a sure roadmap for us. One of the differences comparing our book to the way I've been taught is the Kshanti paramita (patience or forbearance) translated as inclusiveness; the capacity to receive, bear, and transform our suffering. This inclusiveness points us to the idea that our hearts can be large enough to embrace our suffering and pain. The Buddha used an apt example of this, talking about putting a handful of salt into a cup of water making it too salty to drink. But if we put the same amount of salt into a mountain stream, the river has the capacity to receive and transform. The river doesn't suffer and people can drink the water. If our hearts are small, one hurt or injustice makes us suffer a lot. As our hearts grow in compassion, we can make our hearts as big as the ocean, able to take in that same hurt and not suffer at all. For me, this is the touchstone of the bodhisattva path and part of my practice visualizing Kwan The Am as my best meditation partner.

The types of Zen Master Seung Sahn describes are Theoretical Zen, Tathagata Zen, and Patriarchal Zen. In theoretical Zen, the description is "form is emptiness, and emptiness is form;" in Tathagata Zen, it is "no form, no emptiness;" and in patriarchal Zen, "form is form, emptiness is emptiness." Theoretical Zen gives the practitioner a feeling of expansiveness in the understanding that all is one and the one is in all. However, the potential is that it can be a one sided understanding since when we feel at one with everything, we may not have penetrated the understanding of the "one;" what it is and where it goes. In Tathagata Zen, the practitioner achieves an empty mind, one that has no words and no duality. This point is like the Bindu point, an experience of the heart of consciousness, the pearl or dot that in tantra is considered the nucleus of the manifestation of all things. In Patriarchal Zen, the practitioner learns that while the many becomes one and the one becomes many, the practitioner sees reality as it really is and acts in accordance with reality. The practitioner must understand the correct situation, the correct relationship to that situation, and the correct function that she has in that situation and relationship. We then act and speak that truth that is present before thinking. The analogy Master Seung Sahn uses is "Keep a mind that is clear like space, but let your mind function like the tip of a needle." Much like the expression: being in the world, but not of the world, the practitioner experiences and acts on the inter-being-ness of the relative and ultimate dimensions.

In practice, each of these types is present in some degree. In practicing theoretical Zen (although I didn't know the term at the time), learning about the not-self characteristic was an important turning point for me because I felt that I had been pointed in the right direction and then had experienced a connection with all things. However, I really didn't know how to behave with this knowledge and this (imperfect) level of understanding. It would seem like I would have a great sit and yet when I had to drive somewhere, I would be right back in the annoyed at the way people drive state of mind. In Tathagata Zen, there is no need for words and the ultimate reality is all that matters. While it can't be expressed, it can be communicated. The practitioner who has this level of understanding expresses this with the pure stability and presence of their being. While I have had moments of a glimpse of this stability, I have had the good fortune of being around people who have this pure presence and have been touched by this energy. There is an old conversation starter asking people what question would they like to ask of any historical figure. I've always been impressed by the questions people come up with since I can never think of anything good I would ask. But if I had the opportunity to ask the Buddha a question is would be "would you sit with me?" That Tathagata seed is within us all, so we have the opportunity to sit with the Buddha everywhere we turn. The energy that those who have this level of understanding and share it with us through their practice is very valuable. In patriarchal Zen, we are asked to have skillful means in working with each other. Master Seung Sahn explains that substance, truth, and function come together in one point and we know how to answer, how to act, and how to relate to others.

Just starting a sentence "the true Zen is..." is already wrong. In each of the forms of Zen, we can get tripped up when we start thinking or when we turn our experience into a concept. When we're asked if we're the same or different and we confidently say "the same," we're right in a way, but wrong too. When we claim to be different, we're also right in a way, but wrong. When we are present in the moment and aware of all that is around us, that is right in a way, but also wrong because we may be reflecting truth yet not understanding what the correct action is in a given situation. It's more than a little frustrating, since I'm a methodical thinker and would like nothing more than having a step-by-step plan to follow, but each of these types of Zen are doorways to the whole of the Buddha Dharma, not stair steps to heaven. As Master Seung Sahn explains, the three kinds of Zen are only one, but separated out to help with teaching. So the bottom line is that I don't know the true Zen, so cultivating that "don't know" and "try" mind is the practice to lead to experiencing true Zen.

Samadhi is the sixth factor of awakening and is commonly translated as concentration. Thich Nhat Hanh explains that the word is broken down as "sam" meaning together, "a" bringing to a certain place, and "dhi" the energy of the mind. This concentration is one pointed and still and it stays focused naturally and easily. Concentration in and of itself is not necessarily wholesome, since we can concentrate on unwholesome or harmful things. We can concentrate to remove ourselves from the world by becoming so absorbed in our own interests that we are outside of the world and we may try to hide from ourselves. But when we practice the correct concentration, we can have the patience to look deeply on our suffering to develop compassion and liberation. Sitting Zen includes this concentration so that we can experience, as Master Seung Sahn explains, the interpenetration of all phenomena, the insight into the nature of phenomena, and insight into existence.

CHAPTER 12

Korean Buddhism

Korean Zen has a rich history, but one that has not been readily available to those of us in the West. Through new translations of works, and modern commentaries on Korean teachers, we discover a tradition that builds on the foundation brought to Korea that honors its culture and history. By exploring the teachings of Zen Masters T'aego, Ta'Hui, Wonhyo we are introduced to that tradition and wisdom. "The Mirror of Zen: The Classic Guide to Buddhist Practice," truly is a classic and should be in every practitioner's bookcase.

History

In the seventh century, Korea was experiencing many political, social, and religious upheavals and changes. By the 660's, Silla had unified Korea, but there were still regional differences in policies, loyalties, religions, and traditions that exerted their own influence in subtle and not so subtle ways. Throughout East Asian, when Buddhism arrived on the scene, there would be both mutual admiration for the local religious and philosophical thought and contentious disagreements and rivalries. Because the society of Korea included a hierarchy of status; a system that Confucianism is amenable to, not all Confucian leaders embraced the introduction of Buddhism. However, there were conflicts when that hierarchy felt threatened, and it was often prudent for Confucian and Buddhist leaders to work together to try to promote a humane answer to the social and financial issues that conflict produces. Some Confucian teachers could see beyond the superficial teachings and understood the common threads between Confucian thought and Buddhist teachings seeing the goals of reducing suffering to be in alignment with Confucian ideals of social harmony, moral behavior, and proper values. Buddhist teachers, too, used the Confucian values or morality and order to promote harmony, especially in their teachings to those in power.

When any religion seeks to establish an institution in a country, there is a balance that must be reached in being cooperative to the ruling classes' goals and authority, yet also being true to its own values and bring the teachings to the people who can benefit from it. The other factor is competing for scarce resources with other religions in the area. The more dogmatic the religion and the scarcer the resources, the more contention can be found between rivaling factions. Religions also exerted their influence over the populace, insisting on specific types of behaviors which might be to the liking of the ruling classes or might undermine their authority. The favor and influence of any given religion ebbs and flows on the tide of public opinion, the clout of the ruling powers, and being in the right place at the right time. Those with a true understanding of the religion and a desire to help others understand may not always have a high standing in court, but will be true to the teachings and to themselves; some of these teachers have earned a place in history even though they were unappreciated in their own time.

Master Wonhyo was considered the founder of Syncretic Buddhism in Korea. He pursued a "perfect, holistic understanding of the real and ideal" which rose above the sectarian fights of his day. He proposed Harmonizing Disputations and practiced Non-Hindrance. During the period Master Wonhyo lived, there was relative unity in Korea, allowing for an exchange of ideas and he had an exposure to diverse Buddhist ideas and schools of thought and he was able to study under some of the preeminent Buddhist teachers of the day. It is from Master Wonhyo that we get the very famous "drinking water from a skull" story – when he realized that it is our perceptions that rule our judgments about any situation, he realized that there is no Dharma outside the mind. "What else is there to seek?" This experience changed the course of his life and inspired his teachings and writings. He had realized the teaching of Mind-Only through direct experience and had attained enlightenment.

In his practice of non-hindrance, his teaching style was often unconventional – a crazy wisdom style that was controversial. While a number of teachers over the years have used crazy wisdom style teachings to great effect, this is a difficult and dangerous practice and is especially challenging for the student. Unless the student is well grounded in the teachings, there is a very real risk of being seduced by a person who is using their personal charisma for their personal gain and being led further away from the Dharma than toward it. Chögyam Trungpa Rinpoche comes to mind, not because he wasn't an authentic teacher – much of his work is masterful – but because his crazy wisdom lifestyle and teaching methods place some of his teachings in doubt.

When I read his book Spiritual Materialism, the first half of the book or so is something that every Westerner interested in Buddhism should read. But then the book gets denser and harder to understand. Sadly, when I read it I'm struck with the dilemma of wondering if it's simply harder than I'm ready for and I should come back to it, putting it on the back burner for it to simmer. Or, is the problem that he was drunk when he wrote it and it actually makes no sense. I've always felt that the Buddha's basic precepts aren't there to hinder us from having a good time in life, but to protect us and others from harm and keep us safe. They're pretty basic; not a burden to follow at all.

But I digress! When looking at "One Mind" the thing that strikes me as most important is Master Wonhyo's commentary about using the term "one mind." He explains that he's really not talking about a binary construct, but rather, because of non-discrimination, there is no difference between one and two; that "...phenomena at their truest are like empty air." "This truth defies description and abstract thought..." and One Mind lies beyond the realm of relative thought.

Harmonizing Disputations was a concept used in working with discord and conflict by embracing it, showing that everything in the world is interconnected and interdependent, making the whole and the part exist as one. Master Wonhyo was unrestricted in his views and in his dealings with others, making him completely free. He wrote, "if you are free from preconceptions, you and the other person will be equal." A very important point Master Wonhyo makes is about compassion – that freedom without compassion is self-indulgence, but compassion without freedom is passive and not true freedom. They are inseparable with each other and are rooted in the understanding of unity – "the great compassion of unity."

Merit

Buddhist teachers and monasteries often find themselves embroiled in secular issues and concerns. The Buddhist organizations needed the secular/governmental or monarchies to give them permission to build and carry on their activities as well as support for the operations of the monasteries and to finance projects. The rulers of any of the regions sometimes needed the Buddhist organizations to show the people that they were in alignment with their values and beliefs. Sometimes, the ruling classes fought against Buddhism when they felt the tenets of the faith might dissuade people from being "good citizens." Secular patronage is, according to our author, sometimes used as a gage to the spread of Buddhism, but he is quick to point out that this is only part of the story. Buddhist leaders have used the secular leaders maybe not as often as the secular leaders have used them, but the flow of ambition, money, influence, and manipulation is certainly a two way street.

Is this a help or a hindrance? Well, both, really. Without some of this intrigue and posturing, Buddhism might have all but died out – the monasteries and projects did bring a bit of the true meaning of Buddhism with them to people and may have been that drop that started a ripple of understanding. Some of the projects, after all, were sutra copying and libraries, temples, art, statues and sanctuaries that have inspired people through the ages. It certainly hurt Buddhism, though, from the standpoint of disillusioning people of the time (and modern Buddhism isn't immune from this either) who may have lumped Buddhism in with all the other self-serving, self-aggrandizing, and selfish pursuits of people who only care for their own power and ambition.

Merit has been a challenging concept through the ages, because, like karma, it can be used to manipulate people who don't understand what it means. Many beautiful temples have been financed by people who believed that they were accumulating merit to assure an auspicious future life, to buy their way out of bad deeds, or to make themselves look good for their constituency. That goes on today, too –I remember a couple of years ago taking a van full of friends from temple to a monastery on the coast so we could attend a retreat. One of the ladies wanted me to know that I was accumulating merit for this good deed. I don't look at merit as a tally sheet of good deeds like St. Peter or Santa Clause might keep, but rather, the heart of the Bodhisattva path. We recite the sutras, take refuge, help others, support our teachers and friends on the path, meditate, and all the rest to gain merit – then give that merit to those who are suffering and laying it at the feet of the enlightened ones.

I've never looked at the Bodhisattva path as delaying ones enlightenment as some might phrase it, since its only in fully waking up that I will be of the greatest use to anyone else – rather I see it as that act of giving all merit toward that goal of the awakening all sentient beings. By not keeping it for myself, I stay grounded and humble in my efforts. A way to symbolize and remind myself to let go.

Pithy Sayings

"It's like this: the high plateau does not produce lotus flowers; it is the mire of the low swamplands that produces these flowers." The Old Barbarian said, "True Thusness does not keep to its own nature, but according to circumstances brings about all phenomenal things."

The book has so many pithy sayings and quotable phrases, that I'm really glad I got the Kindle version so I can underline to my heart's content (I don't like to mark in books, so I wind up with tons of posty notes in them). For me, the most significant things in the book is Ta Hui's scholarship and knowledge, his encouraging nature toward his students, and his determination to help his students penetrate emptiness. Emptiness is a concept that at first blush seems quite simple to understand, yet the experience of seeing things as empty is as frustrating as trying to figure out an optical illusion with no clues. A Chogyam Trungpa Rinpoche quote that I like, (and it's how I feel when I read the Heart Sutra) "The bad news is you're falling through the air, nothing to hang on to, no parachute. The good news is there's no ground." Good news?? When I've spent much of my life trying to keep ground under my feet, hearing that form is emptiness and emptiness is form is terrifying (I believe the stories about the first people to hear the Heart Sutra fainted.)

Even meditation can feel like a way to gain ground, to be in control – Ta Hui dispels that idea: "If you just manage to cradle the un-crying child in your arms, what's the use?"

Ta Hui goes on to say "This one who fears falling into emptiness – has he been emptied or not? If your eyes aren't empty, how can you see forms? ...if your intellect isn't empty, how can you distinguish the myriad phenomena?" He recognizes that the only way to truly see the flower is to look deeply into it, seeing it's interbeing with everything else; its emptiness. Yet it can be so difficult to look deeply without trying to analyze and figure it out like solving a puzzle, especially when looking at what I'm attached to; what I'm bothered by. It seems easier to figure out the reasons why or to talk myself out of feeling the way I do; I just spend the time beating myself up for not being good enough. In meditation, it can be tempting to think that the goal is blissful quiet; just pushing down the thoughts and feelings so that the mind is under control. Ta Hui will have none of that! "This mind has no real substance: how can you forcibly bring it under control? If you try to bring it under control, where do you put it?" To have faith, he explains, is the key – allowing us to set aside our thoughts and doubts to rest in emptiness; unafraid to fall into it, because we won't make real that which doesn't exist. There is nothing to wait for, nothing to attain, no coming, no going; no birth, no death.

"Does a dog have Buddha-nature or not? Chao Chou said 'No.'" begins the letter on "Contemplating 'No'." I found this letter a very important one. He says "this one word 'no' is a knife to sunder the doubting mind of birth and death." Like the diamond that cuts through illusion, every moment if we can poise our minds between not holding that birth and death are existent nor denying them as non-existent can we stop our discriminating minds. Now that word "no" can be a problem, since in English, we really don't use it the same way as in Asian languages. In Vietnamese, the word "no" is "không" but it's not really completely the word "no." it's also used for the concept of "emptiness" and in everyday use, it's also a modifier to add a negative meaning to a sentence or to is added to an affirmative sentence to make it a question; that last one has an enigmatic feeling for me, seeming to poise the question between pairs of opposites. So contemplating "no" is really to contemplate the emptiness nature of all things. "There are neither humans or Buddhas; the universe is like a bubble on the ocean, all the sages are like flashes of lightning."

And for those of us to puzzle and ponder and figure, believe what our minds tell us, that they are the most important thing, Ta Hui lets us know that it's so very close, "you cannot get this truth out of your own eyes... if you try to receive it by stirring your mind, you've already missed it by eighteen thousand miles." The only way to understand the Truth is to be the Truth.

The other letter I wanted to mention is one that is near and dear to my heart; the advice to a father whose son is ill and not recovering from his illness. This is a very touching section, one that really helps when we get to the bottom line of Buddhist practice. When we think about the cause of suffering being "attachment" (I like the Tibetan word *shenpa* because it is more subtle and doesn't have the cultural connotations that *attachment*, or any of the other terms used to describe this, have.) When we first hear about attachment causing suffering and freeing ourselves from attachment it makes so much sense – wow, just a few sessions of getting to the bottom of someone being mean to me when I was a kid or figuring out that picking up my father's habit energy of this or that, and I can fix myself right up and never have to suffer again, right?

One of the exercises we do with new employees for our hospice is designed to help put them in their patient's shoes. We have them make a nice long list of things that they love, then as we tell the story of learning that they have a terminal illness, they have to start crossing items off the list. When we're down to the last one or two items, the mood in the room is quite somber and some people start to cry as they cross that last item off, some might get ticked off or angry, and others refuse to cross the last item off the list. We have them get up out of their seats and throw the list away; when they return to their seats there is time for discussion about what the exercise meant to them or to share about their own experiences with illness and death. It's a very poignant and tender feeling to get in touch with death, especially in such a raw way. In Buddhist practice, we are instructed to meditate on our death – that meditation was never so powerful and meaningful as when I worked with it shortly after my own diagnosis of breast cancer when, at the time, I didn't know what my prognosis was.

What is Master Ta Hui's advice? With great compassion, he instructs his student to realize that the feelings are very real and natural; not to deny them. I do think that there have been times that I've used meditation as a way to repress my feelings; I sat to convince myself to relax, calm my mind, and force the negative feelings to go away. What I've learned over the years that it is important to sit with those feelings, not to repress the feelings or thoughts, but to stop the story line which only reinforces the shenpa. (And these three years here at PIBS have been instrumental in furthering my growth in the Dharma, not only in knowledge, but in wisdom, and practice as well – thank you for that!) Sitting with the feeling is the hard work – sometimes sitting while on fire. I love Ta Hui's advice: "Keep investigating until your mind has nowhere to go. If you want to think, then think; if you want to cry, then cry. Just keep on crying and thinking. When you can arouse yourself to the point where the habit energy of love and affection within the Storehouse Consciousness is exhausted, then naturally it's like water being returned to water, giving you back your original being, without affliction, without thoughts, without sorrow or joy." And I'll add without hope – finding the courage to set hope aside and experience the full weight of what is happening has been very important on my path.

Where does that leave compassion and our love for those who mean so much to us – our partners, our family, our dear friends? Do we become un-feeling, if serene automatons (or Vulcans, for our sci-fi fan friends)? I don't believe that's the case, and I appreciate that Ta Hui encourages his friend that his feelings are natural and that contemplation of these feelings can be a door to enlightenment; the direct experience of the emptiness nature of father and son, right or wrong, birth and death, sorrow and joy; stepping through the door where true happiness is found in peace.

Time Machine

If I had a time machine and could visit historic people and events, I now have a new person that I would love to meet. I would have loved to have been present at these amazing ceremonies with all their color and grandeur.

I love the language about the robe, especially. Whether T'aego is ceremoniously donning the robe or inviting those assembled to put on the robe with him, the robe is treated as a symbol that is larger than life. Like the stories of masters who spread their robes to cover great areas of land to mark the beginnings of a monastery, or the intimate gathas that are said when putting on the robe mindfully, the robe is a symbol of wrapping us in protection and keeping evil at bay. The form of the kesa is based on a rice field and symbolizes planting the seed of enlightenment, protecting the new sprouts that will nourish all of the world.

I looked back to about a year ago, and I was taking the Precepts class here and we talked about the kesa and I had written in my journal about attending a retreat and spending a lot of the Dharma talk looking at the monk's robe. I felt envious of that robe – I felt that I needed a robe that would protect me from the perils to come, so I would have no fear when the thunderstorms shake the heavens or in my case when surgery and chemotherapy change everything. But as the coming months unfolded, I did have that robe to wrap myself in. In taking the precepts, I do "wear" the Buddha's teachings. Master T'aego invited the assembly to put on the robe of transmission on with him, lifted one corner and said: "Do you see? Not only have all of you put it on along with me, but everything everywhere in all the worlds in the ten directions – the sky and the earth, the dense array of myriad forms, the saintly and the ordinary, the sentient and the insentient – have all put it on at once. Bah!" For me, the Buddha's robe covers the whole universe. Learning to wrap myself in creation and seeing life as my protection is what I want to cultivate.

One of the things that really struck me in this book was the similarity of the section on "How to meditate with Zen cases" and the essentials for reciting the Buddha's name. Because my temple is a Vietnamese Pure Land/Zen school, reciting the Amitabha's name, Nam Mô A Di Đà Phật, is praised for the devotion and aspiration to be "born" in the Pure Land. When considering the Zen cases, these questions are not something to figure out, but to put one's whole self into its examination. T'aego talks about the importance of diligence and focus; like the hen laying on her eggs or the cat waiting to catch a mouse: "Just go on like this, more and more alert and clear... rest but do not stop: contemplate more and more deeply. This is by no means a contrived state of mind [we aim for here]." In that focus, there is no room for an observer; only "just you by yourself" so that thoughts of otherness are identified as delusions. He explains that if we can smash ignorance under the impact of this word *no* "then you are like a man drinking water who knows for himself whether it is cool or warm." "Whether walking, standing, sitting or lying down, twenty-four hours a day, always be aware of it. Just go on studying this way and carefully contemplating *No*."

So, too, in the recitation of the Amitabha Buddha's name; we are to put those words before our minds twenty four hours a day, no matter what we are doing. He explains that the Dharmakaya of Amitabha is everywhere; "mind is Buddha, Buddha is mind. Outside of mind there is no Buddha, outside of Buddha, there is no mind." This illustrates the integral nature of emptiness and form. Exploring my Celtic roots, I found the wonderful phrase *fighte fuaighte* which means "woven into and through each other." In this tradition, this would symbolize that the eternal is not elsewhere; it is not distant. There is nothing as near as the eternal. In Buddhism, we could say the same of the manifestations of the relative world of form and the emptiness of the absolute dimension.

When I first visited the Vietnamese temple I currently practice at, I didn't really like the inside of the sanctuary. I prefer a Japanese aesthetic and the rather, what I considered then, gaudy statues and lights, lots of carvings, and lots of plates of fruits and other offerings on the alter was distracting. But it was in that temple that while reciting a sutra about Quan The Am and her ability to change form to be whatever we need to learn from, be it comforting or terrifying, that it dawned on me that if I entered the Pure Land as I am, making my judgments of good and bad, like and dislike, I wouldn't know what I was seeing. But when I can look with the eyes of the Buddha, instead of being covered in mud and stuck in the roots of the lotus, I can grow and flower above the water line to see the magic of the colorful flowers, the songs of the birds, and the bodhisattvas walking as they chant the sutras. Everything is a dharma lesson. Focusing and purifying the mind is the only way to genuinely recite the Buddha-name and if we do that, "you are just invoking the Amitabha of your own inherent nature."

Essentials

There is so much to love about this book; it's certainly one to savor and return to. One of the themes that I really enjoyed in the book is how careful So Sahn is to show the pitfalls of understanding that many people miss when they start to learn about Zen or the other forms of Buddhism. After all, it's about the experience of emptiness which is ineffable, and yet we must try to communicate with each other. So Sahn uses passages from the sutras, commentary, poetry, and examples from life to inspire understanding.

"The appearance of all Buddhas and Patriarchs in this world can be likened to waves arising suddenly on a windless ocean." The Buddha and the Patriarchs, as all on the bodhisattva path do, come into the world out of great compassion to save all sentient beings from suffering. So Sahn goes on to explain that all beings have original nature and we don't need to be saved. Rather than clinging to the words, even of the Buddha, we practice to understand what they are pointing at and, as he says then they are no longer of any use to us; or maybe we can say that they become our brothers and sisters in the dharma.

In thinking about karma, we tend to think first of the bad kind, hoping to avoid doing things that will have those karmic consequences that aren't so pleasant. Ultimately, though, we need to learn to understand that both bad and good karma are still karma. The chain of karma is something that we can break in order to see the phenomenon around us as empty and act from a very different perspective. There have been some interesting articles I've read recently that talk about the business of meditation, some using the cute catch phrases "McMindfulness and Frozen Yoga" to caution against taking these teachings out of context. It strikes me that the idea of clinging to good karma might be at the heart of these articles.

I do think that it's a good idea to live a good life and to help people. Seems like a pretty straightforward thing to say – do good, fake it til you make it, turn your frown upside down – and the precepts and many of the Buddha's teachings give instructions to lay followers and just regular people on how to live to cause the least amount of harm that we can. That is an important part of life. So what's to be concerned about? One of the pitfalls is when life becomes too comfortable, perhaps. Or when we strive to live a lovely life thinking that when I get that promotion, that better car, loose that weight, get married, or whatever worthwhile goal, I will be happy. Even some of the mindfulness practice groups are all about solving a problem or achieving a goal of stress relief, weight loss, pain reduction, even to calm skin conditions and have been made secular so they will be palatable for a diverse society that might balk at the religious over-tones.

Yet, what are we really doing if we're helping people cling to their happiness, even if it's a form of spiritual materialism? Are we being Bodhisattvas or busybodies? I might create a wonderful world of doing good works, helping others, and being very happy and accomplished, but have I learned to come back to myself and experience life as it really is? Have I really spent my life well unless I've trained my mind to stay and learned to look deeply into the emptiness of all things? Being a fixer and a positive minded person, I'm all for mindfulness clinics and yoga studios that promise that they won't bother people with the deeper spiritual traditions of these practices; after all, adding wholesome activities to people's lives and helping them is worthwhile and a way to make the world a better place. What I do need to watch in myself is becoming too attached to the superficial helping, or the helping that actually takes the other person's ability to help themselves away. Sometimes helping can be a diversion or way to avoid feeling negative emotions like pain and discomfort for a situation. What better way to stop suffering than to fix the problem right up so that everyone feels better, right? Except that I've learned and am beginning to see more clearly that having a direct experience of my suffering is far more valuable. Staying with the feeling and having the training to be able to stay with correct concentration so that I can stay still in order to look deeply at the feeling – the true definition of mindfulness.

So Sahn talks in these pages about the cautions of depending too much on words, yet the dangers of those who would hide their lack of understanding with the wordless gestures that are actually meaningless coming from those who are still deluded. And he brings us back to the essentials; great faith, great courage, and great doubt. It does take great faith or confidence in the Buddha's teachings to take on this practice, and when we've studied and tested it out, we can rest our minds in that confidence because we can understand intellectually that it is true. But it does take a great deal of courage because we're asked to set aside the intellectual understanding and to really look deeply and honestly into our own layers of conditioned responses, peeling them away to our ultimate nature. That's not easy, either! When my mother would ask if I wanted to be right or if I wanted to be happy when I was on one particular high horse or another, my answer was "I want to be happy because I'm right!" I'm kind of a tough case. Being honest about how I feel makes me feel pretty vulnerable because it opens up that I'm not the fixed idea I have about myself of all those good qualities and none of the bad.

And Great Doubt is the third of those essentials. So Sahn even goes so far to say that practicing a koan without great doubt is the gravest disease. This is true of reciting the Buddha's name as well. When we keep the koan or the Buddha's name in our consciousness in all that we do, we can't help but have those doubts. Look at what is happening, can it really be true that everything is empty and all of these nutty people have Buddha nature? Listen to how that person talked to me! Can it really be true that I should soften my heart to them and listen to their side of the story? Surely not! Surely I should armor my heart to protect and stand up for myself – the boundaries will protect them, too, right? And what harm is it to drop the practices just for a few hours to watch a movie, eat junk food, and gossip with friends; it's just a harmless diversion, right? But the seeds of the practice have been planted and rather than beat myself up for my quirks and foibles, those glimpses of being fully present remind me that the practice is a very good use of the rest of my life.

Pure Land

Because I practice in the Vietnamese Pure Land/Zen tradition, which has its roots in Korean syncretic Buddhism, I thought I'd start by sharing what drew me into Pure Land practices. I've written about this before for different classes here but it's worth revisiting, I think. It took me awhile to settle into a school to practice in and most of my early Buddhist teachers were of the Zen persuasion. Thich Nhat Hanh is my root teacher and he emphasizes the Zen part of the Pure Land/Zen combination, so for a long time, I kind of looked down my nose at Pure Land practice. After all, it is touted as the "simple" and "easy" method; something for people who aren't that smart, or who culturally and erroneously worship the Buddha or the Amitabha Buddha as gods. Because I had been ordained into the core community of Thich Nhat Hanh's Order of Interbeing (Tiep Hien) and because he recommended that I find a practice community to spend more time with monastics and join them on retreats, I found Chua Bao An within a pretty reasonable drive from our house.

When I first started attending, the first couple of visits were wonderful; so cool to experience the service and enjoy the people and join them for lunch and kind of be fussed over. I went with some friends and we enjoyed discussing the experience, the importance of ritual, and the scriptural basis of the practice. Over the next weeks, the others dropped off one by one until I was left as the only Westerner sitting in the back of the sanctuary. I debated dropping off, too, but Thay's instructions kept tapping me on the shoulder and I thought I'd give it a few more weeks. I started sitting further up in the sanctuary to be part of the congregation instead of on the periphery, and I looked up the English translations of the sutras that were being chanted in Vietnamese, so I could read along during the service. Some of the ladies there had plans for me, though, and started teaching me how to chant along in Vietnamese and pulling me along for how and when and why to bow before the service. They welcomed me to join in with the working meditations as well, and I started arriving a little early to help sweep the steps and clean the kitchen. We have monthly days of mindfulness and those really became important to me in not only becoming part of the community but for the benefit to my practice as well. The Abbess of our temple invited me to take the precepts during a mini retreat and presented me with a gray robe that she had made for me. I was so touched and felt so at home there.

When I first started attending, the newness was the thing – very exciting and more like being a tourist than a participant. As I started attending on my own, I started noticing the things that I didn't like about it all. I prefer the Japanese Zen aesthetic, so what I saw as the gaudy Asian lights, flowers, too many knickknacks everywhere, and the long periods of chanting Nam Mô A Di Đà Phật seemed like a cultural overlay to the "real" Buddhism that I wondered might be missing. Plus, I was getting a little bit bored by it all. I thought seriously about not going anymore and had lots of excuses, not speaking Vietnamese being the primary one. Who could fault me for that; many paths up the mountain and all that, right? The thing that changed my mind was reading along in the sutra recitation from the Flower Ornament sutra about the qualities of Quan the Am (Quan Yin) and the qualities of the Pure Land. It suddenly clicked that as I was looking at the saturated colors of the lights and flowers, the ornately carved altar and frame around the altar alcove, the statues, bells, and especially the huge Amitabha Buddha on the highest platform that had a halo behind him with a spinning light that glinted rainbow colors that it looked as foreign to me as the Pure Land would look if I looked at it with eyes that only saw the relative reality. I realized that I was coming to the practice with mud on my feet.

The scene in front of me and the people surrounding me were now part of the Pure Land, each teaching me the dharma and supporting my practice, the vivid colors reminding me that my relative, dualistic way of seeing is just a shadow of the truth of the ultimate dimension. The image was of my day to day life being spent in the mud with all of us who suffer from our attachment to the relative world and all I need to do is grow in the dharma to open the lotus blossom of my consciousness to the Pure Land – roots still in the mud and able to walk in that world with compassion that comes from seeing the emptiness in what was causing suffering, and blooming by having a direct experience of things just as they are. It's in my resistance to those things I deem wrong or bad or just don't like and my clinging to those things that I love and like and feel that I have to have to be happy that keeps me from seeing everything as part of the teachings. It was shortly after that that I took the precepts to become a formal member of the temple and I looked at donning the gray robe as my way of supporting this wonderful community and being part of the lineage leading to the Pure Land.

There is a wonderful story about a woman who chanted the name of the Amitabha Buddha day and night for many years. She was well known in her neighborhood for her loud chanting; making sure that everyone heard and was aware of her devotion. She was dutiful in letting others know about their failings, too and never missed an opportunity to point out what others should be doing better. One day a wandering monk was visiting the town and heard about the old woman and heard her chants. He went to her front gate and began shouting her name rhythmically. This went on for over an hour; the duel of the chanting names! When she would try to chant louder to drown out his annoying chanting of her name, he would just chant louder too. Finally, she was exasperated! She came storming out of her house and confronted him – why was he calling her name, didn't he understand that she was chanting her devotion to the Amida Buddha so that she could be reborn in the Pure Land? Wouldn't his time be better spent chanting the Buddha's name himself? Didn't he realize that he was annoying the heck out of her?

When she asked that last question, he smiled. He softly explained that he had been shouting her name without understanding and reverence, just as she was chanting the Buddha's name as a way to puff herself up and make others see how devoted she was. If she was annoyed at hearing her name chanting in this way for only an hour, think of how annoyed the Buddha must be after chanting his name like that for so many years! At that point, her eyes were opened and she bowed deeply; her chants now became a support to her practice, filled with the compassion of the Pure Land.

What I've learned over the years is that holding the name of the Buddha is a koan in its own right and must be approached in the same way. If the chanting is for a goal or to make myself better than, it's no better than trying to figure out a koan intellectually then having pride in having solved the puzzle. When I hold the name of the Buddha or the koan throughout the day, it opens up a different way of interacting with the world. When I'm talking with someone and notice that a button of mine is pushed, because of the practices, some Prajna comes into it – I might not be able to practice on the spot and I might misbehave, but I am aware of that attachment so that I can at least sit with the feeling later without getting carried away with the drama and storyline.

Chanting A Di Đà Phật to myself, sometimes counting the beads of my hand mala is comforting and when done mindfully, it's a similar support to coming back to the breath and is easier for me than using the breath for a support, especially since my surgery. When I have strong feelings, I'm not trying to drown the thoughts or emotions out by chanting, but rather touching them lightly with the name of the Buddha helping me experience that ineffable understanding of emptiness. I look at the chanting of the Buddha's name as an invitation to the Pure Land, the open hand of the Amitabha Buddha with his half smile welcoming me to sit with him. I was asked once what one question I would ask God if I had the chance. I felt tears spring to my eyes when I realized that if I had the opportunity to ask the Buddha a question, the only question I would ask is "will you sit with me?" Sitting in the presence, quietude, and equanimity of the Buddha would be all I would ever need or want in my life.

Fortunately, this is possible – while I still live in the mud, while I still see the world through the lens of the relative reality, I can't see that I'm actually surrounded by bodhisattvas and Buddhas who are more than happy to sit with me. Each one sometimes pointing out a button that I have, often by pushing it, but each time giving me the gift of seeing and processing those buttons so that I can step into the Pure Land button-free. But when I can touch my Buddha nature and see that in each person I meet, the Pure Land is instantly available.

One Mind

Syncretism is the combining of divergent, sometimes even seemingly contradictory beliefs, yet melding the practices illustrating an underlying unity which supports inclusion. The practices of the Korean masters draw from different traditions and help bridge the gap between a variety of schools of Buddhism, allowing people to see that the ultimate goal of awakening can be found in these differing practices when the fundamental purpose of the practices is understood and followed. The main practices are: 1) following the three-fold practice of sila (precepts), samadhi (meditation in its many forms), and prajna (wisdom); 2) sutra recitation or chanting and study; 3) Harmonizing Disputations and the practice of Non-Hindrance; 4) Koan (Kong'an in Korean) and Hwadu practices; 5) the idea of sudden enlightenment and gradual cultivation, and 6) Pure Land practice.

Underlying all of these practices is the understanding of the mind-ground. "There is only one thing, from the very beginning, infinitely bright and mysterious by nature. It was never born, and it never dies. It cannot be described or given a name. What is this 'one thing'?" T'aego explained the qualities of the mind-ground as being limitless light, ineffable, does not falsely engender discrimination, and is silent and motionless in nature; teaching outside this understanding is delusion. This understanding cannot be named, but is called Mind or the Path as an expedient to teaching. He goes on to say that this one thing is always with us and is so vast that it encompasses everything so that all things are within the inter-being-ness of everything else. When this appears in total clarity for the practitioner, all false thinking is obliterated and the mind is quiet and motionless with nothing to rest on because there is no ground on which to rest.

But how is such an abstraction taught? When the Buddha held up a flower and only Mahākāśyapa smiled, the wordless nature of the "one thing" was illustrated beautifully. The "one thing" shows that everyone's original nature is complete as it is; the direct experience of the suchness of all things needs no further embellishment; all of the words even the sutras, and the Buddha and the Patriarchs are of no further use. "All phenomena are beyond names and forms. The sounds of the streams and the colors of the mountains are closest. What is 'closest'? You can only please yourself: how can I speak?" T'aego admonishes the assembly not to revere him or cling to his words: "All of you will think, 'Today an enlightened teacher appears in the world.' What a joke! When I talk like this, it's already sleep talk. Why are all of you sleeping with your eyes open?"

When Master Wonhyo awoke to "One Mind," he was reborn; his wisdom was considered profound and had a lasting impact on Korean Buddhism through his treatise which expounded the importance of sila, samadhi, and prajna, the importance of the innate potential for enlightenment, and the recognition and abandonment of the relative in order to recognize the absolute reality.

Sleeping inside an underground shelter yesterday, I was at ease.
But sleeping inside a tomb last night, my mind was greatly agitated.
Now I understand – when a thought arises, all dharmas (phenomena)
arise, And when a thought disappears, the shelter and the graveyard
are one and the same.

The Three Worlds exist simply in the mind,
And all phenomena are mere perception.
Since there is no Dharma outside the mind,
How can it be sought for elsewhere?

Wonhyo's practice of Muae (non-hindrance) was central to his understanding of One Mind; evoking balance and compassion within the practitioner. He taught that with freedom from duality and delusion, we naturally cultivate compassion because we understand unity and are not crippled by possessive individualism. The purpose of Buddhism is to save all sentient beings and that no matter how great the theory, if it is not practiced in our daily lives, it is of no use.

Chinul explains that "true mind is like space, for it neither ends nor changes." and goes on to demonstrate how the awakened person behaves; that the awakened person is "just so" in any situation and their actions flow naturally from inner peace and compassion. Both Chinul and So Sahn introduce the concept of sudden awakening and gradual cultivation. Chinul reminds us that hindrances and obstacles are formidable and habits deeply ingrained; warning us to continue our practice so that we will not be swept away. So Sahn says: "The sutra teaching transmits only the dharma of One Mind, while Zen meditation transmits only the dharma of seeing one's true nature. Mind can be likened to a bright mirror's clear substance, while our true nature is like the mirror's reflective clarity."

He goes on to emphasize the balance between the importance of having a proper understanding of the sutras and the benefits of a genuine and honest meditation practice. "When you hear sutras being chanted – either by your own voice or by other people – you are cultivating affinity for the teachings and practice. It is a Way that leads to a joyful mind and great spiritual merit. This body is no more stable than a bubble; it will soon disappear. But any efforts made for the sake of truth will never die." and on the other hand, "Pure and clear wisdom that functions with no hindrance arises from correct meditation."

Chinul attained a level of enlightenment from studying a sutra as I'm sure others have, many Masters have experienced awakening during meditation, and others have reached their understanding in unconventional ways of seeing or hearing something seemingly unrelated to the dharma. What these ways have in common is the ripening of the student's mind and their ability to be open to the dharma in whatever forms it takes.

We humans are funny creatures; our habit of distracting ourselves and our conditioned responses are so ingrained, that even the most helpful teaching and beneficial practice can be misused. Master So Sahn maps out both the pros and the cons of each type of practice, helping us see that the sutras can be our guides and our refuge if we allow them to penetrate our hearts giving us wisdom instead of using our knowledge to further solidify our fixed views about the world and ourselves. He also explains that meditation is the way we can have a direct experience of things just as they are and to come back to our true nature, the "one mind." Yet, meditation is not immune from dangers. Instead of a refuge, we can use meditation to repress and retreat from the feelings that arise within us. Instead of softening our hearts, we can become arrogant or believe that meditative bliss is the equivalent of awakening.

Chinul explains that sudden awakening and gradual cultivation are like the two wheels of a cart; neither can be missing. Continuing the training will keep samadhi and prajna equally balanced, helping us hold our insight, yet not be swept away by the unwholesome actions we find in the world which we react to because of our habit energies and conditioning. He further helps us by showing us how the awakened behave, think, and respond. The awakened person is "just so" in any situation; the actions flow naturally from inner peace and compassion. Yet, even as he concludes explaining this in detail, he reminds us not to become complacent or over-confident; ever on guard for those deeply ingrained conditioned and habitual responses.

Balance is important in the teachings for sudden awakening and gradual cultivation because of the recognition of how ingrained our conditioned and habitual reactions are. For me, this is a very important point; especially So Sahn's contention that it is awakening that is the true beginning of our practice. When the practitioner first penetrates the mystery of seeing things as empty, theoretically it is possible that the experience will be so complete that they will be able to see their conditioning and fix it on the spot, thereby experiencing the full awakening of the Buddha.

But my guess is that Chinul and So Sahn are right that, for most practitioners, the ability to see things as empty is a beginning point. They then need to bring prajna into their practice by being able to recognize those conditioned responses and to see when their attachments come up. Practice without words is then a powerful way to work with this habitual way of thinking. At this point, the practitioner does not need the teachings; the teachings have done their work and helped the student perceive emptiness. The student is then able to rest in emptiness and meditate in the full and direct experience of the suchness of things, bringing the full single-pointed focus of the one mind. I have a guilty pleasure in watching corny TV shows and I used to watch the show "Touched by an Angel." In one of the episodes, a man with a crisis of faith meets the pretty lady angel and he talks about his problems, saying that he wished he could have the faith of an angel. She corrected him, saying that she doesn't have any faith at all; she sees God all the time, so she knows him and you don't need faith for what you know for sure. She went on about the importance and value of faith.

I've always remembered that and while faith has slightly different meanings in Buddhism, faith still plays a role in our practice. I like the definition "to place the heart upon" best, but even with all the intellectual evidence and knowledge we can gather to convince ourselves of the truth of the Buddha dharma, there is still an element of faith. When we experience awakening; that experience of seeing things as empty, we no longer need faith – the fighte fuaighte, that beautiful Gaelic phrase that means "woven into and through each other," captures the inter-woven nature of the relative with the ultimate dimensions. Avoiding "falling into emptiness" or as Nagarjuna says that if we become attached to emptiness we're hopeless cases, yet not clinging to the relative reality; we find that delicate balance.

Ta'Hui cautions "In essence the ultimate of the Tao and of things lays neither in speech nor in silence – words cannot convey it, nor can silence." He understood that there is a razor's edge between the pairs of opposites and that the only important thing is for our heart to let go of the self. Chögyam Trungpa Rinpoche once said something along the lines of "The bad news is that you're falling and there is nothing to grab on to. The good news is that there is no ground."

On a clear and bring day,

Clouds gather in deep valleys.

In a remote and silent place,

Radiant sunlight illuminates the clear sky.

The analogy that I think of for the ability to perceive things as empty is trying to explain three dimensions to a two dimensional being. If I draw a Necker cube to illustrate the three dimensions, my two dimensional friend will turn his head one way and the other, but he really won't understand what I'm trying to show him. I can imagine two dimensional beings even teaching others in their two dimensional world about the three dimensions and the

profound spiritual import of it, all the while not understanding what three dimensions are at all. Yet, there may be a day, to use another famous optical illusion as an example, if I have only been able to see the "old hag" in the drawing I might look, perhaps at the prompting of someone explaining it to me or maybe something out of the blue, that I can see the "young lady."

So when the student first perceives a thought or a cloud or a leaf as empty, what to do next is important. Luckily, we have teachers like Chinul and So Sahn who understand and continue to guide us past the pitfalls and encourage us not to give up on our experience or rest on our laurels and not progress to our full potential of being fully awake. It is then that our grounding and living in the ethic precepts, the development of our concentration, and our inner wisdom will support our revelation in order to develop into full Buddhahood.

I practice in the Vietnamese Pure Land/Zen tradition, which has its roots in Korean syncretic Buddhism. I've written about this before for different classes but it is worth revisiting what drew me to Pure Land practices. It took me awhile to settle into a school to practice in and most of my early Buddhist teachers were of the Zen persuasion. Thich Nhat Hanh is my root teacher and he emphasizes the Zen part of the Pure Land/Zen combination, so for a long time I kind of looked down my nose at Pure Land practice. After all, it is touted as the "simple" and "easy" method; something for people who aren't that smart, or who culturally and erroneously worship the Buddha or the Amitabha Buddha as gods. Because I had been ordained into the core community of Thich Nhat Hanh's Order of Interbeing (Tiep Hien) and because he recommended that I find a practice community to spend more time with monastics and join them on retreats, I found Chua Bao An within a pretty reasonable drive from our house.

When I first started attending, the first couple of visits were wonderful; so cool to experience the service and enjoy the people and join them for lunch and kind of be fussed over. I went with some friends and we enjoyed discussing the experience, the importance of ritual, and the scriptural basis of the practice. Over the next weeks, the others dropped off one by one until I was left as the only Westerner sitting in the back of the sanctuary. I debated dropping off, too, but Thay's instructions kept tapping me on the shoulder and I thought I'd give it a few more weeks. I started sitting further up in the sanctuary to be part of the congregation instead of on the periphery and looked up the English translations of the sutras that were being chanted in Vietnamese so I could read along during the service.

Some of the ladies there had plans for me, though, and started teaching me how to chant along in Vietnamese and pulling me along for how and when and why to bow before the service. They welcomed me to join in with the working meditations as well, and I started arriving a little early to help sweep the steps and clean the kitchen. We have monthly days of mindfulness and those really became important to me in not only becoming part of the community but for the benefit to my practice as well. The Abbess of our temple invited me to take the precepts during a mini retreat and presented me with a gray robe that she had made for me. I was so touched and felt so at home there.

When I first started attending, the newness was the thing – very exciting and more like being a tourist than a participant. As I started attending on my own, I started noticing the things that I didn't like about it all. I prefer the Japanese Zen aesthetic, so what I saw as the gaudy Asian lights, flowers, too many knickknacks everywhere, and the long periods of chanting Nam Mô A Di Đà Phật seemed like a cultural overlay to the "real" Buddhism that I wondered might be missing. Plus, I was getting a little bit bored by it all. I thought seriously about not going anymore and had lots of excuses, not speaking Vietnamese being the primary one. Who could fault me for that; many paths up the mountain and all that, right?

The thing that changed my mind was reading along in the sutra recitation from the Flower Ornament sutra about the qualities of Quan the Am (Quan

Yin) and the qualities of the Pure Land. It suddenly clicked that as I was looking at the saturated colors of the lights and flowers, the ornately carved altar and frame around the altar alcove, the statues, bells, and especially the huge Amitabha Buddha on the highest platform that had a halo behind him with a spinning light that glinted rainbow colors that it looked as foreign to me as the Pure Land would look if I looked at it with eyes that only saw the relative reality. I realized that I was coming to the practice with mud on my feet.

The scene in front of me and the people surrounding me were now part of the Pure Land, each teaching me the dharma and supporting my practice, the vivid colors reminding me that my relative, dualistic way of seeing is just a shadow of the truth of the ultimate dimension. The image was of my day-to-day life being spent in the mud with all of us who suffer from our attachment to the relative world and all I need to do is grow in the dharma to open the lotus blossom of my consciousness to the Pure Land – roots still in the mud and able to walk in that world with compassion that comes from seeing the emptiness in what was causing suffering, and blooming by having a direct experience of things just as they are. It's in my resistance to those things I deem wrong or bad or just don't like and my clinging to those things that I love and like and feel that I have to have to be happy that keeps me from seeing everything as part of the teachings. It was shortly after that that I took the precepts to become a formal member of the temple and I looked at donning the gray robe as my way of supporting this wonderful community and being part of the lineage leading to the Pure Land.

There is a wonderful story about a woman who chanted the name of the Amitabha Buddha day and night for many years. She was well known in her neighborhood for her loud chanting; making sure that everyone heard and was aware of her devotion. She was dutiful in letting others know about their failings, too and never missed an opportunity to point out what others should be doing better. One day a wandering monk was visiting the town and heard about the old woman and heard her chants. He went to her front gate and began shouting her name rhythmically. This went on for over an hour; the duel of the chanting names! When she would try to chant louder to drown out his annoying chanting of her name, he would just chant louder too. Finally, she was exasperated! She came storming out of her house and confronted him – why was he calling her name, didn't he understand that she was chanting her devotion to the Amida Buddha so that she could be reborn in the Pure Land? Wouldn't his time be better spent chanting the Buddha's name himself? Didn't he realize that he was annoying the heck out of her?

When she asked that last question, he smiled. He softly explained that he had been shouting her name without understanding and reverence, just as she was chanting the Buddha's name as a way to puff herself up and make others see how devoted she was. If she was annoyed at hearing her name chanting in this way for only an hour, think of how annoyed the Buddha must be after chanting his name like that for so many years! At that point, her eyes were opened and she bowed deeply; her chants now became a support to her practice, filled with the compassion of the Pure Land.

What I've learned over the years is that holding the name of the Buddha is a koan in its own right and must be approached in the same way. If the chanting is for a goal or to make myself better than, it's no better than trying to figure out a koan intellectually then having pride in having solved the puzzle. When I hold the name of the Buddha or the koan throughout the day, it opens up a different way of interacting with the world. When I'm talking with someone and notice that a button of mine is pushed, because of the practices, some prajna comes into it – I might not be able to practice on the spot and I still might misbehave, but I am aware of that attachment so that I can at least sit with the feeling later without getting carried away with the drama and storyline.

Chanting A Di Đà Phật to myself, sometimes counting the beads of my hand mala is comforting and when done mindfully, it's a similar support to coming back to the breath and is easier for me than using the breath for a support, especially since my surgery. When I have strong feelings, I'm not trying to drown the thoughts or emotions out by chanting, but rather touching them lightly with the name of the Buddha helping me experience that ineffable understanding of emptiness. I look at the chanting of the Buddha's name as an invitation to the Pure Land, the open hand of the Amitabha Buddha with his half smile welcoming me to sit with him. I was asked once what one question I would ask God if I had the chance. I felt tears spring to my eyes when I realized that if I had the opportunity to ask the Buddha a question, the only question I would ask is "will you sit with me?" Sitting in the presence, quietude, and equanimity of the Buddha would be all I would ever need or want in my life. Fortunately, this is possible – while I still live in the mud, while I still see the world through the lens of the relative reality, I can't see that I'm actually surrounded by bodhisattvas and Buddhas who are more than happy to sit with me. Each one sometimes pointing out a button that I have, often by pushing it, but each time giving me the gift of seeing and processing those buttons so that I can step into the Pure Land button-free. But when I can touch my Buddha nature and see that in each person I meet, the Pure Land is instantly available.

Chinul and So Sahn both talk about Pure Land practices and clarify how they should be approached. While the cornerstone of Korean Zen practice is kong'an and hwa'du training, Pure Land practice is actually very similar and I believe that is why they valued it and include it as a valid part of Korean Buddhist practice. When the Masters teach hwa'du practice, they both explain what the student should, and just as importantly, should not do. They talk about the importance of one-pointed focus, of being tuned not too loose and not to tight, and about having both great faith and great doubt in order to penetrate the mystery. They also discuss the pitfalls of the ten sicknesses to avoid, including not trying to figure the kong'an out intellectually getting caught in searching for proofs and evidence, not to delude oneself by mimicking the teachers' wordless gestures, and not to abandon everything by falling into emptiness.

Wonhyo taught that Pure Land Buddhism was closely connected to One Mind, contending that anyone can attain enlightenment through skillful means. The key was to find practice that fits the person's abilities and nature. Many people struggle with the complex teachings, doctrine, and philosophies, so the Pure Land practice of chanting the Buddha's name was simple and approachable. That it's said to be for those of inferior spiritual capabilities might seem insulting, but I've come to realize that it's actually true for me. I'm smart, but I'm kind of dense when it comes to these teachings. I'll nod my head and try to contemplate them but find that they either hurt my head or put me to sleep. Those brain teaser kong'ans are just so impenetrable for me; I get what they're supposed to do for me, but I just can't get that insight to happen for me.

On the other hand, both Chinul and So Sahn warned about the improper ways of practice: "Merely chanting with the lips is nothing more than recitation of the Buddha's name. Chanting with a one-pointed mind is true chanting. Just mouthing the words without mindfulness, absorbed in habitual thinking, will do no real good for your practice." That kind of instruction should be very familiar to one who practices hwa'du – the student is exhorted to keep the hwa'du in their mind with everything they do, and warned not to either try to figure it out through cleverness or turn it into another delusion. Chinul believed that, like Zen, Pure Land practices could bring an awakening to the Buddha nature when properly directed in this very lifetime.

In his work *The Essentials of Pure Land Practice*, Chinul gives specific and practical instructions for how to practice. Chinul had a very encouraging nature and this work is no exception as he assures the student that they can do this practice and gives specific advice for the different types of people including those with great sexual desire, great hatred, great mental distraction (squirrel!), or with many karmic obstacles. He explains that when progress is made, not to stop there but to continue practice through the phases of overcoming the impediments, entering the gate of pristine morality, and being unified with the path, pacifying the mind and arriving in Amitabha's Pure Land of ultimate bliss.

Chanting the name of the Amitabha Buddha is cultivated through ten types of recollection: while curbing the body, while curbing speech, while curbing the mind, during activity, during stillness, while speaking, while remaining silent, while contemplating Amitabha's appearance, with no-mind, and in suchness. He goes on to explain that recollection means to maintain and that "Buddha" means to awaken, so the Pure Land practitioner is maintaining their attention on the true mind, remaining attentive to the one thought of thoughtlessness, making it full and bright. "Once it is full and bright and thoughts have been brought to an end, it is called true recollection of the Buddha." In Buddha name recitation, the practitioner asks herself "who is the one who is reciting the Buddha name?" or "who is mindful of the Buddha?" The one mindful of the Buddha is the Buddha within.

Chinul was the first to include hwa'du practice in his approach to Sŏn practice and there were misconceptions about this practice, too. Hwa'du is a so-called shortcut approach that removes the philosophical component entirely and is considered the superior approach for sudden enlightenment. Chinul quotes the Exposition of the Avatamsaka Sutra "First, enter in faith through acquired understanding; later unite with the unimpeded dharma-dhātu through thoughtlessness... The realization of a Buddha leaves behind words... and cuts off thoughts."

Thich Nhat Hanh teaches that in the Pure Land, the teachings are available at all times through the talks of the bodhisattvas, the birds, the clouds, wind, footsteps, or the breath. Gandhi once said: "My life is my message." A dharma practitioner knows that with each step, word, or gesture, he is giving a dharma talk. Each person we meet is a bodhisattva "If we have mindfulness and concentration, everything we see and hear in our daily life becomes a dharma talk. A falling leaf, a flower as it opens, a bird flying by, or the sound of a bird calling are all dharma talks and we say that the one who is giving the dharma talk is Buddha Vairocana, that is the Dharmakaya."

The Pure Land practice is also very similar to the four foundations of mindfulness in that the Buddha taught to have mindfulness of the body in the body, the mind in the mind, the feelings in the feelings, and objects of mind in objects of mind. The Buddha taught that we can expect the fruits of practice within seven years, but also for a week or even a day. In the Amitabha Sutra we also read that if we cannot recollect the name of Amitabha ten times, once will do. When we read this with our heart, we see the great love and compassion that the Buddha has for us; even if we find concentration very difficult, the Buddha tells us "Just try! You can do it."

The Dharmakaya of the Buddha never ceases to teach the dharma. Thich Nhat Hanh wrote this to honor his friend who died young.

The Dahlia Flower:
Standing by the fence,
You smile your wonderful smile.
Looking at you in silence I am amazed
I just heard you singing.
The words of your song
Belong to eternity.
With all my heart, I bow to you in respect.

When we enter the Pure Land, we do not have to go anywhere, we do not have to wait to die; we see the dharma body clearly. We know that in the relative dimension, the birds, flowers, clouds, and all of us exist in a cycle of birth and death, but as far as the Dharmakaya is concerned, all of these things are manifestations of the dharma body and are not phenomena outside of ourselves. When we join our palms to greet one another, this practice can bring us great joy when done in the spirit of mindfulness, concentration, and insight; greeting the other saying "A lotus for you, a Buddha to be." In this way, we enter the Pure Land in our hearts; our minds at ease, open, and free.

CHAPTER 13

Tracing Back the Radiance

"Tracing Back the Radiance: Chinul's Korean Way of Zen" by Robert E. Buswell is a remarkable book that introduces us to the Korean Zen Master Chinul. Chinul was a teacher who not only introduced Zen koan study to Korea, but also took an unmistakable intellectual approach to studying Buddhism. The deep analysis of the sutras and the philosophy was welcomed as a way to understand the concepts in depth. Because Chinul was raised at a time in Korea where there was political strife, the status and stability of any of the religions of the time was in flux. He also recognized corruption of Buddhist ideals by the monastic system, and was dedicated to bringing true Buddhist practice back. He was a prolific writer and often emphasized practice, including instructional documents. Chinul is noted for his ability to connect different ideas and schools of Buddhism, including a syncretic blend of Zen and Pure Land, and did not hesitate to borrow from the sutras reserved by other schools. Chinul developed a devoted following in his life, and we are lucky to have his work available for study.

Chinul

Buswell explains that Chinul had an ecumenical attitude toward Buddhist philosophy and that he developed an eclectic approach to meditation practice. Fundamentally Sŏn in focus, Chinul demonstrated how the various techniques of different sects worked together and could guide students toward the same goal. Chinul recognized what the Buddha had taught was well; that each person has a specific set of talents and ways of learning so that by finding the skillful and expedient means of teaching them, they would be as successful as the person with a natural gift for spiritual capacity. He developed three styles of practice to suit those with inferior, average, and superior spiritual capacity through the balanced approach of sīla, samādhi and prajnā.

In China, and I'm sure in Korea too, many people looked at the Buddhist teachings and doubted that they would ever be able to penetrate the meaning or make spiritual progress in their own lifetime. I certainly relate to this and have bounced back and forth, especially as a younger person, leaving Buddhism behind for a time because it seemed so dense or convoluted or ridiculous to me. But the Buddha Dharma always called me back home because of teachers who, like Chinul, could see that the truth of the dharma has many modes of expression.

It's not surprising to me that Chinul came to see Pure Land practices as a valid approach to awakening considering his emphasis on Hwadu practice. Hwadu practice is a "shortcut" to realization that focuses the student's attention on the one thought of the Hwadu; taking a word from a koan, and bringing the meaning of the word into focus or by focusing on the word itself. In either case, the student has no intellectual ground to cling to; "nothing for the discriminative mind to latch onto for support." The student develops "doubt" and the intensity of the investigation increases, disrupting dualist ways of thinking. The idea is that when the student is at the peak of this balance of perplexity, wonder, concentration, and doubt a catalyst will break through to free the original mind. The student keeps the Hwadu in mind throughout the stages of body, speech, and mind; in no-thought and in suchness, so that the original unity of the awakened mind is restored.

Chinul interprets Pure Land practice in a short work called *Essentials of Pure Land Practice*, a work I looked up when I first read this book for another class and have used in my own practice (I won't refer to it much here, but will talk about it in my detail in my final paper). Buswell explains that Pure Land practice is intended for ordinary people with minimal ability in spiritual matters. This is the point that turns a lot of westerners off about Pure Land practice, and frankly, I was one of those who looked down my nose at this practice. After all, isn't it about wishing to be saved and to go someplace beautiful so there is no suffering anymore? Isn't that what those silly religious folks do; not looking at their own inner peace, but wanting it to come from the outside? While I don't think Mr. Buswell shares my or even Chinul's respect for the practice, I don't believe that Chinul was merely being tolerant or utilitarian in his support of Pure Land practices. The Pure Land School draws from the Avatamsaka and Lotus sutra and the recitation of the Buddha's name is only one part of the practice. Even when only looking at the recitation and later recollection of the Buddha's name, one affects the workings of the mind by suspending the discriminating intellect. While the Hwadu might bring great doubt, the recitation of the Buddha's name brings great faith to the front of the practitioner's mind, suspending the internal dialogue and analysis of thought. Chinul believed that, like Zen, Pure Land practices could bring an awakening to the Buddha nature when properly directed in this very lifetime.

For some people, Pure Land practices might be done simplistically with no understanding of the metaphors and larger truths. It gives them a sense of peace and tranquility that can helps them build merit and hope for a better rebirth. For others, being born in the Pure Land means reaching a state of mental purity and a direct experience of the ultimate reality is achieved. In Buddha name recitation, the practitioner asks herself "who is the one who is reciting the Buddha name?" or "who is mindful of the Buddha?" The one mindful of the Buddha is the Buddha within.

Teachers and Transmissions

Uich'on was a great scholar yet he understood that the true understanding of Buddhism was not about doctrine or being able to answer questions about the sutras perfectly. Perhaps he took to heart the passage in the sutras when the Buddha was asked questions about the nature of gods and the self, but the Buddha was silent. When Ananda asked why he didn't answer the man's questions, the Buddha said that the man only wanted to know facts to then be able to be right. The knowledge wasn't going to help the man wake up. Studying and looking for teachers to help our understanding is very important since for the majority of us, while we might have glimpses of understanding on our own, being given instruction helps us place our minds on the Buddha's teachings, planting seeds that will bear fruit as a result of our practice.

When studying history it's fascinating to see how much has changed and how much has remained the same. I'm so grateful to so many of the historical teachers who sacrificed so much to learn and pass their knowledge on to us. My favorite quote in this reading is "Against the wishes of his father, Uich'on surreptitiously traveled to Sung China..." Now, I have to admit that I had wander lust when I was a young person and for awhile when my mother would answer the phone and it was me, the first thing she would say was "where are you?" Unlike me, though, Uich'on wasn't just out to see the world, but had a desire to study and had the leadership skills to not only see the big picture, but to work toward unity in the two schools. He made impassioned pleas to each side, expressing the value in the other.

In many respects, I think that Buddhism today has some of the same division. The scholars who believe it is more important to have an in depth understanding of the sutras and history, the monastics who believe that their doctrines and rituals are the most important thing, and the schools and practitioners who are skeptical of doctrine and ritual and want to place all of their spiritual eggs in the practice basket all contribute to what is becoming Western Buddhism. Quite a few years ago, along with studying Buddhism, I was a spiritual workshop junky and went to lots of diverse classes and workshops that included academic study, listening to the insights of teachers of a variety of stripes, New Age stuff (some wonderful that I use today like Reiki and some that was so woo that it was hard not to roll my eyes even then). One of the workshops that I attended and went further in was Gabrielle Roth's Five Rhythm movement method of ecstatic dance. I loved the free form movement and world music was wonderful. Interestingly, she developed a method that organized the basic rhythms into: 1) flow, 2) staccato, 3) chaos, 4) lyrical, and 5) stillness. She had lots to say about how we flow through these rhythms yet the primary practice was to move to the music – she would say that her purpose in life was to seduce people into getting out of their heads and into their bodies, and through the body reconnect with the unity of everything. Still, there were people who would balk at any talk of organization and just wanted to experience the practice on their own terms. I found the blending of the two to be most valuable. It didn't help to only listen to the talks or read the books, and it was eventually pretty boring to just do the movement without any understanding. Whether the practice is still or moving, for me, the catalyst to move awareness into wisdom is that blending of steeping my brain in the Buddha's words, then letting them grow within to bear their fruits.

Chinul, whose primary practice was meditation, had an experience of awakening while studying a sutra. This might seem contradictory, but with his study of the Platform Sutra, and initial awakening to the nature of mind, Chinul was able to penetrate the interconnectedness of all forms of practice. Just as walking meditation, working meditation, sitting, sutra recitation and study are equally valid practices when approached as practice, he was able to promote the cultivation of Samadhi and Prajna concurrently. The implications of this, I think, are to illustrate that there are many roads up the mountain. It's a wonderful thing when we find the practice method that works best for us as individuals, but claiming it as an "only way" would not be true for everyone and may not even be true for us. Not to mention that there is a tendency to "fall in love" with our favorite practice which might make it into a form of distraction or diversion instead of a way to find the truth.

I've been listening to Pema Chödrön's talks for the past couple of years, and in one of them, it really cracked me up to hear her talk about how she is a terrible meditator. It was so funny to me, because I've always considered myself a terrible meditator, too. Now, I do it – I sit, usually twice a day, but, like Chinul, it's only been during Dharma talks, reciting the sutras, being with my patients, or during a ritual, that I've really had experiences of oneness or understanding. But then, my teacher explains that everything contains the dharma, and the way I slice the carrots is potentially just as meaningful as sitting. We're cultivating Samadhi and Prajna – each benefits the other.

Sudden vs. gradual awakening are the two approaches of cultivating the steps toward awakening vs. immersing oneself in emptiness. Awakening doesn't occur faster in one than the other, but the two approaches are looking at reality from each point of view. The truth of the dharma is not in question with these two approaches; it is more about the acknowledgement that it isn't possible to teach the reality directly but only from a slight emphasis of either emptiness or form to point to the truth. The passage from the Avatamsaka

Sutra that Chinul appreciated says it best: "the wisdom of the tathagatas is just like this: it is complete in the bodies of all sentient beings. It is merely all these ordinary, foolish people who are not aware of it and do not recognize it."

Chinul never had a long term teacher and did not receive a formal transmission. The majority of his ideas came from his studies of the Buddhist text, and I would add from his on-going and in-depth analysis of the other schools and teachers that were his contemporaries.

My first thoughts on this are that there are advantages and hazards in this approach. On the one hand, it's certainly comforting to think that for the people who do not have a teacher or practice center available to them, it is not necessarily a hindrance to attaining spiritual awakening. On the other hand, this is a dangerous thing unless one has the rigor and honesty to constantly be checking on what the ego is doing. It is an easy thing to believe that we have a depth of knowledge that a deft question from a good teacher can send spinning into uncertainty. We can convince ourselves of our brilliance very easily; a teacher can help bring us back to earth.

Chinul seems to be a brilliant thinker with a one pointed focus on learning and experiencing the truth. I was very impressed by his ability to read doctrinal statement and treatises, the corresponding polemic from the opposing school, then to tease out not only the positive points of each, but to also discern the motivation and reason why choices of doctrine were made. Additionally, he was able to understand and support the idea of the philosophical supporting the Sŏn views, creating a distinctive contribution to Buddhist thought.

These chapters have been wonderful food for thought for me as well. I'm a big fan of study as a form of practice, and I look at the sutras the way I approach artistic expression, even when the sutra seems to be a logic puzzle to be unraveled and understood. Each artist has their own medium and they use that medium to communicate or "transmit" their feeling or experience. I enjoy Salvador Dali's paintings, but only really knew about the more famous surreal paintings. I was able to visit the Dali museum near St. Petersburg, FL and they were having a special exhibition of his religious paintings. I was confronted with the Corpus Hypercubus, which is a huge painting, and it stopped me in my tracks. I found myself looking at the painting without thought – simply drinking it in. It evoked so many feelings; compassion, sorrow, grief, awe, and profound joy. When we can connect in that ineffable way, it doesn't matter if the art form is writing, poetry, dance, painting, or any of the many media that the artist can use, we are touched and we share the power of the experience. Sutras have that power as well, and we can connect with these wonderful teachers over the years.

Cultivating the Mind

Reading Chinul's exposition on Secrets on Cultivating the Mind gives us a picture of Chinul's ideas on practice, a detailed explanation of sudden awakening vs. gradual cultivation, and perhaps more importantly gives a glimpse into the kind of person Chinul was. One of the things that struck me within these passages was how often he used terms like "tragic" and "pitiful" when describing the plight of those of us who do not understand our Buddha nature and true mind yet. I sense an urgency in Chinul's writings and a genuine desire for his students to understand the way. I'm impressed by the lucidity and practicality in his examples and exhortations to his students; he didn't want them to get away with complacency in their practice, yet I got the feeling that he cared deeply that each person who heard his words could be freed from suffering by finding the truth. I've wondered about some of the Buddhist teachers that we've learned about through our courses; what kind of teachers would we consider them if they were alive today. Chinul strikes me as one that would be appreciated as down to earth and authentic.

An interesting point in the text is from the very beginning "true mind is like space, for it neither ends nor changes." That statement seems contradictory to basic Buddhist teachings of impermanence and interdependent co-arising. However, this brings an important point of Mahayana teaching; the Dharmakaya and identifies the "One Thing" that is the ground of being for awakening. Chinul points out the error of thinking that the Buddha is outside the body/mind or that they can receive understanding from anything other than their own efforts, uncovering their true inner nature. Chinul goes on to explain that the "formless thing" that Lin-chi used to express the nature of awakening, is our original mind; the dharma-seal of all Buddhas. He discusses the sudden awakening of following the light to original nature and that this ground of being is no different from the Buddha's. I very much appreciated, though, Chinul's practical side when he talks about the importance of continuing to practice – gradual cultivation in his recognition that even when we "see the light," there are many ingrained habit energies within us that we must continue to practice in order to understand and untangle. A line from the dialogue between the King and Bharati exemplifies this when Bharati is asked "Where is Buddha nature?" and the answer is "This nature is present during the performance of actions." To me, this points to the dynamic nature of emptiness; that its very nature is that of movement and function. In a sense, as we constantly nourish the Tathagatagarbha to remove those habit energies, we are raising our "inner child" again, but this time with a parent who is awake.

My favorite line in this work is "If this body is not ferried across to the other shore in this lifetime, then for which life are you going to wait?" He gives pithy advice to his students, helping us see that the path is not related to knowing or not knowing (frustrating for folks, like me, who like to know the facts and be right) and tells them to clear their minds and listen to him. By relating to the every day, he helps the student understand the truth is statements like "Drawing water and carrying firewood are spiritual powers and sublime functions." so that when he engages his students to really hear the cawing of the crow, he helps them penetrate the relative reality and see the ultimate dimension. In explaining the difference between the Buddhas and the Patriarchs, he says that the only thing that makes them different is that they can protect their minds and thoughts. By seeing that emptiness has no limitations, that there is no inside no outside, no far no near, no coming no going, no birth no death; delusion falls away because there is no longer anything to attain; no longer any obstacle to the mind.

Chinul explains that sudden awakening and gradual cultivation are like the two wheels of a cart; neither can be missing. Continuing the training will keep Samadhi and prajna equally balanced, helping us hold our insight, yet not be swept away by the unwholesome actions we find in the world which we react to because of our habit energies and conditioning. He further helps us by showing us how the awakened behave, think, and respond. The awakened person is "just so" in any situation; the actions flow naturally from inner peace and compassion. Yet, even as he concludes explaining this in detail, he reminds us that hindrances and obstacles are formidable and habits deeply ingrained; warning us to continue our practice so that we will not be swept away. Chinul speaks of treasure in the last lines of his work and his tone speaks of his desire to help, teach, persuade, and to celebrate in the understanding of his students – I get the feeling that he is rooting for all of us still.

True Mind

True mind is used by Chinul to help explain emptiness and our experience of emptiness, it seems to me. He refers to a number of terms that other schools and sutras have used to describe this, while cautioning that what he is talking about transcends knowledge and words. He references the Avatamsaka Sutra for how one can come to understand true mind, "you should know that all dharmas are the own-nature of the mind. The perfection of the wisdom-body does not come from any other awakening." I'm sure Chinul was inspired, in part, by the *Avatamsaka's* descriptions of the ultimate dimension/realm. He poetically expresses the realm of the True Mind "as vast and spacious as the immensity of space..." He explains the names that have been given to this including Bodhi, Dharmadhātu, Tathagata, suchness, dharma-body, Buddha-nature, and that true mind appears in all the sutras. In the most endearing statement, he says "but I cannot cite them all." The names, though, are a block if one does not penetrate one's own true mind.

In *Straight Talk on the True Mind*, Chinul presents a well organized work that expresses what seems to be his over-arching desire to share the salvic message of Buddhism; the awakening of all sentient beings. He systematically approaches the concept of True Mind by defining the term giving descriptions, names, and references to the sutras to illustrate and verify his definitions. He then describes both the essence and the function of true mind, comparing and contrasting each. He goes deeper to explain how true mind can exist amid delusion and how delusion can be extinguished. He relates true mind to the Noble Eightfold Path of Right Thought, and further describes the realm of the true mind. He spends considerable time on practice, explaining the importance of bodhichitta, the qualities of true mind, how one would test the truth of true mind, and the qualities of one who had awakened to their true mind. I found the work to be very accessible, clear, and down to earth. It reads very much like a letter from a teacher who is challenging, encouraging, and who very much believes that the student can be successful.

In describing the essence and functioning of True Mind, Chinul addresses an important and challenging paradox; how can true mind transcend duality, cause and effect, and pervade all places yet also have a function, manifesting in the flow of the universe? If the essence of true mind

Chinul's words certainly remain relevant to practitioners today; in fact, I would think that Chinul's work was rather ahead of his time. Interestingly, when looking at the work of Saicho and the Tendai School, I'm struck with how broadly Chinul is able to view the dharma. While his work comes much later than Saicho, it seems that politically, not a lot had changed over the years with regard to monasteries needing to win courtly favor and prove themselves worthy (superior?) to other schools to assure their place in the system and their survival.

Chinul, I'm sure, had to deal with that as well, however, he often eschews the common controversies and admonishes others not to judge the words of other teachers are inferior or superior, but to look at the time and place; that each master is using skillful means to teach and reach their students. "We should use this bright mirror to illuminate our own minds." Even today, we have practice centers that undergo controversy and divisions. Sometimes, it seems that the reason is so that the leader of the center can copyright his or her work with new terms to describe old ways. Some teachers rise to prominence by design and good marketing; others grow more organically and seem to be reluctant leaders. How refreshing it is to read Chinul's work which strives to cut through to the bottom line, in a sense, not allowing us to dwell on either side of the coin, but flipping it back and forth to give us that chance to see the whole.

For me personally, I find his encouraging words to be the most meaningful. His analysis of the dharma is very helpful as well, but even without that and depending on the teachings of other masters, I find his words of encouragement to be most helpful and personal. Occasionally, I've come across a passage that seems to be sent through time and speaks to me, and Chinul's words do that as well. I used to figure skate when I was young and had a coach who I've always remembered because she had such a good knack for coaching. She knew when to be tough, when to be soft, when to use bribery, and when to cut through the BS to get to the heart of the matter. Buddhist teachers, in some respects, take on the role of a coach at times as well. Helping us with our learning and practice, but also giving us a kick in the pants when we need it and words of encouragement to help convince us that we can be successful even when it seems quite impossible.

As far as implications for my own future teaching, I think that the most important lesson learned is to take Chinul's lead in striving for skillful means in teaching. I tend to talk about the thing that is most meaningful to me at the time. Instead, it is important to understand where the student is and look for ways to make a connection and build on that understanding, rather than indulging my own interests. Learning to be a good coach is an art.

The crux of Chinul's approach to sudden awakening and gradual cultivation is contained in this sentence: "Awakening from delusion is sudden; transforming an ordinary man into a saint is gradual." Perhaps because I'm a fan of the Avatamsaka Sutra and Hua-Yen Buddhist thought, Chinul's approach and explanations resonate with me. It just seems sensible that even when we see the truth, the suchness of things just as they are; we still have work to do to unravel the knots that took at least our own lifetime to tangle. There's a quote from the movie Postcards from the Edge where the director tells the main character that in the movies revelations happen and everything changes dramatically; in real life the revelation happens, but the transformation takes a little longer. While the transformation takes awhile, I would think that while awake, it might not be easier exactly, but at least more aware. Chinul gives us a number of analogies to help us understand, including the dream analogy to help us understand the difference between delusion and awakening. It's a thorny issue, though, when we start sorting through what is real and what is illusion, especially when considering how ingrained our cultural agreements can be. Someplace in the sutras, there is a quote of the Buddha that in following the path, we have to be prepared to go against our very instincts; surrender of the very self that we defend with every fiber of our being is a huge hurdle.

When I was diagnosed with cancer a few months ago, before I knew what my prognosis was, the thought of the closeness of death was very fresh; very raw. One of the things that I did that I'm so glad I had the presence of mind to do was to spend a significant amount of time in our meditation room contemplating my death, using the four foundations of mindfulness as a guide.

Even with a very good imagination, this contemplation in the past paled in comparison to spending time with it knowing that death might actually be near. It's hard to describe the depth of feeling this gave me or the insights; it sounds trite to say. The common wisdom would say that once you've faced and cheated death that it changes you – I agree that's true, but I wouldn't agree that it happens like it does in the movies or Hallmark cards. I do feel that I have a new appreciation for my life and a better sense of where I am; that doesn't mean that any given time in traffic, I'm not muttering under my breath about what an idiot that guy is.

There is a sense, though, that facet of the jewel of my life has come into focus in a way that it wasn't before. It seems to me that the dharma is something of an optical illusion, or gem with many facets, that is difficult to see clearly or wholly given our point of view. Once the wholeness, or suchness, has been seen, the teacher commits to helping his or her students see it as well. They point, cajole, rattle our cages, explain with metaphors and similes; create art and poetry and all the rest, trying to share the experience so that we will experience it ourselves. Looking at my Celtic roots, there is a saying that the spiritual journey is only about an inch long – the length of opening our eyes.

Hwadu or koan practice is considered a "shortcut" approach, although I'm sure that makes students who have been studying koans for many years chuckle. Chinul was concerned that students would develop their understanding based solely on words which would hamper their true understanding. He wanted to stop their thinking so that there was no place left for them to use their minds. So unlike a cat (it always cracks me up to point at something I want one of my cats to look at, but they sniff my finger instead of looking at what it's pointing to), when Hui-k'o saw, he forgot about the finger pointing (the teachings), dropping the intellectual understanding saying: "It is clear and constantly aware; words cannot describe it."

Chinul gives a number of instructions for approaching koans and when to attempt them as well. Perhaps most importantly, is the instruction not to anticipate the breakthrough or expecting awakening. He quotes Ta-hui who explains that anticipating awakening is "...saying to yourself 'I am deluded now.' If you grasp at delusion and wait for awakening, then even though you pass through kalpas as numerous as dust motes, you will never achieve it."

Buddha Nature

"When the waves are choppy,
it is difficult for the moon to appear.
Though the room is wide,
the lamp can fill it with light.
I exhort you to clean your mind-vessel.
Don't spill the sweet-dew sauce."

With the above poem, Chinul invited the monk Yose to the Samadhi and Prajna Community, inviting him to practice Son meditation. We can read the lines as our own personal invitation, too. Chinul coaches, cajoles, admonishes, encourages, and expresses his passion for the dharma; all to let us know what we must do and that he believes we can do it. Chinul wrote extensively about the nature of True Mind, sudden awakening/gradual cultivation, and the practices and aides that lead to realization of True Mind. Chinul quotes Lin-chi to his students: "The four great elements do not know how to expound dharma or listen to dharma. Empty space does not know how to expound dharma or listen to dharma. It is only that formless thing before your eyes, clear and bright of itself, which knows how to expound dharma or listen to dharma." Chinul says: "Since this Buddha-nature exists in your body right now, why do you vainly search for it outside?"

The idea of Buddha-nature is an interesting one and the Tathagatagarbha concept is one that was debated in feudal Japan rather passionately. Tathagatagarbha or Buddha-Nature doctrine states that all beings contain the potential to become a Buddha. Williams explains that the Lankavatara Sutra is the most influential of the literature that posits the Tathagatagarbha as the Buddha-nature within the alaya-vijnana, substratum consciousness. The term Tathagatagarbha is open to a number of nuances when translating the components of the word to understand its meaning. The oldest and most natural meaning would be *containing a Tathagata*, containing a Buddha. The imagery of all sentient beings being compared to lotuses containing a fully formed Buddha homunculus sitting cross-legged in their center would then not be a metaphor, but a reality. In the Yogacara school, literal translations of the sutras are common and often the source of criticism of their ideas when considering the richness of metaphor to explain concepts that are ineffable. The word garbha in Sanskrit also means womb/matrix, seed/embryo, or innermost part; the expression can also refer to all sentient beings having the innermost core of a Tathagata.

The Lankavatara Sutra states: "The Buddha said... now, Mahamati, what is perfect knowledge? It is realized when one castes aside the discriminating notions of form, name, reality, and character; it is the inner realization by noble wisdom. This perfect knowledge, Mahamati, is the essence of the Tathagatagarbha." Master Hyunoon Sunim explains further that "so you need to absolutely believe in this Buddha nature and you have to throw away your common sense. You'll have to discard your stubbornness when you insist on what you think is right or wrong. You need to begin by realizing that maybe your judgments or opinions are wrong. That is how you need to begin looking at yourself. Your biases need to be released, surrendered. Only when opinions and judgments are released can greater things inside start to come forth." This is tough for me! My mom used to ask me if I wanted to be happy or did I want to be right? And my answer was "I want to be happy *because* I'm right!" But a lot of time and effort must be devoted to being right; especially when helping others realize the rightness of the situation. Stepping back can be pretty interesting, though.

During my unit of Clinical Pastoral Education (CPE), I worked with a patient who felt that he could not be close to God because he couldn't go to church. It took some effort for me not to try to fix what I perceived as his misperception. Instead, when we talked as a hospice team about this patient, I asked others (nurses, hospice aides, social workers, the team physician) what they thought – can someone be close to God without being in a church. They had a variety of ideas about that, and I proposed that we develop a team approach to discover what our patient meant by "close to God." One of the hospice aides discovered that he had enjoyed travels with his wife when she was alive in their van as she would read passages from the Bible to him. That simple bit of history shifted all of our feelings about him; in one stroke we understood what "church" and "God" meant to this gentleman. I asked him on my next visit if he would enjoy me reading the Bible to him. He said it would mean the world to him. The hospice aide brought him large print devotionals and sang old-time hymns in her beautiful gospel voice, and the nurses helped him decorate his room with pictures of family; creating a sacred space. Chinul asked his student, "why not trace back its radiance rather than search for it outside?"

Yet we all yearn for that perfect place where everything will be ripe for us to find peace of mind. Even busy abbots, as Hyunoon Sunim related that the busy abbot told him that as an abbot he was so busy, he would need to go off to a hermitage and practice alone. Hyunoon Sunim responded "when you go, where would you go? When you talk about going, where are you going? Right now you can practice, where do you want to go?" We have a workplace mindfulness group that meets twice a month and one of the social workers who has newly joined is having a hard time quieting her mind because of all of her responsibilities. She and one of the other members of the group were talking about how wonderful it would be to find the perfect retreat center to meditate in; beautiful grounds, a waterfall perhaps, flowers of course – so pristine and perfect. I smiled and said, well, until the person next to you has the dreadful habit of that little nose whistle; you know, the one that doesn't happen with every breath, just intermittently and just when you think it won't happen again, there it goes, driving you to distraction. Or when the AC doesn't work right and it's either too cold and I have no sweater or it's too hot and that little drop of sweat is rolling down my spine. They laughed and I told them not to get me wrong; going on retreat is a wonderful experience. It is important, though, not to think that the external perfection is what will give you peace of mind. Chinul helps his students understand that it is not the physical body what performs the actions of life; "they are like images in a mirror or the moon's reflection in water." So when he asks the student to trace back the sounds of the crow calling and listen with his hearing-nature, the student knows how to answer that the place is beyond discrimination.

In the Fifty Verses on the Nature of Consciousness we read: "When delusion is overcome, understanding is there, and store consciousness is no longer subject to afflictions. Store consciousness becomes Great Mirror Wisdom, reflecting the cosmos in all directions. Its name is now Pure Consciousness." Chinul explains "There is no inside or outside... no far or near... no coming or going, no birth, no death... no past no present... no delusion or awakening.. no purity or impurity... no right or wrong, so words do not apply to it. Hence, how can it be anything but originally void and calm and originally no-thing?" He goes on to ask what makes the Buddhas and patriarchs different from other men; "The only thing that makes them different is that they can protect their minds and thoughts – nothing more."

Chinul proposes that meditation is a key to help us stop the whirlwind that pervades our minds. Dr. Ian Prattis explains to modern students that the only way out of the chaos is to train our minds through mindfulness practice; that mind consciousness has the capacity of mindfulness to nurture the wholesome seeds which diminishes the distorting power of manas. That every practice of mindfulness produces transformation at the very core of our consciousness. "The flowers and fruits of awakening will arise from our store consciousness. Mind consciousness has to trust store consciousness just as a gardener has to trust the land. Both roles are important. Remember, though that enlightenment, insight will be brought to you not by mind consciousness, not through your intellectual understanding but through the deeper wisdom of your store consciousness. After transformation, store consciousness becomes the Great Mirror Wisdom, shining forth and illuminating everything."

Chinul emphasizes the importance of keeping and cultivating Prajna and Samadhi as a pair, allowing us to be spontaneous and unconcerned. We become "just so." We are to use Prajna to investigate dharmas and contemplate their voidness, "allowing the mirror of the mind to shine without disturbance..." And to control distracting thoughts with Samadhi, controlling blankness with Prajna. "When this is so, one is truly maintaining Samadhi and Prajna equally, one has clearly seen the Buddha-nature."

Chinul reminds us of how fortunate we are to have a human birth and that we should make the most of this opportunity. I read someplace that the Dalai Lama was puzzled at the amount of unhappiness that people in the Western world expressed, after all, compared to the developing world, we live in luxury and ease. Yet, we suffer. We admonish ourselves to keep things in perspective – at least I do – what do I have to be unhappy about? After all, I have a roof over my head and a lovely family, friends, and pets to love and love me back. Even though I've gone through cancer, I got a lot of good news about my prognosis, so what do I have to complain about? But like all humans, stuff happens and I delude myself into thinking that if only just a few little things were different, I'd have nothing to worry or be annoyed about. I don't even want to win the lottery – just get everyone to drive properly and it's really not too much to ask to have a boss who is professional and competent, right? In other words, kvetch, kvetch, kvetch! Clinging to what is "right" is a strong habit. Recognizing that clinging and annoyance is a good thing and an important thing. Clearing my mind and tracing back the essential nature of what I am experience is such a revelation. When those feelings come up, stopping and relaxing into this basic feeling, shining mindful light on it invites that seed of righteous indignation or anger or impatience not to grow further, cultivating store consciousness into a garden that will support our efforts, not one that is in disarray.

Chinul advises us to practice "as if you were trying to save your head from burning. Death is fast closing in. The body is like the morning dew. Life is like the twilight in the west. Although we are alive today, there is no assurance about tomorrow. Bear this in mind! You must bear this in mind!" After all, he continues, "if this body is not ferried across to the other shore in this lifetime, then for which life are you going to wait?"

CHAPTER 14

Buddha Nature

The book "Buddha Nature" by Thrangu Rinpoche teaches about the Uttara Tantra Shastra, an important treatise examines the idea of each of us having a buddha nature. The idea that we each have a "seed" within us that has the potential to develop, or that we possess an awakened "essence." This is a challenging proposition philosophically, because of the clear teaching of the Buddha of Anatta - no self, or no soul/essence. Rinpoche goes on to explain the more subtle nuances to this position, a uniquely Mahayana one, but one that is grounded in the Buddha Dharma.

Bodhisattvas

This has been such an interesting question to look at. The Uttara-tantra-shastra (Ratnagotravibhaga in Sanskrit and its commentary) preserved in Chinese and Tibetan as verses with commentary, are a transmission of the text by Maitripa, the disciple of Naropa and the guru of Marpa. Traditionally, the sutra is believed to be composed by the Lord Maitreya who is empowered by the Shakyamuni Buddha. Lord Maitreya transmitted the works to Asanga who taught the first three of five teachings, holding back and hiding the last two as too profound and deep to be understood at the time. Our author calls this teaching "the best of the best" and advises us to take this authorship as literally true. The last two sections of the work was then re-discovered and taught by Maitripa after having a vision of the Lord Maitreya, giving him the transmission to understand and teach.

This story is one that is challenging for Westerners, since it promotes the kind of magical visions and transmissions that, speaking for myself, I thought that were only found in other religions since Buddhism is such a rational way of thinking. However, over the years, while I'm still not prepared to believe the stories as literally true as our author suggests, I do look at them as mythic stories in the best meaning of the term mythic. Mythic stories are often fantastic and impossible, yet they inform us of a larger truth through these images, symbols, and the journey of the people. These epic journeys seem so out of our reach, yet we admire the hero and feel inspired by what they learn along the way. Perhaps one day, I'll be able to understand how to believe the stories literally. In practice of relating to the Bodhisattvas, I have often pictures having conversations with these great teachers but haven't been ready to move my consciousness to spend time being the Bodhisattva.

The context of this method of teaching is one that appeals to me personally since I have a linear style of thinking and it can be difficult for me to intuit the meaning of teachings when the emphasis is on emptiness alone. I find a systematic approach a better context for understanding and this teaching gives us the turnings of the wheel of dharma and a layered approach through the topics of the Vajra. As our author says, we can then discover the virtues of the Three Jewels and the path to accomplish them ourselves.

Additionally, the core of the teachings is the understanding of what is meant by Buddha Nature. We hear the term a lot, but doctrinally we need to turn to the Tathagata-garbha sutras to understand what is meant by that term. This is the view that we all have Buddha nature within us; that we are already buddhas or have the "essence," embryo, or kernel of Buddhahood within. This way of teaching integrates the prajna-paramita teachings, which it considers true but incomplete, with the Tathagata-garbha concept of Buddha nature as the completion of the path. It takes the bija seed idea, but makes the Buddha nature a kind of super bija that is the true essence of every living being and the source truth.

What strikes me most in this section is found at the beginning of the chapter on the Buddha – the refuge of fruition. Striving to attain Buddhahood seems pretty daunting whether the method is considered rapid or not (even if "rapid" in Buddhism is often measured in it taking a couple of hundred eons rather than innumerable eons!). Yet fruition is an important thing for us to consider in our practice. For me, Buddhism has always seemed like a solitary pursuit. After all, for many years, I was the only Buddhist I knew and even as I reached out and found others to learn from in person and practice with, I had to return home to practice by myself. Practice has made a huge difference in my life and the teachings have helped me to transform some major suffering from my past into peace. Yet, if I'm being honest, I have to admit that my practice hasn't really been with the goal to attain Buddhahood. That seemed too grandiose and impossible.

But really, I was being lazy as well. I felt I could take my time with study and practice; the practice could comfort me when I'm feeling stressed and that all seemed good enough. It's been working with patients that I'm seeing that putting Buddhism in my pocket isn't good enough. Attaining Buddhahood is unfolding in front of my eyes as the only important thing to do. Two patients in particular the past few weeks have illustrated this beautifully. Each of them was in the active dying stage and I was asked to go to their bedside (this was one of those "is there a chaplain in the house?" situations where I was looking around wondering if one was there, then had to realize – gulp – I'm a chaplain). In each case, it wasn't good enough to recite a prayer and go; I had to be with them – really with them. While I feel fortunate that I have enough practice that the fruit is a tiny apple that I can bring to the situation and hold carefully, how much stronger could my service to those patients be if I am the apple tree?

Since I'm mixing my metaphors a bit here, something I've mentioned in other papers and discussions I've written here, what strikes me most about the term fruition that the text refers to is that fruition comes from our practice but is not something we can make ourselves. If I try to make an apple, the closest I can come to make it myself is something like an apple pop tart. What I can do if I want the real thing, is plant and nurture an apple tree. It seems to me to be the same with practice. Gaining the desire to attain Buddhahood and finding the correct systematic path for me is the most important thing. I'm looking forward to seeing the apple blossoms in the spring.

The Middle Way

The Middle Way of Buddhism, while first presented as the avoidance of the extremes of austerities and over indulgence, was further explained as the understanding that there is neither eternalism nor annihilationism. When this understanding was penetrated, emptiness (shunyata) was clarified. In trying to explain this deep truth, a problem arose; how to explain this truth that is beyond the duality that appears as the real world? I would propose that one can never explain emptiness directly; it can only be directly experienced. When emptiness is explained and taught, the Masters used, by necessity, analogy, logic and reason, metaphor, art, and debate to try to illuminate the meaning. Try as anyone might, it cannot be described head-on, but must be approached obliquely from one side of the coin or the other to point to that razors edge between the pairs of opposites. How can we begin to understand and then describe this perception of the world?

According to Buddhism, there are two kinds of truth, relative or worldly truth (*samvriti satya*) and absolute or ultimate truth (*paramartha satya*). When we look at the conventional world around us, we cling to the reality of things and phenomenon to give us confidence in our world. Things certainly appear to be real. I can knock on the desk and the sound tells me it is sturdy and will hold my monitor and books as I work. But when something happens that takes what I consider permanent and my own, I suffer and feel distress. I may only feel annoyed when I need to replace my computer, but feel pain and anguish when a loved one dies or I become ill and confront my own mortality. Suffering, though, is not objective; it depends on our perception. When we look more deeply, we begin to see and understand the ultimate dimension or emptiness in things and phenomenon. Near the time of his death, the Buddha said:

> *"All conditioned things are impermanent.*
> *They are phenomena, subject to birth and death.*
> *When birth and death no longer are,*
> *the complete silencing is joy."*

We have our own Crouching Tiger, Hidden Dragon story where we enter the path of Buddhism from a relative standpoint and we learn to notice our suffering and joy, learning more about how to see each of those states of being as subjective and temporary, yet they are an echo of what we understand when we transform our perceptions. The Buddha taught an Eightfold Path and Avalokiteshvara told us that there is no path; these two ideas seem to be in opposition to each other, but they are teaching the same thing from two different points of view. Thich Nhat Hahn explains that "we do not have to transcend the 'world of dust' (saha) in order to go to some dust-free world called nirvana. Suffering and nirvana are of the same substance. If we throw away the world of dust, we will have no nirvana."

Nhat Hanh explains the Madhyamika concept of emptiness through the related concept of interdependence. In this analogy, there is no first or ultimate cause for anything that occurs. Instead, all things are dependent on innumerable causes and conditions that are themselves dependent on innumerable causes and conditions. The interdependence of all phenomena, including the self, is a helpful way to undermine mistaken views about inherence, or that one's self is inherently existent. It is also a helpful way to discuss Mahayana teachings on motivation, compassion, and ethics.

Further detailing this idea of emptiness, the Madhyamika philosophy divides into two trains of thought: Rangtong or "empty of self," and Shentong or "empty of other." In Tibetan rang means "self," and tong means "empty," literally "self-empty." Zhen means "other," so Zhentong, or Shentong, means "other empty." Because it can be difficult to understand and explain the nature of emptiness, these two branches attempt to apply logic to the nature of objects and phenomenon through their major arguments into the nature of reality and our perception of it. These two systems "...do not differ in the way they determine all conventional phenomena to be empty, nor do they disagree that the extremes of conceptual elaborations cease during meditative equipoise. Nevertheless, they do differ in terms of the way they use conventional cognitive and verbal expressions during the subsequent state of attainment."

The Rangtong tradition is represented by the *dGe_lugs pa* school (the Yellow Hats) founded in the late fourteenth century and the lineage of His Holiness the Dalai Lama, while the Shentong is associated with the *Jo nag* tradition. Characteristics of the Rangtong tradition include: 1) draws on the *Lankavatara Sutra*, 2) understands the concept in the Madhyamika sense of emptiness, 3) the term Rang sTong means *self-empty* meaning that both Dharmakaya and emptiness itself are empty of intrinsic existence, and 4) looks at these teachings as having a specific purpose to help introduce Buddhism to non-Buddhists by teaching from their paradigm of belief in a Self. The Shentong tradition contains the following characteristics: 1) the teachings are taken literally, 2) they believe there is an absolute reality that intrinsically and inherently exists, 3) refers to its doctrines as the Great Madhyamika and the real teachings of Maitreya and Asanga, and Nagarjuna and Aryadeva, 4) believes that when one goes beyond reasoning and concepts, a real, intrinsically existing Absolute is understood.

The Rangtong teachings consider that the Tathagatagarbha is within all sentient beings and is why we are able to become awakened and it is emptiness that enables us to change; since change is a result of dependent origination and emptiness is the ground of dependent origination, it follows that the Tathagatagarbha is empty in the Madhyamika sense. The Shentong tradition considers that the Tathagatagarbha consciousness is obscured in the unawakened, but is identical to the Dharmakaya or "Essence Body" of the awakened mind.

On the other hand, Brunnhölzl explains that the subdivision of Madhyamika into "self-empty" and "other-empty" is obsolete. He proposes that the Shentong is nothing other than the Yogācāra system. The central point of the Yogācāra system is that everything that we experience always happens in our minds. The term "mere mind" (*cittamātra*) to everything being our subjective experience. The Yogācāra masters were not led to the "conclusion that this consciousness itself is ultimately real or even the only reality... rather, indicative that both the distinct experience and what is experienced are mere projections of our dualistic mind, which thus gets caught in its own web." Realization that it is our own mind that projects our subjective world is a step toward liberation; in seeing things as they really are and having a direct experience of them. "How can the illusion of the world best be accounted for – in terms of *satyadvaya* (the two realities), or in terms of *svabhavatraya* (the three natures)? This is, in all its ramifications, what the debate between Madhyamika and Yogācāra is all about."

Central to Rangtong is the argument of negation. When analyzing a subject, it must be determined if the object is an appearance or something imagined. While a person with an eye disease might have an optical illusion as a result, negating that illusion would not be logical. "Similarly, as long as beings are not free from un-afflicted ignorance, illusion-like appearances to the six modes of consciousness do not stop." Like a rope that is imagined to be a snake, negation only applies to what is imagined and does not conform to facts; it is the mind's fixations. In his Rebuttal of Objections, Nāgārjuna says: "If I were to have a proposition, I would have that fault. Since I have no proposition, I am without fault. If I were to observe something through direct perception or any other means, I would either affirm it or deny it. Since there are no such things, I am beyond censure." Negations play an important role in Nāgārjuna's work through analysis of causes (*Vajra sliver*) and by analyzing results of existent and arising of nonexistent results.

Not all scholars find Nāgārjuna's arguments persuasive. Richard Hayes feels that Nāgārjuna plays on ambiguities in certain terms; then uses the term with his own interpretation rather than the way most Buddhists actually held. Taking an example from Nāgārjuna's writings, Hayes looks at the terms *parabhava* and *svabhava* (own nature) meaning a nature that belongs to the thing itself; the thing's identity. But the word could also be interpreted to mean that the thing comes into being from or by itself and would refer to the things independence. Parabhava which can either mean that which has the nature of another thing, a difference, or coming into being from another thing, a dependence. In Nāgārjuna's writings, we find the statement "surely beings have no svabhava when they have causal conditions. And if there is no svabhava, there is no parabhava." The statement, according to Hayes, can make sense when interpreting it based on common interpretations, making the first statement: "Surely beings have no causal independence when they have causal conditions." That makes sense at face value. Statement two, however, could be "And if there is no identity, then there is no difference." Or it could be "And if beings have no independence, then they have no dependence." which makes no sense at face value. Now, even if statement two makes sense on its face and we decide to pick that meaning, it does not follow from statement one. The ambiguity of the expressions create a lack of clarity which the reader must decide if they are meant to be the crisp logical arguments they are purported to be, or if they are intentionally ambiguous to point to a more esoteric or metaphysical meaning.

The proponents of Rangtong thought are divided further into Svatantrika and Prasangika. The *Svatantrikas* assert non-true existence, refuting the idea that things have their own nature and they assert emptiness. The Prasangika refute the idea that things have true existence or that things have any nature of their own, but they do not assert emptiness, non-existence, or freedom from elaboration. They believe that the ultimate level is beyond being something that can be asserted. Perhaps the Prasangika are the first agnostic Buddhists since it seems that they believed that ultimate truth is beyond any elaborations, thoughts, or expressions. Both of these approaches, though, attempts to logically explain existence and our relative existence.

Shentongpas can consider themselves Rangtongpas since they assert that the two views are a complementary unity, a continuum, and consider that both views are compatible with the Middle Way. That Shentong considers that the ultimate truth is not empty of itself but empty of all other relative phenomenon is logical. Some do interpret this view as proposing or assuming eternalism, but that is not necessarily the conclusion that one must come to. When the ultimate dimension is penetrated, the "dharmadhātu is called 'emptiness' because it is empty of all characteristics that are other than itself, that is, it is empty of all conceptual elaborations or percepts and perceivers." One can argue that, like Nagarjuna, some of the teachings point to direct experience of higher meditative state and this is the fruit of their experiences. Shentong is considered a means of support for practitioners in meditation. Williams asks that if Shentong proponents truly posit an intrinsically existent Absolute, how could this lead to final liberation? He goes on to explain that some scholars have considered "other empty" doctrines as a strange "non-Buddhist aberration." However, the Jo-nang schools have simply taken doctrines literally that were taken literally in India as well as East Asia.

It is helpful as we consider the identity of objects and phenomenon to turn to the Hua-Yen school which attempted to bring the doctrines together in a unified way and looked at the temporal nature of causality. Cook explains that with the six characteristics, Fa-tsang breaks down the aspects of existence to illustrate how objects and phenomena relate to each other. In his treatise, Fa-tsang wants to eliminate any temptation or doubt about viewing life as either eternalistic or annihilationistic. By breaking down "essence" into universality and particularity, "characteristics" into identity and difference, and "function" into integration and disintegration, he illustrates that while each of the three major aspects of reality are not only two sides of the same coin, but are also happening simultaneously. You can't have one without the other. In this schema, we can express that all things are empty and interdependent, therefore have no true difference. He further explains that the "differences which we detect and emphasize are subjective interpretations; our own self-interested values imposed on what otherwise is a valuative no-man's land."

In Fa-tsang's famous analogy of the rafter and the building, he employs the real world example of seeing that a building without its rafter is no longer a whole, so the rafter is the "cause" of the building to further explain these characteristics. The main concern of Fa-tsang is to focus on the process and dynamics of the existence of an object or phenomenon and help to illustrate the difference between eternalism and annihilationism. As he explains, there would be no building (annihilationism) if the rafter did not have the power to wholly cause the building because the building would simply be a collection of parts. If the rafter is removed, the whole building should remain if that were true. If the building were eternal, then we could take pieces and parts from it and it would remain whole. Now, it's easy to balk at this analogy, thinking "oh, of course it's still a building even if imperfect" but it's interesting that when a building is imperfect, we actually pretty automatically start thinking of the parts looking for ways to improve it, salvage parts, etc. but when the building is whole we don't concern ourselves with the parts, we just interact with it in its wholeness. Cook explains that the perception of identity and interdependence help us see the contingency and fragility of our own lives. "In the perception of emptiness, we discover that we owe our being to countless other beings, animate and inanimate, near and far... the Pure Land of Amida is nothing more than this ordinary world, completely pervaded with unconditional respect and gratitude."

These analogies and logic puzzles are important because they help us grasp the relationships that create identity and differentiation that we observe and perceive as real. The bottom line for Fa-tsang and, I think we as

Buddhists, becomes the task of understanding that yes I can place my computer and book on the desk and it will hold them up and be functional; that I can see the component parts, yet I can also understand and see the process that brought it all to manifest here and now and will continue to evolve into something else. All the while, each aspect reflects all the other aspects if I can look deeply at them. The process happens all around us all the time. It is not about rising above to see the folly of the mundane, or, as Cook points out, to banish things that are unworthy or disgusting, but to see the flow of all things as wonderful and good. "The loss and gain are one and the same thing..." The process is a dance and the flow of the dance includes all of life, helping us go deeper into seeing things and having a direct experience of life, just as it is. This meshes well with the scripture (Differentiation of the Middle and Extremes) "no phenomenon exists apart from the dharmadhātu."

For all the talk about emptiness, in Nagarjuna's *MūlaMadhyamikakārikā* comes the pithy statement "Buddhas say emptiness is relinquishing opinions. Believers in emptiness are incurable." Rangtong and Shentong both hold the Cittamātra (mind-only) system with only some minor differences and Verses from the Center gives us beautiful instructions for how to look at our consciousness and ways to practice. Summarizing the Madhyamika systems is to understand that all that is taught is free from the extremes of nihilism and eternalism and the teachings are contained within the three points: ground, path, and fruition. "The flowers and fruits of awakening will arise from our store consciousness. Mind consciousness has to trust store consciousness; just as the gardener has to trust the land. Both roles are important. Remember, though, that enlightenment, insight will be brought to you not by mind consciousness, not through your intellectual understanding, but through the deeper wisdom of your store consciousness. After transformation, store consciousness becomes the Great Mirror Wisdom, shining forth, illuminating everything."

We always have to look deeply into the inter-being-ness of all things, including the Two Truths, to see that they are not two separate things at all, but each contains the other fully. Transcending our lives toward an absolute reality is something much of humanity longs for, but, for me, Buddhism is not about transcending this life for a perfect heaven nor is it about self-improvement of exchanging bad habits for good ones (although that aspect of it has certainly been helpful to me and appreciated by the people around me), but about transforming how we perceive.

Fruition

This short chapter has a lot to offer both in terms of practical explanation and significance for practice. I had never heard the term "refuge in fruition" before and I find that point of view profound. Refuge has always had a great deal of meaning for me on many levels, but because I had been thinking in terms of Dharma as a path, it hadn't occurred to me that taking refuge in fruition is a very important step. Moving toward seeing the truth of cessation and the truth of the path opens up the new question "how do I do that?" I've practiced Buddhism for a long time and it's made a big difference in my life, but I have to be honest that it's only been in the past couple of years that an inkling that attaining Buddhahood is actually possible. It's probably a bit of a tired phrase, but I like it anyway, that maybe it's moving Buddhism from my head to my heart.

While the logic of emptiness seems straightforward and a given, the temptation is to then consider emptiness nonexistence or that the universe is a self-created illusion, which still sets us apart or sets us up as the center of the universe. What was really eye opening for me in this chapter was the idea of things being luminous and empty with luminosity being the potential for phenomena to manifest and be experienced. Rinpoche explains that this is what is what non-duality really means. Rather than thinking that seeing things as they really are means accepting the world as it stands whether I like it that way or not, it seems that Rinpoche is saying that path provides clarity of seeing that emptiness and luminosity are undivided.

We go from seeing our hand and saying "this is a hand," to analyzing the pieces and parts of the hand, logically defining the hand's emptiness, to shifting our understanding to the reality of emptiness and luminosity as the potential for our hand to manifest and for us to experience it. We can stop seeing pairs of opposites and start penetrating the true nature of things. All the while, turning the pages of a book with our hands, sipping a cup of hot tea, being present with a loved one, and moving in this world, for me, with a renewed feeling of gratitude to have been manifested at a time when even a farm girl from Indiana can learn from such amazing teachers from all over the world.

If you've never seen the movie "The Invention of Lying" I highly recommend it. I was shocked when I saw it, not for the racy bits, but for the idea that if we were all perfectly honest and saw the world exactly as it is, we'd likely be so depressed, we would hate our lives or even commit suicide unless we were lucky enough to be good looking and successful. The premise is that people have no hope or future without self delusion or the nicety of all those little white lies that grease the social wheels of conversation and interaction. I found myself mouth agape trying to think of a way to rebut the screenwriters premise. But I think that Rinpoche does explain the difference between Ricky Gervais' view of the world and the Buddhist understanding of seeing things as they really are. In the movie, "things as they really are" is still viewed through the lens of duality while a Buddha isn't as interested in whether or not the baby is cute or ugly; what the "facts" are, (and one of the funniest lines of the movie is "your baby is so ugly, it's like a little rat") but the emptiness/luminosity of the baby.

Freedom

One of the significant things in this chapter for me is the discussion on the qualities of liberation when looking at the sangha as the refuge of fruition. In looking at the freedom from bondage, obstruction, and from inferior views, Rinpoche explains that those sangha members who are endowed with these and the other of the eight qualities are called the noble sangha who are the examples of this liberation. When we are bound to samsara through the poisons of attachment, aggression, and delusion, we are in bondage to our disturbing emotions.

I liked Rinpoche's analogy of having our path obstructed by a wall and being unable to see what's on the other side or to go through the wall. I have many days when I feel that I'm beating my head against that proverbial wall and it gets me nowhere. I've always liked that phrase because it so well captures the futility of trying to understand that barrier through brute force, which I tend to do; trying to muscle my way to understanding by figuring things out logically.

I'm so glad to be taking the Four Foundations of Mindfulness course at the same time as this course. They dovetail very nicely together, especially as we do the meditations on using the body as a support for pure awareness. It's so easy to want to solidify our experience and judge the qualities of what we experience, perceive, or observe. As I practice, I'm finding that it takes a light touch to come back to the present. If I cling to the present moment I crush it and find it doesn't exist; each present moment has gone to the next before I've had a chance to get to the "t" of "this is it." If there is no touch at all, it flutters off and I don't come back. The lightest touch allows those fleeting glimpses into that absolute and relative nature of that wall.

Before going in to see a patient in a nursing home the other day, I used what we're learning in both of these classes to prepare for the visit. There is a retaining pond in front of the parking lot and the surface was very still and it reflected the clouds and birds as they flew by and it struck me that I could emulate the still water with the patient. As we talked, I could see that I would move out of the present moment but I could remind myself, for a moment, to come back. He talked about his frustration with his memory loss and that one of his grandson's had visited and told a joke about grandpa meeting new friends every day. We both laughed, and in that laughter, I was snapped back to the present and felt both the humor and the pain in that moment. I said quietly something to the effect of "that hurts." We sat quietly for a moment and both of our eyes welled with tears as he spoke of the pain in that reality. That experience seemed to me to be a simple level of what the Awakened Ones might perceive on a deeper level of understanding that suffering has no inherent existence yet who have great compassion for us who experience suffering as real. It's encouraging to me that the Noble Sangha perceives me with clarity and recognizes that it's only the clouds that are covering my basic goodness.

Thirdly, the recognition that we must have a Bodhisattva's attitude toward helping others attain their own true nature, that attaining Buddhahood for myself alone is the antithesis of inner wisdom. It's easy to be discouraged, especially when people are so certain that they are solid and unchangeable, I tend to believe it too. It's easy to think "if they would just straighten up and fly right, everyone could be happy!" Yet, that concretizes the other person just as much and doesn't help them or me see through the wall of ignorance.

Qualities

What I found significant in this chapter was the comparison of the qualities of the enlightened essence in principle, the causes that purify the defilements which obscure that essence, and the transcendent qualities of fruition. The causes become a method for achieving the qualities of enlightenment and reflect those qualities that can be embodied both in principle and transcendently. This before, during, and after look at our nature was something I had never considered before since most of my attention has been on the process of the path.

The first quality in principle is purity that is untainted, the cause (cure) that can remove the defilements that obscure this purity is the devotion to the Dharma, and the quality of fruition is transcendent purity. The second quality is being full of qualities and capabilities, the cure is discriminating knowledge - prajna, and the quality of fruition is transcendent identity. The third quality is that the enlightened essence is changeless, the cure is concentration, and the quality of fruition is transcendent bliss. The fourth quality is saturation with compassionate love, the cure is compassion, and the quality of fruition is transcendent permanence.

What I find most interesting is the understanding of the potential, what to do to remove the impurities that cover those basic qualities, then the qualities that shine through in fruition. By cultivating a devotion to the Dharma there is a freshness in practice; rather than considering practice a chore or something to read about, when practice becomes a path "to realize our true condition." In fruition, this purity is the natural state.

Through practice, we develop prajna about the true condition of things and the understanding of ego-less-ness, gaining stability because we're no longer buffeted in our constant striving to maintain and protect our self-identity. Our suffering disappears when this clinging is dropped because we understand that it was an artificial construct. The "transcendent identity" was confusing to me at first since it seems antithetical to what we've been talking about, but Rinpoche explains that this transcendent identity is revealing the true identity that is neither ego nor egolessness since both of these ideas are mental constructs.

By developing the concentration of Samadhi, or right concentration, our fear of suffering disappears, which, in the qualities of fruition; the realization that the state of Dharmakaya is beyond both suffering and happiness, and only transcendent bliss remains. In the translation of the Heart Sutra chanted at our temple, the lines: "Because there is no attainment, The Bodhisattvas, grounded in perfect understanding, find no obstacles for their minds. Having no obstacles, they overcome fear, liberating themselves forever from illusion and realizing perfect nirvana. All Buddhas in the past, present, and future, thanks to this perfect understanding, Arrive at full, right, and universal enlightenment." have always been powerful for me, pointing to that non-duality of things as they are.

Transcendent permanence took me by surprise as well, since it didn't occur to me that the fruition of compassion would be permanence, especially since we're so steeped in the concept of impermanence. But Rinpoche explains that in fruition of the Dharmakaya, we realize the sameness of samsara and nirvana, that they are both essentially non-existent; there is a sameness of nature.

Perfect Knowledge

What struck me as significant in this chapter was the point in the Ten Powers of Perfect Knowledge, knowing fact from fiction. This is an important power to me because I feel that it's important to understand the distinction between "facts and figures" from truth, and to understand the distinction between the perfect knowledge of truth and from creating a fixed view of something that we often call a "fact." I really liked Rinpoche's example of going to a movie. While we understand that we are watching a movie, we can become so absorbed in it that when the lights come up, we almost feel a bit disoriented. In watching the film, we've felt intense emotions, perhaps, and we may think of the characters long after the movie is over as though they were real. Actors sometimes talk about being so closely identified with a character they play that a person might scold them or congratulate them about something that was only part of a story in the movie, but the person has such a fixed view of what they saw, they can't accept that the person might be different from the character. It's our ignorance of the true nature of things just as they are that leads to the confusion of thinking we know the facts, but in reality being deluded by laying our own dramas, storylines, baggage, speculation, and fears on top of the direct experience.

Hand in hand with the perfect knowledge of knowing fact from fiction for me is fearlessness. The quality of stability of mind is something that is very significant to me. Growing up a neglected child, there were many times in my life when I felt that there was no ground under me, no anchor to hold on to. Buddhism has been very appealing to me because of the idea of cultivating an inner stability; that the stability is inside of me and not an anchor within another person or other outside thing. The example of the Buddha as someone with total self-confidence and fearlessness is very comforting to me. Seeing the Buddha (and all of the Buddhas throughout history and who will come to be) as a role model; having qualities that can be attained, gives me a lot of comfort and strength. Not only can I turn to the Buddha in refuge, I'm learning that I can turn to the refuge of fruition and begin to touch these qualities that are already within me.

Unceasing Activity

What I found significant in this chapter was the idea of unceasing activity. What I found most important to understand was that the first impression I had reading just the words "unceasing activity" was "but, I feel like I do that already! And it's not really much fun!" But the examples show that this kind of unceasing activity is spontaneous and effortless, not a perpetual "to do" list. In cultivating the four foundations of mindfulness; mindfulness is to remember to come back to having a direct experience of what is happening or what we are experiencing. In awakening, we no longer need to remember to come back; we're already there, so we have a direct experience of everything just as it is. Our actions, then, would come from this sense of non-effort and ease. The analogies are really lovely to me; the reflection on polished stone, the sound of a great drum, the rain clouds, the sunshine, the earth, and space.

When I reflect on times that I'm tied up in a knot emotionally or with my thoughts, it seems like all of it is in my skull and that small space leaves no room for any way to untangle it all. If there was just a little wiggle room, I could get my fingers in there to untie the knots. What we learn through the four foundations of mindfulness is that there is great space within us and as

Rinpoche explains here, space permeates everywhere... and the qualities of Buddha nature emanate naturally and effortlessly, reaching wherever they are needed. In the universe, there is great space – as much room as we ever will need. It's filled with galaxies and planets and stars, so there's a lot happening – it's not a void – yet, within that activity is lots of room for it to take place without the need for clinging or tying things up in knots.

Practicing the Four Foundations of Mindfulness, one of the things that's making a big difference in my practice is noticing that space. It's helping me see the storylines and baggage that goes with the thoughts and emotions more clearly – just that extra distance, like an impressionistic painting, gives more clarity. When I can see that I can peel away those layers, I can find that the direct experience is just that, the experience. It doesn't need the rest of the layers that I've put on top of it. When I think about my typical actions and reactions, they aren't spontaneous and based on what actually happened, they're the result of all those factors that have gone into my life. When I can come back to the direct experience of what is happening, I feel more present, and respond with stability and being in touch with what is really happening, not what is happening plus what happened years ago on top of what might happen years from now. So, understanding that the level I'm currently practicing is a reflection of the fruition of Buddha nature, is a wonderful insight that gives me a lot of encouragement and is energizing my practice.

Liberation

I believe that the term "idiot compassion" was coined by Chögyam Trungpa Rinpoche, referring to what many of us commonly consider compassion but is often pity, sympathy, or even our own discomfort with another's suffering. During my Clinical Pastoral Education (CPE) unit, I took a course in bereavement counseling and am currently co-facilitating a bereavement support group. One of the topics that came up during the bereavement counseling course was what to do when someone starts to cry. It's common to hand the person a tissue, pat them on the shoulder, give them a hug, or say "there, there." We were challenged to consider why we would have the urge to do any of those things; mostly the message to the crying person is "I really feel uncomfortable with your pain and I wish you would stop to relieve my discomfort." We may genuinely have a kind hearted feeling of empathy for a person who is suffering and turning to us for help, but it is important to look at our conditioned responses more deeply. We want to help, yet sometimes that desire is for selfish reasons; to make ourselves feel better. One of my favorite foibles is how exasperated I get with the way other people drive – why not just follow the rules of the road? We would all get there safer, more efficiently, and with less stress. In other words, if everyone would just shape up, I would be happy! I think there is often an element of this at work when we get frustrated with the injustice in the world. There is injustice and we should certainly stand up to it and be a voice against war, child abuse, torture, and the other evils in the world. Yet, when we speak out, we must caution ourselves to look and listen deeper to those who would perpetrate those evils and avoid having a fixed view of them or ourselves. While I do not have to wait for enlightenment to reach out and pull a child from the path of an on-coming car, only fully waking up will create a future of peace and true compassion for that child to grow up in.

What I found significant in Thrangu Rinpoche's book about Buddha Nature, among so many points in this book, was his discussion of Buddha activity. Compassion is truly the hallmark of Buddhism and Rinpoche explains that "Just as the sun does not deliberately try to shine, but sends forth its rays naturally, automatically, and without any exertion, all the Buddha's wisdom manifestations are constantly ablaze with the radiant qualities of knowledge, compassion, and abilities." Compassion is worthy of deep consideration and contemplation. Rinpoche explains that Buddhas have compassion equally for bodhisattvas on cloud nine as well as those of us who are so engrossed in our conditioning and suffering that we seem beyond help. Often when I have troubled feelings and distress over the suffering caused by cruelty, narrow-mindedness, or ignorance, I find myself trying to figure out what is wrong with the other person. There must be something deeply wrong with them to think the way they do! But this line of thinking, while in a sense true, since all wrong actions are the result of ignorance, is a backward way of approaching the problem. Far more beneficial, I feel, is to approach my feelings as suggested by Rinpoche; what is it in me that has these fixed views that I instantly layer my storylines, conditioned responses, and unwholesome emotions onto what is said or done so that I avoid having a direct experience of things just as they are. In Buddha nature, there is no "I should feel compassion now" there is only the spontaneous compassion that is effortless, pure, and without deliberation.

When the desire for our hearts is to be a limitless ocean of compassion, we are encouraged to take refuge in the fruition of awakening and look to the causes that purify defilements which obscure the awakened essence of Buddha nature. Compassion is one of the causes which give rise to the wish to help all sentient beings uncover their true nature. By cultivating the causes of devotion to the Dharma, discriminating wisdom, concentration, and compassion, we find our practice fresh and valuable. We can give up our disturbing emotions, let go of clinging, develop the confidence needed to be liberated from fear, and open our hearts in a stable, clear, and spacious way. The spaciousness of Buddha nature is a significant concept that applies to practice. "Space naturally permeates everywhere. Life space, the manifestations of the Buddha emanate naturally and effortlessly, reaching wherever they are needed. This example depicts the inconceivable mystery of the Buddha's body and emanations." When we practice, having the experience of having a lot of space within us is very important; it helps us to see what is happening with more perspective but it also opens us to give us room to come back to the direct experience of our circumstances, thoughts, feelings, sense perceptions, objects of mind as they are, letting what we layer on top of that go.

As we begin to feel that space within us, we begin to cultivate confidence and a friendship with ourselves. In practicing with the Four Foundations of Mindfulness, we find that we can begin to come back to ourselves with the confidence of including all that we are experiencing. Practicing the Four Foundations of Mindfulness while learning about Buddha nature puts the practice into a new light. Even if we have practiced like this before, as we learn about the factors and causes of awakening, we can go deeper by exploring these foundations. In working with grief, my own and in my work, Rosenberg touches on something I found important in discussing his own experience with grief. Grief is a self-centered emotion; one that can be challenging to truly experience and allow to ripen fully. There is a lot of clinging in grief. After all, the one thing that we did not want to happen; believed could not happen, that we could not survive if it happened, has happened.

Layers of experience, cultural conditioning, societal expectations, and personal resistance are like hitting a brick wall. In Rosenberg's example from his life; the death of his father, he talks about the self-pity he felt and how difficult it was to break through the barriers to have a direct experience of his sorrow. In my own experience with the death of my mother, it took time to cultivate enough space to have that direct experience of my grief and to see and let go of all the layers of my experiences with her and my longing for the relationship I wished I had that now could never be.

When I was able to sit with my feeling, just as it was; able to say "include" when more layers of feeling were uncovered, there was deep silence. Allowing this silence to work on me was an important step. Interestingly, Rosenberg had a similar experience and uses that in his instructions to his students, advising that when they encounter silence to do nothing; allow this silence which is full of love and compassion to work on you. For me, that love and compassion transformed my grief into relief. I could let go of my fixed view of who I thought my mother should be – I let her off the hook. Through *mudita*, I can genuinely find joy and nourishment from the mother/daughter connection of others that I used to be jealous of. It was only in plumbing the depths of grief that I could let go of my grief over what I did not have, to experience the joy that was always available to me, within me.

The dilemma continues to be, for me, about balancing what I can do now, how can I understand the reasons behind the choices I am making, and how to be sure I that I am on the right track with my practice. In his *Seven Points of Mind Training*, Rinpoche says that "...compassion is founded on the recognition that whether or not you can benefit a person in their immediate circumstances, you can generate the basis for their ultimate benefit." That seems a bit fatalistic to me and I really do not care for the *woo* of positive thoughts sent to someone who needs help being of any value to that person whatsoever. Shantideva helps clarify this point, though. While I may try my best to be present to someone and have a direct experience of them so that true compassion arises and what I do is the best thing for them, I may, and most likely will the majority of the time, only come close. I will learn from my experiences and by continuing to practice, but what of the other person? How should I view what they, and I, are going through?

Suffering also has its worth.
Through sorrow, pride is driven out
and pity felt for those who wander in samsara;
evil is avoided; goodness seems delightful.
                              ~ Shantideva, Way of the Bodhisattva

Our suffering has a positive side; not only does it juxtapose our under-standing of joy; it also humbles us and helps us appreciate the suffering of others. When we feel we are in this thing together with others, we can com-panion them on their journey, too. Our compassion grows as we begin to see what some of the roots of their unwholesome actions might be because we have taken the time to explore our own ugly, embarrassing, jealous, angry; the list goes on and on, thoughts and actions. His Holiness goes on to explain that it is only through compassion for ourselves that we can generate com-passion for others; to understand what they are up against. In his view, with-out self-compassion, what we are doing is more about ego gratification than altruism.

The word compassion has its roots in the idea of joining the other in their suffering; *com* "together with" and *passion* "to suffer." Yet, there is danger in being joined too much with the other's suffering; we may burn out or be overwhelmed and crushed with the feelings. We can learn to touch our suf-fering, listen and look deeply at our own suffering as well as the other's suf-fering, and help ease the burden of suffering through the stability that comes from coming back to the direct experience of what is happening just as it is. Thich Nhat Hanh tells the story that when he was a young monk, he couldn't understand why the Buddha has such a beautiful smile on the statues in his temple; the world was filled with war and such cruelty and pain. Why was the Buddha smiling? Did he not care? What he came to understand is that the Buddha has enough inner strength, self confidence, understanding, and calmness that the suffering does not overwhelm him. We can learn to be aware of suffering in ourselves and others yet retain our clarity, calmness, and strength so we can help transform the situation. "The ocean of tears can-not drown us if karuna is there."

Additionally, Thrangu Rinpoche explains how we can counteract the overwhelming feelings and frustrations when trying to help based on our own efforts. When we develop a sense of fearlessness and self confidence in the dharma, "...that confidence removes the frustration or the misery which otherwise afflicts ordinary compassion. So, when compassion is cultivated in that way, it is experienced as delightful rather than miserable." Tashi Tsering explains that it is important to distinguish between a self-centered mind and a self-confident mind. Self-centeredness and self-concern is one of our primary mental afflictions, driven by ignorance and assumes that our own welfare is always more important than anything else. In cultivating self-confidence, on a basic level, we want to develop confidence in our actions and our practice.

On a higher level, we learn that awakened qualities are permanent, and we have discriminating wisdom. Like a person who mistakes a rope for a snake and is startled, once the error in perception is recognized, they will never make that mistake again. In awakening, we move from faith to self-confidence. "Without addressing our own issues, it is impossible to understand what is going on for anyone else. The Buddha says, 'Whoever loves himself will never harm others.' Those who know exactly what causes pain or happiness for themselves – not intellectually but from the heart – will understand that it is the same with others. Love for both self and others is a deep love, requiring great wisdom and insight."

Being liberated from fear comes from this deep understanding and approaching life with fearlessness and confidence allows us to be present with others with great freshness, clarity, stability, and spaciousness. "Compassion contains fundamental fearlessness, fearlessness without hesitation. This fearlessness is marked by tremendous generosity. This generous fearlessness is the fundamental nature of compassion and transcends the animal instinct of ego. Ego would like to establish its territory, whereas compassion is complete, open, and welcoming. It is a gesture of generosity which excludes no one."

In the instructions listed in the Four Foundations of Mindfulness, are the trainings on cessation and relinquishment. These two contemplations, for me, are about silence and being with the ineffable; letting go of the fixed identity, of concepts, of things; of fear. There is a bittersweet quality about just resting with cessation and relinquishment that is all about silence. Rosenberg talks eloquently about being with silence; letting it work on you, bathing in it, resting in it with no expectation or anticipation.

In our CPE class we were talking about hope and one of the comments I made was that there are times, grief being one of the most important times; that we can try to have the courage to set hope aside. To distract ourselves with well-wishes for a brighter day prevents us from plumbing the depths of our feelings. Legend has it that when asked by the king about the holy Dharma, Bodhidharma answered "nothing holy, just vast space." And when asked who was standing there saying these things to the king, his answer was "I have no idea." Silence can give us the space we need to train our minds in cessation and relinquishment. Leaving behind ideas and concepts, surrendering into the silence, we see things as they really are. Reality becomes vivid, fresh, and clear.

The sutras tell a story of a monk, Baddhiya, who had been a governor who had lived in luxury with great power. Everywhere he went, a regiment of soldiers assisted him and his residence was guarded day and night; he had everything he could possibly want. Yet he lived in constant anxiety, worry, and fear that it would all be taken away from him. When he became a monk and was training in the Four Foundations of Mindfulness, contemplating the desiring mind and relinquishment, he cried out "Oh happiness!" A monk reported this to the Buddha, concerned that the former governor might be regretting his decision to become a monk, so the Buddha called him to him to learn why. Baddhiya explained that through the trainings he had a direct experience of feeling great ease, joy, and peace.

He could live simply like a deer in the forest and the feeling was so wonderful that he raised his voice to say "Oh happiness!" The Buddha praised the monk to the community saying, "The monk Baddhiya is making steady and stable progress on the path of contentment and fearlessness. His are the feelings of joy that even the gods long for." When I consider the complexity of my life with all of the activities, people, and things I can sometimes envy monastics living simply with few possessions spending their days in meditation. But then I realize that it is not the external things and busyness that causes my anxieties and distress; it is my choice to train my mind toward contentment and fearlessness. Shedding the external stuff becomes more of a byproduct of the training; as the mind settles, there is less desire for the distractions and diversions.

"In the *Anguttara Nikaya* (V, 161), the Buddha teaches, 'If a mind of anger arises, the Bhikkhu can practice the meditation on love, on compassion, or on equanimity for the person who has brought about the feeling of anger.' Love meditation is a method for developing the mind of love and compassion. Love has the capacity to give joy. Compassion has the power to relieve suffering." In the Four Foundations of Mindfulness trainings, we turn inward to observe the body in the body, the mind in the mind; the mental formations in the mental formations. We cultivate our inner resources for freshness, stability, clarity, and spaciousness within ourselves, and develop the capacity to then relate to others in a spontaneous way not dependent on conditioned responses, but out of genuine recognition of the human condition. Practicing the compassion meditations helps us learn that love is not contingent on the other person being agreeable or loveable. As our hearts develop great spaciousness and compassion, the love that we feel and express is authentic, allowing us to look and listen deeply. Simply listening with this kind of stability can go a long way to relieve the other person's suffering. "We know that if we do not have peace and joy ourselves, we will not have peace and joy to share with others."

When we learn the discernment to distinguish attachment and clinging from the all-embracing compassionate love of the Buddha, we benefit ourselves and we benefit the world. Because of the Buddha's aspiration to protect all sentient beings and help them uncover their true nature, compassionate love arose from perfect knowledge. Taking the three perfect qualities that benefit others, we learn we must cultivate perfect knowledge from which compassionate love arises, and perfect abilities are based on compassion. The Buddha, carrying only his begging bowl had a tremendous impact on the world due to the strength of the capacity of Buddha nature.

CHAPTER 15

The Diamond Sutra

The Diamond Sutra is part of the Prajnaparamita texts. It illuminates emptiness and compassion with the underpinnings of skillful means. Mu Soeng, in his book "The Diamond Sutra: Transforming the Way We Perceive the World," explores the world of the Diamond Sutra from the historical point of view so that we understand the world view of the time, delves into the many commentaries about it, but also shows how inspiring this sutra can be. Many great thinkers have devoted their time and intelligence bringing the wisdom of this sutra to the world. Mu Soeng brings the understanding that is only in our own world view that any wisdom tradition comes to us, making it possible for us to benefit.

Logic

In section five, the question is about the bodily signs of the Tathagata. The path of the bodhisattva yields the thirty two bodily marks illustrating awakening. Our author asks, what in an ultimate sense could possess these marks. He then jumps right into the Trikaya doctrine, which I really don't see how that leap was made. For me, this passage is much more about the logic problem of emptiness. The Buddha is agreeing that "A" is not "A" even though, up to now, we were taught that A = A. It stops us in our tracks at first. What is "no possession of no marks" pointing to? For me, this is a beginning for looking at emptiness where we are asked to consider that A ≠ A even though that doesn't make sense at first blush. When we keep looking deeper, we begin to figure out that A is made of not-A elements, so A is an illusion until we see A as empty of a unique A quality.

In section six, we get a bit more history lesson from our author, which I really enjoy, but don't find it very helpful in understanding this passage. What I like about this passage of the sutra and find important is the idea of having confidence in the teachings and that we are capable of figuring this out. I like that the Buddha has faith in me – 2557 years ago, give or take, the Buddha put the teachings into motion, knowing that we can learn and apply this stuff. It also admonishes us not to cling to either the dharma or the not-dharma, to use the teachings as tools to understanding.

In section six, our author rightly exhorts us to remember that we should not set the dharma up as an object of knowledge. He goes on to say "The human mind is easily infatuated with what it thinks it knows and tries to establish that knowledge as a statement of truth." I found that statement to be a great way to say what we all try to do. From politicians to religions and just at work or the grocery store; we all know what we know and that's all that we know. And, dammit, that's that! Yet, the Buddha lets us know that we have to use the scientific method with his teachings. We have to follow the formula and see if there is validity and reliability to what he says. Taking his word for it, won't give us the results of the formula.

In eight, we're introduced to the word "chiliocosms" – oddly, this is a Greek word and it is made up of the words "thousand" and "cosmos." Apparently, our author got carried away with this word too and starts reporting on discoveries in cosmology, which I don't really think is the point here. To me, the most important point is putting the teachings in action, even if only a four line gatha from the sutra, sharing that with others will produce great happiness. Like our monk friend from the videos who said that the whole of the Diamond Sutra is contained in the Buddha's actions of going on alms rounds and eating his dinner, we too can be liberated through the wisdom of this sutra. I'm finishing up my unit of Clinical Pastoral Education (CPE) and most of my patients were Christians. I've needed to do a crash course in Christian mythology and scripture to be able to figure out how to relate to different ways of looking at the world. It strikes me, though, that at the last supper, Jesus was asking his disciples to have a direct experience of their meal. To see that he was no separate from everything around them, that they could be with him and his wisdom with each bite. When my mom died, one of the things that really struck me in looking at emptiness around the death of a loved one is that when I see her favorite flower, I find myself smiling and touching the petals. I feel like I'm saying hello to my mom and touching her. All of those not-self elements seem kind of clinical and sterile thinking through them, but looking deeply at them in the reality of dying, they take on a more personal and poignant meaning. I attended a day of mindfulness at our temple today and my morning job was sweeping the front porch and steps. Our temple is on a busy street and when lots of us are around, people tend to watch us curiously. Today as I was doing my sweeping meditation, I found myself wondering if the way I swept the stairs illustrated the teachings of the Buddha. I really enjoyed sweeping this morning.

Emptiness

"If all existence is *shunya* or insubstantial, to what or to whom is compassion directed?" This is a very interesting and, I think, important question. I've written about this before (can't remember which class or format), but I first learned about the not-self characteristic when I was in college – I was very enthusiastic about it and it had brought great feelings of compassion in me, even with a very basic teaching on it. I used to hang out with some archeology grad students and was explaining it to one of them, and asked him if that brought feelings of compassion out in him, too. He said that he thought it all made perfect sense and was certainly in alignment with science, but he couldn't see how the facts of that would make him feel differently than he already did about others. It frustrated me at the time, because it seemed to me that this was a concept that would change the world if everyone were educated about it.

The reader may already be on track for understanding the fatal flaw in my brilliant idea. As our author explains, and as I got eventually, this seeming paradox isn't something that can be figured out with the intellect. That's not to say that Buddhist schools don't enjoy a good philosophical puzzle, I'm looking forward with both dread and anticipation for taking our course on advanced Madhyamika! But as those who study koans are taught, these paradoxical questions are not meant to be brain teasers or riddles, but ways to break through the either/or kind of linear thinking to a more global neither are true/both are true. I've been a vegetarian since I was a kid and have helped a number of people who wanted to become vegetarian and needed advice. That includes people who want to be vegetarian because of their emotional reactions to how animals are treated on factory farms or just had the insight of what an animal goes through when it is killed and their kind heartedness makes them not want to be part of that. However, when that decision and action is based solely on either the idea of it (head knowledge) or the feelings of it (heart knowledge) it can't be sustained forever, sometimes not even for very long.

It's only when we can approach what we're doing in mindfulness, all of those seemingly opposite or disparate parts begin to reveal the interconnection where compassion seems to live.

In John O'Donohue's book Anam Cara, he explains a beautiful Gaelic phrase *fighte fuaighte*, "woven into and through each other." He explains that the eternal world (we might say emptiness) and the mortal world (we might say relative reality) are not separate, not parallel, but that they are fused. There is nothing as near as the ultimate reality of emptiness, even though it feels like we have to work so hard to understand it, thinking that if we understand, we will see. In Celtic, for my Irish friend, *Ta tir na n-og ar chul an ti - tir alainn trina cheile*, "The land of eternal youth is behind the house, a beautiful land fluent within itself."

Oh wait, I haven't answered the question! To whom is compassion directed – that's definitely a tough one to even try to answer. I think that for me, for now, my only answer is that I practice for the stability to be with another person and not drift away, not go somewhere else, not put storylines on them or me, but to have a direct experience of them and be available to them. I still feel sympathy and empathy and all those "pathy's" that aren't really compassion, but get me close to it, I think. But ultimately, being on the spoke of the wheel that is right mindfulness, it's about true understanding of whatever it is that I'm with. Seeing that there is no difference between us brings a feeling of compassion. When my mom went to Ireland to trace our Celtic roots, she stayed in a bed and breakfast. When the young lady preparing breakfast for their group saw my mom come in, being the earliest riser, she asked her if everyone she met had been kind to her. It brings tears to my eyes every time I think of that. Mom gave her a big hug in reply. I guess a big hug is as good as I can do.

Upaya

Upaya is used in Mahayana Buddhism as "skillful means" and the concept has a variety of implications in doctrinal examinations of Buddhism and practical ones in real life. In our daily lives, we can look to the precepts, the eightfold path, and the parables about actions taken to help others. I like that our author brings up the problem of looking at everything as empty with our heads alone that might make us cold to the suffering going on around us. On the other hand, sometimes we can wear our hearts on our sleeves, be in fix-it mode all the time and miss what would actually help the person if we settled down and just listened. The combination of compassion and wisdom, our author credits as skillful means. I think that's a good way to think of it as well. It also helps prevent us from concretizing any one way of helping as an ideology that cannot change or be modified ever again. Upaya gives us a flexibility to respond in the moment in a way that will resonate with the person at that moment.

When I was with patients during this past year, I found this idea very helpful – how could I check my ego at the door and really listen. It was a lot about getting out of my own way to be able to help. It's ironic, I guess, that even that desire to help can get in the way. The visits that I think turned out the best were ones that weren't about my agenda to help, but in letting the patient open up to me in a space that had no picking and choosing of what was ok or not, helpful or not and more about companioning them in what was going on right then.

Shunyata – I had never heard the definition of "bubble" but really like it, being a fan of bubble stuff. Maybe because I've been so steeped in the term "emptiness" I've never looked at it as having an undertone of nihilism that our author mentions, but certainly when I first started reading about Buddhism, most translations were about "void" or "nothingness" and those terms were very confusing and misleading. Over the past ten years or so, I've learned to prefer the Vietnamese term *không* for shunyata or emptiness. Thich Nhat Hanh uses the term emptiness during his talks and writings in English, but không is an interesting word in Vietnamese and very appropriate to getting closer to the intent of the term. In Vietnamese, the word không can be used in a variety of different ways – when added to a statement, it turns the statement into a question; it can change a word into a term that is less specific and more general; it's zero in the number system; it turns a statement into a negative (you'd say "you're thirsty, no?" rather than "you're not thirsty"), and depending on its position in a sentence, it can change the focus of the meaning. There is a quality there that makes the meaning a bit ephemeral and hard to grasp. I was fascinated by the author's discussion about the concept of zero in mathematics and emptiness; I'm not sure if he's implying that zero influenced the Mahayana view, but it is very tempting to dive into the correlations between science and Buddhist thought.

The bottom line, to me, is that even if we found the perfect word for it, that word wouldn't be quite right still. Shunyata is ineffable and we can only point to our experience of it, there will never be a word that we can speak to another person and they will then experience emptiness. We need to get as close as we can so we can be as accurate as possible to prevent further confusion.

Buddha Eye

This section is a very important one, in my way of thinking. It repeats what we heard at the beginning of the sutra, but goes deeper – certainly in a way that I need. Looking at the objects of mind as concepts, even dharmas, we're instructed to look closer at our desire to become a bodhisattva to liberate all beings. Since "there is no independently existing object of mind called bodhisattva. Therefore the Buddha has said that all dharmas are without a self..." When we meditate, then, we need to look deeply to see this, not letting our minds entrap us in words, reasoning, justifications, or speculation. We need to learn how to use non-discrimination so that we see no distinction between living beings and objects, self and no-self, bodhisattvas and normal people.

The sutra goes on to explain the "Buddha eye" that allows us to see in this non-discriminatory way. This seems really daunting, yet, the Buddha was human with human eyes the same as ours. We have the potential to see in this same way. The Buddha looks deeply to have a profound understanding of the human mind and its nature, understanding the various mentalities and ways of thinking. True understanding dove-tails with skillful means, since when we truly understand, compassion is there and we act from that purity.

The most important line – the one that is the bottom line for me, is when looking at our mind "... the past mind cannot be gotten hold of, the future mind cannot be gotten hold of, and the present mind cannot be gotten hold of." When working with the Four Foundations of Mindfulness meditation, we have a chance to really see that flow of thought; that reality of impermanence. This takes that idea even further. We tend to think that we know our minds and can answer questions about our past, the present, and what we want our future to be. I think we've read about this story in one of our other books, but I can't remember which one; there is a story about a monk carrying a copy of the Diamond Sutra, making his way to a monastery wishing to study with a famous abbot. He stopped at an inn just before arriving to spend the night and refresh himself before presenting himself to the abbot. He asked the innkeeper for a meal, and the woman who kept the inn saw the copy of the sutra that he carried and asked him questions about it before she would serve him. One question was something along the lines of 'what kind of mind do you want to point to – past, present, or future?' It's a tough question – if I were that monk, I might say "future" since I would probably be thinking about how to impress the abbot and what it was going to be like studying there. Or I might have been thinking about the journey, the past, or being in the present trying to figure out what was going on. But all of those answers would be wrong because I would be caught in the concepts of what had happened, what was happening, and what will happen. Remembering to come back to myself, I might say that I don't need past, present, or future mind – I'm hungry and need to eat.

Theopathy

Theopathy is the feeling that comes from the experience of the religion. Reading the sutras, listening to the chants, watching and participating in the rituals and the rest have the potential to bring up emotions, feelings of reverence, what might be called a religious experience, bodhichitta, or other transcendent experiences. Our author discusses this in the context of a "framework of not knowing" that the Zen tradition works with using the Koan method and other techniques meant to stop the intellectual, analytical mind and bring forth the feeling heart/mind. This is an important aspect of Buddhism because of our human tendency to want to cling to dogmas and set ourselves apart from other by judging the facts we can spout.

Finding this connection to theopathy, in Buddhist terms perhaps bodhichitta is often through artistic expression as well. When an artist creates a painting or other work of art with the intention of sharing their own inner, ineffable experience brings out feelings that help connect us to their experience or bring about a unique experience that deepens our understanding.

I love this poem about a sunflower by Thich Nhat Hanh:

Come dear, with your innocent eyes,
look at the clear, blue ocean of Dharmakaya.
Even if the world is shattered,
your smile will never vanish.
What did I gain yesterday?
And what will I lose today?

Come dear,
I point my finger
at the world
filled with illusions.
Since the sunflower is already there
all the other flowers turn toward it to contemplate.

It's only when we keep in mind that reality can't be framed, defined, or limited by words, concepts, or rules that we can understand the deepest meaning of the Diamond Sutra or the best poetry, music, art, and all the ways the people have found to point to that deep experience of things as they really are.

Inspired Way

The Prajnaparamita-inspired wisdom "...is the awareness that language is inadequate to express the insights of an awakened consciousness..." The Diamond Sutra was an early example of this attempt to deconstruct the intellectual understanding of the teachings to yield an inner understanding. The sutra starts with the logic puzzle that A ≠ A, then leads us back to A = A in a new way. We have to understand that the flower is empty of a flower element and has no "flower-ness" at all before we can see that it is because the flower is made up of non-flower elements that it is a flower.

The old story about before studying Zen, mountains are just mountains and rivers are just rivers (said with a shrug), when studying Zen, the mountains are no longer mountains and the rivers are no longer rivers (said with the zeal of fresh insight – they're so much more!), when Zen is mastered, the mountains are mountain and the rivers are rivers (said with stability and wisdom).

Our author reminds us that koans are used in this way, too; an attempt to stop us from constructing reality and experience reality. The Diamond sutra uses a method to develop our view based on our direct experience, not our intellectual understanding; to change our perception of the world. The author calls this a "perceptual revolution" and it is contrary to our basic instincts and nearly everything we've ever learned about how the world works.

The Way

I drive bottom-liners crazy. The example of what that is I like to tell is that if I were a restorer of tapestries, I would want to first study the artistry of the tapestry, who made it and their stories, make an analysis of the yarn and materials used, study the patterns on the reverse side, list the symbolic motifs and what they meant during that time in history, and contemplate the overall beauty of the tapestry both from up close and from a distance. The punch line is that my bottom-line boss would say, "Cheryl, just fix the yellow beak on the little bird in the corner and be done with it!"

During my nine month class in Clinical Pastoral Education (CPE), part of the process to birth new chaplains was to email a reflection of the past two weeks to the supervisor who would make comments in the margin and we might discuss it in our private interview time. We had a template to use that included our relationships with our patients and their families, our coworkers, our fellow students, our supervisor, and because CPE is primarily a Christian course of study, our relationship with God. I replaced the "God" section with the "Triple Gem" and my supervisor and I had some very good discussions about my journey in Buddhism and the importance of the three jewels to me. Often, I would end my reflection note with a quote that seemed to sum up the last two weeks, the insights I had gained, or the way I felt about how things were going. My supervisor commented after awhile that he was used to starting a sermon with a scripture or a quote and expounding on that theme, he was enjoying my more inductive approach.

Tackling the Diamond Sutra is, in many ways, like taking on a logic puzzle; testing its validity and reliability. In our text, Mu Soeng explains how this sutra and the early Zen stories which developed into the koan method take Buddhism from theology to theopathy; from the knowing to the feeling. The Diamond Sutra also plays with logic and speaks directly to the deductive reasoning of the theology approach. Deductive reasoning is truth preserving, that is, the conclusion is already shown in the premises.

When we look at the classic example of deductive reasoning that:

- All men are mortal (premise)
- Socrates was a man (premise)
- Socrates is mortal (conclusion)

What we learn would only be that information we might not have been aware and is brought to light, but there is nothing new to expand our knowledge. The truth is contained in the premises. The early teachings gave us signs to recognize the Buddha by, 3,000 chiliocosms filled with seven precious treasures, 500 lifetimes, and enough data to satisfy the most skeptical of students. (Mu Soeng, 2000) Then the Buddha tossed in a black swan. He turned facts into contradictions and demanded that we answer his paradoxical questions. A is no longer equal to A in order to be A.

We can no longer collect all of the good and wholesome concepts, reject the bad and unwholesome ones, and understand the Dharma. "One day we're rich, comforted in our certainties. The next moment we're bereft, deprived of every soothing lie we'd embraced as truth." In the orientation that we give to new staff in our hospice, we have an exercise that helps them look at their own death awareness. We have each person make a list of the ten most important things to them in the world. Then we give them the scenario that they have been diagnosed with a terminal disease and they have to cross off five items. As they think about that and cross off the items, we then continue with this story that they are sicker and must cross off an additional three items.

The story continues and now they cross off another item from the list. This gets harder to do for many of the participants. The story concludes that death is here and the last item must be crossed off the list and when that is done, they are to get up and throw the paper into the waste basket and retake their seat. Some people cry, others cannot cross off the last item, and some have even retrieved their list from the trash after the class. Our concept of our self as real is so strong that we feel great loss and sorrow as we grapple with our personal coming and going. "The meaning of Tathagata is 'does not come from anywhere and does not go anywhere.' That is why he is called a Tathagata."

As Mu Soeng explains, the Diamond Sutra forces listeners to rearrange their conceptual framework, aiming to produce a liberating breakthrough; to shake the mind out of its linear, inductive or deductive reasoning. "Subhuti, what is called a compound is just a conventional way of speaking. It has no real basis. Only ordinary people are caught up in conventional terms." While I think it is a bit risky to look to science, especially physics, for confirmation of philosophical or religious ideas, it is tempting to look at how we come to believe that things are real. We can speculate about what is an illusion or a delusion, perhaps based on whether or not the illusion is shared and the delusion caused by some faulty neurochemical reactions. However, it was common during the Buddha's day to believe that matter was formed by the coming together of atoms, much as we still think of it today. It is only when we look deeper that we find, and have confirmation from our science buddies that matter and energy are actually the "same;" that what exists is a process, continually shifting into other forms as conditions are made right for the object to manifest. So the moment that we speak a word to identify reality, we miss the mark. When we base our understanding of reality on our concepts of the building blocks of reality, we find ourselves stuck. We have identified what we think is true; then deductively preserve this truth without ever being in touch with the true nature of things.

If I am caught in the notion of being and non-being, I am caught in the notion of birth and death. The Diamond Sutra asks me to remove this notion of human nature or personality. There is a deep ecology in this advice, helping us to see that we are made up of not-human elements and that we contain all of the elements of the universe. How can we consider any of the animals, minerals, or sprouts to be less than ourselves? It is when I understand that the flower is only recognizable as a flower when I can see the component parts within it that I understand reality. I must be able to see the beauty of the clouds, rain, and sun making the lovely petals, but also the mud and worms, and the garbage the flower will become going into the compost heap before I can say I recognize the flower.

Yet, just when we think that the Diamond Sutra has explained the non-existence of everything and we are happy to say that all is one and illusion, the Buddha says: "Do not think that when one gives rise to the highest, most fulfilled, awakened mind, one needs to see all objects of mind as nonexistent, cut off from life. Please do not think in that way. One who gives rise to the highest, most fulfilled, awakened mind does not contend that all objects of mind are nonexistent and cut off from life." In the Vietnamese liturgy, we recite "The one who bows and the one who is bowed to, are both, by nature, empty. Therefore the communication between them, is inexpressibly perfect. Our practice center is the net of Indra, reflecting all Buddhas everywhere, and my own person reflects all the Buddhas, to whom with my whole life I go for refuge." When that insight is realized, there is no longer discrimination between myself and anything I would call "other." True communication is only possible from this place, and with this insight and communication flows true compassion; true equality.

As we move closer to death, we begin to have fear about what will happen to us. I have heard people say that they are not afraid to die, but that they are afraid of the process of dying; afraid that they will experience pain. I think that this is only partly true and that the truth is closer to that they cannot wrap their heads around what it would be like to be dead. The first time I saw a dead body, I had to fight with myself not to run away. Because I was young at the time and had not been prepared in other than a clinical way about a person dying, I had no stability to be with the person in mindfulness; I could only gape at what a profound difference there was from living to dead. It was the first time I had honestly thought about putting myself into that place and it was very frightening. During my career as a nurse, most of my encounters with death also had to do with trying to fend death off; to fight tooth and nail to stop the process. As I grew in my career and my practice, I could approach this process with more stability and calm for myself, my patients, and afterwards with their family. As a hospice nurse and budding chaplain, I can bring more of myself to the dying process to see that without dying there can be no life. When I touch my face, I can feel the skull beneath my skin and I know that one day those bones will be ground into the thousands of elements from which they came. While it is terrifying, it also makes life all the more sweet.

There is a corny saying about pain is a given, but suffering is optional; all we need is happiness. But it is suffering that creates true happiness. It is only in looking deeply at the suffering of ourselves or the other person that we can understand the root of their suffering. Understanding gives rise to true happiness and compassion. We have to be as skillful with how we work with the mud and fertilizer as we are in the art of flower arranging. If I believe that I was born and believe that I will die, I am stuck in a notion. Right view transcends the notions of coming and going, birth and death; producing right thinking, right speech, and right action. It has the power to help and to heal.

The Sutra is ended with a poem that guides us in what to do when confronted with this profound teaching:

"All compounded things are like a dream,
a phantom, a drop of dew, a flash of lightening.
That is how to meditate on them.
That is how to observe them."
~ Thich Nhat Hanh

Ford explains that the core expression of the sutra is apophatic; I points the way obliquely, approaching reality by relentlessly rejecting partial truth. It is a direct pointing to our true home. It reveals the Buddha eye and invites us to open that eye that we all possess but rarely open.

May all beings find peace.

CHAPTER 16

Hua-Yen Buddhism

It is not an understatement to say that Hua-yen Buddhism changed my life. The slender volume "Hua-yen Buddhism: The Jewel Net of Indra" by Francis H. Cook, is not a simple book to read, but it is profound. Cook warns us in the preface that Hua-yen is not easy to understand, and we must have a good grounding in the basics of Buddhism to "graduate" to the concepts illuminated in this philosophy. The Flower Garland, or Avatamsaka Sutra, is the principle sutra that the school uses. This sutra has some elements that might be considered more entertaining than enlightening, but at it's heart is the explication of shunyata; emptiness. Hua-yen not only teaches impermanence and interconnectedness, but goes deeper into inter-penetration.

These ideas, especially the metaphor of Indra's Net, might at first blush seem simple and easy to agree with. As we study them, we begin to see that we have to go deep into the meanings and ramifications to come up on the other side. It's a short step over the chasm, but wisdom comes from the journey Fa'tsang takes us on. And artist at heart, Fa'tsang and his famous mirror illustration for Empress Wu is an example of the beauty that is contained in truth. I've always marveled at this illustration and wished that I could have been there to see it when it was new.

Net of Indra

The Jeweled Net of Indra is such a captivating metaphor. We're lucky that, if we have any science training at all, the concept is easier to grasp. Yet an intellectual grasp of the inter-connectedness of all things really doesn't do the image justice. Many modern Dharma teachers talk about interconnectedness – Sharon Salzberg recently posted "Either viewed through Dharma or science, the fundamental condition of reality is wholeness and inter-relatedness." and Thich Nhat Hanh coined the term "interbeing" to express this concept. He has said: "The present moment contains the past and future. The secret of transformation is in the way we handle this very moment." To me, this puts a different spin on the present moment than our new age friends who seem to strive for a bliss of "Now" which is devoid of the past or future, not understanding that as we explore "now," we find a gem that as we turn it, the facets reflect all that has come before and all that will come after if we continue as we are.

At our temple, an opening gatha that we often recite (translated with a little help from my friend):

> *The one who bows and the one who is bowed to*
> *are both, by nature, empty.*
> *Therefore the communication between them*
> *is inexpressibly perfect.*
> *Our practice center is the Net of Indra*
> *reflecting all Buddhas everywhere.*
> *And my whole person reflects all the Buddhas*
> *to whom with my whole life I go for refuge.*

This is followed by many bows to the three jewels and to the bodhisattvas and sets the stage for reciting the sutras for the service. There is a large halo behind the huge statue of the Amitabha Buddha behind and elevated above the alert and its multi-colored lines spiral out so that when the light behind it rotates, sparks of light flash from the little pin holes. It's mesmerizing but it's always reminded me of the net of Indra; the whole is found in each element, yet each element is part of the whole. It's hard, though, to see it that clearly because it's always fluid and flashing a different picture to us at any given moment. It's when we slow down and stop adding to the movement that we can look deeply and begin to see the images and connections. As our author says: "This relationship is said to be one of simultaneous *mutual identity* and *mutual inter-causality*."

The other day I was really annoyed and frustrated by something stupid but I sat with it and realized that I was just stressed about other things and needed some time to be with my true feelings. Later that night, my sister called and she related that she was so annoyed with someone who was over-reacting to something. I had to laugh and say that she would have been annoyed with me earlier in the day, too, but that sometimes the silliest things can seem like the last straw. I hope we can both cut people a bit more slack as we see the inter-connectedness of all things and how easy it can be to get caught in the flashes of movement instead of being able to see the big picture within the gems.

Flower Ornament

When looking at the history of a school or philosophy, my main interest isn't so much in the how, but the why. Our author uses a number of analogies to explain what the Hua-yen school is about and tries to piece together the time line of the school as best as anyone can, with the usual caveats that we can't really know, but this is the best we can come up with. When looking at the underlying purpose of the Hua-yen philosophers, our author says "It was the peculiar mission of Hua-yen to try, on a scale more vast and to a degree more satisfying than any other school of Buddhism, to reassemble all the apparently separate, diverse threads of Buddhist thought and weave them into a seamless whole." The Hua-yen thinkers wanted to present the fullest, most perfect form of the vision of the truth so that people could begin to penetrate the landscape and direct experience of enlightenment.

The Avatamsaka Sutra, or the Flower Ornament Sutra, is a long sutra which is a compilation of a variety of other works which both inspired it and wove these works together to create a whole that is dramatic as well as philosophical. The Hero's Journey is represented as the Buddhist "everyman" Sudhana makes his quest to the lands of Maitreya and is shown truth. The understanding that the Relative dimension that we think we see all around us is actually inter-leaved within the Ultimate dimension of the direct experience of emptiness is what the Avatamsaka portrays and explains.

The Hua-yen school was certainly influenced by the schools of Buddhism that came before and in the Central Asian and Chinese culture and Taoist thought, it also influenced Ch'an and Pure Land schools as well. The founders and developers of Hua-yen, though, were not only interested in creating a beautiful vision and philosophy, they were interested in inviting the reader to take the step into the experience of reality. Many of them were meditators and at the end of the day, it is still important to take all the learning, thoughts, visions, and structures not only to the cushion to look deeply at and realize, but into life to experience. "The Hua-yen picture of existence is grand, beautiful, and inspiring, but it is nothing if it is not a lived reality."

Part of our assignments included posting on the class forum, and having discussions with our peers: I'm struck by your comment about the Hua-yen philosophers giving the idea of emptiness a "more comforting meaning." I've always found the concept of emptiness, and for that matter (no pun intended) the scientific concept of $E=MC^2$ to be quite shocking, un-nerving, and when I'm really open to it, really frightening. On the other hand, when I first learned about the Net of Indra and heard a talk on it that was probably more advanced than I was ready for at the time, I found it to be not comforting but disorienting. It seemed that all that movement and reflection would be something that I would get completely lost in. But that's where I recognized (and mentioned in the other assignment) that I needed to find stability to stop moving to be able to see the flow from a different perspective. Then when I realize that this "I" that I cherish and fear for, is one of the kaleidoscope shapes and that the next configuration is something that I can allow to happen without clinging or picking and choosing.

So, I guess I'm something of a pill - neither explanation gives me any comfort, they both shake me up in different ways. Wouldn't it be nice, though, if we could think it through and figure it out instead of waiting for that shift in perception/consciousness/wisdom. I'm good at figuring things out! But instead, like I learned in CPE class, too, I can't "figure out" the authentic me to bring to my patients, I have to *be* that. When I'm scared about what the next doctor will say, it's been very helpful to stop and allow myself to feel the groundlessness under my feet with curiosity about what will come next. When I talk with people about what's happening, I've let down my guard a bit more, too, allowing the feelings to flow instead of being the brave "good girl" that I was raised to be. I'm finding that while it may make some people uncomfortable, others have welcomed being able to ask the questions about breast cancer that were scaring them.

Ekayana

The word "catholic" is derived from the Greek to mean "universal" or "all embracing"; in that sense the Hua-yen philosophers wanted to create a universal vehicle, "Ekayana," which is all encompassing in scope. They recognized the intrinsic wholeness of the dharma and wanted to include all of the various teachings into one cohesive text and philosophy that could be enfolded into this one vehicle. Our author explains that this is not just a compilation of the teachings that came before, but it is also "one vehicle with distinct teaching." That distinct teaching was the recognition of the interpenetration of all things, infinitely repeated throughout the universe. The concept that All is One, and One is All – Indra's Net.

Sarvam Shunyam means "everything is empty." This concept confronts any illusion that there are irreducible components of existence; that there are entities with a separate, individual reality. All is empty, including the concepts which seem to be the very teachings of the Buddha like the Four Noble Truths and Nirvana. While, at first, this is quite disconcerting, the teaching that there are no obstacles for the mind of the person who penetrates this paradox, it is then understood that having nothing to attain, the person enters into the being-ness of Nirvana. In the poetic language of the Avatamsaka sutra, there is a lot of light, space, and time in the Pure Land. Everyone can walk beautifully, completely free, hearing the Dharma even in the song of the birds; seeing the dharma in the light emanating from the lotus blossoms. In physics, we could talk about the implicate and explicate order of things; concepts proposed to counter the idea that the universe is made of tinier and tinier particles that we need to figure out how to identify. Rather than pieces constructing the universe like a jig saw puzzle, perhaps the universe is like a hologram; the whole contained in each part with modern terms taking the place of Indra's Net and including complex mathematical formulae.

The Tathagatagarbha concept is a bit problematic to describe to non-Buddhists because it would be very tempting to think it as a type of "soul" or "atman." The idea itself is part of the Yogacarins and the bija seed/alaya "store consciousness" way of thinking which blends the germ or potential of human nature, ultimately Buddha nature, with the womb or container which is our human lives. By looking deeply into the energy of each of these seeds, we learn to transform habit energies into wholesome energies which nurture wisdom. By penetrating the ultimate dimension, of seeing the nature of emptiness that is implicate to the nature of relative reality, the "garbha" or seed of the Tathagata can manifest. Nagarjuna approached emptiness from the standpoint of negation to illustrate that things do not exist independently of each other, that there is no explicate order of things. When Fa-tsang approached this problem, he chose to take a different point of view that is just as true and valid, emphasizing the interdependent nature of emptiness to understand phenomena.

By trying to give people an idea of what the world would look like to a Buddha, Fa-tsang uses this positive approach, I would guess, inspired by the poetic language and images of the Avatamsaka sutra. It is important, as our author exhorts us, not to interpret this as making emptiness some kind of positive principle or entity. Far from our New Age friends who would love to leave this physical plane behind to soar in the rarified air of Ultimate Truth, Buddhism explains that the ultimate and relative dimensions cannot exist without each other, but the true bliss of Nirvana is having a direct experience of the reality of the flow of all things into and through themselves. Chinese thought influenced these writings as well, with the Taoist view that the "harmonious co-existence of the phenomena of the world" is good; Fa-tsang came to see emptiness as the ultimate good, harmonizing all things as necessary for the whole to exist. Our author sums this up well by saying that everything is to be valued equally with every other thing, and that value is supreme. After all, everything is empty, therefore everything "contains and teaches that reality which shines from its heart."

Six Characteristics

With the six characteristics, Fa-tsang breaks down the aspects of existence to illustrate how objects and phenomena relate to each other. In his treatise, Fa-tsang wants to eliminate any temptation or doubt about viewing life as either eternalistic or annihilationistic. By breaking down "essence" into universality and particularity, "characteristics" into identity and difference, and "function" into integration and disintegration, he illustrates that while each of the three major aspects of reality are not only two sides of the same coin, but are also happening simultaneously. You can't have one without the other. In this schema, we can express that all things are empty and interdependent, therefore have no true difference. Our author explains that the "differences which we detect and emphasize are subjective interpretations; our own self-interested values imposed on what otherwise a valuative no-man's land."

The analogy of the rafter and the building further explain these characteristics. The main concern of Fa-tsang is to focus on the process and dynamics of the existence of an object or phenomenon and help to illustrate the difference between eternalism and annihilationism. As he explains, there would be no building (annihilationism) if the rafter did not have the power to wholly cause the building because the building would simply be a collection of parts. If the rafter is removed, the whole building should remain if that were true. If the building were eternal, then we could take pieces and parts from it and it would remain whole. Now, it's easy to balk at this analogy, thinking "oh, of course it's still a building even if imperfect" but it's interesting that when a building is imperfect, we actually pretty automatically start thinking of the parts looking for ways to improve it, salvage parts, etc. but when the building is whole we don't concern ourselves with the parts; just interact with it in its wholeness.

These analogies and logic puzzles are important because they help us grasp the relationships that create identity and differentiation that we observe and perceive as real. The bottom line for Fa-tsang and, I think we as Buddhists, becomes the task of understanding that yes I can place my computer and book on the desk and it will hold them up and be functional, that I can see the component parts, yet I can also understand and see the process that brought it all to manifest here and now and will continue to evolve into something else. All the while, each aspect reflects all the other aspects if I can look deeply at them. The process happens all around us all the time and it is not about rising above to see the folly of the mundane, or, as our author points out, to banish things that are unworthy or disgusting, but to see the flow of all things as wonderful and good. "The loss and gain are one and the same thing..." The process is a dance and the flow of the dance includes all of life, helping us go deeper into seeing things and having a direct experience of life, just as it is.

Vairocana

"...Vairocana is the cosmic Buddha, whose body is infinitely large, and whose life is infinitely long." Sounds like we're heading into "God" territory at first blush, and according to the New World Encyclopedia, Francis Xavier in his missionary work, used the term *Dainichi,* the Japanese word for Vairocana, to indicate *God* when he was starting is missions work in Japan. When Francis Xavier learned the subtle differences, he switched to the term *Deusu* to indicate God. (I do have to admire this, though, since it indicates that he actually listened to what the monks had to say.) The Hua-yen taught that the Vairocana Buddha is everywhere, in every time; the whole of the universe – "all these are the sermon of the Buddha."

The implications of this are important because we do need to be cautious as we approach this concept and not jump to conclusions about the identity and function of Vairocana. It isn't accurate to say that Vairocana is a pan-Buddhist concept, but, rather a personification of the Pure Land itself. Our author brings up a good point in looking at why the inter-being-ness of all things is difficult for Westerners to understand. We have been raised to think in terms of dualism in all ways, so for the sacred to be present, the profane must exist. It takes a lot of description to get the concept of emptiness/form inter-penetrating each other, kind of like trying to describe three dimensions to a two dimensional creature. You can try to draw a picture, but it won't really make sense until the two dimensional being can actually see the third dimension. We have the same problem with many of the scientific questions from sting theory, to multiple dimensions, and even time itself. We can understand intellectually, but it takes deep looking to really see. I read an article a couple of years ago about a theory of time that said that time is actually "packets" of information and there was no true "movement" as we perceive. Like looking at a film strip moving through the light, we look at the screen and see movement happening, then look back at the film to see that the reality is that there is no movement, only still pictures in a row. So too, reality seems very "real," as our author relates the story of the gentleman who kicks the rock and feels it is real enough for him! We might have that intellectual understanding of inter-being, yet find that our foot has fallen asleep during meditation and it hurts when we try to take a step – it's happening to me and emptiness seems to disappear at that moment. So in Western thought, what I think of as me I can also accept changes over time – I'm a baby, I grow up, I change my opinions, I learn, etc. – the common thread is the soul. When we look at emptiness/form in Buddhist terms, it is the flow of change that is the thing, the sea of energy is the body of Vairocana – we are Vairocana.

In the quote, it illustrates that Fa-tsang is always concerned throughout his career and writings with the concern that people will misunderstand form and emptiness and think that they are separate things. We could be tempted to believe that Vairocana is an intelligent force or that the Universe itself has a consciousness and intelligence. There are many of our New Age friends that do believe this and that the universe plays with the forms bringing lessons to our consciousness. Fa-tsang clarifies this to emphasize form arising from conditions; if it did not, there could be no awakening nor extinguishing of karma since we would always simply be along for the ride with the whims of the flow. By fully experiencing things just as they are, we then have the ability to "see" the chain of causality in what is happening and we then have a choice to stop the chain of karma and transform our suffering into wisdom.

One of the things that I'm working on is continuing to look deeper at that very thing with my health. Rather than have animosity about my diagnosis, can I stop and break the chain of the reactions which are certainly normal and go deeper to really see? At this point, I'll be going in next month for reconstruction surgery, and my favorite t-shirt says "Yes, they're fake - my real ones tried to kill me!" For now, that feels close enough.

Living in the Net of Indra

I really like our chapter's title "Living in the Net of Indra" because it really helps to remind us that with all of the thought experiments, analogies, and symbolism, there really is life to live. We close our books and wonder how to proceed. When I get up from my chair to answer the phone, what do I say? When an ant crawls across the kitchen counter toward a crumb left behind, what do I do? I've read other essays by people who have had experiences of awe and wonder, of deep spiritual insights or scientific discovery who then feel disconcerted by their entry back into reality. One such thinker found himself feeling embarrassed to relieve himself on a solitary walk through the forest because he had experienced the oneness with all things and recognized the tree as a divine presence and it seemed disrespectful because the mundane had become profane. Another recalls feeling unsteady on his feet after spending a great deal of time examining the building blocks of matter, a bit fearful that his foot might go through the floor since the floor itself isn't the solid that we take for granted. When we see those optical illusions like the one where we either see a young lady or an old crone, our brains flip our perception back and forth and it's difficult to see both at the same time or see the picture as a whole. When I take that first step on the path of the Bodhisattva, what am I really getting myself into?

The Hua-yen thinkers, Fa-tsang especially, brought their holistic approach to the Bodhisattva path, explaining that the first step is the whole path, that each stage is the first cause, "at each stage, one is thus both a Bodhisattva and a Buddha." And, just as Fa-tsang emphasizes so well, this does not mean that the path isn't necessary; in fact, the first step is only the first step relative to the rest of the journey and in the context of the journey. In the Hua-yen universe, the Bodhisattva can see this inter-being-ness and holds all beings with compassion and respect and could not accept the prize of Nirvana if everyone else couldn't enjoy that understanding as well. "The Bodhisattva is 'without an abiding place,' free from attachment to both the mundane and the supramundane." The Hua-yen help us to break down the problems of the Bodhisattva path by asking us to look at both sides of the emptiness and form dichotomy, then looking at the whole as inseparable from its parts. We can't go on flipping from one side of the coin to the other, though, we must find a way to not only understand that we are part of Indra's net, but that we *are* it along with every being and every blade of grass.

Between Heaven and Earth

Vietnamese Buddhism is an interesting mixture. Lineages within Orders are not emphasized very much; an individual monk or nun can trace his or her lineage, but the order they are associated with will commonly be a mixture of lineages. Blending Pure Land and Zen, the services and teachings will lean toward one or the other in greater or lesser degrees depending on the teaching style of the senior teachers or the preference of the lay community. When I first studied Thich Nhat Hanh's writings, he was commonly referred to as a Zen Master and it is true that he leans more to the Zen side of the Vietnamese spectrum because his lineage is through Master Lin Chi (the Rinzai school). Many times, when we think of different schools or sects within schools, we consider the differences in their practices; what do they emphasize or de-emphasize? This is a superficial way of looking at them, but can help in choosing a school to be aligned with since the Buddha understood the concepts of learning styles dubbing it "the 84,000 ways up the mountain."

As I considered which form or school of Buddhism to follow, practice was the principle way I looked to make that choice. Interestingly, what I am finding over the years is that all the practices and forms are actually present within each school and each has its place along the way. When considering the Platform Sutra, the idea of the Middle Way in understanding the interplay between understanding and insight, meditation and wisdom, is key. "If there is a lamp there is light; if there is no lamp there is no light. The lamp is the substance of light; the light is the function of the lamp. Thus, although they have two names, in substance there are not two. Meditation and wisdom are also like this."

There was a time that I kind of looked down at my nose at chanting, especially the chanting of Pure Land Buddhism; this so-called 'easy' form seemed superstitious or just a cultural accretion that our friends striving to form a pure version or agnostic form of Buddhism seem to disdain. I felt that sitting meditation was the superior way to practice and would lead to enlightenment. However, what I am learning is that all of the many forms of sitting, koan practice, chanting, sutra recitation, and doing the dishes mindfully are all valuable ways to bridge the gap between our understanding and experience of the lamp and light. A story I heard about chanting the name of the Amitabha Buddha helped me understand the purpose of reciting the name. The story goes that a man came to the home of a woman who was well known in the community for her devotion to the Amitabha Buddha. She chanted the name over and over in a loud voice from dawn to dusk and then some! But she was also well known to be a rather mean spirited person without a smile on her lips for anyone she met. The man who came to her cottage began to call her name in a loud voice, drowning out her chanting at first. She strengthened her resolve and chanted louder. Eventually, the two were shouting at the top of their lungs. This went on for nearly an hour; the neighbors did not know what to make of all this to say the least. She finally had had enough! She came out of her home and confronted the man: "Don't you realize that I am chanting the name of the Lord Amitabha? Why do you keep calling my name?" The man had a wry smile on his lips, "Madam, I've only been chanting your name for an hour and you are already annoyed with me. You've been chanting the name of the Lord for years; think of how he feels!"

"Merely chanting with the lips is nothing more than recitation of the Buddha's name. Chanting with a one-pointed mind is true chanting. Just mouthing the words without mindfulness, absorbed in habitual thinking, will do no real good for your practice." When we believe that the Pure Land is somewhere outside ourselves that we desire to be, we do not benefit from chanting the name of the Amitabha Buddha, just as when we sit in meditation to escape from our world or ourselves we do not benefit ourselves, but only when we sit in one pointed attention do we gain from the practice. The Platform Sutra exhorts us to practice, saying that to recite the Dharma without practice is "like an illusion or phantom." Yet the Buddha himself declared: "The Pure Land of the Western Paradise is far, far from here. You must pass 100,000 lands, and even 8,000 more regions, in order to reach it." Here, he uses metaphors of distance and space to illustrate the illusory distance between relative reality and ultimate reality that we currently perceive. The Buddha also expresses that "The Pure Land of the Western Paradise is not a faraway place. Why? Because the very mind of sentient beings is the place of Amida Buddha." "Whether we appreciate it or not, we are ceaselessly invoking..." our litany of thoughts of what we want or do not want, what we think and feel, and our judgments and opinions. What should we invoke, then? It is our choice to invoke vow and practice that vow.

In several places in the Platform Sutra, disciples ask the Master to resolve their doubts or transmit knowledge to them. The Platform Sutra teaches that practice while walking or sitting, speaking or silent, moving or still, the practitioner is at peace. In the Zen story about Lung T'an who lived for many years with T'ien Huang. The student felt that he was not progressing on the path could keep silent no longer when he said to his master: 'I have been with you for years, but you have never transmitted anything to me. I beg you to treat me with more compassion." The Master responded to the student with true compassion by pointing out what their interactions had been like over the years, helping him to understand that the day-to-day activities that the student had been taking for granted had been performed by the Master with true awareness and equanimity and had illustrated the teachings for him. The Pure Land was right there all along, but the student had not looked with the eyes of the Buddha. When a teacher asked a student "Where did you come from when you were born and where will you go when you die?" the student thought about it. The master smiled and said, "In the length of a thought, the clouds have crossed a thousand miles."

Nhat Hanh goes on to explain that the authentic mind seal is transmitted in every moment. If we observe the way the master walks, eats, speaks, and perform each act of daily life, we will be receiving the transmission of the Dharma continuously. This transmission, according to Nhat Hanh is available to each disciple in every moment; this is the "real Zen, not just in books but in the living reality of relationships and daily life." At some of our retreats at Bao An Temple we have a ceremonial type lunch. I look forward to these meals as wonderful times to practice and they are very meaningful for me. If not everyone at the retreat is experienced with mindful eating and they just eat in their habitual way, sometimes I find myself becoming impatient with this because I had looked forward to the shared energy of everyone eating mindfully. What I learned to do is to stop and look at the monks and nuns as they eat. Their calmness, the half-smile on their lips; mindfully eating each bite settles me down so that I can continue my meal with that energy. I can practice for myself but also for those around me who might have picked up on my annoyance instead of peace and who might try eating even one bite of their food more mindfully.

So what happened to Mahakasyapa when the Buddha raised his flower? He truly *saw* the flower. The Buddha transmitted his deep understanding to Mahakasyapa mind to mind, thanks to Mahakasyapa's deep looking. The flower was still there and the deeper understanding of the ultimate dimension of the flower was there too. This is the true Middle Way. In the Buddhist context, "middle" does not mean a synthesis between opposing concepts or the phrase 'everything in moderation.' Instead, to penetrate the absolute truth, we must let go of concepts. Using 'negation' can help; looking at emptiness, non-being, and other non-conceptual descriptions. The Platform Sutra helps us by teaching the doctrine of *Mahaprajnaparamita*, explaining that the "capacity of the mind is broad and huge, like the vast sky." The sutra explains that we cannot sit with our minds fixed on emptiness so that we miss the totality of our experience. All of the universe exists in the midst of emptiness, not in spite of it. The meditation practice of *Shikantaza* is another example of the 'middle way.' The word means "just sit" and the practice involves the mind intensely involved in just sitting. The idea is to be as aware as a swordsman facing a skilled opponent. Kapleau explains that it is the mind of somebody facing death. Ideally, one is fully attentive yet relaxed; able to respond effortlessly to the changes that occur. The practitioner is on the razor's edge between the pairs of opposites with perfect equanimity. "But do not for one minute imagine that such sitting can be achieved without long and dedicated practice."

Sitting meditation is a non-conceptual experience according to Nhat Hanh who explains that it is not time to think, reflect, or "lose ourselves in concepts or discriminations. It is also not a time to remain immobile, like a stone or the trunk of a tree. How can we avoid the two extremes of conceptualization and inertia?" This is where we find the direct experience of the present moment in the midst of our experience in the world under the light of the lamp of mindfulness. Just as thinking about drinking our tea and actually drinking it mindfully are not the same thing, we must guard against being 'mindful of being mindful.' One of the challenges of some of the old Zen stories for me is the seemingly violent ones. There are lots of stories of disciples cutting off their arms for whatever reasons or cutting cats in half, and the like. These stories are taking on a new meaning for me as I sit each morning and evening in these days before my surgery. How can I not discriminate? I do not want to have surgery. Intellectually, I know why this is necessary and I know that I will be able to accommodate this new body, yet here I sit thinking of everyone who has had things happen to them that they do not want to have happen; I am no different.

"The moment there is the slightest choice of good and evil, your mind falls into confusion." The constant question is how to avoid picking and choosing. "Chao-Chou answered, 'Between heaven and earth, I alone am the honored one.'." Shen-hui answered the Master that 'it hurt and it also didn't hurt.' when asked if being hit hurt or not. But he was rebuffed for his answer when the Master said "I see and I also do not see... My seeing is always to see my own errors; that's why I call it seeing. My non-seeing is not to see the evils of people in the world. That's why I see and also do not see. What about your hurting and non-hurting?" The Master went on to exhort Shen-hui to practice non-duality in order to experience the ultimate reality and truth for himself. Rather than escape the "bitter sea of birth and death," we can realize that birth and death are not the "vital matters" they seem to be; only realizing that our true nature is the only thing that is important. Loori explains that choice creates a separation and in intimacy, separation dissolves. We need constant reminders not to attach to anything in order to experience the intimacy that encompasses heaven and earth. Yet, understanding intellectually about duality and non-duality can produce a 'unity' that is just another concept.

Nagarjuna's treatise states: "All phenomena can be understood to be in two categories: mind and matter. On the conceptual level, we distinguish mind and matter, but on the level of awakening, all is mind. Object and mind are both marvelous. Mind is matter, matter is mind. Matter does not exist outside of mind. Mind does not exist outside of matter. Each is in the other. This is called the 'non-duality of mind and matter.'" To see the true nature of things is to see the 'interbeing' nature of all things; to perceive their nature of interdependence, not having a separate, independent self. It is only when we can see the nature of the flower before, during, and after it is manifested as a flower can we truly say that we have seen the flower.

I love the saying "Before I studied Zen, the mountains were just mountains and the rivers were just rivers. As I studied Zen, the mountains were so much more than just mountains and the rivers so much more than just rivers (or in some telling's, the mountains were no longer mountains and the rivers no longer rivers). Now that I have mastered Zen, the mountains are mountains and the rivers are rivers." Even while living in the world of conditioned things; in awakening, we are masters of ourselves. The Vietnamese monk Cu'u Chi said: "As long as your activity is based on conceptual discrimination, it is not free. The free person sees all, because he knows there is nothing to be seen. He perceives all, not being deceived by concepts... he lives in peace and freedom... The only way to arrive at awakening; he realizes his calling of awakening in this conditioned world, without thinking whether the world is conditioned or unconditioned."

I have lived through many experiences in this 'full catastrophe' of living. Births and deaths, joy, grief, satisfaction and disgruntlement have all been part of it. Many profound experiences that have taught me so much that I am so grateful for. So now, facing surgery I have a choice to make. Can I join the ranks of those disciples willing to cut off their own arm for the sake of the Dharma, or will I continue to pick and choose? My son and I were talking and I was feeling a little impatient with him because he hadn't done something I wanted accomplished before I go to the hospital; he got a little choked up and when I asked what was wrong, he said that he was trying to be strong for me. I realized right then what a powerful teaching he was giving me. I told him that I don't want him to be strong for me; I want him to be honest with his feelings with me. I realize that I've tried to always be the strong one for others going through a crisis, but what that has done is to bring separation between me and the other person. In picking and choosing, I choose not to be spontaneous and authentic, creating a separateness. Instead, sometimes it has to be OK that things are not OK. In impermanence, I can have the courage to set 'hope' aside, fully confident that things are the way they are and that they will change. All I need to do is step off the edge of the cliff into the void not trying to find ground to stand on.

The Dharma can seem fantastic and inspiring when we feel great and we go forth with great resolve to be perfect people. When things fall apart, we can find ourselves at odds with how we think we should be and how we really are. That's a great moment, though – this moment for me is like that. It's exposing how I really feel, not how I should feel or how I can be strong for someone else or even for myself. So, with no ground to stand on, instead of trying to find security, I want to try to soften, be curious about how I feel, and let my mind grow larger, to put more space around what is happening. I want to try to relax into groundlessness and see what happens. As I go to into that strange anesthesia sleep, I will try to know that I am breathing in and know that I am breathing out.

"There is only one thing, from the very beginning, infinitely bright and mysterious by nature. It was never born, and it never dies. It cannot be described or be given a name. What is this 'one thing'?"

Nam Mô A Di Đà Phật!

Dharma Talk

My favorite program on Animal Planet is *Big Cat Diary*. I love to watch the cats on the Maasi Maura lounge and play, often with behaviors so very much like my cats. But then, they show what those big cats really do well: stalk and catch their prey. The cheetah picks the moment, then takes off running toward the gazelle, often a fawn, the cat's head and eyes parallel with the ground, legs flawlessly running flat out. They are perfectly focused; perfectly one pointed in their goal of catching their prey. They lean to change direction as the gazelle tries to serpentine to get away, but when the cat gets close enough to the fleet footed gazelle, a paw flicks out and trips those long legs that are working so hard to survive. The gazelle is down and the cheetah clamps her mouth on the neck. At first, I'm cheering for the cat and even feel a bit of triumph when the prey is caught. Then the camera shows the eyes of the gazelle, bright and alive. Within moments, that light goes out and the animal is dead. I feel compassion and sorrow for the gazelle. When we study about emptiness, that the all is in one and the one is in all, it seems so logical and reasonable. Then we turn our heads to the world, and all of the times when that flow of energy, form, and life is not a lovely kaleidoscope of color, but a world filled with cruelty, pain, and suffering. Do we relate to the predator or the prey? Are we ready to recognize our own role as either predator or prey in turn? Are we ready to look between that pair of opposites?

Living in the net of Indra is more than understanding with our intellect; accepting that this is the way of the world, and it has to be more than our emotions, feeling pity for the victims of fate or calling our care and concern "compassion." Instead, we must look deeply at everything that crosses our path to truly see each thing, thereby cultivating a compassion that is like "the Love that moves the sun and the other stars." The spark of this feeling might be awakened when we understand that, as Francis Cook explains in his book on Hua-yen Buddhism, "It is not just that 'we are all in it' together. We all are it, rising or falling as one living body." How does Hua-Yen philosophy help me to see the integration between the ultimate reality and relative reality? How do I take these concepts and analogies of mirrors, and rafters and jewels into my understanding and perception of the world?

Thich Nhat Hanh talks at length about *interbeing*, a translation choice from the Avatamsaka Sutra which, along with the Diamond Sutra, are the two sutras he is most influenced by in his teaching. The name of the Order that he founded is the Order of Interbeing in English, *Tiep Hien* in Vietnamese. *Tiep* means "being in touch with" and "continuing." *Hien* means "realizing" and "making it here and now." Understanding these four expressions has been very helpful to me in trying to wrap my head and heart around interbeing. *Being in touch with*, or looking deeply at, reality is to become aware of the processes of the universe. We need to touch our inner processes as well; our feelings, perceptions, and mental formations to uncover our true mind. We pull back the curtain and look clearly at the wonders and beauty of life as well as the suffering. We can develop a unity of mind and world by looking deeply into our mind, and when we are honest, we can see the world. If we look deeply with honesty, we can understand the world and our own mind. *Continuation* is an encouragement to pick up the noble path of the Buddha. He has sown the seeds of awakening and has taught us how to nurture those seeds in the form of our practice. Realization prompts us not to dwell in the world of ideas and concepts, but to express our insights in our personal life. When we touch compassion because of the suffering of another, it is important to reach out however imperfectly to help. We also bring that compassion to ourselves to transform our suffering. We also have the chance to touch the goodness in the world and experience sympathetic joy, sharing our happiness. *Making it here and now*, points us to the present moment as the only moment available to us. The means never justify the ends, the means are the ends; cultivating peace in the present moment is the only way peace can blossom in the future. "There is no way to peace, peace is the way."

When I did a search on the term interbeing to see if there was anything interesting out there to refer to, I stumbled upon a forum with comments about Thich Nhat Hanh and "interbeing." I was puzzled to read that the guy posting felt that Thanissaro Bhikkhu was critical of this term. Luckily, they posted a link to an essay that I eagerly read. The short essay stopped me in my tracks! Rather than critical of the term, it is one of those laser beams of clarity for understanding. Thanissaro explains that in his work with his teacher, his teacher helped him boil down the essence of practice to the phrase "purity of heart." "'You know,' he said, 'the whole aim of our practice is purity of heart. Everything else is just games.'" He went on to define purity of heart as a happiness that will never harm anyone. It seems simple until we realize that ordinary happiness requires that we consume; that we eat. He goes on to relate the first of the Novice's Questions: "What is one? All beings subsist on food." No gentle mirror analogies or gems caught in the net of Indra here – it is feeding. "Interbeing is inter-feeding." Of course, we protest that we must eat to survive and I may try hard to only consume whole foods that cause the least suffering, but I am just making excuses and ignoring the larger impact. Oneness is a pretty primal experience; we are one with our mother in the womb but when we endure the first separation in birth, we are rewarded with the first pleasure of feeding. I love babies – they cry so hard when they are hungry; it hurts them so yet, when they are given the breast or the bottle, they close their eyes in pure bliss. When we look closer at our lives, we begin to see what a challenge it is to keep ourselves feed. We need to keep ourselves occupied with things to feed our bodies, minds, and emotions. We want nutrition, health, fitness, comfort, intimacy, entertainment, experiences, education, intellectual stimulation, and accomplishment as things that certainly seem positive and good. We may even crave less wholesome things at the expense of someone else. While we might believe that most of this is the way the world works and it is ok since, after all, "I'm not attached to these things." If we are really honest with ourselves, we see that when we do not have some of the necessities or wants in life or if we feed ourselves too much junk food of not only food for the body but junk food for the mind and spirit, we can become irritable and unreliable for others.

Cook further explains that in "the one body of Vairocana, surely I can never consider my fate apart from the rest of the body; it must be all or nothing." Whatever individual or phenomenon there is, it exists only in dependence on all other things. But I depend on these other things and phenomenon; I must use them to survive. Rather than sympathy and pity for myself and others, the insight into emptiness itself brings with it compassion, respect, and gratitude. Cook also considers the attitude of fair-mindedness, accepting that we must be prepared that we are made for the use of others as well. His example is that of being eaten by a tiger and I think it is just as important to be able to put ourselves in either place: the cheetah or the gazelle.

"When one sees that form is empty, one achieves great wisdom and no longer dwells in samsara. When one sees that emptiness is form, one achieves great compassion and does not dwell in Nirvana." Fa-tsang worked hard in his career to keep us from dwelling in one side or the other, as we have the tendency to do. Like looking at an optical illusion that is actually two images at the same time, our minds can see one at a time and we have to shift our perception back and forth to see either the young lady or the old crone. So, too, with emptiness and form – the sages who see the interconnectedness can only describe the truth to us in analogies and examples that point to the truth, coaxing us into a direct experience and exhorting us not to dwell in either one. In Celtic mythology this is present in the idea of seeing beyond the veil between this world and the eternal, yet recognizing that the eternal is not distant, that it is *fighte fuaighte* which in Gaelic means "woven into and through each other."

Other Buddhist schools deal with this including the Vajrayana as one of the three vehicles or routes through which one can attain awakening. The fruition of the Vajrayana path is Buddhahood which results from the main areas of practice: view, meditation, and conduct. This point is important – that the practice yields the fruit; the fruit is not something one can go get, create, or be given. Much as a seed contains the whole of the tree and the future fruit, it is not yet a tree until it is planted in fertile soil, watered, and cultivated by the experienced gardener. In Sylvia Plath's *Ode to a Bitten Plum*, she spins a vision of taking a bite of a plum and looking ever deeper at the physical nature of the plum, its colors and textures, then inside the seed to its secret potential as a tree, then further in: "Encased in a wooden shell, enclosed in the small, tight darkness is the pale green twilight; the timeless peace of centuries, the magic hush of deep grass and deeper leaves wreathed in an enchanted garden." Then her consciousness shifts back to reality "Beauty of a bitten fruit, quiet in my warm hand."

So as we practice to go deeper into the aspects of practice, in seeing the truth of the ultimate and relative dimensions, we must remain patient for the seeds to bear fruit. We cannot fool ourselves into believing we have the truth because we can see each image of the young lady and the old crone. If we try to explain three dimensions to a two dimensional being by drawing a cube made of lines on a paper, the two dimensional creature might be able to see the individual planes and might even try to teach his fellows about the wonders of the three dimensional world. But until he actually has a direct experience of the three dimensional world, his understanding and explanations will be merely academic. As I observe the world it is a natural assumption that there are things out there, and my mind and feelings are within me. Yet, if I can still my thoughts and look out the back window to the trees blowing in the wind, my mind does not go outside of me, nor do the trees need to come in. My mind and the trees are one.

> *Forest*
> *Thousands of tree-bodies and mine.*
> *Leaves are wavering,*
> *Ears hear the stream's call,*
> *Eyes see into the sky of mind,*
> *A half-smile unfolds on every leaf.*
> *There is a forest here*
> *Because I am here.*
> *But mind has followed forest*
> *And clothed itself in green.*

Whatever the object, it is not fragmented from the ultimate reality. It, in fact, contains the vast totality of reality. So when we see the cheetah trying to capture the gazelle, in meditation at least, we try not to take sides but to look deeply into both sides of what is happening. While we might want to save the gazelle, we would have to look at the suffering the cheetah would feel deprived of food. When we eat, we must do this as well to develop our own purity of heart. We cannot push away the bad to avoid our feelings of anguish at the suffering of the world or our own. But the point really is not to solve the suffering or rise above it, but to stop – to become immovable before life and death. Schrödinger writes: "Thus you can throw yourself flat on the ground, stretched out upon Mother Earth, with the certain conviction that you are one with her and she with you.... As surely as she will engulf you tomorrow, so surely will she bring you forth anew to new striving and suffering. And not merely 'someday': now, today, every day she is bringing you forth, not *once* but thousands and thousands of times, just as every day she engulfs you a thousand times over. For eternally and always there is only *now*, one and the same now; the present is the only thing that has no end."

In the Avatamsaka Sutra, we read "All things are birthless. All things have no extinction. You are also like that. If you know how to look at things this way, you can see and touch all the Buddhas at any time." When I think of the Net of Indra, it kind of makes me feel dizzy. The universe is infinite and all things are reflected in everything else, all moving and flowing into, around, and through each other. For me, it is important to remember to stop. Rather than try to chase the processes to understand them and keep up with them, to take a step back to see and enter the Avatamsaka realm. That realm has all of the light, space, and time that I feel I lack. Each flower shines with the light of learning, each bird sings a song of wisdom, and each being there is a bodhisattva speaking the dharma. This realm is not separate from the relative reality and not a fantasy to escape in. For me, visualizing entering the Pure Land becomes a refuge for meditation and realizing that everything that I encounter is teaching me the dharma. If I have confidence in the idea that all is in one and one is in all, then I need to practice until I can see myself in my loved one, in the butterfly or flower but also in the cruel terrorist, the tortured prisoner, the starving child, the dying person; in the speck of dust, or in the most distant galaxy. The blooming of the flower will bring the fruit of compassion, tolerance, and letting go. True compassion goes hand in hand with peace, seeing all beings as a bodhisattva; seeing myself in the other.

Thich Nhat Hanh relates the story of a Vietnamese man who left home to go to the States to live and when he misses his mother, he looks at his hand and feels better. Before he left, she told him "Whenever you miss me, look into your hand, my child. You will see me immediately." Such a deep teaching – one that encompasses so much: identity, time and space, contin- uation, emptiness, and compassion. Thanissaro Bhikkhu further identifies the importance of practice to cultivate true and unconditioned happiness within ourselves. He explains that it is imperative for "only an unconditioned happiness can guarantee the purity of your behavior. Independent of space and time, it's beyond alteration. No one can threaten its food source, for it has no need to feed." You can trust and be trusted in your actions because you lack for nothing. "Purity of heart is to know this one thing."

CHAPTER 17

The Platform Sutra

The Platform Sutra has been highly influential on many schools of Buddhism, and has its roots in China. Much of the story surrounding the Platform Sutra include legends, political intrigue, history, power, and even paperwork. This sutra is comprised of the sayings, commentaries, and teachings of Hui-neng, the Sixth Patriarch of Ch'an Buddhism. The Platform sutra is a "transmitted" sutra, meaning that it was given during a ceremony of ordination, as a robe, would be confirming that the student understood the teachings. Placing the sutra in an historical context is challenging, but more important for the purposes of using academic study to further practice, is to explore the position the sutra takes on the intersection of intellectual understanding and practice.

Wall Gazing

The first section of the assignment summarizes some of the history preceding the writing of the Platform Sutra including political intrigue, cultural upheavals, legend, and lineage. When Buddhism was introduced to China, many of the texts and techniques were translated and then practiced by the Chinese who adopted the practices. Meditation was an integral part of the Chinese practice as it had been in India, and while there were wandering ascetics who devoted themselves entirely to meditation, communities of monks were eventually formed. In these communities, the priest Hung-jen came to prominence and became known as the Fifth Patriarch. He trained monks who then went out to establish schools of their own. These groups formed the genesis of Ch'an Buddhism. This history led to the story of Hui-neng, the Sixth Patriarch whose teachings form the Platform Sutra of the Sixth Patriarch. Our author explains that these biographies and histories are not fixed and were embellished later to "bring emotional appeal and authenticity" to their characters and to give the lineage legitimacy equal to Indian Buddhism.

My favorite phrase in this section of the book is "teachings of wall gazing;" makes me think of "watching paint dry." In the history, we learn about the development of the fame and regard of great teachers like Bodhidharma and Hui-neng for Ch'an Buddhism. Even if we'll never really know the details or be able to separate out fact from fiction about these people, it is still a fascinating history and enjoyable to imagine what it was like during that time of Empresses and wandering monks through the pristine countryside of ancient China. For me, the most important thing I take away from any history of Buddhism is how grateful I am to those who came before. They overcame obstacles and suffered persecution and hardships to keep the Buddha Dharma alive. When I bow at temple when I first arrive, the first bow is to all the people who keep things running there and all the hard work that takes, the second is to all the ancestral teachers who kept the Dharma alive through the ages, and the third is to the Buddha who started the wheel in motion.

In the second section, the sutra sets the scene of disciples and the Fifth Patriarch in a time of transition when a successor might be named. When the Fifth Patriarch preaches, he says "for people in this world, birth and death are vital matters. You disciples make offerings all day long and see only the field of blessings, but you do not seek to escape from the bitter sea of birth and death." He goes on to explain the importance of understanding our self-nature. When he reads the verse by Shen-hsiu, then confronts him about what he wrote, he exhorts him to "...enter the gate and see your own original nature."

Not to "escape from the bitter sea of birth and death" is such a powerful phrase. When we look at the full catastrophe of our lives and those around us, it is so easy to be swept away in that sea. We happily go about our lives thinking that things will always be the same or we hope for the best. Then something happens that knocks us out of our complacent mind-set. Called to the hospital just a few days ago to be with a friend who has learned that he will need to be on renal dialysis soon and may need to be on a transplant list for a new kidney, I was brought again to that sea. For me, this introduction places the Dharma in the most important setting; how to enter the gate to see our own original nature – the gate being oh so close to the shore of that sea.

History

What I found most significant in the first section was that the history that our author chronicles is not only rich in legend and intrigue; it also illustrates impermanence really well. The temples that were favored by the elite or those in power enjoyed the largess heaped upon them and grew opulent and rich. Yet, after a time, they fell out of favor and fell into disrepair, crumbling to dust. Just as each of us strives to find our place in the world, excelling in school, getting a good job, making ourselves physically attractive – hoping for the favor of those in power or getting the kind of mate and family we feel we deserve. The American dream, right? Yet, we fall out of favor and begin to find that all that we've built up is beginning to crumble (with perhaps an interval during our mid-life crisis) and we're left in a heap ourselves unless we've taken the time to look deeper within ourselves.

The Platform Sutra seems to me, in this first part, to be kind of a Cliff Notes of basic Buddhism. I particularly appreciate this quote: "Never under any circumstance say mistakenly that meditation and wisdom are different; they are a unity, not two things. Meditation itself is the substance of wisdom; wisdom itself is the function of meditation." This is Samadhi; that non-dualistic state of mind, observant yet not attached so that we can experience the flow of things just as they are. The quote reminds us that understanding must be integral to experience and vice versa; we could even say "form is emptiness and emptiness is not other than form." This is important for me when there are times that meditation becomes just another thing to do to feel better – like the poster I used to have in my office "I meditate, I light candles, I drink green tea... and still, I want to smack someone!" I wrote this quote and have it propped up in front of my cushion to contemplate this week; now to find those moments of unity.

Legends of Awesomeness

To be honest, I had a hard time concentrating on the history of Chinese Buddhism and all the intrigue this week. I kept hearing the theme song to "Kung Fu Panda" in my head with all these names and legends and forms – "legends of awesomeness... sweet!" One of the things that did strike me though is that the rise and fall of these groups and teachers is kind of a broken record – none of them really learned from history. Guess that's not too surprising since we refuse to learn from history even today. At any rate, I'm just happy that Buddhism has survived the trip through history.

This is my first time with the Platform Sutra and one of the things that struck me in this section was the list of good advice. The pieces and parts of the sutra were really familiar because I've heard many of the phrases expanded on as a theme in a dharma talk. But because it was so action packed with ideas, it reminded me of Polonius in Hamlet with his lists of good advice and bromides. However, this gem stuck with me this week "The capacity of the mind is broad and huge, like the vast sky. Do not sit with a mind fixed on emptiness. If you do you will fall into a neutral kind of emptiness. Emptiness includes the sun, moon, stars, and planets, the great earth, mountains and rivers, all trees and grasses, bad men and good men, bad things and good things, heaven and hell; they are all in the midst of emptiness. The emptiness of human nature is also like this." I love that! When I work with the four foundations of mindfulness, the most helpful aspect is bringing more space into the situation or my feelings. So this passage really speaks to me that the space within my heart/mind is vast enough to contain universes; plenty of room for me to work on my worries and anxieties and ignorance. Bringing that space into this week was a big help – I wasn't less worried, but the worry didn't consume me or make me unhappy if that makes sense. I could sit with my feelings and fears and bring a lot of space in; I had room to feel what I felt without feeling overwhelmed by it or that I had to do something to get back control of what was happening.

Water and Waves

In the first section, what is most interesting to me is the legendary nature of the history of the Patriarch. While out author doesn't elaborate too much; it's fun to imagine the stories played out in a movie like Crouching Tiger, Hidden Dragon with all the beautiful photography and special effects. The metaphors are so beautiful of beautiful light appearing at the birth, the baby refusing his mother's milk yet at night, the universe provides special nectar for him – while he's in the world, he's not of the world and his nourishment is provided by the heavens. When he spreads his sitting cloth to accommodate those who would hear the Dharma, the cloth unfurls to cover the whole region and Devas join in to guard the four directions so that the Dharma can be illuminated.

Most significant in the sutra is the metaphor of water and waves. On this shore, we are buffeted by the waves; we see the rise of birth and death, creation and destruction. On the other shore, the sutra explains, we have put an end to birth and death and we go along with the flow of the water. "Thus it is called 'reaching the other shore,' in other words, paramitas." The sutra admonishes us to remember that this isn't something that we merely recite, but something that we must understand with our heart/mind. In the sutra's praise of the Prajnaparamita and Diamond Sutras, he also differentiates between one limited in capacity to understand and faith is not generated by hearing these sutras with the person who hears it clearly, gaining awakening. The water metaphor continues with the example of the great dragon who sends a deluge of water on the land, washing away the houses and crops while when the rain is upon the ocean, the water level neither rises or falls. In our history, the Master tames a dragon who is wrecking havoc at the Buddha pool by tricking it into making itself small, then preaching the Dharma to it so that it leaves its earthly body. We're often buffeted by the storms and waves of life and when we lack stability, it's pretty distressing and painful. When we can allow ourselves to surrender to the flow of what is happening, we find ourselves able to be in these situations with peace and equanimity.

The dragon image was a good one for me this week, especially since there were a number of unexpected changes that were happening with Greg, with work, and with my health. I would find myself feeling like that huge dragon was "wrecking havoc" and trying to fight him so that things would settle down and so I could take control back. When I could remember to shrink him and teach him the dharma, first I would find myself smiling, picturing him like Mushu the dragon from the Disney movie Mulan, then I would ask myself how I needed to teach myself the dharma in this moment. Rather than looking for an anchor in the storm, I asked myself how I could let go and be swept along with the flow rather than fighting it. I wasn't always able to find that calm centeredness, but sometimes I could and it helped me see that I can find it.

Biography

I found the end of the chapter on the attempt to piece together the biographical history of Hui-neng's life quite poignant. I sense some wistfulness on the part of our author in his desire to see through the mists of time to understand and visualize the Master who he admires. A couple of years ago, one of my cousins did a project of researching our family history. She uncovered a number of our ancestors and even discovered old photographs, letters, and records. She put it all in a book and shared it with our large family. I remember turning the pages and bringing past memories to life yet the more pages turned, the more distant these people seemed. Yet even with the names, like Recompense Murphy (is that a great name or what?), I would look at their faces, sepia toned and serious and wonder what they would tell me if they could speak from the page. What was their life like? What did they love; what did they pick and choose? And so it is with the man credited with writing this influential sutra; what do we know, but what is important that we know? With my own ancestors, I know there is a chain of life that led to me today, typing on a computer keyboard that they would never have imagined. With the Dharma Masters, regardless of what details are correct or mythic, that chain led to what we understand today. Is there a ring of truth to what we read? For me there is, so that has to be enough of what I know of Master Hui-neng or even Recompense.

In this section of the sutra, and dove-tailing with the assignment this week in the Precepts class, is the recognition of our attachment to what we perceive as the dual nature of the world and our lives. The verse that is recommended to the laity to practice includes the line "if they always make clear the guilt within themselves, then they will accord with the way." I bought this as a used book and I've been interested and sometimes bemused by what the previous owner underlined or wrote in the margins. He underlined the words "guilt within themselves" and put a big question mark next to it. I would love to hear why he did that; maybe he felt that Buddhism isn't about guilt and shame or renunciation, that the phrase seems judgmental. I think that the passage and this verse point to that quality of honesty that we need to practice the Dharma; the acknowledgement of the part we have played in making the world what it is. The verses go on to explain that the relative dimension and the ultimate dimension are part and parcel of each other, interleaved together and impossible to separate. We try to ignore or discount the world around us as we search for the sublime, but the transcendental world does not exist outside the mundane. It's only when we smash our notions of duality that we can gain awakening, taking that one inch long journey of opening our eyes.

Copies

In the first section, our author talks a little more at length about the copies of the Platform Sutra that were given to prove that the student had proper understanding of its meaning. Yet now we discover that the many of the texts that have been found have problems of errors and questions of authorship. I've often heard a critique of oral traditions that question how well an orally transmitted work can survive intact. I bought into that until I started attending services where sutra recitations are a key part of the service. There are older ladies there that have those sutras memorized in every detail. Now, granted today we have our books that we read from for the sake of people like me who need that as a crutch, but I can just picture the days when the monks would recite the sutras making a mistake – they would be corrected quite promptly. In the description of the problems with the transcribed words, it's a perspective worth remembering that things that are written aren't necessarily as certain as they might seem.

The part of the sutra that is most significant to me is the beginning verse of part 37: "The Master said: 'Good friends, if all of you recite this verse and practice in accordance with it, even if you are a thousand li away from me, you will always be in my presence. If you do not practice it, even if we are face to face, we will always be a thousand li apart. Each of you yourselves must practice. The Dharma doesn't wait for you." When I was young, I had kind of a crazy quilt kind of practice since the teachers I could find were kind of few and far between. When I finally found my teacher and committed to be his student, I had total confidence in his teachings, but what bothered me was the distance between us. He lives over-seas and as the years have gone by, I have had less and less direct contact with him. I wondered if because I have had issues with my own father who was emotionally distant, I was unconsciously picking a teacher who was distant as well. It's been years ago now, but the feeling is still fresh when I read the letter he sent about these concerns that I had written to him about. He explained that whatever teacher I learned from, while it is tempting to want to receive the special attention of the teacher; the most important thing the teacher can do is practice well. Because he loves all of his students, he does his best to practice – that his practice is the way he manifests his love for each of us. Then when we feel that the miles are great and the emotional distance is difficult, we can sit beautifully, knowing that our teacher is still sitting as well. I can think of people I've been in the same room with yet we weren't present to each other at all; we may as well have been in different countries. Yet every time I sit on the cushion in my meditation room, I feel I'm sitting next to my teacher like those precious days when I could talk with him directly.

Free Your Mind

The first part of our reading talks about the historical texts and places them in the time frame of Japanese history. It's certainly always interesting and colorful to imagine those days and to find those markers that place something in its historical context. I hung out with some archeology students when I was in college. I'd go on digs with them to the mounds of central Indiana. It was fun to get muddy with them, but what was the most fun for me was watching them and having them share their passion for the details of it all. We'd talk about the plains Indians who created the mounds and speculate on what they were used for. They'd explain how one object was consistent with the time period, but how another didn't belong, and how another thing was just a piece of junk. I got to take home the little pieces of junk or glass or pottery that stuck my fancy, but meant nothing to their work. I'd park them on the window sill and they made me smile when I did the dishes and I could wonder the path that little thing took to get there. Now, I can wonder where those little pieces of flotsam and jetsam have gone now.

So while the history of these texts is not my passion, I do appreciate the care and insight of historians like Mr. Yampolsky as they map out the journey of this sutra so that it carries its meanings and insights to us.

For me, the significant part of the sutra is the interaction between Master Hui-neng and Shen-hui. Shen-hui asks the Master if he sees or not, and is answered by being hit three times and asked if it hurts or not. Shen-hui gives what seems like a good answer; but it is an answer that comes from intellectual learning, not from the experience of practice and the Master recognizes this. Master Hui-neng says "My seeing is always to see my own errors; that's why I call it seeing. My non-seeing is not to see the evils of people in the world. That's why I see and also do not see...." He exhorts Shen-hui to practice for himself since the understanding of the Master cannot take the place of his delusions. Master Hui-neng emphasizes the honesty that we all must have in Buddhist practice; that we must look at our actions and thoughts without justifying them or intellectualizing them. Instead, we must practice and have a direct experience ourselves; not worrying about what anyone else is up to. That Shen-hui bowed to the Master and became his disciple shows that he did have a great deal of insight; many people would become offended and leave. It's a really good lesson that the teachings we most need are not necessarily always soft and fluffy; sometimes we need that kick in the pants to shake us out of our pat answers.

The secret meaning? I think it's in that interchange between Master and student – that we must practice and see for ourselves, whether it's the meaning in a shard of pottery or being whacked with a staff; learning to be self-aware enough to recognize how we're deluding ourselves then practicing to rid ourselves of that delusion is the task. Or in the words of Morpheus: " I'm trying to free your mind, Neo. But I can only show you the door. You're the one that has to walk through it."

CHAPTER 18

Stages of Emptiness

The book "Progressive Stages of Meditation on Emptiness" by Khenpo Tsultrim Gyamtso Rinpoche is a remarkable one. Rather than an academic approach to emptiness, it is a book on practice instructions. The essays that follow are rather unconventional because they are my personal responses to doing the meditations. Week by week, practicing these meditations, the writings served as a diary of sorts to share insights, or sometimes not, to the work.

First Meditation

Most significant for me in this first section is the importance of the investigation of experience in a methodical way. The foundation is the Four Foundations of Mindfulness but builds on this through a logical progression and the four kinds of authoritative cognition; perception, inference, testimony, and analogy. (somewhere in Jay Garfield) Having a methodical way to work through the not-self characteristic is definitely in my tribe as a way of approaching things and thinking about things.

The simple statement in the book is "So the Shravaka approach is to investigate experience by simply being as aware as possible every moment." The word "aware" is deceptively simple, and I find it important to remember that this awareness seems to me to point to a direct experience of what is happening right here and right now. What Chogyam Trungpa Rinpoche called "the gap," and Zen might call "just sitting," seems to be the essence of the work – looking deeply into the nature of the aspects of being.

This has been an interesting week with this material. So far, I love this book and the Rinpoche is one of those authors who I wonder where he's been all my life. Backing up to the past few months, I've been working with the Four Foundations of Mindfulness a lot. After taking the class with Laura, I kept working with that method by listening to Pema Chodron's tape and re-reading Thich Nhat Hanh's work, and, of course, doing the meditations. Soon after my diagnosis of breast cancer, I felt that it was important to continue working with this material. Before I had a plan of care or a prognosis, I spend a significant amount of time meditating on dying and there is nothing quite like doing that meditation without having to rely on your imagination. Far from being morbid, I felt that it opened me up to approaching the process in an honest way.

The past couple of weeks before the course started, though, I felt that I have been fighting with myself (funny turn of phrase, isn't it? especially when contemplating not-self). In some respects, it seems that my meditation has been more about talking myself out of my feelings rather than accepting them whether it was about work, food, side effects from medication, house-work, money, or whatever; looking for some kind of transformation... or something. At any rate, I've been eager to take this course and read the book and am pleased that I like the writing. I set up my schedule of about 20 mins in the morning and 20 mins in the evening (pretty much my normal routine) but enjoyed sprucing up the meditation room and have been following the instructions of taking refuge before and dedicating merit after. The instructions for this first chapter are a nice deepening of the four foundations and the sessions have been nice, well, until Thursday morning that is.

I woke up earlier than planned with leg pain (my medication causes joint pain, among other side effects) so I figured I would just get up and meditate since staying in bed wasn't working to fall back asleep. Well, after starting as instructed, my reflection on emptiness became a pretty heated argument; giving Rinpoche what for. I had some pretty cogent arguments against this whole concept, too – after all, the pain in my leg woke me up from sleep; no concept of self caused this suffering. And what is the other pain that we humans feel? Is it fair to separate out physical pain from psychological or existential pain? The comment he made that I felt was too much of a leap was "So consciousness can only ever be momentary, and such a momentary phenomenon would never quality for the title of 'self.' Thus, the mind or awareness that seems to behind all our experience cannot be the self either." I certainly do not posit a soul, being something of a materialist, but I considered ideas that I agreed with earlier in the week to now be patronizing and unfeeling of the pain and suffering in the world; too simplistically boiling it all down to that one unsubstantiated point. When I was afraid that I would die, or only had five years to live, that was a powerful experience for me; to reduce it to me "clinging" to a childish notion of the "self" seems too precious and dismissive. People suffer far more than I did and it seemed to diminish them as being "silly."

I glanced at the time and it was over 20 mins and I was really feeling tired. I rang the bell lightly and sat quietly to listen to the sound, got up, bowed, and returned to the bedroom. I reset the alarm for an extra half an hour, figuring that I could make up an excuse for being late to work later, and shaking my head – wow, less than two quarters to having a master's in Buddhist doctrine, all those retreats, books, practice, going to temple, and all the rest, but I suck at meditation and now don't believe in non-self – I'm a fraud! I surprised myself by falling right to sleep.

When I woke up, far from feeling defeated, I felt refreshed; I felt like I had been honest finally – not about not believing the concepts that I actually do agree with, but that instead of being a "good Buddhist girl" I hadn't tried to fix myself or figure out how to agree, I actually said "no" to the parts that are difficult and seem unfair; wrestling with the concepts. I spent my lunch hour rereading the chapter, but in a different mindset – not one so eager to agree, but just reading, listening to the "voice" of the Rinpoche, allowing it to soak in. The passage that spoke to me was: "Then the mind (when focused inwardly on the absence of self in the skandhas) can rest peacefully in empty space. Through meditation in this manner all subtle doubts are worn away and the mind can rest naturally in emptiness." Maybe I had become attached to emptiness as a concept and been as Nagarjuna says, hopelessly incurable. Just that simple statement "absence of the self in the skandhas" shifted me away from *Emptiness* toward *empty of*. During my treatment for cancer, I had quite a few people tell me that they were amazed at how well I did, that

I had a great attitude and all that; but the bottom line is that I was able, albeit imperfectly, to take each step at a time; to avoid clinging. I would go deeply into my feelings at each step, resting in the reality of how I felt. Each new morning was fresh; walking meditation was lovely seeing the clear blue sky, green grass, breathing with the pain and leaning into it – all of it was a meditation on impermanence. Now, shaking up my way of looking at emptiness, this will be an important process to work with.

I'm sort of using these assignments as a diary of the experience and that's helpful, too.

Yogacara

This chapter is such a pithy and good distillation of the Yogacara philosophy and the consciousness-only school is one I'm very interested in. This idea of consciousness and the concept of what is real and what isn't real is food for thought and lots of people have tackled this in scholarly and artistic work of all sorts. I'm a fan of science fiction and fantasy and I thought of many of the stories that I've read or watched that addressed this through asking questions about creating environments that would be perceived as real yet were not (holograms or magical or neurological) and could that be used for good or evil; entertainment and enrichment, or punishment and suffering. We wonder if others can read and manipulate our thoughts and dreams, or can we ourselves learn to control our dreams and use them to our benefit or enhancement? What happens when our brains are injured or become ill and we suffer memory loss, personality and behavior changes, hallucinations, or other breaks with what we collectively call reality?

The Cittamātra school focuses on mind or consciousness only where we think of our experience as a stream of consciousness. While this avoids solipsism because of the understanding of emptiness of self, so the world is not an invention of the mind, the idea is to have a direct experience of every moment as it arises.

My father had schizophrenia and while I didn't have a chance as an adult to talk with him about his experience, I do believe that he had hallucinations. It was watching the movie "A Beautiful Mind" when the character asks an assistant if she can see the person who is addressing him and when she says she can, he acknowledges that he needs to be certain considering his condition that made me realize my father had done the same thing with my sister and me. Now, he would never approach that situation that directly. He would ask my sister or me about the person but he would ask us to comment on their appearance or clothes or something and as I remember it, if my sister or I were looking at the person and engaged, he never asked (my guess is that he watched us and saw that we were seeing what he was seeing and could be confident that the person was real, but if we were distracted and not paying attention, he wasn't as sure). I've never had a hallucination, so I really can't imagine what it would be like or how it would affect me, but reflecting on my father is a good support to this practice. On the other hand, relating to my fear of losing touch with reality is important, too – as the child of a parent with a mental illness, that fear is on the periphery, wondering if that can happen to me, too, and what would cause it to happen.

The focus on dreams and the three natures was very helpful and I really spent a lot of time both in meditation as advised and thinking about the nature of the dream world and waking world. One of the interesting things that happened was that one night – and I've had a bad cold, so taking cold medicine and not sleeping well takes its toll – I had a very vivid dream. I was painting our van and a man who seemed to be a friend was painting his car in a driveway. We were painting the cars with the markings of koi fish and discussing how realistic the spots looked – the dappled edges, shapes of the markings, and the colors (mine were mostly white on the maroon background of the van). Then we flashed to a river and we were standing in the water talking about how the rocks and plants looked under water and how different our view of how things looked depending on our point of view and perspective. Then the man lunged with his hands into the water suddenly and caught a fish – he brought it out of the water and I was looking at it with its shiny, wet scales; its mouth opening and closing. Just as suddenly, we were back at the driveway painting the cars and he asked "so, are you a painter dreaming she's a fish, or..." And I suddenly realized that it was a dream and said "hey! This is a dream!" and it felt very much like a lucid dream for that moment. I woke up very alert and awake and got up to meditate. During meditation, I felt very peaceful and stable within that feeling of things being empty of...

Methodical

Most significant in this chapter is the methodical approach used to work through the levels of consciousness illustrating the lack of self-nature in each. Albert Einstein said that "...for us physicists believe the separation between past, present, and future is only an illusion, although a convincing one." when explaining that there may be an arrow to time, but it's only our perception of time that make it seem to move forward. Essentially, despite all of the exhortations to "be in the moment" or the power of "now," there really is no "now." Nagarjuna was ahead of Einstein in his analysis of consciousness, claiming that you can never find the truly existing moment of consciousness or experience that could define it or give it a self-nature.

The Svatantrika approach further fine tunes the understanding of the relative and ultimate dimensions and explains that "the true nature of things cannon be conceptualized as wither existent, non-existent, both or neither." They explain that the Chittamatrins conceptual teachings are provisional rather than definitive since they use concepts that need to be interpreted. Instead, the Svatantrika approach establishes emptiness, including the concept of emptiness as the ultimate nature of all relative dharmas.

In the instructions, I really appreciated the instruction to "abandon all doubts" and "rest the mind in that vast open space..." In a very real way, it was like putting some puzzle pieces together – I can understand the arguments and analysis regarding the not-self characteristic, having worked with the four foundations of mindfulness, I've experienced putting space around the object of my meditation, and I've had those moments of direct experience. What I haven't really done is "abandon all doubts." In our psychology classes here at PIBS, a couple of discussions hit on framing the way we talk about what we do in terms of always saying "I'm choosing to do..." rather than saying things like "I can't... or I have to..." Taking responsibility for my actions and being more honest about what I do just through my language, and I've noticed a change in my attitudes about a lot of things by making that change. Funny, my first Zen teacher would ask us "why are you choosing not to be enlightened... choosing not to wake up." I thought it was just one of those California Zen things for a long time.

During my meditation sessions this week, I wrote the phrase "abandon all doubts" on a piece of paper for the front of the altar. I found the sessions to be restful, but it was during our Wed night service at temple that was the most interesting. We have some visiting monks and they participated in the Wed night chanting service. I love going to temple in the evening because the light is so beautiful coming into the sanctuary and it is very meditative with a quieter atmosphere than regular Sunday services. Because a service is similar to the instructions, I thought this would be a good time to use this approach. I felt that I did have a direct experience of what was happening; resting my mind in that empty space. As with other times that I've had direct experiences; I felt very open and my heart very full of compassion and love. In touching that compassion in the past, I've noticed that for awhile that compassion comes with me and everything is brighter and clearer; the faces of people more beautiful, but there always seems to be a letdown (a hang over?) During the service I realized that in those times I had "fallen in love" with everything around me and had taken my feeling of compassion and love to a form of attachment. I could feel that "falling in love" thing happening, but then brought my mind gently back to having the direct experience. I hadn't realized that before I was adding a layer onto the experience. I'm sure I still am adding a subtle layer, but as I continue to practice, I can be on the lookout and continue to peel that onion.

During the week, I took the advice of our author as well as my previous teacher and contemplated how vivid things appear despite their emptiness and asked myself why I was choosing not to have a direct experience of things as they really are all the time.

Relative and Absolute

Most significant in this chapter is taking the approach of relative and absolute to a finer level of understanding. Taking the previous approach further, the Prasangika break down time's arrow into discreet packets, showing that things do not arise, stay, or perish. In a sense it's like the laws of physics; on a day to day level, Newtonian physics work just fine and we really don't need any further detail whether it's striking a match, turning on a light, or catching ourselves from a trip on a crack in the sidewalk. However, if we want to look at the universe on a very large or very small scale, those tools won't serve us. Some of the concepts are so difficult to wrap our minds around, often because we're asking questions that don't make sense in the context of these scales. It would be like asking 'where is the middle point of an infinite space?' the question only makes sense on the level of the day to day. So the Prasangika help us to stop asking questions that make no sense and to realize that emphasizing that "as well as things not being truly existent and not arising, they are also not truly existing and not non-arising. Such positions being equally unsatisfactory."

The Prasangika approach explains that the Svatantrika system is still subtly conceptual due to their dependence on establishing emptiness based on reason. According to the Prasangika, the conceptual mind is always in error and can never give a direct experience of the suchness of reality. By not positing anything either positive or negative and systematically refuting all conceptual attempts at describing the true nature of reality, they leave no alternative than a non-conceptual view of the absolute nature of reality; emptiness.

All that said, I found this method to be both challenging and effortless. It was such a relief to find those last couple of paragraphs – I've always been one to feel that I had to work at using a strong emotion as an object of meditation and to look deeply at it and transform it. Those methods from the four foundations of mindfulness, *shamatha*, and *vipassana* have been really helpful to me, and I don't think that I would have known what to do with this instruction when starting out. During my meditations this week, I had a variety of situations to work with; we had a mini retreat at our temple, my son and I worked on cleaning out the garage, and I went to dinner with my ex-husband. During the retreat was a very nice time to really relax my mind – the mindful energy, beautiful surroundings, and encouragement of the monks made that feel natural. Working is also a good meditative practice, allowing the mind to relax into spaciousness when happy, worried, too hot, thirsty, satisfied, laughing and joking; allowing the day to unfold.

Having a meal with my ex-husband was challenging because it reminded me of that reminder that between sessions, we still have to deal with everyday life, where we see cause and effect working. His complaints about his health and his anger over the way he is being treated at work, really sucked me in. I found myself joining in with issues at my own work over how I'm being treated by the corporate office. But it was really good food for thought

– how to be around someone who is complaining and miserable without being sucked in, and how to respond to the situations at work. Do I "stand up for myself" and say what I think, do I do my best to be reasonable, but basically not rock the boat for my last few years working there? And how do I do either of those things (both or neither) without getting myself worked up and upset?

I keep coming back to the Rinpoche's advice "Whenever strong passions like anger, desire, or jealousy arise, letting the mind rest without contrivance is sufficient remedy..." So I think that I really don't have to protect myself from the people I deem unreasonable, or prove myself right to them – I just need to do my best to help where it's needed and stop distracting myself from the path. After all, I'm not really helping when I join someone in their complaints and dramas, I'm building up my own ego in wanting to be right or the fixer. It's a tough one to let go, but beautifully relaxing for those short moments when I do.

Rest Naturally

Over this past week, my experience with this practice deepened as I continued to look at how I was feeling and responding to the meditation. One of the things I noticed was that I found that I was holding tension about things. It's like I feel I have to have a tension in the back of my mind about things I care about or feel are important; otherwise, it would be like I don't care about those things if I'm not, on some level, worried about them or trying to generate some control over them. It was good to think about that. Even though I know that the world will keep spinning even if I'm relaxed and not worried about it, there still is that Midwestern work ethic that makes that sense of total rest a bit suspicious. After all, what would happen if everyone just let go of their worries? We might spin off our axis and into all sorts of anarchy.

When I was taking my unit of Clinical Pastoral Education (CPE) one of the students talked about being called to a patient room by a nurse on her last nerve – the patient was over the top unhappy and anxious, so the chaplain was called to "settle her down, or something!" So my fellow student went in to do her best to help – she tried guided imagery, talking with her, anything she could think of. The patient finally asked her "what is your agenda here?" The student claimed she had no agenda other than helping her, but by that time the patient was so worn out that she wanted to go to sleep. In our class, as we discussed what had happened and what we thought we might do in a similar situation, what dawned on me was that she did go in with an agenda; she wanted to do what the nurse had asked her to do – settle the patient down. I certainly don't share the story as a criticism of her, but because when she shared her story, it helped me see that I do that, too. I go in with all the good intentions in the world, but really I have an agenda to fix or please someone or make myself feel better in an uncomfortable situation. When confronted with suffering, there is that tension in the back of my mind; that discomfort. So, under the guise of compassion, I work to fix the situation so that the person will stop suffering – I'm glad they feel better, but I'm really glad I feel better. When it doesn't work, I feel quite frustrated about it. That simple statement "...one should let the mind rest naturally without contrivance in the natural emptiness of mind" is so powerful; helping me understand why I don't have to hold the control and tension. Compassion isn't about how much I can fix – thank goodness, really, since I can't actually fix very much!

The other point at the end of the chapter is about resting the mind when the mind is happy so it becomes spaciousness and peace as well as with suffering I found to be very valuable. I had a really good weekend this weekend and this morning was just ideal. I made muffins early in the morning, the rain from the day before had washed the air clean and it was cool and just lovely. I got to the temple early so I could meditate before the service and a few of us sat together outside in front of our large Quan The Am statue. There wasn't a cloud in the sky and a gentle breeze was perfect. I was very happy and I remembered that part of the chapter. It was, ok, how to explain – taking the feeling of happiness into the spaciousness of the natural emptiness of mind was so restful. When I've meditated when happy before, there was still an aspect of clinging I'm realizing – kind of thinking that the meditation would help me keep that feeling/mental state longer. When I practiced with my first Zen teacher and would come to him with either the meditation was difficult or whatever, he would say to keep sitting, that the feeling would go away; when I came to him because the meditation was blissful and wonderful, he would say the same thing. I didn't realize at the time that that was a quintessential Zen answer, and even when I did realize it was a good Zen answer I didn't really get it; I thought it was an in-joke and that of course the enlightened mind must be happy. What I am realizing over the years and especially with this meditation, is that true happiness isn't the emotion or feelings of being happy because of conditions that I like and want more of. It's hard to put into words the feeling of being so beautifully at rest for those moments, but I do know that I am very happy to have been introduced to this book.

No Effort

Most significant in this section is the distinction between Shentong and Cittamātra and Rinpoche is able to explain this difference, even when other authors of doctrinal books try to define them as one in the same. He explains that consciousness is not truly existent as in Cittamātra thought and explains the non-conceptual Wisdom Mind which has absolute and true existence and which must be experienced directly.

It seems to me that the bottom line of the Shentong approach is the contention of the experience of the Clear Light Nature of Mind. When we spend a long time cutting through illusion and creating a strong habit of negation, that even when the Clear Light Nature of Mind shines through, the meditator subtly tries to negate it. So, in the Shentong approach, the third wheel of the doctrine is turned to remedy this fault of the Rangtong through the Tathagatagarbha teachings. Understanding that the mind's nature is Clear Light and our true nature is Tathagatagarbha, allowing us to go through a process of purification from which the Buddha nature emerges.

I've had to read this chapter a few times and will read it a few more. The differences between Cittamātra and Shentong are subtle, but important and I'm sure it will take me awhile to wrap my head around them. In my practice this past week, I did feel that I was letting go of my habit to cling to issues, acknowledging that not clinging is not the same as not caring – that I really don't keep the earth spinning on its axis. I realize that this stage is one that a teacher trained in this approach is necessary, but I do appreciate the last paragraph explaining that working on this process is keeping me moving in the right direction. I did feel that I was allowing my feelings and thoughts to be like a river flowing with me sitting with stability on the river bank, not getting swept away with them. The other thing I noticed was that during the day

I would find myself coming back to a moment of non-meditation quite naturally. Before, it's been more of an "oops, I should be more mindful – should be breathing – should be..." putting a layer of fault on a realization that I had been swept away. Several situations happened this past week that would have normally annoyed me and stayed with me, and I noticed myself not being nearly as bothered and allowing my feelings of annoyance to flow away – like Rinpoche says "whatever thoughts arise, there is no need to try to stop them; in that state they simply liberate themselves. ...like the waves on an ocean that simply come to rest by themselves. No effort is required to still them."

Go With the Flow

How has your experience from last week changed? How has your understanding deepened? Questions that are hard to answer, really. I missed one session this week because of being ill – I was awake all night with severe leg pain and spent the day with a bad headache and feeling sick, so the morning session was spent sleeping. But during the night, I kept feeling pulled back to awareness and instead of wondering how meditation could help me through this, I kept thinking "it has always been thus..."

Having back and sciatic pain the past few months have been challenging, but perhaps most challenging because of the thought in the back of my head that it might be metastatic bone cancer. I had an MRI (which was a lot of fun, really – it's like a sweat lodge meditation. The young girl who was the technician kept apologizing for how long it was taking, and couldn't really believe me when I told her to take her time and do her best job; I was happy meditating – well, she said, you are holding perfectly still and that's making my job easier) and the results of the MRI have revealed that I do not have mets in my spine, but do have some degenerative changes causing the pain.

When I contemplated the pain during the night, instead of my "argument" with Rinpoche a few weeks ago, I used the method of examination to take myself through the pain; to find its essence. In thinking of the anatomy, the nerves, picturing the MRI in my mind and hearing the explanation of the nodes and pressure on the nerves, thinking back through the aging process, considering, my family history with back issues, even human evolution, and peeling back each of the layers of cause and effect and the psychological layers of worry, anticipation, and fear. I was left with no essence of pain at all; only the present reality of it to be present with. Instead of fighting my pain, I chose to companion it through the night. Going back to the basics of a body scan, using Reiki to help guide the scan, helped me relax my muscles and become stable. Then going back to my favorite advice from the book to set aside all doubts and rest the mind in the vast space of emptiness. With pain, I want to fight it; to fix it, however, in recognizing its emptiness, I could set that fight (the doubt that it truly is empty) aside, allow myself to see the spaciousness, and simply be with it. It was a bit like being a rag doll riding some turbulent waves, but there were times when my mind was still and tranquil and patient to companion the pain until it subsided, which, as it must, did subside allowing me to sleep. Why do I continue to doubt impermanence? Simply by settling and watching the thoughts, physical sensations, emotions; impermanence plays itself out like a river flowing – it's my choice to jump in and be buffeted by the waves and rocks, or to sit on the bank and watch it flow; looking deeply at its nature and beauty.

Meditation Through the Years

When I look back at my relationship with meditation over the years, I remember a young girl who spontaneously found a sense of stillness that awakened a sense of wonder and prompted a search for learning more; a recognition that there was something different from the prayers and sermons that the family found so meaningful but seemed lacking to me. Over the years, I learned and practiced a number of meditation techniques from Buddhist teachers and other more New Age sources and enjoyed using these techniques, more often than not with a goal in mind – fixing my insecurities and relationships, making me a better person (sometimes it was me wanting to be better than others), or wanting to transcend; to transcend what, I am not sure I ever identified. When I started studying with Thich Nhat Hanh, the primary meditation he recommended was the Four Foundations of Mindfulness. These age old techniques continue to inform my meditation practice and are like old friends that I can turn to and rely on in times of trouble or in times of joy.

Through the years I have had a developing sense of what meditation is good for. Sometimes it was from a well placed question from someone who had never meditated or maybe had only heard of the word before. They might ask "what are you doing when you meditate?" or "what is meditation good for?" and those are good questions; questions that I used to have good answers for. But for many years, I think that my main goal has been control; to be on the side of what is right, and to be in control of myself to be right. There are certainly sutras and quotations that would seem to support that if you do not read too deeply into them, that is. There are many pithy quotations about the monkey mind, wild horse mind, or even a raging elephant with the teacher exhorting us to get that unruly mind under control. This was very appealing to me; in fact, I would say it would be my greatest hope for everyone to get themselves under control. It is still a source of irritation to me when someone is out of control; in my life and in my profession it has always been the ultimate indulgence to lose control, especially in an emergency situation, an indulgence that I have contempt for. Instead of actually learning to have the discipline to liberate and transform my mind, I was using the techniques to control my thoughts; to fix myself, or so I thought.

But even when practiced imperfectly, the practices have allowed wisdom to soak through and I have been able to confront my mistaken views and to look deeply at the suffering that brought many of them into manifestation. Instead of trying to change the world, even though I was telling myself that I was helping, I am learning to stop complaining about the external factors and change myself. Luckily, I have an honest streak and even though it can take some time to get down from a particular high horse or another, there is always that little tickle in the back of my mind that asks if I am really being honest with myself. Shantideva wrote: "To cover all the earth with sheets of hide – where would such amounts of skin be found? But simply wrap some leather around your feet, and it's as if the whole earth had been covered!" Shantideva further explains in his chapter on *Taming the Mind* of the great *Bodhicaryāvatāra* that we cannot use a harness or harsh austerities to control our minds because the aim is to tame the mind, to turn it into an ally to help us transform our suffering. Instead we are encouraged to use gentleness, to protect our wounds and pay attention to them, finding what they need to be healed. When I worked in Neonatal Intensive Care, my work was about being responsive to the tiny baby that was my patient. I learned to understand how the baby was communicating pain or contentment; how to identify when the baby's condition was getting better or worse. The baby could not talk to me, I had to learn how to listen and be watchful. What I am learning is to give my own mind that same attention and care.

Ritual has been a powerful force for me as well. Finding a Buddhist temple and hearing the temple bells ringing, the voices of the people reciting the sutras, the incense, the presence of the monks and nuns all add to a feeling of centeredness and stability. It creates a sacred space to do the work of being honest with myself. I especially appreciate the ritual space that Rinpoche creates in each of the practice procedures in each chapter – bowing to the three Jewels, taking refuge, arousing bodhichitta, dedication of merit to all beings, all set the stage for the contemplations and meditation.

Gyamtso explains that "the clinging to the idea that one has a single, permanent, independent, truly existing self that is the root cause of all one's suffering." The Rinpoche goes on to explain how normal it is for us to try to remove pain and discomfort when it arises, that it is instinctive, automatic, and normal. We act as though we have a self to protect and preserve. Many Buddhist schools have given a number of analogies and logical explanations for emptiness. When we look deeply into the Four Foundations of Mindfulness, we see this as well; a systematic approach for convincing us of the truth of the not-self characteristic.

Gyamtso shows, with each progressive stage, that part of the time we spend in this approach is to examine the arguments and proposals that each school presents. We are given the problem of matter and encouraged to pick an object apart so we understand that it has no essential essence, no self. We are encouraged to consider what dreams are made of and to wonder about the differences between the object and its observer. I wrote in another paper or maybe two, about an experience when I was a college student. I was studying with a free-spirited Zen teacher, only recently having found someone who could explain more to me about Buddhism than I had read in books and to begin guiding my meditation practice. I was also learning about science and the rudiments of what energy and matter are. I was amazed at this interconnectedness of all things and it brought out a feeling of bodhichitta in me. In talking to a fellow student about it, he was puzzled. He agreed that science supported that idea that we do not have a soul and found that to be satisfying in and of itself but he did not understand why it would prompt anyone to have compassion – after all, relativity is only a formula that describes the reality of the universe. I had to laugh "only the reality of the Universe? I think that's something!"

Rinpoche explains what I could not at that point – that we do need to convince our minds of the reality of the nature of reality, the two truths, and emptiness but then we need to let it go and rest our minds in the spaciousness of emptiness. "...one focuses on the emptiness of each moment of consciousness by not creating any concepts of there being a difference in substance between the inner perceiving aspect and the outer perceived aspect... the mind rests in the vast expanse of emptiness." From the *Ekottara Agama*, before his death the Buddha said "All conditioned things are impermanent. They are phenomena, subject to birth and death. When birth and death no longer are, the complete silencing is joy." Or as Thay Nhat Hanh says, mirroring the logic of the diamond sutra, "A rose is not a rose. That is why it is an authentic rose. We have to remove our concept of rose is we want to touch the real rose."

The Buddha also uses tool of relative truth to help us make friends with our fears and to help us appreciate the here and now. The Buddha encouraged his disciples to recite the Five Remembrances:

"I am of the nature to grow old.
There is no way to escape growing old.

I am of the nature to have ill-health.
There is no way to escape having ill-health.

I am of the nature to die.
There is no way to escape death.

All that is dear to me and everyone I love
are of the nature to change.
There is no way to escape being separated from them.

My actions are my only true belongings.
I cannot escape the consequences of my actions.
My actions are the ground on which I stand."

~ Thich Nhat Hanh

I have found the remembrances to be very helpful for understanding the truth of reality and to help me not waste my precious life by pretending that this is not the truth. It seems contradictory to recite these remembrances and then say that there is "no birth, no death; no coming, no going" yet we do need the relative world (it's where I keep all my stuff!) but I still need to touch the ground of my being and "not allow relative truth to imprison us and keep us from touching absolute truth." Rinpoche explains that we need to spend time understanding the conceptual points in order to have the confidence to let them go. He encourages us to understand the different ways of meditating so that we move in the right direction and can know the subtle faults of conceptual effort. But most important is to "rest the mind in its Clear Light Nature" allowing the thoughts, like waves on an ocean, to simply come to rest by themselves. It is light and effortless.

I truly appreciate that working with this book over the past two months has deepened by practice. I am sure that the instructors here might chuckle over how often I am amazed by the wonderful teachers we are introduced to and I often wonder where a particular teacher has been all my life. The added depth of understanding prompted by this slim volume has been remarkable. The discipline of creating these courses and guiding the students through them is also remarkable; something I hope only continues to grow. That said, there are still more questions than answers and I still struggle with those questions whether I fight with the material or myself. I found this quote from Rainer Maria Rilke last year and it holds great comfort for me: "Be patient toward all that is unsolved in your heart and try to love the questions themselves. Do not now seek the answers, which cannot be given you because you would not be able to live them. And the point is to live everything. Live the questions." It is a wonderful object of meditation.

CHAPTER 19

Conclusion

This paper was written reflecting on a analyzing Karl Brunnhölzl's book "The Center of the Sunlit Sky: Madhyamika in the Kagyü Tradition." It also became a thank you letter to my instructors and fellow students at the Prajna Institute for Buddhist Studies. It was an interesting, challenging, profound, and joyous time in my life. I went on to continue my studies, earning a Master's in Divinity in Buddhist Studies, and a PhD in Biblical and Religious Studies, but continue to look at this time with fondness - it was a special time indeed.

Conclusion

It has been an amazing couple of years. My mother died, I started this program which is now (unbelievably) almost over, I was diagnosed with breast cancer, a number of changes at work both good and bad, my former husband has been fighting a number of health and emotional problems, my son moved to start a new life, I have been on a number of retreats, and I have worked with some amazing teachers. The work I have done in these classes has been so valuable to me – it is important to me to learn and think through all the details so I can commit to practice wholeheartedly. The teachers I have been introduced to in the courses here at PIBS have been life changing – I am sure that you instructors have chuckled at my comments about how in awe I am of some of these authors, how grateful I am, or my question "where has this book been all my life?" But the fact is, my practice has benefited so much from everything that has happened the past couple of years, and I think that the exploration of Hua-Yen and the schools of thought within the Madhyamika have been what has set the stage for a new chapter in my meditation and understanding. I have done a paper on the comparison of Shentong and Rangtong and have done a lot with the logic puzzles of the Diamond Sutra, Lotus, and Hua-Yen. Rather than writing this paper on the intellectual exercises (which is always tempting and enjoyable for me), I would like to explore some of the insights about my behavior and emotions that I have experienced over the past few months.

As Rinpoche Gyamtso recommends in his book *Progressive Stages of Meditation on Emptiness*, it is important to do the intellectual work of understanding the nature of the relative reality and emptiness through metaphor, thought puzzles, understanding the fruit of the practice, ritual, and analysis. Then it is important to know that we can investigate experience by being as aware as possible every moment. But there comes a time when the investigation is no longer needed and, in fact, once we have confidence in the study, to keep returning to investigation is like switching the light on and off without any purpose – the light is on; leave it on. "At the meditation stage of your practice there should be no more need for reflection. One should just rest in the meditation without any hesitation." For now, I feel like I need to take the training wheels off and practice. And who better to guide my practice than Shantideva, the Madhyamika guide for the bodhisattva path, and to reflect on how far I have come...

"You're like an egg, aren't you? Smooth, contained, graceful; no edges... maybe it's time to put a crack or two in that eggshell..." This was said to me about 20 years ago when I attended a workshop that offered a number of talks on spiritual topics. The first day was a sampler of talks that everyone attended. Workshop intensives were held for the rest of the weekend where you chose one presenter. The first night after we had been sitting all day listening, we were all treated to a session with Gabrielle Roth and a small group of musicians leading us through her Five Rhythms. She explained briefly that the rhythms of life can be summed up as 1) flowing – the rhythm of the ocean waves and the feminine, 2) staccato – the rhythm of the heart beat, stepping out into the world; the masculine, 3) chaos – liberation, throwing off convention, wild and free, 4) lyrical – surrender and soulful, graceful and sweet, 4) stillness – the resonance of silence, where we are led to by the other rhythms. Then we all got up and danced. The evening event was intense, really fun, out of my comfort zone, and exciting. I had signed up for another presenter, but went to the organizers to see if there was a space in Gabrielle's workshop and was able to switch. When the workshop started, she talked for a bit and then led us through the basics of the five rhythms. We danced through them with the percussionists. She worked with each of us on where we were stuck, where the movement touched our emotions, and warned of the shadow side of each of the rhythms. We were to sweat our prayers, connect our head with our heart with our feet, and crack the egg shell of convention, self-consciousness, and conformity. With the maxim that an ounce of practice is worth a ton of theory, the majority of the time in the workshop was spent exploring the spontaneity and honesty of movement – it was exhausting, too.

During the session, her comment about me being like an egg was an important symbol of where I was in my journey, and it turned out to be a good frame of reference for what can happen when we get into our practice; sometimes things seem worse and get pretty messy because we allow those cracks to form and break open the eggshell that we think is holding it all together. Recognizing when we are stuck, even when it seems to the outside like the rhythm we are in is a good one – like being a flowing, lovely egg – hide the fact that we may be using that flow to avoid stepping into our own power and strength; we might be hiding in chaos so that we do not have to think about our pain, marching along doing all the right things so that the world will not attack us, or even sitting still, looking so spiritual, but hiding an apathy and sluggishness that prevents us from the direct experience of things just as they are.

When we study the Madhyamika, we find ourselves working to find the center; emptiness. All of the logic, philosophy, analogies, arguments, and analysis have an important place in our study. Exploring the evolution of thought and the fine points of the arguments sometimes feel that we are shifting our perception to one side or the other (form or emptiness) like when we close one eye then the other making the object on the table move back and forth. Which one is correct, the one on the right, the one on the left, or the one in the middle? The explorations of the nature of reality, the difference between illusion and delusion, what is relative and what is absolute are important parts of our understanding and a good use of our intelligence. It gives us a framework to build our practice on. "All of these branches were taught by the Sage for the sake of knowledge. Therefore, those who wish for suffering to subside should develop knowledge." But what happens when we close the book?

Shantideva provides specific instructions for those who wish to follow the Madhyamika path. His Holiness, the Dalai Lama explains that when we take the Buddha's gradual method of examination, starting with generosity, we ground ourselves in the relative truths, like cause and effect, so that we are protected from the philosophical extremes of nihilism or eternalism. But when we go on to study the Prajnaparamita, the Diamond Sutra, and other texts we learn that there is a distinction with regard to knowable things; between the relative and absolute truth. Quoting Shantideva, "Relative and ultimate, these two truths are declared to be. The ultimate is not within the reach of intellect, for intellect is said to be relative." To me, understanding the not-self characteristic, or emptiness, is a balancing act – walking a tight rope, passing over the razor's edge, shifting the gaze between the young lady or the old woman – no true ground beneath my feet and knowing that if I alight too long on either side, become rigid, or stop moving I will fall. But I find that I constantly fight with myself as well, arguing this hand or the other hand, looking too often for what is right, but sometimes looking for what is true.

So, how did I become an egg? Growing up was a challenging time for my sister and me. Our dad had schizophrenia and the consistency and stability children need from their parents was not always present for us. Dad had his own balancing act; he strove to behave normally yet his inner demons created behavior that caused a lot of suffering. It was not until I saw the movie A Beautiful Mind that I understood one of my father's behaviors. At the end of the movie when he has learned how to cope with his hallucinations, John Nash is approached by a man who is giving him some good news. A student is there too, and Nash asks the student if anyone is there and the student confirms that there is. Nash says "Okay. I am always suspicious of new people. Now that I know you're real, who are you, and what can I do for you?" What our father would do was more subtle; he would watch us and if my sister and I were looking at the person he would interact with him, if we were distracted, dad would ask one of us a question about the person like what color his shirt was or something like that to confirm there was someone there. Sometimes our answer would be "oh, daddy, you're so weird" then he knew it was a hallucination I suppose. He died before I was able to talk with him about his experiences. The razor's edge he walked spilled over to me even though I have never experienced a hallucination because there was a battle of being in and out of control.

We were to be in control of our emotions and selves because he couldn't tolerate the stress of others crying or being upset. Passion and excitement over something was too much for him and we were to be good girls. On the other hand, if we did not get all worked up about something that was affecting him, it was interpreted that we did not care. Our mother pretty much checked out; she had a very low self-esteem because of her own upbringing. My sister was three years younger, so for many years, I was the only responsible one in the family and took care of everyone. There was always a "on the one hand" and "on the other hand" for me, so I actually did like my parents and appreciated a lot of things about them; their humor, their efforts to make things work, and their talents. But, all in all, it was terribly confusing. It was also a gift – looking for a way to understand reality led me to Buddhist practice.

When I started meditation it was about giving my mind a break from the world; a time to rest and renew. When I learned more about practice, I tended to be goal oriented. I thought I could control my mind with meditation and that way I could keep my natural calm which I considered valuable and was the face I wanted to show the world. If I could keep that aspect and get rid of the rage I felt underneath, there would be order in my mind and in my world. One of the things that I learned and that started to come up for me was cracking that egg – getting more in touch with those aspects that I did not want to admit to myself, let alone show anyone else. My mom would use that old chestnut when I got on my high horse about something "do you want to be right, or do you want to be happy?" and my response was usually "I want to be happy because I'm right!" Shantideva says: "To cover all the earth with sheets of hide – where could such amounts of skin be found? But simply wrap some leather around your feet, and it's as if the whole earth had been covered!" My way of wanting to cover the earth, or getting rid of what I do not like or approve of, was pretty aggressive really.

One of the insights I have started to recognize is the conflict I feel between wanting to find a peaceful heart with caring about things that are important to me. From the environment to social justice; taking good care of those weaker than ourselves to simply being polite and kind, I often feel that if I do not get worked up about it, it means that it is not important or will fall by the wayside. How do I stand up for myself, set boundaries, and get my due if I do not hold on tight to what is right? Yet the anger and righteous indignation is invigorating and covers the soft spot of vulnerability. I get so frustrated with myself (and if I am honest, ashamed) when I become furious at the smallest slight. Looking past the anger to the soft spot that it covers, though, finds a little girl pretty scared at having the responsibility to take care of her family and wishing someone would step in and help. One of the phrases I have heard that really helps is "just like me" – that just like me, that person who is not being polite to me, not helping me, wants to be happy and wants to be free of the habitual nature that is causing their suffering. But our society and culture cultivate that black/white, right/wrong attitude. You cannot watch television without hearing this kind of polarization in the news, action movies or programs glorify the violent solution to the problem with the bad guys.

One of the things that Thich Nhat Hanh teaches that just drives me crazy is when he talks about the person who is making us suffer having reasons for acting the way he or she does. TNH will talk about maybe their loved one is very sick or some other serious problem and I just want to roll my eyes and shake my head and reply "Oh, please! They're just jerks!" I am very happy to be the arbiter of who is deserving of their suffering, judging the person who does bad but has a good reason for their suffering a better person than someone who does bad but who does not have an adequate reason. That righteous indignation gives me a boost of feeling superior and plays out that energy of my parents who believed that conflict was the ultimate sin and we should never indulge in losing control. Shantideva taught in an eighth-century Indian monastery, yet he wrote "Pain, humiliation, insults, or rebukes – we do not want them either for ourselves or those we love. For those we do not like, it's quite the opposite!" So I guess I am not alone! Except that darn it, sometimes things really are right and wrong – if someone thinks it is ok to abuse a child or an animal, I do not care what caused their problems nor do I forgive them.

But when I can stop and add a sense of softness, I can see that it is in that fundamentalist kind of thinking that I feel very closed in; that there is very little space to even breathe. Opening up to my feelings about what I am experiencing, what is happening to me or in the world does not mean that I am condoning what is happening. Getting worked up does not illustrate how much I care, in fact, getting worked up closes down my feeling of compassion and bodhichitta. So TNH turns out to be right, it is just that those reasons for suffering are complex and personal, not something I can easily evaluate, let alone judge.

"Those who wish to overcome the sorrows of their lives, and put to flight the pain and suffering of beings, those who wish to win such great beatitude, should never turn their back on bodhichitta." Shantideva reminds us that we wish for all sentient beings to be free of suffering, even those who are flat out wrong, even when I refuse to give them any space, locking them into their wrong headedness and not helping them bring some space into their fundamentalism either. A fact may be a fact, but is it really skillful means for me to be the educator of all, correcting their ideas as though that will make everyone happy? Does that mean that I have to chase down everyone who is in error?

"Good works gathered in a thousand ages, such as deeds of generosity, or offerings of the blissful ones – a single flash of anger shatters them." Oh no no no – Shantideva cannot possibly mean this – not to mention that maybe my anger is justified, or understandable, or that we approve of. Don't I have to be angry to make sure justice is done or that it is a motivator to get change to happen? Looking back at my habit energy, this argument of mine seems pretty old and it seems that I am using anger to cover that soft spot of vulnerability that when looked at from the bodhisattva's point of view reminds me that the other person is armoring or covering their soft spot with their habit energy of rigidity, anger, and aggression. The Dalai Lama explains that we can look to the teachings on the nutriments to understand that we must learn to eradicate the fuel of the aggressive, angry energy. Acting on our anger never makes things better but only serves to make things worse. Thich

Nhat Hanh says: "When another person makes you suffer, it is because he suffers deeply within himself, and his suffering is spilling over. He does not need punishment; he needs help. That's the message he is sending."

Not acting on our anger is not the same thing as suppressing our feelings though. This is a point that is very important, one that I tried to use meditation in a wrong way for quite awhile. In working with Thich Nhat Hanh, this is a very important theme in his teachings, to have the humility to be honest about how you feel. What we do when anger comes up is the key. Being able to stop putting up barriers and pretending that everything is ok is not honest and it will not help us learn the underlying reasons for our reaction; nor will it cultivate trustful and loving relationships with others.

Shantideva says on the one hand that "All things, then, depend on something else; on this depends the fact that none are independent. Knowing this, we will not be annoyed at objects that resemble magical appearances." teaching that emptiness has qualities of being like a dream and why would we become angry at actions from a dream? But on the other hand, "'Resistance,' you may say, 'is out of place, for what will be opposed by whom?' The stream of suffering is cut through by patience; there's nothing inappropriate in wanting that!" He stands the intellectual arguments of emptiness philosophy on their ear and encourages us to help reduce suffering in a tangible way. Thich Nhat Hanh gives us a number of tools for working with our strong emotions including sitting with the emotion, breathing space into it, and holding the emotion the way a mother would hold her baby who is crying, to take good care of it; bringing the energy of mindfulness to it.

When I feel pain, anger, or upset, my first reaction is to resist the feeling and try to push it away. A formulaic way to approach suffering might be: Suffering = Pain x Resistance. I think that is a pretty brilliant way to put that teaching in a nutshell. When we resist our feelings, we tense up, become anxious and fearful, and close down. Resistance really is futile (I am Borg) because it does not help anything – it is only in softening and bringing space into and around the feeling that we can see the big picture and experience what is actually happening fully, unencumbered by all the drama, baggage, story lines, or conditions. "Thus, when enemies or friends are seen to act improperly, be calm and call to mind that everything arises from conditions." By bringing in space, not acting on or repressing our feeling of anger, we can see more clearly and have patience with the situation when we realize how complex and sometimes crazy the reality of situations as they really are. We will never have the full picture of all of the conditions that brought about the current situation, but we can keep from adding fuel to the fire.

These complex and sometimes contradictory feelings are common for many of us and are never so important than at the end of our lives. It can be a powerful and profound time to deal with feelings of anger and guilt when the end of life is near and hopes and dreams have, perhaps, not come to fruition or if we have waited to find happiness until all conditions were right only to find it is too late, or if we feel that something we have done is unforgivable. In hospice chaplaincy, patients who are veterans can have strong spiritual conflicts or despair around unresolved feelings about their military service. Some of these patients may have repressed their feelings about their service because of the culture of stoicism in the military or because of their own conflicted feelings or guilt over what they did or witnessed.

Healthcare professionals may be conflicted as well in working with these patients because of their own moral, cultural, spiritual, or political beliefs about war and other conflicts. In her chapter about forgiveness, Deborah Grassman gives examples of how to help soldiers move toward forgiveness, but cautions clinicians not to bring their own agendas and opinions to the interaction. For some of these patients, they may have rigid views about right and wrong and may feel that others who they believe have transgressed should be punished and forgiveness is not an option, making it harder for them to be able to ask for forgiveness for themselves. They may have inner conflicts especially at the end of life when they may long for forgiveness, yet feel that they do not deserve anyone's forgiveness, not even to forgive themselves. Grassman relates her experience with a soldier who told her about some of the things he did during the war, the first time he was ever able to speak the words out loud to anyone, challenging her to show him how he could possibly be forgiven for what he did. She warns against using platitudes like "you were just following orders," or "that was a long time ago," and for clinicians to watch their body language and their own hostility about the events a solider might relay. The stories that are shared may be pretty chilling, yet the clinician has the opportunity, as Grassman puts it, to bear witness to the stories. In Buddhism, we would talk about being present with stability, in chaplaincy we talk about the ministry of presence. These men show great courage in their path toward forgiveness; how much courage do I need to muster to forgive myself and them? It shines a light on the fact that all of us deserve to find peace.

One of the things that I believe is important in our personal meditation practice or working with someone who is suffering is to realize that the goal is not for these feelings to go away, to somehow be miraculously made to disappear, never to be remembered or experienced again. One of my primary resistances to the concept of emptiness has been that it almost seems like a trite or pat answer to the profound nature of the human experience. On a superficial level it almost sounds like we are saying "oh, that's nothing, it's just empty – get over it!" but that is an interesting thing about the truths of Buddhism; they can seem simplistic and almost foolish at first glance.

Yet, when I breathe into my resistance and bring in as much space as I can, I can work through my anger, pain, or suffering systematically to try to find its essence. When I have physical pain, I can think of the anatomy, the nerves, picture the MRI in my mind and hear the explanation of the nodes and pressure on the nerves, think back through the aging process, consider my family history with back issues, even human evolution, and peeling back each of the layers of cause and effect and the psychological layers of worry, anticipation, and fear. I am left with no essence of pain at all; only the present reality of it to be present with. Instead of fighting my pain, I can choose to companion it. The pain will still be there, just as memories of other suffering that I have experienced will never go away, nor do I want them to go away. The pain and the experiences are part of my life and add to the richness of my experience; making joy that much sweeter. In the book *Progressive Stages of Meditation on Emptiness*, the advice is to set aside all doubts about the nature of emptiness and to rest the mind in the vast space of emptiness. With pain, I want to fight it; to fix it.

However, in recognizing its emptiness, I could set that fight (the doubt that it truly is empty) aside, allow myself to see the spaciousness, and simply be with it. It can be a bit like being a rag doll riding some turbulent waves, but there are times when my mind is still and tranquil and I have the patience to companion the pain until it subsides, which it does, as it must. Why do I continue to doubt impermanence? Simply by settling and watching the thoughts, physical sensations, emotions; impermanence plays itself out like a river flowing – it's my choice to jump in and be buffeted by the waves and rocks, or to sit on the bank and watch it flow; looking deeply at its nature and beauty.

"Energy moves in waves. Waves move in patterns. Patterns move in rhythms. A human being is just that – energy, waves, patterns, rhythms. Nothing more, nothing less. A dance. Movement is my medium and my metaphor. I know that if a wave of energy is allowed to complete itself, it yields a whole new wave, and in fact that is all I really know. Riding these waves means joining the cosmic dance that, as Dante says, 'moves the sun and the other stars.'" Whether we call it a matrix, Indra's net, the ultimate dimension, the Pure Land, Clear Light Nature of Mind, or Nirvana our practice progresses toward an "experience of the ineffable quality of the realization of emptiness and then we can rest our mind in that non-conceptual state. The waves on the ocean simply come to rest by themselves. No effort is required to still them."

"Anger cannot be overcome by anger. If a person shows anger to you, and you show anger in return, the result is a disaster. In contrast, if you control your anger and show its opposite--love, compassion, tolerance, and patience--then not only will you remain in peace, but the anger of others also will gradually diminish. No one can argue with the fact that in the presence of anger, peace is impossible. Only through kindness and love can peace of mind be achieved."

There are so many people to thank for their impact on my practice and life – teachers near and far, historic and contemporary, Buddhist or not. It was a great feeling to cut the cake on my 60th birthday and realize that I am happier than I have ever been, am on a journey of learning that does not have to end, and have access to a practice that gives me remarkable support as I endeavor to wake up. The courses here have supported me in no small measure. The discipline of creating these courses and guiding the students through them is also remarkable; something I hope only continues to grow. That said, there are still more questions than answers and I still struggle with those questions whether I fight with the material or myself. I found this quote from Rainer Maria Rilke last year and it holds great comfort for me: "Be patient toward all that is unsolved in your heart and try to love the questions themselves. Do not now seek the answers, which cannot be given you because you would not be able to live them. And the point is to live everything. Live the questions." It is a wonderful object of meditation.

I bow down.

Bibliography

Introduction to Buddhism

Bhikkhu Bodhi. *"A Look at the Kalama Sutta."* *Access to Insight*, June 5, 2010, www.accesstoinsight.org/lib/authors/bodhi/bps-essay_09.html.

Chödrön, P. (1996). *Awakening Loving Kindness.* Boston (1st ed.), MA: Shambhala Publications, Inc.

Chödrön, P. "Bodhichitta: The Excellence of Awakened Heart," *Shambhala Sun,* September 2001.

Five Mountain Order Buddhist Seminary (FMOBS). (accessed 2010). *Introduction to Buddhism Hinayana Handout.*

Foster, J. (accessed 2010). *Three Yanas, Two Yanas, One Yana.* Audio file lecture on the Five Mountain Buddhist Seminary student portal site.

Fry, V. "Improving End of Life Care" *Patient Care: The Practical Journal for Primary Care Physicians.* November 15, 2000.

Gyatso, T. Dalai Lama XIV. (1994). *The Way to Freedom, Core Teachings of Tibetan Buddhism* (1st ed.). San Francisco, CA: Harper Collins.

Harvey, P. (1995). *An introduction to Buddhism: Teachings, history, and practices* (1st ed.). New York, NY: Cambridge University Press.

Harvey, P. Website "Works" biography page, retrieved October 8, 2010, from: seacoast.sunderland.ac.uk/~os0phr/works.html

Huynh, C. (translator, 2001). *Nghi Thuc Tung Niem.* Sugarland, TX: Trung Tam Phat Giao, Chua Viet Nam.

"Karaniya Metta Sutta: Good Will" (Snp 1.8), translated from the Pali by Thanissaro Bhikkhu. *Access to Insight*, July 11, 2010, http://www.accesstoinsight.org/tipitaka/kn/snp/snp.1.08.than.html.

Kleinman, A. "On Caregiving" *Harvard Magazine*, July-August 2010. http://harvardmagazine.com/2010/07/on-caregiving

Kumar, N. "Kuan Yin, the Compassionate Rebel." *Exotic India Magazine*. March, 2007.

O'Donohue, John. (1998). *Anam Cara: A Book of Celtic Wisdom*. New York, NY: Harper Collins.

Patrul Rinpoche. (1996). *The Words of my Perfect Teacher*. Boston, MA: Shambhala Publications.

Plath, Sylvia. (1950). "Ode to a Bitten Plum." *Seventeen*. November.

Ray, Reginald A. (2001). *Secrets of the Vajra World: The Tantric Buddhism of Tibet*. Boston, MA: Shambhala Publications.

Salzberg, Sharon. (2000; retrieved October 8, 2010). "A Heartfelt Faith: The stages of faith on the Buddhist path". *Tricycle: the Buddhist Review*, excerpt from:

http://www.beliefnet.com/Faiths/Buddhism/2000/04/A-Heartfelt-Faith.aspx

Shantideva; Bachelor, Stephan. (translator, 1992). *Bodhisattvacharyavatara: A Guide to the Bodhisattva's Way of Life* (6th ed.). Ithaca, NY: Snow Lion Publications.

Thich Nhat Hanh. (1988). *The Heart of Understanding: Commentaries on the Prajnaparamita Heart Sutra* (1st ed.). Berkeley, CA: Parallax Press.

Thich Nhat Hanh. (1992). *The Diamond That Cuts Through Illusion: Commentaries on the Prajnaparamita Diamond Sutra* (1st ed.). Berkley, CA: Parallax Press, Inc.

Thich Nhat Hanh (1998). *The Heart of the Buddha's Teaching: Transforming Suffering into Peace, Joy, and Liberation* (1st ed.). Berkeley, CA: Parallax Press.

Thich Nhat Hanh. (1999). *Going Home: Jesus and Buddha as Brothers* (1st ed.). New York, NY: Riverhead Books of Penguin Putnam, Inc.

Zasep Tulku Rinpoche. (1998). Bodhichitta. Vancouver, BC, Canada. Union of Sutra and Tantra Series.

Life of the Buddha

Armstrong, K. (2001). *Buddha*. New York, NY: Penguin Putman.

Arnold, E. (1879). *The Light of Asia*. London, England:

Austin, J. (1999). Zen and the Brain: Toward an Understanding of Meditation and Consciousness, Cambridge, MA: The MIT Press.

Bullitt, J., editor. (2010) "Jhana: *jhana."Access to Insight*. www.accesstoinsight.org/ptf/dhamma/sacca/sacca4/samma-samadhi/jhana.html.

Chödrön, P. (1996). *Awakening Loving Kindness*. Boston (1st ed.), MA: Shambhala Publications, Inc.

Chödrön, P. "Bodhichitta: The Excellence of Awakened Heart," *Shambhala Sun*, September 2001.

Craig, E. (1998). *Routledge Encyclopedia of Philosophy*. New York, NY:Taylor and Francis Books.

Grubin, David. "The Buddha: The Story of Siddhartha." *Public Broadcasting Service (PBS)*, 2010.

Harvey, P. (1995). *An introduction to Buddhism: Teachings, history, and practices* (1st ed.). New York, NY: Cambridge University Press.

Jackson, N., et al., editors. (2010) "Mudita: The Buddha's Teaching on Unselfish Joy", four essays by Nyanaponika Thera, accesstoinsight.org/lib/authors/various/wheel170.html.

Samkhya. (2011). In *Encyclopedia Britannica*.

Thanissaro Bhikkhu, translator. (2010). "Anapanasati Sutta: Mindfulness of Breathing." (MN 118). *Access to Insight*, accesstoinsight.org/tipitaka/mn/mn.118.than.html.

Thanissaro Bhikkhu. (2010). "No-self or Not-self?" *Access to Insight*, www.accesstoinsight.org/lib/authors/thanissaro/notself2.html.

Than, M., editor (1997). *The Seeker's Glossary of Buddhism*. (2nd ed.). Taipei, Tawain: The Corporate Body of the Buddha Educational Foundation.

Thich Nhat Hanh (1998). *The Heart of the Buddha's Teaching: Transforming Suffering into Peace, Joy, and Liberation* (1st ed.). Berkeley, CA: Parallax Press.

Williams, P. (2008). *Mahayana Buddhism: The Doctrinal Foundations* (2nd ed.). New York, NY: Routledge.

The Four Noble Truths

Hagen, S. (1997). *Buddhism Plain and Simple: The Practice of Being Aware, Right Now, Every Day*. New York, NY: Broadway Books.

The Precepts

Loori, J. (2009). *The Heart of Being: Moral and Ethical Teachings of Zen Buddhism* (2nd ed.). Mount Temper, NY: Dharma Communications Center.

Thich Nhat Hanh. (1987). *Interbeing: Fourteen Guidelines for Engaged Buddhism* (3rd ed.). Berkeley, CA: Parallax Press.

Thich Nhat Hanh, editor. (1993). *For a Future to be Possible: Commentaries on the Five Mindfulness Trainings*. Berkeley, CA: Parallax Press.

The Doctrine of Mahayana

Armstrong, K. (2001). *Buddha*. New York, NY: Penguin Putman.

Arnold, E. (1879). *The Light of Asia*. London, England: Kessinger Publishing Co.

Batchelor, S. (2000). *Verses from the Center: A Buddhist Vision of the Sublime*. New York, NY: Riverhead Books.

Becker, U. (1994). *The Continuum Encyclopedia of Symbols*. New York, NY: Continuum.

Berger, D. (2005). "Nagarjuna." Carbondale, IL: Southern Illinois University.

"Bhikkhuvagga: Monks" (Dhp XXV), translated from the Pali by Thanissaro Bhikkhu. *Access to Insight*, September 19, 2010, www.accesstoinsight.org/tipitaka/kn/dhp/dhp.25.than.html.

Campbell, J. (1968). *The Hero with a Thousand Faces*. (2nd ed.) Princeton, NJ: Princeton University Press.

Campbell, J. (1974). *The Mythic Image*. Princeton, NJ: Princeton University Press.

Chödrön, P. "Bodhichitta: The Excellence of Awakened Heart," *Shambhala Sun,*September 2001.

Cleary, J. (1992). *Meditating with Koans*. Freemont, CA: Asian Humanities Press.

Conze, E. (1993). A Short History of Buddhism. (2nd ed.) Oxford, England: Oneworld   Publications, Ltd.

"Digha Nikaya: The Long Discourses", edited by John T. Bullitt. *Access to Insight*, August 1, 2010, www.accesstoinsight.org/tipitaka/dn/index.html.

Eiseley, L. (1978). The Star Thrower. New York, NY: Harcourt Brace Jovanovich.

Friedman, R. E. (1995). *The Disappearance of God: A Divine Mystery*. New York, NY: Little, Brown, and Company Ltd.

Friedman, R. E. (1989). *Who Wrote the Bible?* (2nd ed.) San Francisco, CA: Harper Collins.

Garfield, J. (1995). *The Fundamental Wisdom of the Middle Way: Nagarjuna's Mulamadhyamakakarika*. New York, NY: Oxford University Press, USA.

Gyatso, K. (1995). *Ocean of Nectar: The True Nature of All Things*. Glen Spey, NY: Tharpa Publications.

Gyatso, T. (2002). *Atisha's Lamp lecture, part 2*. Melbourne, Australia: lamrim.com.

Harvey, P. (1995). *An introduction to Buddhism: Teachings, history, and practices* (1st ed.). New York, NY: Cambridge University Press.

Jung, C.G. (1979). *Word and Image*. Princeton, NJ: Princeton University Press.

Kaufman, G. (1989). God and Emptiness: An Experimental Essay. *Buddhist-Christian Studies, 9*, 175-187. oi:10.2307/1390011

Karuna, V. *Sudden or Gradual Enlightenment*. Los Angeles, CA: International Buddhist Meditation Center.

Khandro.net. (2010). "Nagas" and "Nagas and Nagini." khandro.net/mysterious_naga.htm

Kinh Nhât Tung. (2001) Orlando, FL: Chua Bao An

Moyers, B. (1996). *Genesis: A Living Conversation.* (1st ed.) New York, NY: Doubleday Dell Publishing Co.

Nattier, J. (2003). *A Few Good Men: The Bodhisattva Path according to the Inquiry of Ugra.* Honolulu, Hi: University of Hawaii Press.

O'Donohue, John. (1998). *Anam Cara: A Book of Celtic Wisdom.* New York, NY: Harper Collins.

Page, T. (2008). *The Mahayana Mahaparinirvana Sutra - Last and most impressive teachings of the Buddha about Reality and the True Self.* Suwannee, GA: FLepine Publishing.

Prattis, I. (2003). Consciousness as Food. Ottawa, Canada: Carlton University.

Powers, J. (2007) *Introduction to Tibetan Buddhism.* Ithaca, NY: Snow Lion Publications.

Radha, S. (1978). *Kundalini Yoga for the West.* Boston, MA: Shambhala Publications, Inc.

Ray, R. (2004). *Three in One: A Buddhist Trinity.* Halifax, Nova Scotia, Canada: Shambhala Sun.

Ray, R. (2010). "The Three Lineages." *Buddhadharma: The Practitioner's Quarterly.* Halifax, NS, Canada: Shambhala Sun Foundation.

"Samyutta Nikaya: The Grouped Discourses", edited by John T. Bullitt. *Access to Insight,* November 6, 2010, www.accesstoinsight.org/tipitaka/sn/index.html.

Shantideva; Bachelor, Stephan. (translator, 1992). *Bodhisattvacharyavatara: A Guide to the Bodhisattva's Way of Life* (6th ed.). Ithaca, NY: Snow Lion Publications.

Stein, D. (1995) *Essential Reiki: A Complete Guide to an Ancient Healing Art.* Toronto, Canada: Crossing Press

Suzuki, D.T. (1999). *The Lankavatara Sutra: A Mahayana Text* (1st ed.). Philadelphia, PA: Coronet Books.

Than, M. editor. (1997). *The Seeker's Glossary of Buddhism.* Taipei, Taiwan: Buddha Educational Foundation.

Thanissaro Bhikkhu, translator. (2010). "Samaññaphala Sutta: The Fruits of the Contemplative Life" (DN 2), *Access to Insight.* accesstoinsight.org/tipitaka/dn/dn.02.0.than.html

Thanissaro Bhikkhu (translator). (2010). "Uposatha Sutta: The Observance" (Ud 5.5). *Access to Insight.* www.accesstoinsight.org/tipitaka/kn/ud/ud.5.05.than.html.

Thera, N. translator. (2010). "The Discourse on the Snake Simile: Alagaddupama Sutta (MN 22)", *Access to Insight.* accesstoinsight.org/lib/authors/nyanaponika/wheel048.html

Thich Nhat Hanh. (1990). *Present Moment, Wonderful Moment: Mindfulness Verses for Daily Living* (1st ed.). Berkeley, CA: Parallax Press.

Thich Nhat Hanh. (1993). *Thundering Silence: the Sutra on Knowing the Better Way to Catch a Snake.* Berkeley, CA: Parallax Press.

Thich Nhat Hanh. (1998). *The Heart of the Buddha's Teaching: Transforming Suffering intoPeace, Joy, and Liberation.* (1st ed.). Berkeley, CA: Parallax Press.

Thich Nhat Hanh (editor). (2000) *Plum Village Chanting and Recitation Book.* Berkeley, CA: Parallax Press.

Thich Nhat Hanh. (2001). *Transformation at the Base: Fifty Verses on the Nature of Consciousness.* Berkeley, CA: Parallax Press.

Thich Nhat Hanh. (2004). *The Ultimate Dimension: and Advanced Dharma Retreat on the Avatamsaka and Lotus Sutras.* Boulder, CO: Sounds True.

Veitch, J. translator. (1901). *Descartes' Meditations.* Dayton, OH: Wright State University Press.

Vogel, J. (1926). *Indian Serpent Lore or The Nagas in Hindu Legend and Art.* Whitefish, MT: Kessinger Publishing, LLC.

Walser, J. (2005). Nagarjuna in Context: Mahayana Buddhism and Early Indian Culture. New York, NY: Columbia University Press.

Williams, P. (2008). *Mahayana Buddhism: The Doctrinal Foundations* (2nd ed.). New York, NY: Routledge.

Madhyamaka

Brunnhölzl, K. (2004) *The Center of the Sunlit Sky: Madhyamaka in the Kagyü Tradition*. Ithaca, New York: Snow Lion Publications.

Cook, F. H. (1977). *Hua-Yen Buddhism: The Jewel Net of Indra*. University Park, Pennsylvania.

Jamgön Kongtrul Lodrö Tayé (2007) *Frameworks of Buddhist Philosophy: A Systematic Presentation of the Cause-Based Philosophical Vehicles*. Ithaca, New York: Snow Lion Publications.

Hayes, Richard P. (2003), *Nagarjuna: Master of Paradox, Mystic or Perpetrator of Fallacies?* Presentation at Smith College.

Thich Nhat Hanh. (1988). *The Heart of Understanding: Commentaries on the Prajnaparamita Heart Sutra*. Berkeley, CA: Parallax Press.

Thich Nhat Hanh. (1997). *All in one, One in All.* Dharma talk given at Plum Village Monastery: Dordogne, France.

Thich Nhat Hanh. (2001). *Transformation at the Base: Fifty Verses on the Nature of Consciousness*. Berkeley, CA: Parallax Press.

Williams, Paul. (2008). *Mahayana Buddhism: The Doctrinal Foundations* (2nd ed.). New York, NY: Routledge.

The Myth of Freedom

Campbell, J. (1949). *The Hero with a Thousand Faces*. (2nd ed.) Princeton, NJ: Princeton University Press.

Campbell, J. (1968). *The Masks of God*. New York, NY: Penguin Books.

Chödrön, P. (2007). *No Time to Lose, A Timely Guide to the Way of the Bodhisattva*. Boston (1st ed.), MA: Shambhala Publications.

Deutsch, S. & Bain, B. (producers) and Ward, V. (Director). (1998). *What Dreams May Come [motion picture]*. United States: Interscope Communications.

Hamilton, E. (1942). *Mythology*. Boston, MA: Little, Brown, and Company.

Nhat Hanh. (2001). *Anger: Wisdom for Cooling the Flames*. New York, NY: Riverhead Books.

Nhat Hanh. (1987). *Interbeing: Fourteen Guides for Engaged Buddhism*. Berkeley, CA: Parallax Press.

Than, M. editor. (1997). *The Seeker's Glossary of Buddhism*. Taipei, Taiwan: Buddha Educational Foundation.

Tri Duc. (2011, July). *The Amitabha Buddha in the Pure Land*. Novice Retreat conducted at the Chua Bao An Buddhist Center in Orlando, FL.

Trungpa, Chogyam. (2005). *The Myth of Freedom and the Way of Meditation*. Boston, MA: Shambhala Publications, Inc.

Shakespeare, W. (c. 1600). *Hamlet*. London, England.

Shantideva; Bachelor, Stephan. (translator, 1992). B*odhisattvachar-yavatara: A Guide to the Bodhisattva's Way of Life* (6th ed.). Ithaca, NY: Snow Lion Publications.

Immeasurables and Paramitas

Bullitt, J.T., editor. (accessed 2011) "Dhamma: *dhamma*." *Access to Insight*, 21 February 2011, http://www.accesstoinsight.org/ptf/dhamma/index.html .

Tashi Tsering, Geshe. (2006). *Buddhist Psychology: The Foundation of Buddhist Thought, volume 3*. Somerville, MA: Wisdom Publications.

Tenzin Gyatso, the 14th Dalai Lama. (accessed 2011). *The Eight Verses of Thought Transformation*. Essay on the http://bodhicitta.net website.

Than, M. editor. (1997). *The Seeker's Glossary of Buddhism*. Taipei, Taiwan: Buddha Educational Foundation.

Thich Nhat Hanh. (1998a). *The Heart of the Buddha's Teaching: Transforming Suffering into Peace, Joy, and Liberation*. (1st ed.). Berkeley, CA: Parallax Press.

Thich Nhat Hanh. (1998b). Teachings on Love. Berkeley, CA: Parallax Press.

Agnostic Buddhism

Batchelor, S. (1990) *The Faith to Doubt: Glimpses of Buddhist Uncertainty*. Berkeley, CA: Parallax Press.

Batchelor, S. (1996, June) "The Agnostic Buddhist: A Secular Vision of Dharma Practice." Speech presented at the Rochester Zen Center, Rochester, New York (edited version on the Upaya.org website, retrieved on 5/12/2012).

Batchelor, S. (1997) *Buddhism Without Beliefs: A Contemporary Guide to Awakening*. New York, NY: Riverhead Books.

Batchelor, Stephen. (1997) *Buddhism Without Beliefs: A Contemporary Guide to Awakening*. New York, NY: Riverhead Books.

Batchelor, S. (2011) *Confessions of a Buddhist Atheist*. New York, NY: Spiegel and Grau. Kindle e-file, unpaginated.

Bhikkhu Bodhi, (1998) "Buddhism Without Beliefs" from the Journal of Buddhist Ethics. Pennsylvania, PA.

Campbell, Joseph. 1991. *The Power of Myth*. New York, NY: Anchor Books.

Haraway, Donna. 1991. "Situated Knowledges: The Science Question In Feminism and the Privilege of Partial Perspective," in *Simians, Cyborgs, and Women: The Reinvention of Nature*. New York: NY: Routledge.

Thich, Thien-An. 1975. *Zen Philosophy, Zen Practice*. Berkeley, CA: Dharma Publishing.

Thich Nhat Hanh. (1992). *The Diamond that cuts through Illusion: Commentaries on the Prajñaparamita Diamond Sutra*. Berkeley, CA: Parallax Press.

Venerable Dr. Wonji Dharma. Personal Correspondence. Buddha Dharma University. February 2016.

Japanese Buddhism

Batchelor, S. (2000). *Verses from the Center: A Buddhist Vision of the Sublime*. New York, NY: Riverhead Books.

Brunnhölzl, K. (2004). *The Center of the Sunlit Sky: Madhyamaka in the Kagyü Tradition.* Ithaca, New York: Snow Lion Pubs.

Cleary, J.C. (1992). *Meditating with Koans.* Fremont, CA: Jain Publishing Company, Inc.

Cook, F. H. (1977). *Hua-Yen Buddhism: The Jewel Net of Indra.* University Park, PA: The Pennsylvania State University Press.

Groner, P. (2000). *Saicho: The Establishment of the Japanese Tendai School.* Honolulu, HI: University of Hawai'i Press.

Jamgön Kongtrul Lodrö Tayé. (2007). *Frameworks of Buddhist Philosophy: A Systematic Presentation of the Cause-Based Philosophical Vehicles.* Ithaca, New York: Snow Lion Publications.

Suzuki, D.T. (1999). *The Lankavatara Sutra: A Mahayana Text* (1st ed.). Philadelphia, PA: Coronet Books.

Thich Nhat Hanh. (2001). *Transformation at the Base: Fifty Verses on the Nature of Consciousness.* Berkeley, CA: Parallax Press.

Williams, Paul. (2008). *Mahayana Buddhism: The Doctrinal Foundations* (2nd ed.). New York, NY: Routledge.

The Compass of Zen

Sahn, Seung. (1997). Compass of Zen. Boston, MA: Shambhala Sun Publications, Inc.

Korean Buddhism

Boep Joeng. (2006) *The Mirror of Zen: The Classic Guide to Buddhist Practice by Zen Master So Shan.* Boston, MA: Shambhala Publications, Inc.

Buswell, Robert. (1983). *The Collected Works of Chinul: The Korean Approach to Zen.* Honolulu, HI: University of Hawai'I Press.

Buswell, Robert. (1991) *Tracing Back the Radiance: Chinul's Way of Korean Zen.* Honolulu, HI: University of Hawai'I Press.

Cleary, J.C. (2006) *Swampland Flowers: The Letters and Lectures of Zen Master TaHui.* Boston, MA: Shambhala Publications.

Cleary, J.C. (2001) *A Buddha From Korea: The Zen Teachings of T'aego*. Boston, MA: Shambhala Publications, Inc.

Jeong, Byeong-Jo. (2010). *Master Wonhyo: An Overview of his Life and Teachings*. Published by Diamond Sutra Recitation Group.

Nhat Hanh. (2003). *Finding Our True Home: Living in the Pure Land Here and Now*. Berkeley, CA: Parallax Press.

O'Donohue, John. (1998). *Anam Cara: A Book of Celtic Wisdom*. New York, NY: Harper Collins.

Tracing Back the Radiance

Batchelor, S. (2000). *Verses from the Center: A Buddhist Vision of the Sublime*. New York, NY: Riverhead Books.

Buswell, R. (1991). *Tracing Back the Radiance: Chinul's Korean Way of Zen*. Honolulu, HI: University of Hawaii Press.

Hyunoon Sunim. (1996, September). "Thinking Mind and Correct View." Dharma talk given at the Sixth Patriarch Zen Center, Berkeley, CA.

Prattis, I. (2011). "Consciousness as Food." *Pine Gate Sangha Newsletter*. Ottawa, Canada.

Thich Nhat Hanh. (2001). *Transformation at the Base: Fifty Verses on the Nature of Consciousness*. Berkeley, CA: Parallax Press.

Williams, Paul. (2008). *Mahayana Buddhism: The Doctrinal Foundations* (2nd ed.). New York, NY: Routledge.

Buddha Nature

Tashi Tsering, Geshe. (2006). *Buddhist Psychology: The Foundation of Buddhist Thought, volume 3*. Somerville, MA: Wisdom Publications.

Tenzin Gyatso, the 14th Dalai Lama. (2006). *For the Benefit of All Beings: A Commentary on the "Way of the Bodhisattva"*. (3rd ed.) Boston, MA: Shambhala Publications, Inc.

Thich Nhat Hanh. (1998). *The Heart of the Buddha's Teaching: Transforming Suffering into Peace, Joy, and Liberation.* (1st ed.). Berkeley, CA: Parallax Press.

Thich Nhat Hanh. (1990). *Transformation and Healing: Sutra on the Four Establishments of Mindfulness.* Berkeley, CA: Parallax Press.

Thrangu Rinpoche. (2004). *The Seven Points of Mind Training.* Crestone, CO: Namo Buddha Publications. Retrieved on 23 February 2012.
http://www.rinpoche.com/teachings/sevenpoints.htm

Thrangu Rinpoche. (1996) *The Reason we Practice Meditation: a Dharma talk.* Seattle, WA: Kagyu Shenpen Osel Choling. Retrieved on 23 February 2012.
http://www.rinpoche.com/reason.html

Thrangu Rinpoche. (1993). *Buddha Nature.* (2nd ed.) Kathmandu, Nepal: Rangjung Yeshe Publications.

Rosenberg, L. (2004). *Breath by Breath: The Liberating Practice of Insight Meditation.* Boston, MA: Shambhala Publications, Inc.

Sangharakshita. (2010). *Living with Awareness: a Guide to the Satipatthāna Sutta.* (3rd ed.) Cambridge, UK: Windhorse Publications, Inc.

Diamond Sutra

Ford, J. (2001, November). "Stealing our Delusions: Introducing the Diamond Sutra and the Prajñāpāramitā." Dharma talk given at Boundless Way Zen Center.

Mu Soeng. (2000). *The Diamond Sutra: Transforming the Way we See the World.* Boston, MA: Wisdom Publications.

Thich Nhat Hanh. (1992). *The Diamond that cuts through Illusion: Commentaries on the Prajñāpāramitā Diamond Sutra.* Berkeley, CA: Parallax Press.

Thich Nhat Hanh, editor. (2000). *The Plum Village Chanting and Recitation Book.* Berkeley, CA: Parallax Press.

Thich Nhat Hanh. (2011, September). "Free From Notions: The Diamond Sutra." Dharma talk given at Deer Park Monastery, Escondido, CA.

Hua-Yen Buddhism

Cook, F. H. (1977). *Hua-Yen Buddhism: The Jewel Net of Indra.*University Park, Pennsylvania.

Plath, Sylvia. (1950). "Ode to a Bitten Plum." *Seventeen*. November.

O'Donohue, John. (1998). *Anam Cara: A Book of Celtic Wisdom*. New York, NY: Harper Collins.

Thanissaro Bhikkhu. (2006) "Purity of Heart", *Access to Insight*. http://www.accesstoinsight.org/lib/authors/thanissaro/purityofheart.html accessed on 11/15/2012.

Thich Nhat Hanh. (1987). *Interbeing: Fourteen Guidelines for Engaged Buddhism* (3rd ed.). Berkeley, CA: Parallax Press.

Thich Nhat Hanh. (1988). *The Sun My Heart.* Berkeley, CA: Parallax Press.

Thich Nhat Hanh. (1997). *All in one, One in All.* Dharma talk given at Plum Village Monastery: Dordogne, France.

Ray, Reginald A. (2001). *Secrets of the Vajra World: The Tantric Buddhism of Tibet*. Boston, MA: Shambhala Publications.

Schrödinger, E. (1964). *My View of the World*. London, England: Cambridge University Press.

Platform Sutra

Boep Joeng. (2006). *The Mirror of Zen: The Classic Guide to Buddhist Practice* (2nd ed.). Boston, MA: Shambhala Publications, Inc.

Kapleau, P. (1965). *The Three Pillars of Zen* (3rd ed.). New York, NY: Bantam Doubleday Dell Publishing Group, Inc.

Loori, J. (2009). *The Heart of Being: Moral and Ethical Teachings of Zen Buddhism* (2nd ed.). Mount Temper, NY: Dharma Communications Center.

Thich Nhat Hanh. (1995). *Zen Keys: A Guide to Zen Practice* (3rd ed.). New York, NY: Bantam Doubleday Dell Publishing Group.

Yampolsky, P. (1967). *The Platform Sutra: The Text of the Tun-Huang Manuscript*. New York, NY: Columbia University Press.

Progressive Stages of Emptiness

Chödrön, Pema. (2005). *No Time to Lose: A Timely Guide to the Way of the Bodhisattva*. Boston, MA: Shambhala Publications.

Gyamtso, Hookham, & Ghatsal. (2001) *Progressive Stages of Meditation on Emptiness*. Auckland, NZ: Zhyisil Chokyi Ghatsal Publications.

Thich Nhat Hanh. (1998). *The Heart of the Buddha's Teaching: Transforming Suffering into Peace, Joy, and Liberation.* (1st ed.). Berkeley, CA: Parallax Press.

Conclusion

Shantideva; Bachelor, Stephan. (translator, 1992). *Bodhisattvacharyāvatāra: A Guide to the Bodhisattva's Way of Life* (6th ed.). Ithaca, NY: Snow Lion Publications.

Shantideva: Crosby & Skilton (translators, 1995).*The Bodhicaryāvatāra: A New Translation*. New York, NY: Oxford University Press, Inc.

Brunnhölzl, K. (2004). *The Center of the Sunlit Sky: Madhyamaka in the Kagyü Tradition*. Ithaca, New York: Snow Lion Publications.

Chödrön, Pema. (2005). *No Time to Lose: A Timely Guide to the Way of the Bodhisattva*. Boston, MA: Shambhala Publications.

Doka, K. and Tucci, A., editors. (2013) *Improving Care for Veterans Facing Illness and Death: Part of the Living with Grief® Series.* Oregon, IL: Quality Books, Inc.

Gyamtso, Khenpo Tsultrim. (2001) *Progressive Stages of Meditation on Emptiness*. Auckland, NZ: Zhyisil Chokyi Ghatsal Publications.

Gyatso, Tenzin. (1979). *Healing Anger: The Power of Patience From a Buddhist Perspective.* Ithaca, NY: Snow Lion Publications.

Gyatso, Tenzin. (1994). *For the Benefit of All Beings: A Commentary on "The Way of the Bodhisattva."* Boston, MA: Shambhala Publications, Inc.

Nhat Hanh. (2001). *Anger: Wisdom for Cooling the Flames.* New York, NY: Riverhead Books.

Roth, Gabrielle. (1989). *Maps to Ecstasy: Teachings of an Urban Shaman.* Novato, CA: Nataraj Publishing.

Acknowledgements

There are many people to acknowledge and thank, especially when an education journey has taken place over this many years. First to thank is Dr. Darlene Eddy, Humanities Professor at Ball State University. Even though I was in nursing school, I took an honors program in English and the Humanities, and she was my advisor throughout my four years of undergraduate work. She may have been a bit disappointed that I did not change my major to English, but her introduction to the Humanities, classic literature, mythology, comparative literature, and especially Shakespeare, set a journey of lifelong learning in motion for me.

I will be forever grateful to Thich Nhat Hanh and the monastics of the Order of Interbeing whose teachings and example have led me to want to know the Dharma better, and have opened the doors of practice and insight. The Abbess of our temple, Chua Bao An, Su'co Lieu Ha, and Su'co Tinh Tuyen have given constant support, help with translations, understanding, and lovely examples of practice. When times are hard, just knowing that they are there, practicing beautifully, is such a comfort.

I would also like to thank my Clinical Pastoral Education supervisor, the Reverend Chuck Weinrich who encouraged me to pursue finding a way to earn a Master's of Divinity with an emphasis in Buddhism. He helped me look for ways to better prepare myself to help my patients and develop an identity as a chaplain. The faculty and staff at Prajna Institute of Buddhist studies motivated me to study the Dharma more deeply and in an academic way. Laura Bonyon Neal was a mentor, fellow student, and instructor who was encouraging and insightful.

Professor Diane Moore of Harvard Divinity School has been a tremendous inspiration and mentor for my work in religious studies, exploring the intersections between the academic study of religion and personal practice for discovering meaning. I am very proud to consider her a mentor, teacher, and friend. The Venerable Dr. Wonji Dharma has been encouraging and has given valuable feedback and inspiration as I completed this phase of my formal education. I feel very blessed by all of these wonderful teachers. A big thank you goes to my editor Sarah Bee. I had a post-it note on my monitor with WWSBS "What Would Sarah Bee Say" during this process. Her guidance sharpened my writing, and inspired me to be better.

I would also like to acknowledge and thank my family. My son Chris and partner Matt have been such a strong support throughout this adventure in learning. Even though they have had to put up with my late nights, helping me through frustrations with the computer, and listening to me go on and on about some new idea or concept, they were always there for me. It has been quite a ride.

Lastly, I must thank my bestie and mother-in-law, Carol Foster without whom this book would not exist. In her own adventures in writing, I have learned a lot about editing, book publishing, book design, and realized that I could make this happen. We have learned together, and I look forward to more fun with books!

Cheryl Barnes-Neff

About the Author

Cheryl Barnes-Neff, a registered nurse for over 40 years, has worked in a variety of healthcare settings from neonatal intensive care to hospice care.

Cheryl has lived a rich life both professionally and personally. Travelling the world with Up with People as their nurse, working in several areas of the U.S., trying out different aspects of nursing and healthcare quality, and starting a family have been enriching pursuits. Always interested in culture and religion, she has explored learning and immersing herself in both. This interest has enabled her to integrate patient care in not only the physical, but the psychosocial, spiritual, and cultural dimensions. She found her calling in hospice care, and has spent over twenty years as a hospice nurse, educator, quality manager, and chaplain.

With a commitment to lifelong learning, she has earned certifications in Religious Studies and World Religions from the Harvard Divinity School, a Master's degree in Buddhist Doctrine, a Master's of Divinity in Buddhist Studies, and a Doctorate in Biblical Studies with a distinction in Religious Studies. She is currently an Assistant Professor in Buddhist Studies and Chaplaincy at the Buddha Dharma University.

www.ingramcontent.com/pod-product-compliance
Lightning Source LLC
Chambersburg PA
CBHW031230090426
42742CB00007B/141